Collins

175 YEARS OF DICTIONARY PUBLISHING

easy learning
English
Idioms

D0185176

HarperCollins Publishers
Westerhill Road
Bishopbriggs
Glasgow
G64 2QT

First edition 2010

Reprint 4

© HarperCollins Publishers 2010

ISBN 978-0-00-734065-1

Collins ® is a registered trademark of
HarperCollins Publishers Limited

www.collinslanguage.com

A catalogue record for this book is
available from the British Library

Typeset by Davidson Publishing
Solutions, Glasgow

Printed in Great Britain by Clays Ltd,
St Ives plc

Editorial staff

Project manager: Lisa Sutherland

Senior Editors:
Penny Hands
Kate Woodford

Contributors:
Sandra Anderson
Katharine Coates
Kate Mohideen

For the publishers:
Lucy Cooper
Kerry Ferguson
Elaine Higgleton

Collins Easy Learning English Idioms is designed for anyone who wants to improve their knowledge of English. Whether you are preparing for exams, need a quick look-up guide to English idioms, or you simply want to browse and bring some fun and colour into your English, *Collins Easy Learning English Idioms* offers you the information you require in a clear and accessible format.

What is an idiom?

An idiom is a special type of phrase. It is a group of words that can be difficult to understand even if you know all the words contained in it. In some cases, you can make a good guess at the meaning, because the idiom creates an image which represents an idea in our head. For example, it is easy to see that someone who is described as *a pain in the neck* is annoying; however, in many other cases, it is almost impossible to work out the meaning of an expression.

How to find an idiom

Idioms are listed under headwords, which are ordered alphabetically. In order to find the idiom you are looking for, you will first need to see if the idiom contains a noun. If it does, the idiom will be found under the headword for the **first noun** that occurs within it. So, for example, *call it a day* will appear at **day**, and *the life and soul of the party* will appear at **life**.

If there is no noun in the idiom, look for the **first adjective** or **first adverb**. Examples of these types of idioms would be *drop dead* (found under **dead**, or *leave someone cold* (found under **cold**).

Finally, if there is no noun, adjective, or adverb, look for the **first verb**. An example of this type of idiom would be *give it up for someone*, which appears under **give**.

Remember, then, that the ordering system works as follows:

- first noun
- first adjective
- first adverb
- first verb

One exception to this rule is that idioms like *hard as nails* or *fresh as a daisy* (called 'similes') are found under their **first adjective** rather than their noun. This is because there are often several nouns that can go with the adjective, and so it is more useful to see them all together in the same place.

Finally, please note that idioms are always placed under their headword in the form in which they appear in the idiom. So, for example, *pick holes in something* will be found under **holes**, not **hole**.

We hope you enjoy finding out more about this fascinating area of the English language. For more information about Collins dictionaries, visit us at **www.collinslanguage.com**.

guide to entries

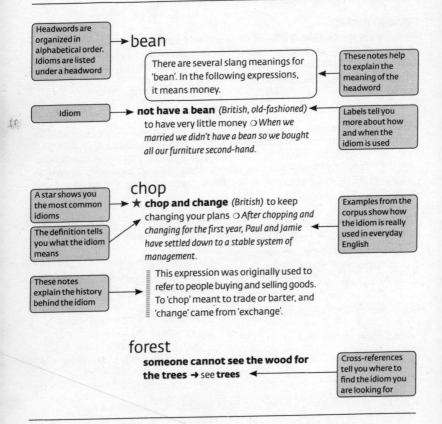

Headwords are organized in alphabetical order. Idioms are listed under a headword

bean

There are several slang meanings for 'bean'. In the following expressions, it means money.

These notes help to explain the meaning of the headword

Idiom

not have a bean (British, old-fashioned) to have very little money ○ *When we married we didn't have a bean so we bought all our furniture second-hand.*

Labels tell you more about how and when the idiom is used

A star shows you the most common idioms

chop

★ **chop and change** (British) to keep changing your plans ○ *After chopping and changing for the first year, Paul and Jamie have settled down to a stable system of management.*

The definition tells you what the idiom means

Examples from the corpus show how the idiom is really used in everyday English

These notes explain the history behind the idiom

This expression was originally used to refer to people buying and selling goods. To 'chop' meant to trade or barter, and 'change' came from 'exchange'.

forest

someone cannot see the wood for the trees → see **trees**

Cross-references tell you where to find the idiom you are looking for

Aa

accounting

there's no accounting for taste
said to mean that you think that what
someone likes is unpleasant or strange
○ *Daisy ordered her favourite pepperoni and
pineapple pizza (there's no accounting for
taste).*

ace

> In many card games, the ace is the
> card with the highest score.

the ace in your hand (British)
something that you have, and that you
can use to your own advantage ○ *You
have to convince your opponent that you have
the ace in your hand. Especially in politics.*

come within an ace of something or
be within an ace of something
(British) to very nearly succeed at doing
something ○ *The defendant was intent on
murder and he came within an ace of
succeeding.*

> In this expression, 'ace' refers to a
> score of one on a dice, rather than a
> playing card.

have an ace in the hole to have
something which you can use to gain
an advantage ○ *He doesn't usually risk
that much unless he thinks he has an ace in
the hole.*

> In 'stud' poker, you have an ace in
> the hole when you have an ace as
> your 'hole' card: see 'hole card' at **hole**.

play your ace to do something clever
and unexpected to give yourself an
advantage ○ *Just as the race was nearly
over, Hackett played his ace and pulled ahead.*

aces

hold all the aces to have all the power
or advantages in a situation ○ *When I was
an adolescent, I thought girls held all the aces.*

> In many card games, the ace is the
> card with the highest score.

acid

★ **the acid test** an experience or situation
that proves how skilful or effective
someone or something is ○ *My first really
stressful day when things go wrong: that will
be the real acid test.*

> Nitric acid can be used to test whether
> a metal is pure gold because it
> corrodes most metals but does not
> affect gold.

acquaintance

a passing acquaintance or
a nodding acquaintance
1 someone you know, but only slightly
○ *After a while a man came in who was
evidently a passing acquaintance of the
family and stopped at their table to chat.*
2 slight knowledge of something ○ *We
chatted for a little about poetry, with which
he showed considerably more than a nodding
acquaintance.*

act

> The metaphors in these expressions
> relate to performers entertaining
> audiences.

★ **a balancing act** a situation in which
you try to satisfy two or more opposing
groups or sets of ideals ○ *Mr Alia is
performing a delicate balancing act. He talks
of reform, but clings to old certainties.*

★ **be caught in the act** to be seen doing something secret or wrong ○ *The men were caught in the act of digging up buried explosives.*

⁞ In this expression, 'act' refers to the act of doing something.

★ **a class act** someone, for example a sports player or a performer, who is very good at what they do ○ *Koeman is a class act. He's got great control and can hit passes from one side of the pitch to the other with amazing accuracy.*

★ **clean up your act** to improve your behaviour and start to act in a more socially responsible way ○ *The Minister warned the press that privacy laws would be implemented if newspapers didn't clean up their act.*

★ **get in on the act** or **be in on the act** to start doing something which someone else was doing first, so that you share their success or win an advantage ○ *The company's reputation has reached the United States, and American investors have been trying to get in on the act.*

★ **get your act together** to take control of yourself and organize your activities more effectively in order to be more successful ○ *We're going to be 22 points down by Monday, and we've got to get our act together.*

★ **a hard act to follow** someone who is so impressive or effective that it is difficult for anyone else who comes after them to be as good ○ *He was a hard act to follow – a brilliant intellectual with long experience as an observer of the economic scene.*

action

★ **fight a rearguard action** to try hard to stop something happening, without much hope of success ○ *National telephone companies are fighting a rearguard action against competition from beyond their frontiers.*

⁞ The rearguard of a retreating army is a unit which separates from the rest and acts as a defence while the rest of the army is getting away.

★ **a slice of the action** (mainly British) or **a piece of the action** involvement in an activity which seems exciting and likely to succeed or make money ○ *As the British rap scene grows in strength, the Americans are becoming keener to grab a slice of the action.*

actions

actions speak louder than words said to mean that people show what they really think and feel by what they do, rather than by what they say ○ *The government needs to understand that actions speak louder than words.*

✓ Adam

not know someone from Adam to not know someone at all, and be completely unable to recognize them ○ *The man greeted me like an old friend, but I didn't know him from Adam.*

⁞ According to the Bible, Adam was the first human being.

ado

✓ **much ado about nothing** (journalism) a lot of fuss about something which is not important ○ *French newspapers described the international row as much ado about nothing.*

⁞ 'Much Ado About Nothing' is the title of a play by Shakespeare.

agenda

★ **a hidden agenda** a situation in which someone secretly tries to achieve a particular thing while they appear to be doing something else ○ *The unions fear these tactics are part of a hidden agenda to reduce pay and conditions throughout the company.*

⁞ An agenda is a list of things that need to be dealt with, for example at a meeting.

air

★ **be left hanging in the air**
if a question or remark is left hanging in the air, people avoid discussing it because they do not want to deal with it or the issues involved ○ *The presenter made intelligent points but never challenged anybody, so we were left with a lot of questions hanging in the air.*

be walking on air or
✓ **be floating on air** to feel very happy or excited because something good has happened to you ○ *I can't believe that I've won. I'm floating on air!*

★ **clear the air** to deal openly with misunderstandings, problems, or jealousy, and try to get rid of them ○ *I get angry and frustrated with Hannah's temper, but I'm a great believer in expressing my feelings to clear the air.*

★ **disappear into thin air** or
vanish into thin air to disappear completely ○ *Her husband disappeared into thin air for years.*

★ **hot air** false claims and promises ○ *In a sense, all the rhetoric about heightened co-operation can be seen as just so much hot air. There are still endless disputes.*

★ **in the air** if a change, idea, or feeling is in the air, people are aware of it or think it is going to happen even though it is not talked about directly ○ *Great excitement was in the air that week in London.*

★ **out of thin air** or
from thin air if something appears out of thin air, it appears suddenly and unexpectedly ○ *A crisis had materialized out of thin air.*

pull something out of the air or
pluck something from the air
to suddenly state something without considering it carefully or using correct information ○ *She pulled a figure out of the air, an amount she thought would cover several months' rent on an office.*

★ **up in the air** not yet decided or settled ○ *At the moment, the fate of the Hungarian people is still up in the air.*

airs

airs and graces (British) if someone has airs and graces, they behave in a way which shows that they think they are more important than other people ○ *Ian is such a nice bloke. He has no airs and graces.*

put on airs and graces (British) or
put on airs to behave in a way which shows that you think you are more important than other people ○ *We're poor, honest folk, and we never put on airs.*

aisles

roll in the aisles to laugh so much that it is hard to stop ○ *It's all good knockabout stuff that has them rolling in the aisles.*

The aisles in a theatre or cinema are the gaps between the blocks of seats.

alec

The form 'aleck' is the usual spelling in American English. People sometimes spell 'alec' and 'aleck' with capital initials, as names.

a smart alec (British) or
a smart aleck (American) someone who thinks they are very clever and has an answer for everything ○ *They've got a smart alec lawyer from London to oppose bail.*

Alec or Aleck is a shortened form of the name Alexander.

alive

★ **alive and kicking** if someone or
✓ something is alive and kicking, they are still active or still exist, even though a lot of people might have expected them to have stopped or disappeared a long time ago ○ *Romance is still alive and kicking for a couple who will be celebrating their 50th wedding anniversary this week.*

eat someone alive
1 to cause someone great pain or distress ○ *The pain ate him alive; the world was nothing but fire and pain.*
2 to repeatedly bite someone ○ *'Can we*

go out?' 'Outside? The mosquitoes will eat us alive!'

skin someone alive

1 to make someone suffer a lot in order to get an advantage for yourself ○ *They are fiercely competitive. If they can skin us alive in business, they will.*

2 to punish someone severely ○ *Who let the cat out? You catch that animal, Ernie, or I'll skin you alive!*

someone will eat someone alive

said to mean that someone will completely defeat someone else ○ *Sid will be eaten alive by the hardened criminals at the jail.*

all

that's all she wrote *(American)* said when there is no more to say or when something is finished ○ *He got hurt, and he didn't play much anymore. That's all she wrote.*

alley

★ **a blind alley** something that is useless and will not lead to anything worthwhile ○ *Sooner or later they will have to realize that this is a blind alley and that they need to rethink their own strategies.*

A blind alley is a street which is closed at one end.

be right up someone's alley to be exactly what someone likes or knows about ○ *I thought this little problem would be right up your alley.*

all-singing

all-singing, all-dancing *(mainly British)* very modern and advanced, with a lot of additional features ○ *As long as you don't expect the latest all-singing, all-dancing Japanese marvel, this camera is an excellent buy.*

This phrase originally appeared on a poster advertising the first ever Hollywood musical film, Broadway Melody (1929), described as 'all talking, all singing, all dancing'.

altar

be sacrificed on the altar of something to suffer unfairly or be harmed because of a particular set of ideas or an activity ○ *They agreed that the interests of twelve million farmers could not be sacrificed on the altar of free trade.*

An altar was a large stone on which animals were killed during the worship of a god or goddess in former times. The killing of an animal in this way was called a sacrifice.

angel

a fallen angel someone once good or successful who has become bad or unsuccessful ○ *Without an away League win all season, Leeds United quickly became the fallen angels of the Premier League.*

angels

be on the side of the angels to be trying to do what you think is morally right ○ *The President is on the side of the angels when it comes to racial tolerance, the environment and Indian rights.*

answer

★ **not take no for an answer** to continue trying to make someone agree to something, despite their refusals ○ *Gerry, whose persistence has been known to wear down the resistance of many executives, refused to take no for an answer.*

ants

have ants in your pants to be very restless or impatient ○ *Before, there would be no way I would sit down and take it easy. It was like I had ants in my pants.*

ante

In card games such as poker, the ante is the amount of money which each player must place on the table before the game begins.

★ **up the ante** or
raise the ante
 1 to make greater demands or take greater risks in a dispute or contest, and so increase the amount that you will eventually lose or win ○ *Whenever they reached their goal, they upped the ante, setting increasingly difficult challenges for themselves.*
 2 to offer a higher gambling stake or financial investment ○ *Its network television division upped the ante by paying an estimated $2 million a year for a deal.*

ape

go ape (*informal*) to become extremely angry or very excited about something and start shouting or behaving in an uncontrolled way

 People who behave in a violent or uncontrolled way are being compared with apes.

appetite

★ **whet someone's appetite** to make someone start to want something very much ○ *Winning the World Championship whetted his appetite for more success.*

 To whet a knife means to sharpen it.

apple

the apple of your eye the person that you like more than anyone else ○ *I was the apple of my father's eye.*

 In the past, the pupil in the eye was sometimes called the apple.

★ **a bad apple** or
a rotten apple a dishonest, immoral, or unpleasant person who has a bad influence on those around them ○ *They made it clear that they were not going to tolerate a bad apple in the United States Senate.*

 If a rotten apple is stored with good apples, it causes the good ones to rot.

applecart

upset the applecart to cause trouble or spoil something ○ *His departure at this critical stage could upset the whole applecart.*

apple pie

American as apple pie typical of American culture or the American way of life ○ *Jeans are as American as apple pie and old jeans show a touch of class.*

 Apple pie is a traditional dessert that is thought of as typically American.

in apple-pie order (*old-fashioned*) very neat, tidy, and well-organized ○ *Apart from the plastic sheeting that still remained, they found everything in apple-pie order.*

 This expression is perhaps derived from the French for 'from head to foot', referring originally to a well-kept suit of armour or military uniform.

apples

apples and oranges (*mainly American*) two completely different things that it is useless to compare ○ *To compare one with the other is to compare apples and oranges.*

apron

apron strings
 1 the feelings that keep you dependent on your mother after the age when you should be independent ○ *At 21, I just had to get away, to cut those apron strings.*
 2 the control that one country or institution has over another even though it should be independent ○ *The Prime Minister has the rough outline of a blueprint for Australia as an independent nation, free of British apron strings.*

 These expressions were originally used to refer to a child, particularly a boy, who remained too much under the influence of his mother at an age when he should have become independent.

area

★ **a grey area** a situation or subject that is not clear or understood and that nobody really knows how to deal with ○ *The court action has highlighted the many grey areas in the law affecting stolen animals.*

ark

be out of the ark (British) to be very old-fashioned ○ *The car's steering was simply dreadful, and the driving position was straight out of the ark.*

something went out with the ark (British) said to mean that something is not used now because it is so old-fashioned ○ *Tyres are not made from rubber any more; that went out with the ark.*

> According to the Bible, the ark was the boat in which Noah and his family survived the flood.

arm

at arm's length if one person or organization is at arm's length from another, they are not closely connected, for example because it would be wrong for them to influence each another ○ *Relations between the bank and the committee will be at arm's length until the report is delivered in July.*

chance your arm (British) to do something risky or adventurous in order to get something you want ○ *Instead of going on the dole I chanced my arm on a business.*

cost an arm and a leg to cost a lot of money ○ *It cost us an arm and a leg to get here. But it has been worth it.*

★ **keep someone at arm's length** to avoid being friendly with someone or getting emotionally involved with them ○ *Brian had tried to get close, but his father had kept him at arm's length.*

put the arm on someone (American) to try to force someone to do what you want ○ *Women like you are not only writing checks, but you're putting the arm on other people to give to charity as well.*

someone would give their right arm to do something or
someone would give their right arm for something said to mean that someone wants something so much that they would do almost anything to get it ○ *I would give my right arm to be able to start again.*

> Most people are right-handed, and so consider their right arm to be more important than their left.

twist someone's arm to try hard to persuade someone to do something ○ *I didn't twist your arm to make you come. You wanted to because you sensed a story.*

arms

★ **be up in arms** to be angry and protesting strongly about something ○ *More than one million shopkeepers are up in arms against the new minimum tax. They are threatening a day's closure in protest.*

> 'Arms' in this expression means weapons.

★ **with open arms**
1 if you greet or welcome someone with open arms, you show that you are very pleased to see them or meet them ○ *We got out of the trucks to greet them with open arms. We had gifts ready, we were high on the idea of the meeting.*
2 if you welcome an event or new development with open arms, you are very pleased that it has happened ○ *Watchdog organizations welcomed today's guidelines with open arms.*

arrow

a straight arrow (American) someone who is very conventional, honest, and moral ○ *I was very much a product of my environment. I was very traditional, a real straight arrow in lots of ways.*

art

have something down to a fine art
to know the best way of doing something
because you have practised it a lot and
have tried many different methods
○ *They've got fruit selling down to a fine art.
You can be sure that your pears will ripen in
a day.*

ask

a big ask something which you have
been asked to do that is very difficult or
demanding ○ *It's a pretty big ask to run
faster in the second half of the race.*

atmosphere

**you could cut the atmosphere with
a knife** said to mean that the
atmosphere in a place is extremely tense
or unfriendly ○ *As soon as we entered the
house, you could cut the atmosphere with a
knife.*

awakening

★ **a rude awakening** a situation in which
you suddenly realize the unpleasant
truth about something ○ *Instead of quick
profits, Johnson got a rude awakening.*

axe

'Axe' is spelled 'ax' in American English.

an axe is hanging over someone said
to mean that someone is likely to lose
their job soon ○ *I wouldn't say there's an
axe hanging over him but he's only got
another season to put everything right.*

an axe is hanging over something
said to mean that something is likely to
be destroyed or ended soon ○ *The axe was
hanging over 600 jobs at oil giant BP last
night.*

get the axe or
be given the axe
1 to lose your job ○ *This time, it's the
business managers, executives and technical
staff who are getting the axe.*
2 to be cancelled or ended suddenly
○ *There will be cuts of $170 billion in defense,
and almost $120 billion in domestic spending.
Do you have any idea what specific programs
will get the ax?*

★ **have an axe to grind** to have
particular attitudes and prejudices about
something, often for selfish reasons
○ *Lord Gifford believed cases should be
referred by an independent agency which does
not have an axe to grind.*

There are several explanations for the
origin of this expression. One is a story
told by Benjamin Franklin about a man
who managed to get his own axe
sharpened by asking a boy to show
him how his father's grindstone
worked.

Bb

babe

'Babe' is an old-fashioned word for a baby or small child.

a babe in arms *(mainly British)* someone who is very young ○ *The family have always cycled, and Chris has been going to races since he was a babe in arms.*

a babe in the woods an innocent person with no experience who is involved in a complicated situation that they do not understand ○ *By this time I wasn't such a babe in the woods, and one thing I insisted on was that they sign a contract.*

An old story tells of two young orphans who were left in the care of their uncle. If the children died, the uncle would inherit the family fortune. The uncle ordered a servant to take them into a wood where they died and their bodies were covered with leaves by the birds. There is a pantomime based on this story.

baby

leave someone holding the baby *(British)* to make someone responsible for a problem that nobody else wants to deal with. The usual American expression is **leave someone holding the bag**. ○ *If anything goes wrong on this, Agnes, it's you and I who'll be left holding the baby.*

throw the baby out with the bath water to reject something completely, the good parts as well as the bad ○ *Even if we don't necessarily like that, we're not going to throw the baby out with the bath water.*

back

the back of beyond a place that is a long way from any other towns, houses, etc. ○ *He was born in a little village in the back of beyond.*

★ **be glad to see the back of someone** *(mainly British)* to be pleased that someone has gone because you do not like them ○ *Nick said last night that Court was a 'vile man'. He added: 'We are glad to see the back of him.'*

be on someone's back to annoy someone by criticizing them and putting a lot of pressure on them ○ *The crowd aren't forgiving, and as soon as you make a mistake they are on your back.*

break the back of something
1 to deal with the most difficult parts or the main part of a task ○ *The new government hopes to have broken the back of the economic crisis by the middle of this year.*
2 to do something in order to make something weaker so that it is destroyed after a time ○ *The government made a big effort late last year to break the back of the black market.*

break your back to work extremely hard to try to do something ○ *When you're breaking your back to make an enterprise work, it's going to cut into your time with family.*

do something behind someone's back to do something secretly in order to harm someone ○ *He had discovered that it was safer to have the Press on his side than to have correspondents sneaking around behind his back.*

get off someone's back *(informal)* to stop criticizing someone and leave them alone ○ *He kept on at me to such an extent* that occasionally I wished he would get off my back.

get your own back → see **own**

★ **have your back to the wall** to have very serious problems or be in a very difficult situation, which will be hard to deal with ○ The European Union has its back to the wall: it must choose between a reform of its working methods or its dilution into a large free trade area.

off the back of a lorry (British) if something has fallen off the back of a lorry, or you got something off the back of a lorry, you have bought something that was stolen ○ The only evidence of any criminal tendencies is that Pete once bought the boys a bicycle cheap off the back of a lorry.

on the back of an envelope quickly and without enough thought or planning ○ But the screenplay sounds as if it has been written on the back of an envelope and the whole thing has an improvised air about it.

on the back of a postage stamp if everything that someone knows about something could be put on the back of a postage stamp, they know very little about it ○ What she knew about children would have fitted on the back of a postage stamp.

put someone's back up (British) or **get someone's back up** to annoy someone ○ I thought before I spoke again. The wrong question was going to get her back up.

This expression may refer to the way cats arch their backs when they are angry.

put your back into something to start to work very hard in order to do something successfully ○ Eighty miles across the mountains could be done in six days walking, if she put her back into it.

★ **say something behind someone's back** to say unkind and unpleasant things about someone to other people ○ I knew behind his back his friends were saying, 'How can he possibly put up with that awful woman?'

★ **stab someone in the back** to do something which hurts and betrays someone ○ She seemed to be incredibly disloyal. She would be your friend to your face, and then stab you in the back. ○ People begin to avoid one another, take sides, be drawn into gossip and back-stabbing.

★ **turn your back on someone** to ignore someone and refuse to help them ○ We appeal to this conference – do not turn your back on the poor. Do not turn your back on the unemployed.

★ **turn your back on something** to stop thinking about something and paying attention to it, or to reject it ○ He intends to turn his back on his Communist past and form a completely new party with which to challenge for power.

when your back is turned when you are away or involved with something else ○ They are quite happy to question you, though, and are not averse to having a look through your personal items when your back is turned.

you scratch my back and I'll scratch yours said to mean that one person helps another on condition that the second person helps them in return ○ The chemist knew his business and, willing to play the game of 'you scratch my back and I'll scratch yours', charged Eve for only the ingredients he used.

backs

live off the backs of someone to use the money and resources of another group of people to survive, and give nothing in return ○ For too long the fat and decadent rich have lived off the backs of the working-class.

backwards

★ **bend over backwards** to try very hard to do something and to help or please someone, even if it causes you trouble ○ We are bending over backwards to ensure that the safeguards are kept in place.

know something backwards
(mainly British) or
know something backwards and forwards (American) to know something very well ○ *I thoroughly enjoy lecturing and I know my subject backwards.*

bacon

save someone's bacon (mainly British) to get someone out of a dangerous or difficult situation ○ *Your mother once saved my bacon, did you know that? She lent me money when I needed it.*

bag

a bag of nerves → see **nerves**
a bag of worms → see **worms**
★ **in the bag** certain to be obtained or achieved ○ *After being 23-16 up at the break, it seemed victory was in the bag for Ponty.*

The bag referred to here is a hunting bag, in which hunters carry home the animals and birds they have shot.

leave someone holding the bag
(mainly American) to make someone responsible for a problem that nobody else wants to deal with. The usual British expression is **leave someone holding the baby**. ○ *If a project goes bust, investors are left holding the bag.*

★ **a mixed bag** something that contains things that are of very different kinds or qualities ○ *The papers carry a mixed bag of stories on their front pages.*

The bag referred to here is a hunting bag containing the different kinds of animals and birds that the hunter has shot.

someone's bag of tricks a set of special techniques or methods that someone uses in their work ○ *The album is a delightful offering with Griffin going through his bag of tricks to great effect.*

This expression refers to the bag in which conjurers carry the equipment they need for their performances.

something is not someone's bag
(informal) said to mean that someone is not very interested in something or not very good at it ○ *'Being an umpire is not my bag,' Mr. Anders says. 'I'd rather be a player.'*

This expression may have originated in the slang spoken by American jazz musicians. They sometimes referred to the type of jazz they played, or to their own distinctive style of jazz, as their 'bag'.

bags

★ **pack your bags** to suddenly leave where you live or work, usually because of a disagreement ○ *If things go wrong and our conditions are not met, we will simply pack our bags and leave.*

bait

fish or cut bait (American) to stop wasting time and make a decision to do something ○ *Morale and stamina were said to be low after seven weeks of stalemate – the time had come to fish or cut bait.*

The literal meaning behind this expression seems to be that it is time for someone to make a definite decision either to start fishing, or else to prepare the bait so that other people can fish.

take the bait or
rise to the bait to react to something that someone has said or done in exactly the way that they wanted you to react, usually by getting angry ○ *It's important not to rise to the bait and get cross.*

In fly-fishing, the fish rise to the surface of the water to take the bait, and so they get caught.

baker

a baker's dozen (old-fashioned) thirteen ○ *Alan Else, series co-ordinator, has picked out a baker's dozen of top events between April and September.*

Bakers in medieval England had a bad reputation for cheating their customers by selling underweight loaves. After regulations were introduced to fix the standard weight of loaves, bakers began to add a thirteenth loaf to each dozen to make sure they were not breaking the law.

balance

★ **in the balance** if a situation is in the balance, it is not clear what is going to happen ○ *One of the judges had died unexpectedly and the choice of his successor was in the balance.*

A balance is a set of scales which consists of two dishes suspended from a horizontal bar.

★ **throw someone off balance** to suddenly confuse or surprise someone ○ *She was trying to behave as if his visit hadn't thrown her off balance.*

ball

a ball and chain someone or something that limits your freedom to do what you want ○ *Our national debt is an economic ball and chain dragging us down, keeping longer term interest rates high.*

In the past, prisoners were sometimes chained by the leg to a heavy metal ball to prevent them from escaping.

★ **the ball is in someone's court** said to mean that it is someone's responsibility to decide what to do next in a particular situation ○ *The ball is now in his court. I, and indeed others, have told him quite clearly what we think. He has to decide.*

This expression refers to the game of tennis.

behind the eight ball (mainly American) in trouble or in a difficult situation ○ *If a child doesn't get the basics in primary school they are way behind the eight ball.*

In the game of pool, the 'eight ball' is a ball with a number 8 on it, which

players have to pot last. If the eight ball is between the cue ball and the ball which the player is trying to hit, the player is likely to hit the eight ball first, which is a foul shot.

be on the ball to be quick to notice what is happening and quick to respond to things ○ *You can't bumble along in this business. You have to be on the ball.*

In football, the player who is on the ball has the ball at their feet and is in control of it.

★ **a crystal ball** a way of saying what will happen in the future ○ *What you need to help you select your new car is a crystal ball to tell you how much it will be worth a few years down the road.*

A crystal ball is a glass ball used by some traditional fortune-tellers to predict the future. They say that they can see visions of future events within the ball.

drop the ball (mainly American) to do something stupid or something that shows you have no skill ○ *There are people who'd like to see me fail, I know that. But I'm not afraid. I won't drop the ball.*

★ **have a ball** to enjoy yourself very much ○ *Why not go out and see if there's some place we can dance? Let's go and have a ball.*

In this expression, a 'ball' is a formal dance.

a new ball game or
a different ball game a situation that has changed so much that people will have to change the way they deal with it or consider it ○ *If military force were to be used, then that could be a completely different ball game.*

'Ball game' is often used in American English to refer to a game of baseball.

★ **play ball** to do what someone has asked you to do, or to work with them in order to achieve something that you both want ○ *The Association of British Insurers has threatened to withdraw its support if the banks and building societies refuse to play ball.*

★ **set the ball rolling** or
start the ball rolling to start an activity or do something which other people will join in with later ○ *The big supermarket rivals are all cutting prices. Sainsbury set the ball rolling last week with 30 per cent discounts on a wide range of brands.*

take the ball and run with it to take an idea or plan that someone else has started and develop it in order to see if it will be successful or useful ○ *It's up to him. If he studies, fine. If not, there's nothing we can do. He's the one who has to take the ball and run with it.*

▤ The game referred to here is American football.

the whole ball of wax *(mainly American)* the whole of something. The usual British expression is **the whole caboodle**.
○ *Perry wanted it all, the whole ball of wax. He wanted the Society for himself.*

ballistic

go ballistic to get extremely angry and start shouting or behaving in an uncontrolled way ○ *The singer went ballistic after one member of his band failed to show for a sound check on the recent American tour.*

▤ This expression uses the image of a ballistic missile, and the powerful explosion which it causes.

balloon

the balloon went up *(mainly British)* said to mean that a situation has become very serious or something bad has just happened ○ *On the Saturday the balloon went up. Sara told him to take his things and not to come back.*

▤ In the First World War, balloons were used both to protect targets from air

raids and to observe the enemy. The fact that a balloon had gone up therefore indicated that trouble was coming.

ballpark

A ballpark is a park or stadium where baseball is played.

a ballpark figure or
a ballpark estimate an approximate figure or quantity ○ *But what are we talking about here – a few thousand, millions, two bucks? Give me a ballpark figure.*

be in the same ballpark as someone or something to be as good or important as another person or thing ○ *As a general investigative agency, they're not in the same ballpark as the FBI.*

in the ballpark or
in the right ballpark approximately right ○ *A piece of subtle surgical equipment cost about £5 – an underestimate, maybe, but in the right ballpark.*

balls

keep balls in the air to deal with many different things at the same time ○ *They had trouble keeping all their balls in the air. They were trying to do too much and things were starting to break down.*

▤ This expression uses the image of juggling, where someone has to keep throwing and catching a number of balls at the same time.

banana

★ **slip on a banana skin** or
slip on a banana peel *(British)* to say or do something that makes you look stupid and causes you problems ○ *Most of the nation would enjoy seeing mighty Liverpool slip on a banana skin in front of millions.*

▤ Comedies and cartoons often use the device or image of a character slipping on a banana skin, falling over, and looking foolish.

band

★ **a one-man band** someone who does every part of an activity themselves, without help from anyone else ○ *The chef was a one-man band, taking orders, and cooking and serving at table.*

> A one-man band is a street entertainer who plays several different instruments at the same time.

bandwagon

★ **jump on the bandwagon** to get involved in an activity or idea because it is likely to succeed or it is fashionable at the time ○ *There will always be inexperienced people ready to jump on the bandwagon and start teaching classes in whatever is fashionable.*

> In American elections in the past, political rallies were often publicized by a band playing on a horse-drawn wagon which was driven through the streets. Politicians sat on the wagon and those who wished to show their support climbed on board.

bang

bang goes something (*mainly British*) said to mean that it is now obvious that something cannot succeed or be achieved ○ *Bang goes his influence, maybe his job, if the two countries reach a real understanding.*

more bang for your buck a bigger quantity or better quality of something for the same amount of money ○ *With this program you get more bang for your buck.*

not with a bang but a whimper if something happens not with a bang but a whimper, it is less effective or exciting than people expected or intended ○ *The festival finished yesterday not with a bang but a whimper, as thousands of disappointed festival-goers left early.*

> This is the last line of T. S. Eliot's poem 'The Hollow Men' (1925): 'This is the way the world ends Not with a bang but a whimper.'

bank

★ **break the bank** to cost too much money ○ *Porto Cervo is expensive, but there are restaurants and bars that won't break the bank.*

> If one gambler wins all the money that a casino has set aside to pay all the winning bets, they are said to have broken the bank.

laugh all the way to the bank to make a lot of money very easily or very quickly ○ *Investors who followed our New Year share tips are laughing all the way to the bank.*

> This expression was used by the American entertainer Liberace to describe how he felt when he read bad reviews of his shows.

baptism

★ **a baptism of fire** a first experience of a new situation that is very difficult or unpleasant ○ *They have given themselves a baptism of fire by playing what many would consider the four best teams in the world.*

> This expression originally referred to the deaths of martyrs by burning. It was later used by the French Emperors Napoleon Bonaparte and Napoleon III to refer to someone's first experience of battle.

bark

someone's bark is worse than their bite said to mean that someone seems to be much more severe or unfriendly than they really are ○ *My bark is definitely worse than my bite. When people get to know me, they'll tell you I'm just a big softy really.*

barn

closing the barn door after the horse has gone ➔ see **door**

barrel

have someone over a barrel to have put someone in a position where they cannot possibly win ○ *The unions wish they had more options. Jobs are tight, they know that, and they feel management has them over a barrel.*

This expression may refer to a method used in the past to save someone who had almost drowned. The person was placed face down over a barrel, which was then rocked gently backwards and forwards until all the water had drained from their lungs.

scrape the bottom of the barrel or **scrape the barrel** to use something or do something that is not very good, because you cannot think of anything better to use or do ○ *The game designers were scraping the bottom of the barrel for ideas when they came up with this one.*

barrelhead

on the barrelhead or **on the barrel** (*American*) if you pay cash on the barrelhead or on the barrel for something, you pay for it immediately and in cash. The British expression is **on the nail**. ○ *Customers usually pay cash on the barrelhead, so bad debts aren't much of a problem.*

The most likely explanation for this expression comes from the days when settlers first started living in the American West. Saloons often consisted of just a room with a barrel of drink in it, and customers who wanted to drink had to put their money on the top of the barrel before being served, as credit was not given.

barrels

give someone both barrels or **let someone have it with both barrels** to attack or criticize someone fiercely and aggressively ○ *Let him have it with both barrels and then get out of the situation while you can.*

This expression refers to the firing of both barrels of a double-barrelled gun.

base

In baseball, players have to hit the ball and then run round all four corners or bases to score a run.

get to first base to begin to make progress with your plans ○ *We couldn't get to first base with any U.S. banks. They didn't want to take the risk.*

★ **off base** (*mainly American*) mistaken or wrong ○ *I don't think the church is off base at all in taking a moral stand on this.*

In baseball, if a player is caught off base, a member of the opposite team gets them out while they are between bases.

touch base to speak or write to someone, often when you have not spoken to them or seen them for a long time ○ *Being there gave me a chance to touch base with and make plans to see three friends whom I had not seen for a year.*

In baseball, batters have to touch the first, second, and third bases to score a run.

bases

touch all the bases or **cover all the bases** to deal with or take care of all the different things that you should ○ *He has managed to touch all the bases necessary, and trade goes on.*

In baseball, batters have to touch the first, second, and third bases to score a run.

basket

★ **a basket case**

1 a country or organization whose economy or finances are in a very bad state ○ *The popular image about Latin America a few years ago was that it was a basket case.*

2 (*informal*) a crazy or mentally ill person ○ *You're going to think I'm a basket case when I tell you this, but we used to play with toys when we were about twenty.*

This expression was originally used to describe someone, especially a soldier, who had lost all four limbs. It may have come about because some of these people had to be carried around in baskets.

bat

do something off your own bat (British) to decide to do something yourself rather than being told to do it ○ *I'm certain whatever she did, she did off her own bat; it was nothing to do with me.*

In cricket, players can score runs either by hitting the ball themselves, or when their partner hits it, or when the ball is not hit at all but goes beyond the wicket.

go to bat for someone or
go in to bat for someone to give someone your support or help ○ *She was just fabulous in going to bat for me, in not being judgmental and helping me work it out.*

This expression refers to a baseball player who joins in the game and takes the place of another batter.

like a bat out of hell very quickly ○ *He said 'Thank you, sir,' and departed like a bat out of hell.*

In this expression, 'bat' is used to refer to a small, flying mammal. Bats are often associated with the devil, probably because they usually fly at night.

play a straight bat (British)
1 to try to avoid answering difficult questions ○ *But last Saturday her interviewee played a straight bat, referring all inquiries to his solicitors before driving off.*
2 (old-fashioned) to do things in an honest and simple way because you have traditional ideas and values ○ *Amit, then 14, was very surprised to find that playing a straight bat was not considered all that important in his new school.*

In cricket, to play a straight bat means to play very correctly and cautiously, in order not to risk being out.

right off the bat (mainly American) immediately or at the very beginning of a process or event ○ *He learned right off the bat that you can't count on anything in this business.*

The image here is of a ball bouncing quickly off a baseball bat.

bath

take a bath (journalism) to lose a lot of money on an investment ○ *Investors in the company took a 35 million dollar bath on the company, which entered bankruptcy proceedings 18 months ago.*

take an early bath (British) to stop doing something that you are involved in and leave before you have finished ○ *Nineteen of the country's most experienced referees have been invited to take an early bath.*

baton

pass the baton to give responsibility for something to someone else ○ *Does this mean that the baton of leadership is going to be passed to other nations?*

pick up the baton to take over responsibility for something ○ *In the 1980s, councils really picked up the baton of public concern and became the standard bearers in the quality of life versus nature debate.*

In a relay race, team members pass on a baton as they finish running their stage of the race.

bats

have bats in the belfry (informal) to be crazy ○ *What maudlin nonsense! Don't say that to anyone else or they'll think you've got bats in the belfry.*

The belfry is the top part of a church tower where the bells are kept, and bats resting there would fly about wildly when disturbed by the bells being rung. In this expression, the belfry represents the person's head.

batteries

★ **recharge your batteries** to stop working or doing an activity for a period and relax so that you feel better when you start working or doing the activity again ○ *After playing in the Divisional Championship, I took a long break from the game to recharge my batteries.*

When people recharge batteries, they put an electrical charge back into the batteries by connecting them to a machine that draws power from another source of electricity.

battle

★ **the battle lines are drawn** said to mean that opposing groups or people are ready to start fighting or arguing, and that it has become clear what the main points of disagreement are ○ *The battle lines were drawn yesterday for the fiercest contest in the history of local radio.*

a battle of nerves → see **nerves**

a battle of wills an argument or conflict in which the people involved are refusing to accept each other's demands ○ *It was a battle of wills, and Grace's was the stronger.*

a battle of wits a competition or disagreement in which each person involved uses their intelligence and mental ability to beat their opponents ○ *With chess you're involved in a battle of wits from start to finish.*

★ **fight a losing battle** to try to achieve something when you are very unlikely to succeed ○ *Miss Bennett fought a losing battle against her depression.*

join battle to decide that you are going to try to beat someone in an argument or contest ○ *This new company intends to join battle with Cellnet and Vodafone in the mobile telecoms market.*

★ **a running battle** an argument or fight with someone that continues over a long period of time ○ *For the past year, customers have inspired a running battle between the two mobile phone providers.*

someone has won the battle, but lost the war said to mean that in a struggle, someone has gained one small thing but lost something that is much more important ○ *The strikers may have won the battle, but they lost the war.*

bay

★ **keep something at bay** or **hold something at bay** to stop something from attacking you or affecting you badly ○ *By salting the meat, bacteria were kept at bay, preserving the meat for future use.*

When a hunted animal is at bay, it is trapped by the hounds and forced to turn and face them to defend itself. However, if the animal is successfully defending itself in this position, you can say that it is holding the hounds at bay. This second use seems the most likely origin of the expression.

bead

draw a bead on something (*mainly American*) to aim your weapon at someone or something ○ *There was only one spot where the light through the trees would have enabled him to draw a bead on his target.*

The bead is the small marker on top of the end of the barrel on some guns, which is used to aim at the target.

be-all

★ **not the be-all and end-all** not the only thing that is important in a particular situation ○ *Results are not the be-all and end-all of education.*

beam

be way off beam (*British*) to be completely wrong or mistaken ○ *The writer was hilariously way off beam in his criticism of soccer.*

This refers to the use of a radio signal or beam to direct aircraft which were coming in to land. A radio transmitter on one side of the runway transmitted dots, or short tones, while one on the other side transmitted dashes, or long tones. If pilots were coming in on the right course, the dots and dashes merged and the pilots heard a continuous tone.

bean

> There are several slang meanings for 'bean'. In the following expressions, it means money.

a bean counter someone who is only interested in how much money a business makes and spends and does not care about more important things ○ *The reason for America's failure is that we have bean counters running our companies.*

not have a bean (British, old-fashioned) to have very little money ○ *When we married we didn't have a bean so we bought all our furniture second-hand.*

beans

full of beans happy, excited, and full of energy ○ *Jem was among them, pink-cheeked and full of beans after a far longer sleep than anybody else had got.*

> This originally referred to a horse that was well-fed and therefore full of energy.

★ **spill the beans** to reveal the truth about something secret or private ○ *He always seemed scared to death I was going to spill the beans to the cops.*

> This expression has a number of possible explanations. One is derived from an ancient practice of voting by placing coloured beans in one of a number of jars or pots, then tipping the beans out and counting them. Another is an informal description of vomiting.

bear

be like a bear with a sore head (mainly British) to behave in a very bad-tempered and angry way ○ *Ever since we arrived here, you've been like a bear with a sore head.*

loaded for bear (American) ready and eager to do something ○ *We could notify the mainland police, and they could go charging in there with guns and bullhorns, loaded for bear.*

> Someone who is loaded for bear has ammunition which is powerful enough to kill a bear, even though they may be hunting smaller animals.

beat

★ **beat your breast** or **beat your chest** to show regret or anger very publicly about something that has gone wrong in a way that is usually not sincere ○ *He is very thoughtful with the players. He doesn't go around beating his chest all the time. He knows when a quiet chat is what's needed.* ○ *His pious breast-beating on behalf of the working classes was transparently bogus, but it was a clever public relations job.*

not miss a beat to always know what is happening and so be able to take advantage of every situation ○ *This time we played like machines. The longer the game went the stronger we got, and we never missed a beat.*

> The 'beat' referred to here is probably a heartbeat, although it may refer to a beat in music.

without missing a beat without pausing or hesitating ○ *She was asked point-blank whether she should bow out. But, without missing a beat, she replied: 'I do not believe it is appropriate for me to withdraw my nomination.'*

beaver

an eager beaver someone who is very enthusiastic about work or very anxious to please other people ○ *George was like a sneaky kid. He lied, boasted, was an eager beaver without the ability to live up to his promises.*

> Beavers are often associated with hard work, as they spend a lot of time building shelters and dams out of mud and wood.

beck

at someone's beck and call always ready to do what someone tells you to do, even when their orders are unreasonable ○ *Your child must understand that you can't always be at his beck and call for every little thing.*

> 'Beck' is an old word meaning a gesture, for example a nod or a movement of the hand or forefinger, which represents a command such as 'Come here.'

bed

get into bed with someone to make an agreement to work with another person or group. This expression is usually used showing disapproval.
○ *The BBC might have been criticized for getting into bed with Sky TV last summer, but it's easy to see now why they did.*

not a bed of roses not all pleasant, having some difficult or unpleasant aspects ○ *Life as a graduate is not a bed of roses.*

> The bed referred to here is a flower bed.

put something to bed to achieve a plan or task or complete it successfully
○ *Before putting the agreement to bed, we still had to satisfy Fran Murray.*

> On an old-style printing press, the bed is the flat part that holds the type. If journalists talk about putting a newspaper or magazine to bed, they are talking about making the final changes before printing.

someone got out of bed the wrong side or
someone got out of bed on the wrong side said to mean that someone is in a very bad mood without there seeming to be any obvious reason for it
○ *Sorry I was so unpleasant when I arrived this morning. I must have got out of bed the wrong side.*

> This relates to the old superstition that it was unlucky to put your left foot on the ground first when getting out of bed. 'Get off on the wrong foot' is based on a similar belief.

someone has made their bed and will have to lie on it said to mean that someone has to accept the unpleasant results of a decision which they made at an earlier time ○ *For Sara, marriage was for life – in her eyes she had made her bed and would have to lie on it.*

bee

the bee's knees (British) something or someone that you like very much ○ *Back in the '80s it was the bee's knees but now it looks horribly out of date.*

> Some people believe that this expression refers to the way in which bees transfer pollen from their bodies to pollen sacs on their back legs. However, it seems more likely that it dates from the 1920s, when other similar expressions such as 'the cat's pyjamas' began to be used.

have a bee in your bonnet to feel very strongly about something and keep talking or thinking about it. This expression is considered old-fashioned in American English. ○ *I've got a bee in my bonnet about the confusion between education and training.*

> Two images are suggested by this expression. The first is of thoughts buzzing inside someone's head like bees. The second is of someone who has a bee trapped in their hat and is anxious to get it out before they are stung.

beeline

make a beeline for something to go straight to something without any hesitation or delay ○ *The boys headed for computer games while the girls made a beeline for the dolls.*

> It used to be believed that bees, having collected the pollen, flew back to the hive in a straight line. In fact, this belief has been proved to be incorrect. 'As the crow flies' is based on a similar idea.

beer

not all beer and skittles (British) not always as enjoyable or as easy as other people think ○ *It's not all beer and skittles when you get to be famous.*

> The game of skittles is associated with beer because it is traditionally played in pubs.

★ **small beer** (British) something that is not important when compared with another thing ○ *The present series of royal scandals makes the 1936 abdication look like pretty small beer.*

> 'Small beer' originally meant weak beer.

beggars

beggars can't be choosers said to mean that you must accept an offer or a particular course of action, because it is the only one which is available to you ○ *'So would you be happy to work wherever you got a job?' 'Yes. You've got to take anything that comes around because beggars can't be choosers.'*

begging

be going begging to be available to be used or bought because other people are not interested ○ *Nearly half a million holidays for the busiest six weeks of the year are still going begging.*

bell

ring someone's bell (mainly American, informal) to be very attractive, exciting, or satisfying to someone ○ *After a couple of comedies that didn't exactly ring my bell, I thought I'd like to do something that was different.*

saved by the bell said when something happens at the last possible moment which allows you to escape from a difficult situation ○ *There was another period of silence. It was broken by the sound of Eleanor's car pulling up outside the front door. 'Saved by the bell,' I said.*

> This expression refers to the bell which signals the end of a round in a boxing match.

something rings a bell said to mean that something is slightly familiar to you and you are aware that you have heard it before, although you may not remember it fully ○ *'Who?' he queried, 'Passing Clouds? I simply don't remember them. Their name doesn't ring a bell.'*

bells

bells and whistles special features or other things which are not necessary parts of something, but which are added to make it more attractive or interesting ○ *People are still buying luxury cars with all the bells and whistles, but cheaper systems are becoming more popular.*

> In the past, organs were used in cinemas to accompany silent films. Some of these organs had devices attached to them which produced sound effects such as bells and whistles.

pull the other one, it's got bells on it → see **pull**

★ **set alarm bells ringing** or **set warning bells ringing** to cause people to begin to be aware of a problem in a situation ○ *The islanders' fight for compensation has set alarm bells ringing round the world.*

bellyful

have had a bellyful of something (informal) to find something very irritating or boring, and not want to experience it any longer ○ *I have had a bellyful of excuses. It's always someone else's fault.*

belly-up

★ **go belly-up** if a company goes belly-up, it fails and does not have enough money to pay its debts ○ *Factories and farms went belly up because of the debt crisis.*

This expression may refer to dead fish floating upside down near the surface of the water.

belt

below the belt unfair or cruel ○ *These kinds of blows below the belt are the surest way to destroy a friendship or love affair.*

In boxing, it is against the rules to hit an opponent below the level of their belt.

a belt and braces approach (British) a situation in which you do something extra in order to make sure that something is safe or works properly ○ *He described airport security as a belt and braces approach, at huge cost to industry.*

Trousers that are held up by a belt as well as a pair of braces are not likely to fall down.

★ **have something under your belt** to have already achieved or done something ○ *After a few years, I had enough recipes under my belt to put them into a book.*

★ **tighten your belt** to spend less and live more carefully because you have less money than you had before ○ *Clearly, if you are spending more than your income, you'll need to tighten your belt.*

bend

drive someone round the bend (mainly British, informal) to annoy someone so much that they feel they are becoming crazy ○ *Can you make that tea before your fidgeting drives me completely round the bend?*

★ **round the bend** (mainly British, informal) crazy ○ *If anyone told me a few months ago that I'd meet a marvellous person like you I'd have said they were round the bend.*

benefit

★ **give someone the benefit of the doubt** to decide to believe that what someone is saying or doing is honest and right, even though it is possible that they are not telling the truth or that they are doing something wrong ○ *I am basically a trusting person. I make it a practice to give everyone the benefit of the doubt.*

berth

give someone or something a wide berth to deliberately avoid someone or something ○ *Having lived all my adult life in Africa I have a very healthy respect for snakes and have always tried to give them a wide berth.*

A berth is the amount of space which a sailing ship needs to manoeuvre safely.

best

the best of both worlds → see **worlds**

bet

★ **a good bet** or
a safe bet
1 a sensible or useful thing to do ○ *When you're unfamiliar with your guests' likes and dislikes, poultry is a safe bet for the main course.* ○ *If you really want to keep your home safe from robbery, your best bet is still to buy a burglar alarm.*
2 something that is very likely to happen or someone who is very likely to do something ○ *But they will not enjoy reading this book; it is a safe bet that few will read more than 100 pages.*

bets

all bets are off said to mean that it is impossible to say how a particular situation may develop ○ *This election year all bets seem to be off. In fact, even the folks who make a living predicting what the voters will do find themselves on shaky ground.*

★ **hedge your bets** to avoid making decisions, or to decide on more than one thing, so that you will not make a mistake whichever way the situation develops ○ *Political forecasters are hedging their bets about the likely outcome of this Saturday's Louisiana governor's race.*

When bookmakers accept a large bet, they often try to protect themselves against heavy losses by laying bets with other bookmakers. This practice is called 'hedging'.

big

In the second expression, 'britches' is also spelled 'breeches'.

get too big for your boots *(British)* or **get too big for your britches** *(American)* to behave as if you are much more important or clever than you really are ○ *Nobody in England will ever allow us to get too big for our boots.*

Britches are trousers which reach as far as your knees.

bike

on your bike *(British, informal)* said to tell someone to go away or stop behaving in a foolish way ○ *It was a heated game, and when I got Alec I just said something like 'You're out mate, on your bike.'*

bill

★ **be given a clean bill of health**
1 to be told by a doctor that you are completely healthy and not ill in any way ○ *He had a full medical late last year and was given a clean bill of health.*
2 to be examined or considered and then judged to be in a satisfactory condition ○ *Fourteen seaside resorts failed to meet the environmental and safety standards, while 43 were given a clean bill of health.*

A bill of health was a certificate which was given to a ship's master to present at the next port the ship arrived at. It stated whether or not there was an infectious disease aboard the ship or in the port it was departing from.

★ **fit the bill** to be exactly the right person

or thing that is needed in a particular situation ○ *I wanted someone who really knew their way around film-making and I knew that Richard would fit the bill.*

The 'bill' in this expression is a public notice advertising something such as a show or a play.

★ **foot the bill** to pay for something ○ *Police will have to foot the bill for the slight damage to both cars.*

This expression may come from the practice of someone paying a bill and signing it at the bottom, or 'foot'.

sell someone a bill of goods *(American)* to deceive someone or tell them something that is not true ○ *I began to realize that I'd been sold a bill of goods, that I wasn't in any way incompetent or slothful.*

bind

be in a double bind to be in a very difficult situation, because you have problems that cannot be solved easily or without causing more problems ○ *Women are in a double bind: they are expected to act like men, but they are criticized when they do.*

bird

the bird has flown said to mean that someone has escaped or disappeared ○ *He was supposed to follow the woman to work. Instead he'd wandered off, come back an hour later, and found the bird had flown.*

a bird in the hand or
a bird in the hand is worth two in the bush said to mean that it is better to keep something you have than to try to get something better and risk having nothing at all ○ *Another temporary discount may not be what you want, but at least it is a bird in the hand.*

a bird of passage someone who never stays in one place for long ○ *Most of these emigrants were birds of passage who returned to Spain after a relatively short stay.*

an early bird someone who gets up early in the morning or who does something before other people ○ *We've always been early birds, up at 5.30 or 6am.* ○ *An early-bird discount is sometimes available at the beginning of the season.*

the early bird catches the worm said to mean that if someone wants to do something successfully then they should start as soon as they can ○ *If you're going to make it to the Senate, you need to start right now. The early bird catches the worm.*

eat like a bird to eat very little ○ *She always orders two larger chops and one smaller chop because her daughter eats like a bird and her husband eats a lot.*

a little bird told me said to mean that you are not going to say how you found out about something or who told it to you. This expression is considered old-fashioned in American English. ○ *Incidentally, a little bird told me that your birthday's coming up.*

a rare bird someone or something that is different from most other people or things ○ *Diane Johnson's book is that rare bird, an American novel of manners.*

> 'A rare bird' is a translation of the Latin expression 'rara avis', which was used by the Roman writer Juvenal in the 2nd century AD to describe a black swan. At the time, black swans were unknown, although they were later discovered in Australia.

birds

the birds and the bees the facts about sex and sexual reproduction, as told to a child ○ *At the age of 16, I remember having yet another discussion about the birds and the bees with my father.*

> People sometimes explain sex and sexual reproduction to children by telling them how animals reproduce.

birds of a feather two or more people who are very similar in many ways ○ *She and my mother were birds of a feather. You felt something special between them that left you out.*

birds of a feather flock together said to mean that people from the same group or with the same interests like to be with each other ○ *Birds of a feather flock together. Basically, people seek out neighborhoods that are most congenial to them.*

for the birds stupid, boring, or worthless ○ *This journal business is for the birds. It's a waste of time.*

> This expression refers to horse manure, which is of use only to small birds in search of nest material or food such as seeds.

kill two birds with one stone to manage to achieve two things at the same time ○ *We can talk about Union Hill while I get this business over with. Kill two birds with one stone, so to speak.*

biscuit

take the biscuit (British) to be very extreme or behave extremely ○ *This ban takes the biscuit. The whole idea is ridiculous and bureaucratic and not fair on the children.*

> This expression has a similar origin to 'take the cake', which refers to the practice in the past of awarding cakes as prizes in competitions.

bit

> A bit is a piece of metal which is held in a horse's mouth by the bridle and reins.

champ at the bit or
chomp at the bit to want very much to do something, but be prevented from doing it, usually by a situation that you have no control over ○ *Foremen had been champing at the bit to strike before next week's meeting.*

get the bit between your teeth to become very enthusiastic and determined about doing a particular job or task ○ *You're persistent when you get the* bit between your teeth, I'll say that for you.

The bit should be positioned at the back of a horse's mouth, behind its back teeth. When a horse bolts, it sometimes takes the bit between its teeth, which makes it very difficult for a rider or driver to use the reins to control it.

bite

bite off more than you can chew

to try to do too much ○ Don't bite off more than you can chew simply because everything is going so well.

a second bite at the cherry (British) a second chance to do something, especially something that you failed at the first time ○ We might, if we push hard enough, get a second bite at the cherry in two years' time.

take a bite out of something

(American) to take away a part of a sum of money or other quantity ○ The government is going to be taking a bigger bite out of people's income than ever before.

biter

the biter gets bit (British) said to mean that someone suffers as a result of their own actions, especially when they were trying to hurt someone else ○ Sympathy seldom abounds when the biter gets bit.

'Biter' is an old word meaning a swindler or con man.

bitten

once bitten, twice shy said to mean that a recent and unpleasant experience has made someone not want to get involved in similar situations in the future ○ I'm certainly not looking for new boyfriends or thinking of having any more kids. Once bitten, twice shy.

black

★ **black and blue** badly bruised ○ I spent that night in hospital and was released the

next day with minor head and neck injuries. My face was black and blue.

★ **black and white** a way of considering things that is too simple, judging things either as right or wrong ○ That is not, any more, an accurate portrait of much of British society. People do not see these things purely in black and white. ○ It's just not a black and white issue.

★ **in black and white** written down ○ We have a strict, clear rule in black and white, that sexual harassment will lead to expulsion.

★ **in the black** not owing anyone money ○ Last year, the company was back in the black, showing a modest pre-tax surplus of £4.6 million.

This expression comes from the practice in the past of using black ink to fill in entries on the credit side of a book of accounts.

blank

Originally, to draw a blank meant to be given a losing ticket in a lottery.

★ **draw a blank**

1 to not be able to find someone or something or find out about something ○ I searched among the bottles and under and behind and inside everything I could think of and drew a blank.

2 (mainly American) to be unable to remember something or to answer a question you are asked. ○ Why do we recognize a face, but sometimes draw a blank when it comes to the name?

3 (mainly British, journalism) to not score any goals or points, or win any races in a sports competition ○ Goal-shy Raith drew a blank at home yet again.

blanket

a wet blanket

1 someone who spoils other people's fun because they are boring or miserable ○ 'Hey', said Thack, looking at Michael. 'Stop being such a wet blanket.'

2 something that makes an event or situation less successful or enjoyable than it would otherwise have been ○ *The weather threw a wet blanket over the championship final yesterday.*

blanks

fire blanks (British) to fail to achieve anything although you are trying very hard ○ *Dalian and his fellow attackers continued to fire blanks against Norwich and it was left to full-back Steve Staunton to provide Villa's first goal.*

Blanks are gun cartridges which contain explosive but do not contain a bullet, so that they do not cause any injuries or damage when the gun is fired.

bleed

★ **bleed someone dry** to make a person, organization, or country weak, for example by forcing them to use up all their money or resources ○ *He extorted money from me on a regular basis for five years. But he was careful not to bleed me dry.*

In the past, doctors often treated patients by bleeding them, which involved extracting some of their blood.

blessing

★ **a blessing in disguise** an event that causes problems and difficulties at first, but later brings advantages ○ *Franklin's illness proved a blessing in disguise, for it gave him strength and courage which he had not had before.*

blind

blind as a bat unable to see well ○ *Without my glasses I was blind as a bat.*

Most bats are active only at night and find their way by sending out sounds and sensing objects from the echoes, rather than by using their eyesight.

the blind leading the blind said to mean that the person in charge is just as incapable of doing a task as the person who they are meant to be helping or guiding ○ *I'm afraid it's the blind leading the blind as I've never actually used this software before myself.*

This expression comes from one of the stories that Jesus tells in the Bible (Matthew 15:14). He says that if a blind person tries to guide another blind person, they are not likely to be successful in getting what they want.

fly blind to be in a situation where you have nothing to help or guide you ○ *We will be flying blind into a world we don't know anything about.*

A pilot is flying blind when they are piloting an aircraft without using visual navigation, but relying solely on their instruments.

swear blind (British) to insist that you are telling someone the truth, even though they are not sure whether or not to believe you. The American expression is **swear up and down**. ○ *He had a reputation for being a bit of a philanderer but he swore blind that he had met the right girl in me and said he wanted to settle down.*

blink

on the blink not working properly ○ *We had to have the washing done at the laundry because our machine was on the blink.*

block

★ **on the block** (American) offered for sale at auction. The British expression is **under the hammer**. ○ *Last week, after months of rumors, the company officially put itself on the block.*

put your head on the block or **put your neck on the block** to risk your reputation or job by taking a particular course of action ○ *He really put his neck on the block there and it's great to see his bravery being rewarded.*

The 'block' here is a special piece of wood on which a prisoner was made to place his or her head before being beheaded.

★ **a stumbling block** a problem which stops you from achieving something
○ *Your inability to choose between material security and emotional needs is a major stumbling block to your happiness.*

> This expression comes from the Bible (Romans 14:13), where people are advised not to do anything that might stop other people from being successful.

blocks

> These expressions come from athletics, where sprinters put their feet against pieces of equipment called starting blocks to help them start quickly when the race begins.

off the blocks or
off the starting blocks

1 used for describing how quickly someone starts to do something
○ *The Liberal Democrats were first off the blocks with their manifesto on Monday.*
2 succeeding in starting to do something, often despite difficulties
○ *People thought I was totally mad and, if they think that, then you just can't get off the starting blocks.*

blood

★ **bad blood** feelings of anger or hatred between two people or groups because of arguments they have had in the past
○ *The situation has reached crisis point because of the bad blood between the two.*

> People used to think that feelings such as anger and resentment were carried in the blood.

bay for blood (British) to demand that a particular person should be hurt or punished, because of something that person has done ○ *The travel company had just buried itself with debts of more than £12m and thousands of disappointed holidaymakers were baying for blood.*

> This expression compares the people's demands to the sounds that hounds make on a hunt.

be after someone's blood to want to harm or punish someone, because they have harmed you or made you angry
○ *Adam has upset Broderick, who is after his blood.*

blood and thunder (British) full of exaggerated feelings or behaviour
○ *In a blood and thunder speech, he called for sacrifice from everyone.*

★ **blood is shed** or
blood is spilled

1 (journalism, literary) said to mean that people are being killed in fighting ○ *All the signs are that if blood is spilled the countries will be at war.*
2 said to mean that trouble or suffering is caused as a result of a change taking place ○ *Given the political blood that was spilled over the deficit reduction package, few observers believe the president will start spending more.*

blood is thicker than water said to mean that people are more loyal to their family than to people who are not related to them ○ *Families have their problems and jealousies, but blood is thicker than water.*

blood on the carpet serious trouble as a result of a struggle between people or groups inside a company or other organization ○ *The issue is highly emotional and will cause a lot of blood on the carpet.*

★ **blood, sweat, and tears** great effort or suffering that is involved in a task or project ○ *It's almost as if the end product – the songs themselves – are less important than the blood, sweat, and tears that went into them.*

> This expression is originally derived from a wartime speech by the British Prime Minister, Winston Churchill, in which he said, 'I have nothing to offer but blood, toil, tears and sweat'. He

used the expression several times in other wartime speeches.

have blood on your hands to be responsible for a death, or for the deaths of several people ○ *I want him to know he has my son's blood on his hands.*

★ **in cold blood** in a calm and deliberate way, rather than in anger or self-defence. People often use this expression to express shock or horror at a killing. ○ *They murdered my brother. They shot him down in cold blood.* ○ *This is just another attempt to excuse the cold-blooded murder of an innocent woman.*

In medieval times, some people believed that certain emotions changed the temperature of the blood.

★ **in your blood** used for describing something that is a very important part of you and seems natural to you, for example because it is traditional in your family or culture ○ *Trilok has music in his blood. 'I was born into a family of musicians.'*

it is first blood to someone or **someone draws first blood** *(journalism)* said to mean that someone has had a success at the beginning of a competition or conflict ○ *The picture had looked bright as the Scots drew first blood with a drop goal from Gregor Townsend.*

like getting blood out of a stone or **like getting blood out of a turnip** *(American)* said to mean that it is very difficult persuading someone to give you money or information ○ *The goods have to be returned to their rightful owner and getting money back from the seller is like getting blood out of a stone.*

★ **make your blood boil** to make you very angry ○ *This statement is untrue and makes my blood boil.*

In medieval times, some people believed that certain emotions changed the temperature of the blood.

make your blood run cold *(literary)* to frighten or shock you very much ○ *It makes my blood run cold to think what this poor, helpless child must have gone through.*

In medieval times, some people believed that certain emotions changed the temperature of the blood.

★ **new blood** new people who are brought into a company or organization in order to improve it ○ *The July Ministerial reshuffle is a chance to freshen up the government and make way for new blood.*

out for blood intending to attack someone, or to make them suffer in some other way ○ *They seem to be out for blood, and they're attacking everywhere where their enemy is.*

scent blood to sense a weakness in your opponent and take advantage of it ○ *Right wing parties, scenting blood, have been holding talks aimed at building an alternative coalition.*

taste blood to have a small victory which encourages you to think that you can defeat your opponent completely ○ *The real opposition to the Government continues to be its own backbenchers who have now tasted blood for the first time.*

sweat blood to work very hard to achieve something ○ *I sweat blood to write songs with tunes that you can remember.*

young blood young people who are brought into a company or organization in order to provide new ideas or new talent ○ *The selectors have at last shown some bravery and forward thinking and gone for some young blood, fielding a side whose average age is just 26.*

blot

a blot on the landscape a building or some other structure that is ugly and spoils a place which would otherwise be very attractive ○ *The power station is both a blot on the landscape and a smear on the environment.*

blow

★ **soften the blow** or
cushion the blow to make an
unpleasant change or piece of news
seem less unpleasant and easier to
accept ○ *Although attempts were made to
soften the blow, by reducing what some
people had to pay, the tax still met with
widespread opposition.*

★ **strike a blow for something** to do
something which supports a cause or
principle, or makes it more likely to
succeed ○ *Her appointment would strike a
blow for women's rights in Poland.*

blows

★ **come to blows** to disagree so strongly
about something that you start to fight
○ *Some residents nearly came to blows over
this proposal.*

blue

★ **out of the blue** unexpectedly ○ *Turner's
resignation came out of the blue in the after-
math of his team's 3-0 defeat at Portsmouth.*

This expression compares an
unexpected event to a bolt of lightning
from a blue sky. The expressions 'out of
a clear blue sky' and 'a bolt from the
blue' are based on a similar idea.

bluff

★ **call someone's bluff** to put someone
in a position in which they are forced to
do what they have been threatening to
do because you do not believe that they
will really do it ○ *Mr Lukanov warned that
he would deal severely with any protest
actions in the universities. Now, the students
have called his bluff.*

In poker, a player who is bluffing is
playing as though they have a strong
hand when in fact they have a weak
one. If another player calls the first
player's bluff, they increase their stake
to the required amount and ask the
first player to show their cards.

blushes

★ **spare someone's blushes** or
save someone's blushes *(British)*
to do something that prevents someone
from being in an embarrassing situation
○ *Andy Gray spared Tottenham's blushes last
night, scoring a superb goal against Enfield.*

board

★ **above board** honest and legal ○ *Anyone
who wants to inspect our books can see for
themselves that we are totally above board.*

This expression comes from card
games in which players place their
bets on a board or table. Anything that
takes place under the table is likely to
be against the rules, whereas actions
above the table, where other players
can see them, are probably fair.

★ **across the board** if a policy or development applies across the board, it applies
equally to all the people or areas of business
connected with it ○ *The compromise
proposal reduces funding across the board.*

This was originally an American
expression which was used in horse
racing. If someone bet across the
board, they bet on a horse to win or to
come second, third, or fourth.

★ **go back to the drawing board** to
start again or try another idea because
something which you have done has not
been successful ○ *His government should
go back to the drawing board to rethink their
programme in time to return it to Parliament
by September.*

Drawing boards are large flat boards,
on which designers or architects place
their paper when drawing plans or
designs.

go by the board *(British)* or
go by the boards *(American)* to be
abandoned and forgotten ○ *You may find
that all your efforts go by the board when he
is away at university.*

'To go by the board' originally meant to fall or be thrown over the side of a ship.

sweep the board (British) to win all the prizes or seats in a competition or election ○ *The government swept the board in yesterday's first contested National Assembly elections.*

This expression comes from card games where players place the money they are betting on a board or table. The image is of the winner sweeping his or her arm across the table to collect all the money.

★ **take something on board** (British)
1 to understand or accept an idea, suggestion, or fact ○ *I listened to them, took their comments on board and then made the decision.*
2 to accept responsibility for a task or problem and start dealing with it ○ *All you have to do is call us. Our co-ordinator will take your problem on board and solve it.*

The literal meaning of this expression is to take something onto a boat or ship.

boat

float someone's boat (informal) to seem exciting, attractive, or interesting to someone ○ *I can see its appeal. But it doesn't float my boat.*

★ **in the same boat** in the same unpleasant or difficult situation ○ *If baldness is creeping up on you, take heart – 40 per cent of men under 35 are in the same boat.*

push the boat out (British) to spend a lot of money in order to have a very enjoyable time ○ *I earn enough to push the boat out now and again.*

This expression may come from people having a farewell party before setting sail on a voyage.

★ **rock the boat** to do something which might cause trouble in a situation ○ *Diplomats are expecting so much*

instability in a power struggle after his death that they argue it's unwise to rock the boat now.

Bob

Bob's your uncle (British) said to mean that a process or series of events ends exactly as expected or in exactly the right way ○ *If the boiler ever gets too hot, the safety valve releases all the excess steam, and Bob's your uncle. No problem.*

This expression dates back to a political scandal in Britain in 1886. The Prime Minister Robert Cecil gave his nephew the position of Chief Secretary for Ireland, and many people criticized him for this. The name 'Bob' is short for 'Robert'.

body

★ **body and soul** with all your energy or skill ○ *They worked body and soul to make this day a success.*

★ **a body blow** (mainly British, journalism) something which causes you great disappointment or difficulty ○ *The result will deliver a body blow to Conservative party confidence.*

In boxing, a body blow is a punch between the breast-bone and the navel.

keep body and soul together to earn enough money to buy the basic things that you need to live ○ *20-year-old Rafael says he's selling firewood to keep body and soul together.*

over my dead body said to mean that you dislike a plan or action that has been suggested, and will do everything you can to prevent it ○ *They will get Penbrook Farm only over my dead body.*

boil

be on the boil (British)
1 if a situation or feeling is on the boil, it is at its point of greatest activity or strength ○ *Across the border in Sweden, a similar debate is on the boil.*
2 to be performing very successfully

○ *All three players are obviously on the boil at the moment in the Italian league.*

come to the boil (British) or
come to a boil (American) if anger comes to the boil, it increases until it reaches a very high level ○ *Their anger came to the boil last week when they protested at a media campaign against them.*

go off the boil (British)
1 to be less successful than in the past ○ *Sandy Lyle says it pays to go back to the fundamentals when your game goes off the boil.*
2 to become less strong or intense ○ *If a relationship seems to be going off the boil, it is a good idea to appraise the situation.*

bold

bold as brass not ashamed or embarrassed, although your behaviour is shocking or annoying to other people ○ *Their leader, bold as brass, came improperly dressed, while all the others were wearing black ties.*

This expression may be based on an incident that occurred in Britain in 1770, when the London Evening Post illegally published a report of Parliamentary proceedings. As a result, the printer was put in prison. The Lord Mayor, Brass Crosby, released him and was punished by being imprisoned himself. There were public protests and Crosby was soon released.

bolt

★ **a bolt from the blue** or
a bolt out of the blue an event or piece of news that surprises you because it was completely unexpected ○ *Mrs Thomas says the arrest had come 'like a bolt out of the blue'.*

This expression compares an unexpected event to a bolt of lightning from a blue sky. The expressions 'out of a clear blue sky' and 'out of the blue' are based on a similar idea.

someone has shot their bolt (British) said to mean that someone has done everything they can to achieve something but has failed, and now can do nothing else to achieve their aims ○ *The opposition have really shot their bolt; they'll never ever get any more votes than this.*

This expression uses the idea of an archer who has only one arrow or 'bolt' and is defenceless once he has fired it.

bomb

go like a bomb (British, informal) to move very fast ○ *Once I had a Russian motorbike. It was built like a tank, weighed a ton, went like a bomb and was pure joy to ride.*

put a bomb under something (British) to completely change the way an old-fashioned organization or system operates ○ *One half of us admired and valued the BBC's high standards, the other half longed to put a bomb under it and propel it into innovation.*

bombshell

★ **drop a bombshell** to suddenly tell someone a piece of bad news which they were not expecting ○ *My ex-wife is on the phone and she drops a bombshell. Sue, our beloved daughter, is leaving the country to live in Australia.*

bone

★ **a bone of contention** a problem that people have been arguing about for a long time ○ *Pay, of course, is not the only bone of contention.*

close to the bone or
near to the bone if a remark or piece of writing is close to the bone, it makes people uncomfortable, because it deals with subjects which they prefer not to be discussed ○ *This isn't strictly satire, it's far too close to the bone to be funny.*

★ **cut something to the bone** to reduce resources or costs as much as possible

○ We managed to break even by cutting costs to the bone.

have a bone to pick with someone
to be annoyed with someone about something, and want to talk to them about it ○ 'I have a bone to pick with you.' She felt justified in bringing up a matter that she had been afraid to discuss before.

This expression may refer to the fact that dogs often fight over bones.

bones

★ **the bare bones** the most basic parts or details of something ○ We worked out the bare bones of a deal.

feel something in your bones to feel very strongly that you are right about something, although you cannot explain why ○ Joe, I have a hunch you're going to lose tonight. I just feel it in my bones.

★ **make no bones about something** to not hesitate to express your thoughts or feelings about something, even though other people will not like what you say ○ There will be changes in this Welsh team until we get it right. I make no bones about that.

This expression may refer to gambling. 'Bones' is an old word for dice, so a gambler who 'makes no bones' throws the dice after just one shake, rather than performing an elaborate ritual.

book

★ **bring someone to book** (British) to punish someone officially for something wrong that they have done ○ No-one has yet been brought to book for a crime which outraged Italy.

Originally, if someone was brought to book, they were ordered to prove that something they had said or done was in keeping with a written rule or agreement.

a closed book (British) something or someone that you know or understand very little about ○ Economics was a closed book to him. It constituted a strange, illogical territory where two and two didn't always make four.

close the book on something
to cause something to end, especially a difficult or unpleasant situation ○ Lawyers say they are happy to close the book on one of the most frustrating chapters of the company's history.

★ **do something by the book** or **go by the book** to do something correctly and strictly, following all the rules ○ Modern man is often dull, studious, careful, safe. He does everything by the book.

★ **in someone's book** said to state someone's own belief or opinion, especially when it is different from the beliefs or opinions of other people ○ People can say what they like, but in my book he's not at all a bad chap.

an open book a person's life or character that you can find out everything about, because nothing is kept secret ○ Her long life is not a completely open book, but it is full of anecdotes and insights into her part in Hollywood history.

read someone like a book to know exactly what someone is thinking and planning ○ There are a number of books on the market which suggest that it is possible to learn to read a person like a book.

throw the book at someone to give someone the greatest punishment that is possible for the offence that they have committed ○ 'If this is found to be true, then we will throw the book at the clubs involved,' Barry Smart, the chairman of the league, said yesterday.

This expression refers to a book in which laws are written down.

you can't judge a book by its cover
said to mean that you should wait until you know someone or something better before deciding whether you like them, because your first opinions may be wrong

○ *You can't judge a book by its cover. Just because someone looks strange doesn't mean they're not a nice person.'*

books

be in someone's bad books (British)
to have done something that has annoyed someone ○ *Sir John was definitely in the Treasury's bad books for incorrect thinking on economic prospects.*

be in someone's good books (British)
to have done something that has pleased someone ○ *I never really was that bothered about being in the teacher's good books.*

cook the books to dishonestly change the figures in your financial accounts in order to deceive people ○ *She knew that when the auditors looked over the books there would be no hiding the fact that she had cooked the books and £3 million was missing.*

≡ The 'books' in this expression are books of accounts.

boot

the boot is on the other foot
→ see **foot**

★ **get the boot** or
be given the boot (informal) to lose your job ○ *The chief reason he got the boot was because the Chancellor didn't trust him any more.*

put the boot in (British, informal)
to attack another person by kicking or hitting them ○ *Policemen who are tempted to put the boot in occasionally will have to tread more carefully in future.*

★ **put the boot into someone or something** or
put the boot in (British, informal) to criticize a person or thing very severely or be very unkind about them ○ *There's no one quite like an unpublished novelist for putting the boot into established reputations.*

boots

die with your boots on to die while you are still actively involved in your work ○ *Unlike some businesspeople who die with*

their boots on, he has very sensibly left the entire running of Seamark to his son.

≡ This expression was originally used to refer to a soldier who died in battle.

fill your boots (British) to get as much of something valuable or desirable as you can ○ *As soon as the company was sold off, the bosses were always going to fill their boots with cut-price share options.*

get too big for your boots
→ see **big**

lick someone's boots to do everything you can to please someone, often because they are powerful or influential and you want something from them ○ *Even if you didn't have an official position you'd still be a big shot locally, everybody would be licking your boots.*

quake in your boots to be very frightened or anxious about something that is about to happen ○ *If you stand up straight you'll give an impression of self confidence even if you're quaking in your boots.*

step into someone's boots (mainly British) to take over from another person in sport who has been injured or who has given up their position ○ *Michael Kinane, the leading Irish jockey, has turned down the chance to step into Steve Cauthen's boots and ride for Sheikh Mohammed next season.*

bootstraps

Bootstraps are straps attached to a boot which you use for pulling it on.

pull yourself up by your bootstraps to improve your situation by your own efforts, without help from anyone else ○ *It was his ability to pull himself up by his bootstraps which appealed to Mrs Thatcher.*

to your bootstraps (Australian) if someone is, for example, British to their bootstraps, they are typically British ○ *Lord McAlpine and all his friends are law and order men to their bootstraps.*

bored

bored to death or
bored to tears or
bored stiff extremely bored ○ *There are no jobs, there's nothing to do; these young people are bored to death.*

boss

show someone who's boss to prove to someone that you have more power or control than they do ○ *It was a classic strategy: show new students who is boss at the very beginning and everything will then go smoothly.*

bottle

hit the bottle to start drinking too much alcohol, usually because something very unpleasant or upsetting has happened to you ○ *One newspaper even said I'd started hitting the bottle. Complete rubbish.*

bottom

at the bottom of the heap → see **heap**
at the bottom of the pile → see **pile**
be at the bottom of something or **lie at the bottom of something** to be the real cause of an undesirable attitude or situation ○ *Remember that pride is at the bottom of all great mistakes.*
the bottom falls out of something or **the bottom drops out of something** if the bottom falls out of a market or industry, people stop buying its products in as large quantities as they did before ○ *But just as quickly, the bottom fell out of the American home video game market.*
bump along the bottom (*British*) to reach a low level of performance, and not get any better or any worse ○ *New car sales are continuing to bump along the bottom as the motor industry shows little sign that it is going to revive substantially this year.*
from the bottom of your heart → see **heart**

★ **get to the bottom of something** to solve a problem or mystery by discovering the truth about it ○ *The attack was quite severe. We intend to get to the bottom of things and, if needs be, ensure that action is brought against those responsible for it.*
scrape the bottom of the barrel → see **barrel**

bounds

★ **out of bounds**
1 if a place is out of bounds, you are not allowed to go there ○ *The area has been out of bounds to foreigners for more than a month.*
2 if a subject is out of bounds, you are not allowed to discuss it ○ *The private lives of public figures should be out of bounds to the press and public.*

bow

> 'Bow' is pronounced with the same vowel sound as the word 'how'.

bow and scrape to be too respectful towards a powerful or famous person ○ *Having a hereditary title can be a drawback because some people feel they have to bow and scrape.*

> If you bow, you bend your body towards someone as a formal way of greeting them or showing respect. In the past, 'scraping' was a form of bowing which involved drawing back one leg and bending the other.

take a bow (*mainly British, journalism*) written before or after a person's name to congratulate that person or show admiration for them ○ *When you've got the best camerawork and the best commentators – Martin Tyler, take a bow – it's hard to go far wrong.*

box

a black box a process or system that produces a particular result although it is not understood how it works ○ *Only a* decade ago cancer was a black box about which we knew nothing at the molecular level.

In an electronic or computer system, a black box is a self-contained part. You can understand its function without knowing anything about how it works.

out of the box

1 (mainly American) if you come out of the box in a particular way, you begin an activity in that way. If you are first out of the box, you are the first person to do something ○ Arco is definitely first out of the box with an alternative gas for cars without catalytic converters.

This refers to the game of baseball. A player runs out of the box, which is the marked area where the batter stands, towards first base after hitting the ball.

2 if you buy something such as a computer or software and you can use it out of the box, you can use it immediately, without having to do or learn complicated things first ○ The computer industry has yet to sell a PC which can be used by a novice, straight out of the box.

think outside the box to think about something in a way that is new or different and shows imagination, especially in business ○ She goes on to urge companies to think outside the box and challenge the old ways of working.

boy

someone's blue-eyed boy (mainly British) or

someone's fair-haired boy (mainly American) a man who someone has a very high opinion of and gives special treatment to ○ He'd lost interest in Willy by that time – I was the blue-eyed boy.

a whipping boy someone or something that people blame when things go wrong, even though they may not be responsible for what has happened

○ Businessmen fear that they and the hard-won free-market reforms will be the whipping boys for the economic ills that confront the new administration.

A whipping boy was a boy who was educated with a prince and was punished for the prince's mistakes because tutors were not allowed to hit the prince.

boys

boys will be boys said to excuse the noisy or rough way a boy is behaving by saying that it is normal for boys to be noisy and rough ○ 'Your troubles are just beginning,' they would say, shaking their heads. 'Boys will be boys.'

★ **one of the boys** a man who is accepted as belonging to a group of men who behave in ways which are considered typically masculine ○ His overly enthusiastic efforts to seem just one of the boys were sometimes embarrassing.

brain

get your brain into gear (informal) to start thinking clearly about something, so that you can achieve what needs to be done ○ All I want is to get my brain into gear and get back to the top.

have a brain like a sieve to have a bad memory and often forget things ○ Grandad's lost the car keys again – his brain's like a sieve.

brains

pick someone's brains to ask someone for advice or information, because they know more about a subject than you do ○ I'd like to pick your brains about something. Nothing urgent.

★ **rack your brains** to think very hard about something or try very hard to remember it. The old-fashioned spelling 'wrack' is occasionally used instead of 'rack' in this expression. ○ Reformers are racking their brains for a way to slow down these processes.

brass

the brass ring (American) success or a big reward or profit ○ *There are good and bad features to living among people who are all young, on the make and going for the brass ring professionally.*

On some merry-go-rounds, a brass ring was placed just out of the reach of the riders. If a rider managed to grab it, they won a free ride.

cold enough to freeze the balls off a brass monkey (British, informal) extremely cold ○ *It was a cold snap in the middle of spring with winds cold enough to freeze the balls off a brass monkey.*

A brass monkey was a plate on a warship's deck on which cannon balls were stacked. In very cold weather the metal contracted, causing the stack to fall down.

get down to brass tacks to begin to discuss the basic, most important aspects of a situation ○ *The congress was due to get down to brass tacks today with a debate on the party's performance during the last five years.*

The usual explanation for this expression is that in Cockney rhyming slang 'brass tacks' are facts.

bread

the best thing since sliced bread or **the greatest thing since sliced bread** something that someone thinks is very good, original, and exciting ○ *When your programme first started I thought it was the best thing since sliced bread. But over the last three months I think you have adopted an arrogant attitude.*

bread-and-butter most basic or important ○ *On major bread-and-butter issues, there's little difference between the two candidates.*

bread and circuses used to describe a situation in which a government tries to take attention away from real problems or issues, by providing people with things which seem to make their lives more enjoyable ○ *Metternich proceeded to neutralize political dissent through a policy of bread and circuses.*

This is a translation of a phrase in a satire by the Roman poet, Juvenal. It refers to the fact that, in ancient Rome, the authorities provided the people with public amusements and food in order to prevent possible rebellion.

cast your bread upon the waters (literary) to do something good or take a risk, usually without expecting very much in return ○ *You should make time to offer assistance to others. It's a case of casting your bread upon the waters – who knows how the favour will be repaid.*

This expression comes from the Bible (Ecclesiastes 11:1), where people are advised that if they are generous and helpful (by 'throwing their bread to the waters'), they will be rewarded, but possibly only after a long time.

know which side your bread is buttered on to understand fully how you are likely to benefit from a situation, and know what to do or who to please in order to put yourself in the best possible situation ○ *Donald was a man who knew with utter clarity which side his bread was buttered on.*

★ **your bread and butter** the main way that you earn money ○ *'Who's your audience?' 'We play maybe a hundred colleges a year. That is our bread and butter.'*

breadline

live on the breadline or **be on the breadline** to be extremely poor ○ *They should be stripped of everything they own but the bare essentials. Let them feel what it is like to be on the breadline.*

In times of hardship, particularly in the last century in the United States, poor people used to line up outside bakeries or soup kitchens for free or very cheap bread.

break

★ **give me a break** (informal)
1 said to show that you think that someone is being very annoying or ridiculous ○ Give me a break! Why quote feminists on a decision that concerns the rights of all women? Why can't they quote mothers, teachers, nurses, or dancers?
2 said to tell someone to stop criticizing or annoying you and leave you alone ○ Anxious families yesterday begged youngsters, 'Give us a break', after dozens of cars were wrecked by the gangs.

never be given an even break or **never get an even break** to not get the same chances or opportunities to do something as other people ○ He kept talking about how she never got an even break from the family.

> 'Never Give a Sucker an Even Break' is the title of a film starring W. C. Fields (1941).

breast

beat your breast → see **beat**
make a clean breast of something to start to be completely truthful about something, so that you can begin to deal properly with a problem ○ If you make a clean breast of your problems, creditors, whether secured or unsecured, are much more likely to deal fairly and leniently with you.

breath

★ **a breath of fresh air** someone or something that is pleasantly different from what you are used to ○ Basically, I was bored. So Mike, my husband, was a breath of fresh air.

★ **hold your breath** to wait in an anxious or excited way to see what happens next ○ She had been holding her breath and hoping that the agreement would be signed.

★ **in the same breath** if someone says one thing and then in the same breath says something different, they are saying two things that do not agree with each other ○ For politicians to demand firm immigration controls and argue against racism in the same breath is a deep contradiction.

someone is wasting their breath said to mean that there is no point in someone continuing with what they are saying, because it will not have any effect ○ He wanted to protest again, but the tone of her voice told him he was wasting his breath.

★ **take your breath away** to amaze and impress you ○ 'Tell me again about the picture.' 'It's beautiful. It's so beautiful it takes your breath away.'

★ **with bated breath** feeling anxious or excited to see what happens next ○ They got the people in the villages interested in what was going to happen, so they were then watching with bated breath as the experiment began.

> 'Bate' is an old form of 'abate', which in this context means 'control' or 'hold back'.

breeze

shoot the breeze to talk with other people in an informal and friendly way ○ Goldie does what she likes doing best: shooting the breeze about life, love, and her bad reputation.

> The sense of 'shoot' used here is presumably the same as 'shoot the rapids', suggesting riding or being carried along by the flow of a conversation.

brick

come up against a brick wall to arrive at a situation in which something is stopping you from doing what you want and preventing you from making any progress ○ I was tired, I had been working real hard for a long time and I felt that I'd come up against a brick wall.

drop a brick (British) to say something that upsets or offends other people ○ After his comments on the live TV programme, Mr Freeman was immediately aware that he had dropped a political brick of the worst kind.

drop something or someone like a hot brick → see **drop**

bricks

make bricks without straw to do a job, or try to do it, without the proper resources that are needed for it ○ *His job was apparently to make education bricks without straw – that is to say, to be inspiring without having much money.*

This expression is from the Bible (Exodus 5:7), and refers to Pharaoh's order that the captive Israelites should not be given any straw to make bricks.

bridge

someone will cross that bridge when they come to it said to mean that someone intends to deal with a problem when, or if, it happens, rather than worrying about the possibility of it happening ○ *'You can't make me talk to you.' 'No, but the police can.' 'I'll cross that bridge when I come to it.'*

bridges

★ **build bridges** to do something to help opposing groups of people to understand each other or behave well towards each other ○ *We look for ways to build bridges between our two organizations.*

brief

hold no brief for something (*British, formal*) to not support a particular cause, belief, or group of people ○ *This newspaper holds no brief for a committee that has done nothing to distinguish itself in the past.*

In law, a brief is all the papers relating to a particular client's case that are collected by the client's solicitor and given to the barrister who will represent them in court.

bright

bright as a button (*mainly British, old-fashioned*) intelligent, full of energy,

or very cheerful ○ *She was as bright as a button and sharp as anything. If it had been her running the company, it might still be OK.*

bright-eyed

bright-eyed and bushy-tailed lively, keen, and full of energy ○ *But for now, go and sleep awhile. I need you bright-eyed and bushy-tailed tomorrow.*

The comparison in this expression is to a squirrel.

britches

get too big for your britches → see **big**

broke

★ **go for broke** to decide to take a risk and put all your efforts or resources into one plan or idea in the hope that it will be successful ○ *In London's West End there is a reluctance to take risks with new plays while going for broke on musicals.*

If a gambler goes for broke, they put all their money on one game or on one hand of cards.

★ **if it ain't broke, don't fix it** said to mean that things should only be changed if they are wrong. The word 'ain't' is a form of 'isn't' which is used in informal or non-standard English. ○ *With regard to proposals for some grand reorganization of the intelligence community: If it ain't broke, don't fix it. And I believe it is not broke.*

The first recorded use of this modern proverb is by the American Bert Lance, President Carter's Director of the Office of Management and Budget (1977). He was referring to governmental reorganization.

broom

a new broom someone who has just started a new job in an important position and is expected to make a lot of changes ○ *We had a new, exceptionally young headmaster and he was a very active new broom.*

brown

brown as a berry having a very dark skin from being in the sun ○ *Steve Hobbs had just come back from his holiday. Brown as a berry he was, when he came round here the following Monday.*

> The reference may be to juniper or cedar berries, which are brown, as most other berries are red, purple, or white.

brownie

★ **brownie points** a reward or congratulations for doing something good ○ *Mr Stein would almost certainly win extra brownie points for taking an ultra-cautious view and removing uncertainty from the share price.*

> The Brownies is an organization for young girls. Members are expected to be well-behaved and helpful.

brunt

★ **bear the brunt of something** to suffer most as a result of a problem or difficult situation ○ *In 37 years with British Rail, I saw how station staff always bore the brunt of public anger over fare rises.*

brush

tar someone with the same brush to assume that someone behaves as badly as other people in a particular group ○ *I am a football supporter and I often have to explain that I'm not one of the hooligan sort, because we all get tarred with the same brush.*

> This expression comes from the use of tar to mark all the sheep in one flock to distinguish them from another flock.

bubble

★ **the bubble has burst** said to mean that a situation or idea which was very successful has suddenly stopped being successful ○ *The bubble has burst. Crowds at the team's World League games are down from last year's 40,000 average to 22,000.*

> The bubble referred to in this expression is the South Sea Bubble, a financial disaster which took its name from The South Sea Company. In the early 18th century, this company took over the British national debt in return for a monopoly of trade with the South Seas. A lot of people invested in the company, but it crashed in 1720 and many investors became bankrupt.

on the bubble (*American*) in a difficult situation, and very likely to fail ○ *Hewlett was on the bubble after a difficult round yesterday.*

> The reference may be to a bubble which is about to burst, or to the bubble on a spirit level, which will move off centre if the level is not kept exactly horizontal.

buck

> In poker, the buck was a marker or object which was passed to the person whose turn it was to deal the next hand. This person could either keep the marker or pass it on, in order to avoid dealing and being responsible for declaring the first stake.

★ **the buck stops here** or
the buck stops with me said to mean that a problem is your responsibility, and that you are not expecting anyone else to deal with it ○ *If you are going to blame anyone, it must be the man in charge and that's me. The buck stops here.*

> This expression is often associated with U.S. President Truman, who had it written on a sign on his desk in the Oval Office to remind him of his responsibilities.

★ **pass the buck** to fail to take responsibility for a problem, and to expect someone else to deal with it instead ○ *He is our responsibility. Canada is the only place he has ever known and to* deport him is simply passing the buck because of a legal loophole.

bucket

kick the bucket to die. This expression is used to refer to someone's death in a light-hearted or humorous way. ○ *All the money goes to her when the old man kicks the bucket.*

≣ The origins of this expression are uncertain. It may refer to someone committing suicide by standing on a bucket, tying a rope around their neck, then kicking the bucket away.

bud

★ **nip something in the bud** to stop a bad situation or bad behaviour at an early stage, before it can develop and become worse ○ *It is important to recognize jealousy as soon as possible and to nip it in the bud before it gets out of hand.*

≣ This expression may refer to extremely cold weather damaging a plant and stopping it flowering. Alternatively, it may refer to a gardener pruning a plant in bud to prevent it flowering.

buffers

hit the buffers (*British, journalism*) if an idea, plan, or project hits the buffers, it experiences difficulties which cause it to fail ○ *Their plans may not get very far before they hit the buffers.*

≣ Buffers are barriers at the end of a railway track.

bug

★ **be bitten by the bug** to become very enthusiastic about something, and start doing it a lot ○ *Bitten by the travel bug, he then set off for a working holiday in Australia.*

bull

a bull in a china shop someone who says or does things which offend or upset people in situations where they should be more careful ○ *In confrontational*

situations I am like a bull in a china shop.

a red rag to a bull (*mainly British*) or **a red flag before a bull** (*mainly American*) something which always makes a particular person very angry ○ *This sort of information is like a red rag to a bull for the tobacco companies but it really needs to be exposed.*

≣ It is a common belief that the colour red makes bulls angry. In bullfighting, the matador waves a red cape to make the bull attack.

take the bull by the horns to take definite and determined action in order to deal with a difficult situation ○ *This is the time to take the bull by the horns and tackle the complex issues of finance.*

≣ In bullfighting, the matador sometimes grasps the bull's horns before killing it.

bullet

★ **bite the bullet** to accept a difficult or unpleasant situation ○ *The same stressful event might make one person utterly miserable, while another will bite the bullet and make the best of it.*

≣ During battles in the past, wounded men were sometimes given a bullet to bite on while the doctor operated on them without any anaesthetic or painkillers.

get the bullet or **be given the bullet** (*British, informal*) to lose your job. ○ *The banks are still making money but they only have to have one bad year and everybody gets the bullet.*

bum

a bum steer (*mainly American, informal*) information that is wrong and misleading ○ *Did you give me a bum steer about your name and address?*

≣ This expression may refer to a worthless bullock. Alternatively, it may refer to someone being given directions which are not correct.

get the bum's rush *(informal)* to be completely ignored or rejected in an unexpected and upsetting way ○ *He turned up there at 2.45 and sat down to lunch with European royalty, so we got the bum's rush.*

> A bum is a person who has no permanent home or job, and very little money. This expression refers to a bum being thrown out of a place by force.

bums

bums on seats *(British, informal)* if a performer or performance puts bums on seats, they are very popular and succeed in attracting large audiences ○ *He's always been like that and will never change. That's why he gets bums on seats – he's a showman.*

> In British English, your bum is your bottom.

bundle

a bundle of nerves → see **nerves**
drop your bundle *(mainly Australian)* to give up and stop trying to win or succeed when you are failing at something ○ *At 25-6 University were losing badly, but to their credit they did not drop their bundle.*

bunny

not a happy bunny *(British)* annoyed or unhappy about something. You use this expression to be humorous or ironic. ○ *Arthur stared into the cup, worriedly. He was not a happy bunny.*

> 'Bunny' is a childish word for a rabbit, and the expression is meant to sound like part of a children's story.

burn

★ **burn your boats** *(British)* or
burn your bridges to do something which forces you to continue with a particular course of action, and makes it impossible for you to return to an earlier

situation ○ *I didn't sell it because I didn't know how long I would be here. I didn't want to burn all my bridges.*

> During invasions, Roman generals sometimes burned their boats or any bridges they had crossed, so that their soldiers could not retreat but were forced to fight on.

burner

★ **put something on the back burner** to decide not to do anything about a situation or project until a later date, because you do not consider it to be important at the time ○ *She put her career on the back burner after marrying co-star Paul Hogan two years ago, spending her time making a home for them in Australia.*

> A burner is one of the rings or plates on the top of a cooker.

bush

the bush telegraph *(British, old-fashioned)* the way in which information or news can be passed on from person to person in conversation ○ *No, you didn't tell me, but I heard it on the bush telegraph.*

> This expression refers to a primitive method of communication where people who are scattered over a wide area beat drums to send messages to one another.

not beat about the bush *(British)* or
not beat around the bush to say what you want to say clearly and directly, even though it is not pleasant ○ *I decided not to beat around the bush. 'I'm at Sam's,' I told her. 'Eddie didn't come back from his paper route yet. Nobody knows where he is.'*

> In game shooting, beaters drive birds or small animals out of the undergrowth by beating it with sticks. They may have to do this cautiously as they do not know exactly where the birds or animals are.

bushel

hide your light under a bushel
to say little about your skills and good
features, instead of being confident
and telling other people about them
○ *Don't be tempted to hide your light
under a bushel for fear of upsetting other
people.*

This is from the Bible (Matthew 5:15),
where Jesus says that no one lights a
lamp and then hides it under
something; instead, they put it on
a stand so that it can give light to
everyone.

bushes

beat the bushes (*mainly American*)
to try very hard to get or achieve
something ○ *He was tired of beating the
bushes for work, and he did not want to ask
for help or accept charity.*

business

be in business (*spoken*) to be able to
start doing something because you have
got everything ready for it ○ *It plugs in
here, right? Okay, we're in business. Let's see
how it works, guys.*

business as usual said to mean
that everything is continuing in the
normal way, even though something
unpleasant or unexpected has happened
○ *Mr Fitzwater told reporters: It is business
as usual; this isn't the kind of crisis that
requires us to drop everything else.*

do something like nobody's business
to do something a lot or very well
○ *I mean Geoffrey can chat like nobody's
business.*

do the business (*informal*) to do
what is needed to achieve a result.
Compare with **do the trick**. ○ *Now I
could be judged solely on my achievements
as a player, and I was absolutely determined
to prove I could still do the business.*

★ **mean business** to be serious and
determined about what you are doing

○ *One of them poked a shotgun at me.
I could see he meant business.*

busman

a busman's holiday (*mainly British*)
a situation in which someone spends
part of their holiday doing or
experiencing something that forms
part of their normal job or everyday
life ○ *A fire crew's Christmas outing turned
into a busman's holiday when their coach
caught fire.*

This expression may refer to bus
drivers at the beginning of the
20th century when buses were horse-
drawn. Drivers sometimes spent their
day off riding on their own bus to
make sure that the relief drivers were
treating the horses properly.

busy

a busy bee or
busy as a bee if someone is a busy bee
or busy as a bee, they enjoy doing a lot of
things and always keep themselves busy
○ *He is busy as a bee designing every
production in London.*

butter

**butter wouldn't melt in
someone's mouth** said to mean that
although someone looks completely
innocent, they are capable of doing
something bad ○ *He may look as though
butter wouldn't melt in his mouth, but I
wouldn't trust him.*

butterflies

have butterflies in your stomach
to feel very nervous about something
that you have to do ○ *He seemed so full of
enthusiasm that I felt foolish still having
butterflies in my stomach.*

butterfly

break a butterfly on a wheel (*British*)
to use far more force than is necessary to
do something ○ *They have had their
ideology combed over, examined,*

misinterpreted and rewritten. Talk about breaking a butterfly on a wheel.

> This is a quotation from 'Epistle to Dr Arbuthnot' (1735) by Alexander Pope. In the past, the wheel was an instrument of torture. A person was tied to it and then their arms and legs were broken or they were beaten to death.

button

★ **do something at the touch of a button** to do something very easily and quickly, usually because of new technology ○ *Specially trained staff will be able to trace obscene and threatening calls at the touch of a button, and pass the information to police.*

★ **a hot button** (*American*) a subject or problem that everyone is interested in or arguing over ○ *If crime is the city's issue most known to outsiders, rent control is the city's hot button for its residents.*

on the button exactly ○ *He said he'd meet us at 10.00 on the button.*

press the right button or

press all the right buttons to cleverly or skilfully do the things which are necessary to get what you want in a particular situation ○ *In what it describes as a well-judged performance, the newspaper says he pressed all the right buttons to please the representatives.*

right on the button correct about something ○ *'Am I right?' 'Right on the button.'*

Cc

caboodle

the whole caboodle or
the whole kit and caboodle (British)
all of something. The usual American
expression is **the whole ball of wax**.
○ I would probably find that I could borrow
the whole caboodle.

'Caboodle' may come from the Dutch
word 'boedal', meaning 'property'.

cage

rattle someone's cage to do or say
something that upsets or annoys
someone ○ I don't rattle their cages and
they don't rattle mine.

Cain

raise Cain to get very angry about
something ○ I figure she'd raise Cain if we
tried to stop her.

The reference here is to the Bible
story in which Cain murdered his
brother, Abel, in a fit of rage
(Genesis 4:1-9).

cake

★ **have your cake and eat it** to get the
benefits of two different situations or
things, when you should only get the
benefit of one of them ○ The Chancellor
can't have his cake and eat it: interest rates
will go up, but tax revenues will go down.

Although 'have your cake and eat it' is
now the most common form of the
expression, the original was 'eat your
cake and have it'. Some people
consider the recent version illogical,
since it is certainly possible to have a
cake and then eat it but not the other
way round.

take the cake said to express surprise or
anger at someone's extreme behaviour or
qualities ○ Officers say they get to see some
pretty odd things but that just about takes
the cake.

Cakes have been awarded as prizes in
competitions since classical times but
this expression is thought to have its
origin among African-Americans in the
southern United States in the time of
slavery. The competitors walked or
danced round a cake in pairs, and the
cake was awarded to the couple who
moved the most gracefully.

cakes

cakes and ale a time or activity when
you enjoy yourself greatly and have no
troubles (British) ○ You can't deny other
people cakes and ale just because you've never
enjoyed them yourself.

This expression is used in
Shakespeare's 'Twelfth Night'.
Sir Toby Belch says to Malvolio,
'Dost thou think, because thou art
virtuous, there shall be no more cakes
and ale?' (Act 2, Scene 3). 'Cakes and
Ale' is also the title of a novel by
Somerset Maugham, which was
published in 1930.

calf

kill the fatted calf to celebrate and do
everything possible to welcome a person
○ He went off to make movies, and when he
returned, his record company didn't exactly
kill the fatted calf.

This expression comes from the story
of 'the prodigal son' (Luke 5:3-32),
which is told by Jesus in the Bible. In

this story, a young man returns home after wasting all the money his father has given him. However, his father is so pleased to see him that he celebrates his return by killing a calf and preparing a feast.

call

★ **a close call** a situation in which someone only just manages to avoid an accident or disaster ○ *'That was a close call,' Bess gasped, as the boat steadied and got under way.*

calm

★ **the calm before the storm** a very quiet period that it is likely to be followed, or was followed, by a period of trouble or intense activity ○ *Things are relatively calm at the moment, but I think this is probably the calm before the storm.*

camp

a camp follower a person who likes to be seen with a particular person or group, either because they admire them, or because they hope to gain advantages from them ○ *Even in my day as a player, we had our camp followers.*

Originally, camp followers were civilians who travelled with an army and who made their living selling goods or services to the soldiers.

pitch camp to settle somewhere or have control of a certain area for a period of time ○ *As reporters pitched camp outside their home, the family's political differences became a public concern.*

can

a can of worms → see **worms**

★ **carry the can** (British) to take the blame for something even though you are not the only person responsible for it ○ *It annoys me that I was the only one who carried the can for that defeat.*

This was originally a military expression referring to the man

chosen to fetch a container of beer for a group of soldiers.

in the can successfully completed ○ *We've got the interview in the can.*

Old cinema film is stored in circular metal containers called cans.

candle

burn the candle at both ends to try to do too much, by regularly going to bed very late and getting up early in the morning ○ *Most people need six or seven hours each night and you're burning the candle at both ends if you regularly sleep for less than five.*

not worth the candle (British) not worth the trouble or effort that is needed in order to succeed ○ *If it means falling into my present state afterwards, writing isn't worth the candle.*

This expression originally referred to a game of cards where the amount of money at stake was less than the cost of the candle used up during the game.

someone can't hold a candle to someone said to mean that the first person mentioned is not in any way as good as the second ○ *There are football players now valued in the £2m bracket who can't hold a candle to Ian in terms of ability.*

This expression implies that the first person is not worthy even to hold a light to help the other person to see.

candy

like taking candy from a baby very easy ○ *Stealing the stuff was like taking candy from a baby.*

cannon

★ **cannon fodder** soldiers who are considered unimportant by their officers and are sent to fight in the most dangerous areas, where they are likely to be killed ○ *The fifty-five to sixty-five year-olds would be sent to the front as cannon-fodder. They were to attack ahead of the* *regular troops and absorb the enemy's fire.*

▤ Fodder is cheap food such as hay or straw that is used to feed animals.

★ **a loose cannon** a person who could cause problems for other people because they do bad or silly things that no one expects ○ *There is a widespread worry that the military command has turned into a loose cannon beyond the control of the government.*

▤ This expression refers to the cannons which used to be carried on the decks of warships. If one of the cannons was not properly fastened down, it could spin round and make a hole in the ship.

canoe

paddle your own canoe to control what you want to do without anyone else's help or influence ○ *As far as the rest of Europe is concerned we've just got to paddle our own canoe.*

cap

cap in hand (*mainly British*) very humbly and respectfully. The usual American expression is **hat in hand**. ○ *On holiday, if you rely on cash and lose the lot, you could end up going cap in hand to the nearest British consulate.*

▤ The idea is of a servant or person of low rank removing their hat in the presence of someone important.

if the cap fits, wear it (*British*) said to suggest that someone should consider whether unpleasant or critical remarks which have been made about them are true or fair. The American expression is **if the shoe fits**. ○ *I have not mentioned any names yet, but I told the team what I think and I told them that if the cap fits, they should wear it.*

put your thinking cap on or **get your thinking cap on** to try hard to solve a problem by thinking about it ○ *She decided to put her thinking cap on: there must be a job somewhere that she could do.*

▤ This expression may refer to the cap which judges used to wear when passing sentence or judgment.

capital

★ **... with a capital ...** said to draw attention to a particular word and emphasize its importance ○ *Students thought studying psychology would tell them something about Life with a capital L.*

carbon

★ **a carbon copy** a person or thing that is very similar to someone or something else ○ *She's always been quiet. She's a carbon copy of her mother – her mother always hated making a fuss.*

▤ A carbon copy of a document is an exact copy of it which is made using carbon paper.

card

a calling card something that someone possesses or has achieved, that gives them a lot of opportunities ○ *He says the actor used the New York magazine cover story about him as 'his calling card'.*

▤ In American English, a calling card is a small card printed with your name and other personal information, which you give to people when you visit or meet them.

a wild card someone or something that causes doubt, because nobody knows how they will behave or what effects they will have ○ *I was always a bit uneasy about him; I liked him, but he was a bit of a wild card.*

▤ In games such as poker, a wild card is a card that can have any value a player chooses.

cards

keep your cards close to your chest to not tell anyone about your plans or thoughts ○ *The Prime Minister was said yesterday to be keeping his cards close to his chest after an informal discussion at cabinet on Thursday.*

This is a reference to card-players holding their cards close to their chest so that nobody else can see them.

lay your cards on the table or
put your cards on the table to tell someone the truth about your feelings and plans ○ *Put your cards on the table and be very clear about your complaints. This should clear the air.*

The reference here is to players in a card game laying their cards face up for the other players to see.

★ **on the cards** (British) very likely to happen. The American expression is **in the cards**. ○ *There's no need to look so surprised. This has been on the cards for a long time.*

This is a reference to Tarot cards, or to other cards used to predict the future.

play your cards close to the vest (American) to not tell anyone about your plans or thoughts ○ *He plays his cards very close to the vest, causing some attorneys with whom he's worked to describe him as secretive and manipulative.*

play your cards right (mainly British) to use your skills to do all the things that are necessary in order to succeed or gain an advantage ○ *Soon, if she played her cards right, she would be head of the London office.*

The reference here is to a player in a card game who can win the game if they use their cards well enough.

carpet

on the carpet (British) in trouble for doing something wrong. The usual American expression is **called on the carpet**. ○ *The bad boy of English cricket was on the carpet again this week for refusing to wear one of the club's sponsored shirts.*

This expression may refer to a piece of carpet in front of a desk where someone stands while being reprimanded. Alternatively, it could refer to an employer calling a servant into one of the best rooms in the house, which would have a carpet, in order to reprimand them.

roll out the red carpet to give someone a special welcome and treat them very well ○ *The museum staff rolled out the red carpet; although it was a Sunday, the deputy director came in especially to show us round.*

It is customary to lay out a strip of red carpet for royalty or other important guests to walk on when they arrive for an official visit.

★ **sweep something under the carpet** (mainly British) to try to hide and forget about something because it makes you embarrassed or ashamed. The usual American expression is **sweep something under the rug**. ○ *People often assume if you sweep something under the carpet the problem will go away, but that is not the case.*

carrot

★ **carrot and stick** rewards and threats that are offered in order to persuade someone to do something ○ *But Congress also wants to use a carrot and stick approach to force both sides to negotiate.*

The idea behind this expression is that an animal such as a donkey can be encouraged to move forward either by dangling a carrot in front of it or by hitting it with a stick. The carrot represents the tempting offer and the stick represents the threat.

★ **offer someone a carrot** to try to persuade someone to do something by offering them a reward if they do it ○ *He is to offer the public a new carrot by reversing this week's doubling of petrol prices.*

The image here is of someone encouraging a donkey to move forward by holding a carrot in front of it.

carry

carry all before you (British) to achieve great success in a task or competition ○ *Newcastle United were carrying all before them, winning all their matches.*

cart

put the cart before the horse to do things in the wrong order ○ *Creating large numbers of schools before improving school management is putting the cart before the horse.*

cartload

a cartload of monkeys (British, old-fashioned) if someone is as cunning or as clever as a cartload of monkeys, they are extremely cunning or clever ○ *They are engaging creatures, cunning as a cartload of monkeys.*

case

In these expressions, a case is one that is being dealt with by a lawyer or doctor, not a box or suitcase.

be on someone's case or
get on someone's case (informal) to keep criticizing someone in an annoying way, because you think that they have behaved badly ○ *I don't need my friends getting on my case and telling me what to do as well.*

on the case dealing with a particular problem or situation ○ *I am on the case, and as soon as I have a solution to the problem, I'll let you know.*

cash

a cash cow a source of money that continues to produce a large amount of profit over a long period, without needing a lot of funding. ○ *The park has been a cash cow for the city. Sales taxes there account for approximately 15 per cent of the city's general fund.*

The reference is to something that produces money as freely as a cow produces milk.

castles

castles in the air unrealistic plans or hopes for the future ○ *'Along the way I have to become very, very rich.' He shook his head in wonder at her. 'You're building castles in the air, Anne.'*

cat

★ **cat and mouse** or
a game of cat and mouse a situation in which a person tries to confuse or deceive another in order to defeat them ○ *He would play cat-and-mouse with other riders, sometimes waiting until the fourth lap to come from behind and win.*

The reference here is to a cat playing with a mouse before killing it.

the cat's whiskers or
the cat's pyjamas the very best person or thing (British, old-fashioned) ○ *She had this great dress on and she thought she was the cat's whiskers as she came out along the gallery.*

These expressions were originally American and became popular in Britain during the 1920s. 'Cat's whisker' was also the name of a fine wire in a crystal wireless receiver.

★ **a fat cat** a person who uses their great wealth and power in a way that seems unfair ○ *They want higher taxes for the bulk of the population, not just the fat cats.*

fight like cat and dog to frequently have violent arguments ○ *They had fought like cat and dog ever since he could remember, and he wondered how they'd got together in the first place.*

grin like a Cheshire cat to do a big smile, often because you are pleased with yourself ○ *Charles was sitting in his place, grinning like a Cheshire cat, when I joined him.*

The Cheshire cat is a character from 'Alice in Wonderland' (1865) by the English writer Lewis Carroll. This cat gradually disappears until only its huge grin remains. Alternatively, it may have come from signboards of inns in Cheshire, many of which had a picture of a grinning lion on them.

let the cat out of the bag to reveal something secret or private, often without intending to ○ *'The Mosses didn't tell the cops my name, did they?' 'Of course not,' she said. 'They wouldn't want to let the cat out of the bag.'*

like a cat on hot bricks or
like a cat on a hot tin roof very nervous or restless ○ *He's like a cat on hot bricks before a game.*

'Cat on a Hot Tin Roof' is the title of a play by Tennessee Williams.

like a scalded cat very fast, as though suddenly frightened or shocked *(British)* ○ *Scrambling around to recover his glasses, the scientist darted to his car like a scalded cat and clambered quickly in.*

like the cat that got the cream *(mainly British)* looking very satisfied and happy ○ *Did you notice Hugh acting like the cat that got the cream?*

look like something the cat dragged in to look very untidy ○ *It is quite possible to be an intelligent and successful woman and look like something the cat has dragged in.*

look what the cat's dragged in said when someone arrives, to express your dislike or disapproval of them, or as a light-hearted way of greeting them ○ *In strolls Babs. 'Now look what the cat's dragged in,' says Jeanie, with a nod.*

put the cat among the pigeons or
set the cat among the pigeons *(British)* to cause trouble or upset ○ *Once again she set the cat among the pigeons, claiming that Michael was lying.*

see which way the cat jumps *(mainly British)* to delay making a decision or taking action on something until more is known about how the situation will develop ○ *I'm going to sit tight and see which way the cat jumps.*

This expression could be connected with the old game of 'tip-cat', in which players waited to see which way a short piece of wood called the 'cat' moved before hitting or 'tipping' it.

there isn't room to swing a cat *(mainly British)* said to mean that a place is very small and has very little space ○ *Inside, there isn't room to swing a cat, and everything you see and touch is the most basic junk.*

The 'cat' in this expression is probably a 'cat-o'-nine-tails', a whip with nine lashes which was used in the past for punishing offenders in the army and navy. However, the expression could be connected with the practice in the past of swinging cats by their tails as targets for archers.

there's more than one way to skin a cat there are several ways to achieve something ○ *There is more than one way to skin a cat; keep positive and try another method of reaching your goal.*

when the cat's away, the mice will play said to mean that people do what they want, or misbehave when their boss or another person in authority is away ○ *While the bosses are out of the room, the workers watch the game – a case of while the cat's away the mice will play.*

catbird

in the catbird seat *(American, old-fashioned)* in an important or powerful position ○ *If I can run around the world and buy that particular group, then I'll be in the catbird seat.*

This expression became widely known in the 1940s and 1950s, when it was used by the baseball commentator Red Barber. Catbirds are North

American songbirds. The expression may be explained by the fact that catbirds often sit very high up in trees.

Catch

a Catch 22 an extremely frustrating situation in which one thing cannot happen until another thing has happened, but the other thing cannot happen until the first thing has happened ○ *There's a Catch 22 in social work. You need experience to get work and you need work to get experience.*

This expression comes from the novel 'Catch 22' (1961), by the American author Joseph Heller, which is about bomber pilots in the Second World War. Their 'Catch 22' situation was that any sane person would ask if they could stop flying. However, the authorities would only allow people to stop flying if they were insane.

cats

it's raining cats and dogs *(British, old-fashioned)* said to mean that it is raining very heavily ○ *'Could you see how he looked?' 'Not really. It was raining cats and dogs by then.'*

There are several possible explanations for this expression, but none of them can be proved. It may refer to the days when drainage in towns was so poor that cats and dogs sometimes drowned in heavy rainfall. Alternatively, 'cats and dogs' could be a corruption or misunderstanding of the Greek word 'catadupe', meaning 'waterfall', so the expression would originally have been 'it's raining like a waterfall'. The origin may also be in Norse mythology, where cats and dogs were sometimes associated with the spirit of the storm.

caution

★ **throw caution to the wind** or **throw caution to the winds** to do something without worrying about the risks and danger involved ○ *This was no time to think, he decided. He threw caution to the winds and rang the bell of the ground-floor flat.*

ceiling

★ **go through the ceiling**

1 to suddenly increase very rapidly ○ *Sales went through the ceiling and pharmacists began reporting shortages of the drug.*
2 to suddenly become very angry sometimes shouting at someone ○ *'If he did what she said, she was happy, but if he didn't, she went through the ceiling.'*

cent

not have a cent to your name → see **name**
not a red cent or
not one red cent *(mainly American)* no money at all ○ *But investors have to remember that with many shows they won't get a red cent back.*

The American one-cent coin used to be made from copper, but is now made from a mixture of copper, tin and zinc.

centre

'Centre' is spelled 'center' in American English.

★ **centre stage** the position in which someone or something gets the most attention ○ *The summit is the first time he has occupied centre stage at an important international gathering since coming to power last year.*

The stage referred to is in the theatre. The centre of the stage is the position where actors are most prominent. 'Centre stage', 'stage left' and 'stage right' are used in theatre directions for actors, along with 'up stage' and 'down stage'.

cents

your two cents' worth *(mainly American)* your opinion about something.

The British expression is your **two penn'orth**. ○ *Your father kept telling me to hush up and don't be a damn fool, but you know me, I had to put in my two cents' worth.*

chain

yank someone's chain *(mainly American, informal)* to say something to annoy someone ○ *When would I learn to smarten up and ignore her when she yanked my chain?*

chalice

a poisoned chalice *(mainly British)* a job or an opportunity that seems to be very attractive but may in fact, lead to failure or a very unpleasant situation ○ *The contract may yet prove to be a poisoned chalice.*

≣ A chalice is an old-fashioned cup or goblet, usually made of metal and shaped like a wine glass.

chalk

by a long chalk *(British)* said to add emphasis to a statement, especially a negative statement or one that contains a superlative ○ *Where do you think you're going, Kershaw? You haven't finished by a long chalk.*

≣ This expression may refer to the practice of making chalk marks on the floor to show the score of a player or team. 'A long chalk' would mean 'a lot of points' or 'a great deal'.

chalk and cheese *(British)* if you describe two people or things as chalk and cheese, you mean that they are completely different from each other ○ *Our relationship works because we are very aware of our differences, we accept that we are chalk and cheese.*

chance

chance would be a fine thing *(British)* said to mean that something that you would like to happen is very unlikely ○ *Everyone needs a day in bed sometimes.*

If you've got kids you're probably thinking 'chance would be a fine thing'.

★ **not a snowball's chance in hell** or **not a chance in hell** *(British)* no chance at all of something happening ○ *If I was caught with all the film on me I had not a snowball's chance in hell of talking my way out of it.*

≣ The original expression was 'as much chance as a cat in hell without claws'.

change

★ **a change of heart** a new and different attitude towards something ○ *At the last minute, she had a change of heart about selling it. It had been in her family for generations.*

get no change out of someone to get no help at all from someone *(British)* ○ *You won't get any change out of him, so don't expect it. And no promotion, either.*

changes

★ **ring the changes** *(British)* to make changes to the way something is organized or done in order to vary or improve it ○ *The different varieties enable you to ring the changes so that your cat never gets bored with his food.*

≣ In bell-ringing, to 'ring the changes' means to ring a number of church bells, each of which gives a different note, one after the other in every possible combination.

chapter

chapter and verse full and accurate information about something ○ *I explained everything to Lapiere. I gave him chapter and verse.*

≣ This expression refers to the practice of giving precise chapter and verse numbers when quoting passages from the Bible.

a chapter of accidents *(British)* a series of unlucky events in a short time ○ *In fiction, however, such a chapter of accidents can end up seeming comic.*

This expression has been used many times by various writers. One of the earliest uses is 'the chapter of accidents is the longest chapter in the book', the book being the story of a person's life or a record of a particular event.

charity

charity begins at home said to mean that you should deal with the needs of people close to you before you think about helping other people further away ○ *Charity begins at home. There are many tasks right here on campus that need volunteers as well.*

chase

cut to the chase to start talking about what is really important ○ *He talked about the need to see all points of view, then he cut to the chase: 'Well, it looks like there is nothing here for me. I'm planning to fly back.'*

In films, when one scene ends and another begins the action is said to 'cut' from one scene to the next. If a film 'cuts to the chase', it moves on to a car chase scene. This expression compares the important matters to be discussed or dealt with to the exciting action in a film, such as car chases.

cheek

★ **cheek by jowl** very close together ○ *After about seven years, all this living cheek by jowl began to irritate people.*

'Jowl' is an old-fashioned word for 'cheek'.

★ **turn the other cheek** to decide not to take any action against someone who harms or insults you ○ *It's better to learn how to avoid a situation where you have either to defend yourself or turn the other cheek.*

This expression comes from Jesus's words to His followers in the Bible (Matthew 5:39). He tells them that

they should not fight against bad people, and that if a bad person hits them on the cheek, they should simply offer the other cheek.

cheese

a big cheese (*informal*) a person who has an important and powerful position in an organization ○ *During the conference big cheeses from the State Department were dropping in and out all the time.*

The word 'cheese' in this expression may be a corruption or misunderstanding of the Urdu word 'chiz' or 'cheez', meaning 'thing'. This started being used in English in about 1840 because of the British presence in India. Later the word came to refer to a person or boss.

cheque

'Cheque' is spelled 'check' in American English.

★ **a blank cheque** complete authority to do whatever you think is best ○ *De Klerk had, in a sense, been given a blank cheque to negotiate the new South Africa.*

This expression is often used literally to mean that someone gives another person a cheque without an amount of money written on it.

chest

beat your chest → see **beat**

★ **get something off your chest** to talk about a problem that has been worrying you for a long time, and to feel better after doing this ○ *My doctor gave me the opportunity to talk and get things off my chest.*

chestnut

★ **an old chestnut** (*mainly British*) a statement, story or idea that has been repeated so often that it is no longer interesting ○ *The feminist struggle is too important to become an old chestnut over which people groan.*

chicken

chicken and egg

1 a situation where you cannot decide which of two related things happened first and caused the other ○ *It's a chicken-and-egg argument about which comes first: Do people create this lifestyle? Or does the environment influence how people live?*

2 a problem that is impossible to solve because the solution is also the cause of the problem ○ *Until we get promotion, we won't get the top players. But until we get top players, we won't win promotion. It's a chicken and egg situation.*

This expression comes from the unanswerable question, 'Which came first, the chicken or the egg?'

chicken feed

1 a very small amount of money ○ *The £70,000-a-year that we receive from our sponsors is chicken feed compared to the £20m budgets available to some of our rivals.*

2 something unimportant, especially in comparison to another thing ○ *Ordinarily, this late in the campaign, presidential candidates don't play around with chicken feed like this.*

★ **like a headless chicken** *(British)* in an uncontrolled or disorganized way, and not calmly or logically ○ *Instead of running round like a headless chicken you're using your efforts in a more productive way, more efficiently.*

Chickens have been known to run around for a short time after they have had their heads cut off.

chickens

don't count your chickens or **don't count your chickens before they're hatched** said to mean that you should not make plans for the future because you do not know for certain how a particular situation will develop ○ *When dealing with important financial arrangements, it is imperative that you do not count your chickens before they are hatched.*

child

★ **child's play** something that is very easy to deal with ○ *He thought the work would be child's play.*

chin

keep your chin up to remain calm or cheerful in a difficult or unpleasant situation ○ *Richards was keeping his chin up yesterday despite the continued setbacks.*

lead with your chin to behave very aggressively ○ *This game is no place for a player who cannot lead with his chin.*

This expression comes from boxing, and refers to a boxer fighting with their chin sticking out, making it easy for their opponent to hit it.

★ **take it on the chin** to bravely accept criticism and not to make a fuss about it ○ *When the police arrived, he took it on the chin, apologizing for the trouble he'd caused them.*

This refers to someone being punched on the jaw but not falling down.

chink

'Armour' is spelled 'armor' in American English.

a chink in someone's armour a person's weakness that you can take advantage of, although they appear to be very strong and successful ○ *Opposition leaders hope to use their annual conference to attack what they see as the most vulnerable chink in the government's armour.*

A chink is a small hole or opening.

chip

a chip off the old block a person who is very similar to one of their parents in appearance, character or behaviour ○ *Lewis's lawyer said 'He is a chip off the old block – a hothead and a bully just like his dad.'*

The 'chip' in this expression is a small piece that has been cut off a block of wood.

★ **a chip on your shoulder** a feeling of anger and resentment because you think that you have been treated unfairly in the past ○ *My father had a chip on his shoulder; he thought people didn't like him because of the way he looked.*

≡ There is a story that in America in the past, men sometimes balanced a small piece of wood on one shoulder in the hope that someone would knock it off and give them an excuse to start a fight.

chips

> In the following expressions 'chips' are the coloured tokens or counters which are used to represent money in casinos.

call in your chips (mainly British) to decide to use your influence or social connections in order to gain an advantage over other people ○ *That point needs making, before the President's friends in the labour unions and the steel and textile industries try to call in their chips.*

≡ In gambling, if you call in your chips, you ask people to pay you all the money that they owe you.

cash in your chips to sell something such as your investments, in order to raise money ○ *ICI was small in over-the-counter drugs in the States. It decided to cash in its chips at a surprisingly good price.*

≡ In a casino, if you cash in your chips, you exchange them for money at the end of a gambling session.

have had your chips (British) to have completely failed in something that you were trying to do ○ *After the 4-1 defeat, most of the 10,000 crowd were convinced they'd already had their chips.*

≡ This may refer to gamblers who have lost all their chips and so have to stop playing.

★ **when the chips are down** in a particularly difficult or dangerous situation ○ *There will be no panic. We are at our best when the chips are down.*

≡ In a casino, the players lay their chips down on the table to make their bets.

choice

of choice used after a noun for describing something that is chosen most often by a particular group of people or for a particular purpose ○ *Now we have conclusive evidence that oat bran is the fibre of choice for those who want to keep their cholesterol levels out of the risk zone.*

chop

★ **chop and change** (British) to keep changing your plans ○ *After chopping and changing for the first year, Paul and Jamie have settled down to a stable system of management.*

≡ This expression was originally used to refer to people buying and selling goods. To 'chop' meant to trade or barter, and 'change' came from 'exchange'.

★ **for the chop** (British, informal)
1 about to lose your job ○ *There are rumours that he is for the chop.*
2 not allowed to continue or remain ○ *He won't say which programmes are for the chop.*

chord

★ **strike a chord** to make you respond in an emotional way, for example by feeling sympathy or pleasure ○ *It is a case which has shocked America – and one which has struck a chord with every family with teenagers.*

church

a broad church (British) an organization, group or area of activity that includes a wide range of opinions, beliefs or styles ○ *Rock music in France is a very broad church indeed.*

cigar

close but no cigar said to someone to mean that they have failed in what they were trying to achieve or make you believe ○ *It was a case of close but no cigar for a group of illegal immigrants intercepted by customs officials on their way to the train station.*

In the past, cigars were sometimes given as prizes at fairs. This expression may have been used if someone did not quite manage to win a prize.

circle

★ **come full circle** or
the wheel has come full circle said to mean that something is now exactly the same as it used to be, although there has been a long period of changes ○ *Her life had now come full circle and she was back where she started, in misery, alone.*

This may refer to the medieval idea of the wheel of fortune which is constantly turning, so that people who have good luck at one time in their lives will have bad luck at another time.

★ **square the circle** to try to solve a problem that seems to be impossible to solve ○ *All have the same hope: that foreign markets and, especially, foreign investment will somehow provide enough jobs to square the circle.*

★ **a vicious circle** a situation where one problem has caused other problems which, in turn, have made the original problem even worse ○ *The economy has been caught in a vicious circle: the economy couldn't create large numbers of jobs because consumers weren't spending; consumers weren't spending because the economy wasn't creating jobs.*

This refers to the error in logic of trying to prove the truth of one statement by a second statement, which in turn relies on the first for proof. The expression is a translation of the Latin 'circulus vitiosus', meaning 'a flawed circular argument'.

circles

go round in circles (British) to not achieve very much because you keep coming back to the same point or problem over and over again. In American English, you say that someone **is going around in circles**. ○ *They have been going round and round in circles about treatment methods. And their solution, in the end, was perfectly straightforward.*

run round in circles (British) to have very little success in achieving something in spite of trying hard, because you are disorganized. In American English, you say that someone **is running around in circles**. ○ *She wastes a lot of energy running round in circles, whereas more careful planning could save a lot of effort and achieve a great deal.*

circus

a three-ring circus (mainly American) a lot of noisy or very chaotic activity ○ *They might fight among themselves, but grief was a private thing, not something to be turned into a three-ring circus by newspaper reporters.*

clam

shut up like a clam to become very quiet and withdrawn ○ *When they are worried, they may well shut up like a clam, definitely not wanting to tell you what is wrong.*

clanger

drop a clanger (British) to make a very embarrassing mistake ○ *'You wouldn't have thought that Jimmy of all people would drop such a clanger.'*

This expression probably comes from comparing an obvious and embarrassing mistake with the clang or loud ringing noise made when a heavy metal object is dropped.

clappers

like the clappers (British) very quickly ○ *What is it that makes people run like the clappers for a train?*

≣ The clapper of a bell is the part inside
≣ it which strikes it to make it ring.

claws

get your claws into someone
1 to control or influence someone in a
selfish way ○ *These people had got their
claws into him and he didn't know how to
get clear of them.*
2 to form a selfish and uncaring
relationship with someone ○ *Sadly for
Jackie, Amanda got her claws into Gavin first.*

clean

clean as a whistle
1 having done nothing wrong ○ *There are
no scandals. His private life is as clean as a
whistle.*
2 completely free from dirt ○ *It leaves
your face feeling clean as a whistle but not
bone-dry.*

★ **come clean** to tell the truth about
something ○ *I had expected her to come
clean and confess that she only wrote these
books for the money. But, no, she insists that
she takes them all very seriously.*

★ **squeaky clean** morally very good with
no character faults ○ *As a country-dweller
myself, I can truthfully say that not all people
living in the countryside are as squeaky clean
as they like to think.*

≣ Clean surfaces sometimes squeak
≣ when you wipe or rub them.

cleaners

take someone to the cleaners
to make someone lose a lot of money in
an unfair or dishonest way ○ *Just for a
change, the insurers discovered that they had
been taken to the cleaners.*

≣ This developed from the expression
≣ 'to clean someone out', which has been
≣ used since the 19th century. People say
≣ that they have been 'cleaned out' when
≣ they have lost all their money and
≣ valuables, for example through being
≣ robbed or cheated.

clear

clear as a bell very easy to hear and
often understand ○ *Her words, when she
finally spoke, were as clear as a bell.*

clear as crystal obvious and very easy
to understand ○ *I read the instructions –
they were as clear as crystal.*

clear as day in a way that is very easy
to see, or very obvious and easy to
understand ○ *Suddenly she stepped out
from behind a tree less than ten yards from
me. I saw her face as clear as day.*

clear as mud confusing and difficult to
understand ○ *'It's all written down there!
Self-explanatory! Clearly.' 'Clear as mud.
Even I can't understand it, and I'm pretty
smart.'*

in the clear
1 free from blame or suspicion ○ *Their
possessions had not been searched so they
were not officially in the clear.*
2 no longer in danger or trouble ○ *She
and her husband underwent an agonising
48-hour wait for the results of tests before
discovering he was in the clear.*
3 ahead of other people in a competition
or contest ○ *There was more gloomy news
for the Prime Minister in an opinion poll
yesterday which showed The Conservative
Party five points in the clear.*

★ **steer clear** to deliberately avoid
someone or something ○ *Steer clear of
foods made from artificial preservatives.*

clever

box clever *(British)* to be very careful
and clever in the way that you behave in a
difficult situation, so that you can get an
advantage over other people ○ *By boxing
clever with your personal tax allowances, you
could save over £900 a year.*

cloak

★ **cloak-and-dagger** done in secret
○ *They met in classic cloak-and-dagger style
beside the lake in St James's Park, both
tossing snacks to the ducks.*

This expression is taken from the name of a type of 17th century Spanish drama, in which characters typically wore cloaks and fought with daggers or swords.

clock

★ **round the clock** or
around the clock continuously, throughout the day and night ○ *Fire crews were working round the clock to bring the huge blazes under control.*

★ **wish you could turn back the clock** to wish to return to an earlier period, for example because you think it was a very good time or because you would like the chance to live your life differently ○ *He said if he could turn back the clock, he would act differently.*

clockwork

★ **like clockwork**
1 very smoothly and exactly as expected ○ *The journey there went like clockwork – flying out on Friday from Gatwick it took seven hours door-to-door.*
2 regularly, always at the same time ○ *They would arrive like clockwork just before dawn.*

clogs

pop your clogs (British, informal) to die ○ *The kids want to know that the person they're paying to see isn't going to pop their clogs during the performance.*

This expression may refer to an old sense of 'pop', meaning to pawn something. Clogs used to be the normal footwear of people such as mill workers, especially in the north of England.

close

★ **something is too close to call** said to mean it is impossible to say who will win ○ *The presidential race is too close to call.*

cloth

cut from the same cloth (mainly British) very similar in character,
attitudes or behaviour ○ *London critics are all cut from the same cloth: they are white, male, middle-aged, middle-class and university-educated.*

cut your coat according to your cloth (mainly British) to make plans and decisions that are based on what you have and not what you would like ○ *It is up to organizations which were supported by the taxpayer to cut their coats according to the cloth available.*

have cloth ears (British) to be unable to pay attention to or understand something properly ○ *The audience had been sitting there for two hours with cloth ears.*

made of whole cloth (American) completely untrue and not based on fact ○ *There are those who say that story was made of whole cloth.*

clothes (British, journalism)

steal someone's clothes to take another person's ideas or policies and pretend that these ideas or policies are your own ○ *The Chancellor has tried to steal our clothes but he has done it in a cheap and shoddy way.*

cloud

★ **every cloud has a silver lining** said to mean that there is always a good or pleasant side-effect of a bad or unpleasant situation ○ *As they say, every cloud has a silver lining. If we hadn't missed the plane, we would never have met you.*

★ **on cloud nine** very happy because something very good has happened to you ○ *I never expected to win, so I'm on cloud nine.*

This expression is probably derived from the numbered cloud categories used by the US Weather Bureau. Cloud nine, cumulonimbus, is the highest and occurs at about 30,000 ft. At this height and above, clouds consist of ice crystals rather than water vapour.

★ **under a cloud** suffering from disapproval or criticism because of something that you have done or are believed to have done ○ *He was under a cloud after his men failed to find who had placed the bomb in the office.*

clover

in clover happy because you have a lot of money and are enjoying a luxurious lifestyle ○ *For the next ten days I was in clover at Vicky and Allen's house. They took me to all the town's attractions and its restaurants.*

Clover is a plant which often grows in fields of grass. Cows are said to enjoy grazing in fields which contain a lot of clover.

club

join the club said to indicate that you have had the same experiences or feelings as someone who has been telling you about their problems or how they feel ○ *Confused? Then join the club.*

clue

★ **not have a clue** (*informal*) to not know anything about something or to have no idea what to do about something ○ *I don't have a clue what will happen now.*

coach

drive a coach and horses through something (*mainly British*) to severely weaken or destroy an agreement or an established way of doing something ○ *The judgment appeared to drive a coach and horses through the Hague agreement.*

coalface

at the coalface (*mainly British*) doing a particular job and not just discussing it ○ *The key is to listen and learn from those at the coalface about how improvements could be made.*

In a coal mine, the coalface is the part where the coal is being cut out of the rock.

coals

haul someone over the coals (*British*) to speak to someone very severely about something wrong that they have done ○ *I heard later that Uncle Jim had been hauled over the coals for not letting anyone know where we were.*

This expression may refer to a practice in medieval times of deciding whether or not someone was guilty of heresy, or saying things which disagreed with the teachings of the Church. The person was dragged over burning coals. If they burned to death they were considered guilty, but if they survived, they were considered innocent.

rake over the coals (*mainly British*) to talk about something that happened in the past which you think should now be forgotten or ignored ○ *Let us not waste time raking over the coals when there is hard work to be done.*

send coals to Newcastle to provide someone with something that they already have plenty of ○ *Sending food to that region is like sending coals to Newcastle. There is plenty of food, the problem is the breakdown of the distribution system.*

The city of Newcastle was the main centre of England's coal-mining industry for over 150 years.

coast

the coast is clear said to mean that you are able to do something which someone does not want you to do, because they are not there to see you or catch you doing it ○ *Midge stepped aside, nodding that the coast was clear, and Lettie ran through the lobby and up the main staircase.*

This expression may refer to smugglers sending messages that there were no coastguards around and it was safe to land or set sail.

coat-tails

'Coat-tails' is usually written as 'coattails' in American English.

★ **on the coat-tails of someone** because of the success or popularity of another person or activity, and not because of your own efforts ○ *She was looking for fame and glory on the coat-tails of her husband.*

A tail coat is a man's coat with the front covering only the top half of the body and the back reaching down to the knees in a pointed 'tail'. It is now usually worn only for formal weddings, or as part of formal evening dress.

cobwebs

blow away the cobwebs to make you feel more alert and lively, when you have previously felt tired or dull ○ *We have a cottage in the Cotswolds, and getting back there after a few days in London really blows the cobwebs away.*

cock

a cock and bull story a story that you do not believe ○ *They'll be believed, no matter what kind of a cock and bull story they tell.*

This expression may come from old fables in which animals such as cocks and bulls could talk. Alternatively, it may come from the names of inns, such as 'The Cock' and 'The Bull', where people gathered and told each other stories and jokes.

cockles

warm the cockles of your heart (old-fashioned) to make you feel happy and contented ○ *In the bold black and white setting, the sunny yellow color of the house warmed the cockles of my heart.*

Cockles are a type of shellfish. They are associated with the heart because they have a similar shape. The zoological name for cockles is 'Cardium', which comes from the Greek word for 'heart'.

coffee

wake up and smell the coffee said when you are telling someone to be more realistic and more aware of what is happening around them ○ *It would really serve you well to wake up and smell the coffee and quit acting like a teenager!*

coin

★ **the other side of the coin** the other, very different, aspect of a situation ○ *Of course, I get lonely at times. But the other side of the coin is the amazing freedom I have.*

pay someone back in their own coin to treat someone in exactly the same, bad way that they have treated you ○ *We need to tell them that if they don't actually cease their attacks they could face the prospect of being paid back in their own coin.*

'Coin' is an old-fashioned word for currency.

cold

catch someone cold (mainly British, journalism) to score against someone in a sports game because they are not prepared for your attack ○ *They maintained their two-point lead at the top of the Third Division with a 29-14 win after Barrow had caught them cold to lead 8-4 at the interval.*

cold as ice acting in a very unfriendly way ○ *He sat cold as ice through breakfast, ignoring Claire's hand on his shoulder as she passed his chair.*

★ **come in from the cold** to become popular, accepted, or active again after a period of unpopularity or lack of involvement ○ *Over the past two years, Swedish investors have come in from the cold.*

'The Spy who Came in from the Cold' is the title of a novel by the English writer John Le Carré, published in 1963.

★ **leave someone cold** to not excite or interest someone at all ○ *Given the world situation, chat about shopping and hairdos leaves you cold.*

★ **leave someone out in the cold**
to ignore someone and not ask them
to take part in activities with you
○ *The developing countries must not be
left out in the cold in current world trade
talks.*

**when one person sneezes, another
catches cold** (*mainly British*) said to
mean that the things that happen to one
country or person have a great effect or
influence on other countries or people
○ *And when the American economy sneezes,
the City of London catches cold.*

collar

hot under the collar annoyed about
something ○ *Judges are hot under the collar
about proposals to alter their pension
arrangements.*

colour

'Colour' is spelled 'color' in American
English.

the colour of someone's money
proof that a person has enough money
to pay for something ○ *He made a mental
note never to enter into conversation with a
customer until he'd at least seen the colour
of his money.*

colours

'Colours' is spelled 'colors' in American
English.

A ship's colours are its national flag.

nail your colours to the mast
1 (*British, journalism*) to state your
opinions or beliefs about something
clearly and publicly ○ *Let me nail my
colours to the mast straightaway. I both like
and admire him immensely.*

Battleships used to lower their colours
to show that they were surrendering.
Sometimes the colours were nailed to
the mast as a sign of determination to
fight to the end.

2 (*British, journalism*) to say clearly and
publicly that you support a particular
person, idea or theory ○ *In the Thatcher
years, the young MP nailed his colours to
Mrs T's mast more firmly than many.*

sail under false colours
to deliberately deceive people
○ *This report sails under false colours. The
author had reached his basic conclusions long
before he even began gathering any fresh
evidence.*

When pirate ships spotted a treasure
ship, they often took down their own
flag and raised the flag of a friendly
nation, in order to get close enough
to the ship to attack it.

★ **see someone in their true colours**
to suddenly become aware that a person
is not as moral or honest as you thought
they were ○ *When my boyfriend was involved
in a road rage incident it was as if I was seeing
him in his true colours for the first time.*

Once a pirate ship had got close to a
treasure ship by 'sailing under false
colours', it then revealed its true
identity by raising its own flag.

★ **with flying colours** very successfully
○ *She thought she was on a fast track to a
good job as a medical assistant when she
passed the entrance exam with flying colors.*

The image here is of a victorious
battleship sailing back into port with
its national flag flying.

comb

with a fine-tooth comb or
with a fine-toothed comb very
carefully and with great attention to
detail ○ *I have taken the responsibility of
going through Ed's personal papers and
letters with a fine-tooth comb.*

A fine-tooth comb is a comb with very
thin teeth set very close together. It is
used to remove nits and lice from
people's hair.

come

★ **come out fighting** to be prepared to do everything possible in order to win ○ *The crude oil producers have come out fighting, claiming the West is using environmental issues as a way of cutting back on oil.*

> If boxers come out fighting, they leave their corner as soon as the bell rings and attack their opponent immediately.

where someone is coming from the reasons for someone's behaviour, opinions, or comments ○ *I do see where he's coming from – as a company, we're not great at innovation.*

comfort

★ **cold comfort** encouragement that does not in fact make a difficult or unpleasant situation better ○ *Finding out more about this disease can be cold comfort, as no cure and virtually no treatment are available.*

commas

★ **in inverted commas** (British, spoken) said to mean that a particular word or phrase is not an accurate or suitable description. ○ *So, in what sense do you see the students as disadvantaged, in inverted commas?*

common

common as muck (British, offensive) lower-class ○ *Leary guessed correctly that his guests were as common as muck and planned the menu accordingly.*

concrete

set in concrete fixed and impossible to change ○ *With expenditure plans now set in concrete for three years, slower growth would mean higher taxes.*

converted

preach to the converted to present an opinion or argument to people who already agree with it ○ *While I was encouraged by the positive receptions we had received in August I was essentially preaching to the converted then.*

> The converted are people who have converted, or changed their religious beliefs and become Christians. Preaching is the activity of speaking to non-Christians to persuade them to convert.

cookie

be caught with your hand in the cookie jar (mainly American) to be caught stealing or doing something wrong. The usual British expression is **have your hand in the till**. ○ *The banker had been caught with his hand in the cookie jar. Had my client not been aggressive he would have lost 35,000 dollars.*

a smart cookie a clever person who has good ideas ○ *As soon as movie film had been invented, around 1890, smart cookies started thinking about how to accompany pictures with sound.*

that's the way the cookie crumbles said to mean that you should accept the way that things happen, even if it is bad ○ *Even after he failed, he didn't give up. That's the way the cookie crumbles he said.*

a tough cookie a person who is very determined to get what they want ○ *Behind that sweet smile, there lies one tough cookie.*

cooks

too many cooks or
too many cooks spoil the broth said to mean that something may not be successful if too many people try to do it at the same time ○ *So far nothing had worked. It was simply a case of too many cooks.*

> This expression comes from the proverb **too many cooks spoil the broth**.

cool

cool as a cucumber very relaxed, calm, and not emotional ○ *Never once did she* gasp for air or mop her brow. She was as cool as a cucumber.

★ **keep your cool** to control your temper and stay calm in a difficult situation ○ The manager has kept the pressure off the players by keeping his cool and it has paid off.

★ **lose your cool** to suddenly get angry and behave in a bad-tempered or uncontrolled way ○ At this I lost my cool and shouted 'For goodness sake, stop!'

coop

fly the coop to leave a situation, for example because you do not like it or because you want to have more freedom ○ It should be a proud moment when a senior stylist flies the coop to set up in a salon of his or her own.

≣ A coop is a small cage in which chickens or small animals are kept. 'Coop' is also American slang for a prison.

cop

not much cop (British, informal) not very good ○ She looked round the big room: 'there's no one here but us, this place can't be much cop.'

≣ In early twentieth century slang, 'cop' meant 'value' or 'use'.

copybook

blot your copybook (British) to damage your reputation by doing something wrong ○ I'm proud of my family heritage and I don't want to blot my copybook.

≣ In the past, schoolchildren had 'copybooks'. These were books of examples of handwriting, with spaces for the children to copy it.

cord

cut the umbilical cord or
cut the cord to start acting independently ○ I'll never forget all you've done for me, but it's time to cut the umbilical cord. I want you to go away. I need time alone to think.

≣ An unborn baby's umbilical cord is the tube connecting it to its mother, through which it receives oxygen and nutrients.

core

★ **to the core** very much; deeply ○ Father Carney said the community was shocked to the core.

corn

earn your corn to be successful and therefore justify the money that has been spent, for example on training (British) ○ The back four got us through the match. They earned their corn against Middlesbrough and that's why we came off with a win.

corner

★ **fight your corner** (British) to state your opinion openly and defend it strongly ○ The future of Britain lies in the EU and we must fight our corner from within using honest and intelligent arguments.

≣ In a boxing match, each boxer is given a corner of the ring. They return to their corner at the end of each round.

★ **in a tight corner** or
in a corner in a situation which is difficult to deal with or escape from ○ I was horrified at what I had done and knew I was in a tight corner and that everything depended upon my keeping my head.

in your corner supporting you and helping you ○ Harry and I were encouraged. We felt we already had Bob in our corner.

≣ In a boxing match, each boxer is given a corner of the ring. Trainers and helpers come into a boxer's corner between rounds and give help and encouragement.

★ **just around the corner** about to happen ○ With summer just around the corner, there couldn't be a better time to treat your home to a bright new look.

paint yourself into a corner or
box yourself into a corner to find

yourself in a difficult situation where you have to act in a certain way
○ *I've been watching her these last few years. She's painted herself into a corner. She is trapped.*

'Paint yourself into a corner' refers to someone who is painting a floor and ends up in a corner of the room with wet paint all round them. 'Box yourself into a corner' refers to a boxer being forced into a corner of the ring and having no means of escape.

turn the corner to begin to recover from a serious illness or a difficult situation ○ *At last, Joe turned the corner.*

corners

★ **cut corners** to save time, money or effort by not following the correct procedure or rules for doing something ○ *Don't try to cut any corners as you'll only be making work for yourself later on.*

four corners of the world or
four corners of the Earth all the different parts of the world ○ *A foreign correspondent makes friends in all four corners of the world.*

cost

★ **count the cost** (*mainly British*) to consider how much damage or harm has been caused ○ *The government is today counting the political cost of the dispute which has already prompted the resignation of one government minister.*

couch

★ **a couch potato** a person who spends most of their time sitting around watching television ○ *In fact, we sit, like a pair of couch potatoes in front of television, and watch her eat.*

This expression is a complicated pun based on the American slang term 'boob tube' meaning the TV, and the fact that a potato is a variety of tuber or root vegetable.

count

> The following expressions refer to a 'count' in boxing. If a boxer is knocked to the ground and does not get up before the referee has counted to ten, they lose the contest.

down for the count (*mainly American*) having failed in something that you are doing ○ *Without this business, our little town was down for the count.*

out for the count asleep or unconscious ○ *At 10.30am he was still out for the count after another night disturbed by the crying baby.*

counter

under the counter (*mainly British*) secretly. The usual American expression is **under the table**. ○ *Most of the trading was done under the counter, through some form of black-market barter.*

In Britain, during the Second World War, shopkeepers sometimes kept articles that were in great demand under the shop counter. They only sold them to special customers, often charging very high prices for them.

country

★ **go to the country** (*British*) to hold a general election ○ *The Prime Minister is about to call a snap election even though he doesn't have to go to the country for another year.*

courage

Dutch courage (*mainly British*) an alcoholic drink that someone believes will increase their confidence ○ *The survey also noted how some performers used a little Dutch courage to overcome inhibitions.*

In the past, the Dutch had a reputation for drinking a lot of alcohol.

course

★ **on course for something** likely to achieve something ○ *We're well on course for a victory in a general election.*

★ **run its course** or
take its course to develop gradually and come to a natural end ○ *The real recovery for the auto industry won't come until the recession runs its course.*

★ **stay the course** to finish a difficult or unpleasant task, even though you have found it hard ○ *In Canada, where the infantry is open to women, very few have stayed the course.*

court

★ **hold court** to be surrounded by people who pay you a lot of attention because they consider you interesting or important ○ *She used to hold court in the college canteen with a host of admirers who hung on her every word.*

> 'Court' in this expression refers to the court of a king or queen.

laughed out of court not taken seriously ○ *When one London architect suggested a similar idea to a British developer he was laughed out of court.*

> A plaintiff who is 'out of court' has lost the right to be heard in a court of law.

rule something out of court (mainly British) to make something impossible because of a situation ○ *I was going to start studying medicine in September but then in August I caught polio which clearly ruled it out of court.*

Coventry

send someone to Coventry (British) to ignore and refuse to talk to someone because you disapprove of something they have done ○ *There is a strong feeling of hostility towards his decision. He has been sent to Coventry.*

> Various origins have been suggested for this expression. During the English Civil War, Royalist prisoners from Birmingham were sent to prison in Coventry. Another suggestion is that the people of Coventry disliked soldiers so much that they refused to talk to any woman who was seen talking to a soldier. As a result, soldiers did not like being sent to Coventry.

cover

cover your back to do something to protect yourself, for example against criticism or against accusations of doing something wrong ○ *"Perhaps the greatest singer of his generation." A well-placed "perhaps" always covers your back.*

cow

have a cow (American, informal) to become very upset or angry ○ *Don't tell Dad; he'll have a cow if he ever finds out.*

a sacred cow a belief, opinion or tradition that people are not willing to criticize, question or change ○ *The trade unions were, perhaps, the greatest sacred cow in British politics during the 1960s and early 1970s.*

> In the Hindu religion, cows are regarded as sacred.

cows

until the cows come home for a very long time ○ *Your child will enjoy this lively tape until the cows come home!*

> The full form of this expression is 'until the cows come home unbidden' or without being asked.

crack

at the crack of dawn very early in the morning ○ *He was scheduled to get up at the crack of dawn for an interview on 'Good Morning America'.*

★ **have a crack at something** to try to do something difficult ○ *I've decided now to have a crack at the world cross country race.*

cracked

★ **not all it's cracked up to be** not as good as many people say ○ *Package holidays are not always all they're cracked up to be.*

cracking

get cracking (*informal*) to start doing something immediately and quickly ○ *I realized that if we got cracking, we could make the last 700 miles to St Lucia within our deadline.*

cracks

fall through the cracks or
slip through the cracks (*mainly American*) to not be helped by a system which is supposed to help you. The British expression is **slip through the net**. ○ *This family slipped through the cracks in the system so they are not eligible for aid.*

★ **paper over the cracks** (*mainly British*) to try to hide the fact that something has gone badly wrong ○ *Accepting the minister's resignation will only serve to paper over the cracks of a much more serious rift.*

cradle

cradle-snatching (*British*) having a relationship with a person who is very much younger. The American expression is **robbing the cradle**. ○ *His uncle said: 'His dad and I just can't believe it. The woman is even older than his mother. It's cradle snatching.'*

from the cradle to the grave throughout all of a person's life ○ *The health service is said to provide for every emergency from the cradle to the grave.*

rob the cradle (*American*) to have a relationship with a person who is much younger. The British expression is **cradle-snatch**. ○ *'I'll always be younger,' he said, 'and there'll always be those who might accuse you of robbing the cradle.'*

crash

crash and burn to suddenly fail badly as a result of extreme tiredness or a big mistake ○ *Stress can cause over-achievers to crash and burn, and they can end up suffering from emotional disorders.*

▤ This may be a reference to a plane crashing into the ground and bursting into flames.

crazy

crazy as a bedbug (*American, informal*) not at all sensible or practical ○ *By now she'd concluded that Skolnick was crazy as a bedbug.*

▤ Bedbugs are small wingless insects that live in beds and bedding. They feed by biting people and sucking their blood.

cream

the cream of the crop the best people or things in a particular set or group ○ *The first Midlands media degree show features the cream of the crop of this year's graduates in photography, film, and video.*

creature

creature comforts modern sleeping, eating and washing facilities ○ *Each room has its own patio or balcony and provides guests with all modern creature comforts.*

▤ An old meaning of 'creatures' is material comforts, or things that make you feel comfortable.

creek

up the creek or
up the creek without a paddle (*informal*) in a very difficult situation ○ *We're up the creek because we don't know where to go from here.*

▤ A creek is a narrow bay. The idea is of being in a boat such as a canoe without being able to control it.

crest

on the crest of a wave very successful at what you are doing ○ *They are on the crest of a wave, winning games even when they don't play well.*

▤ The crest of a wave is its highest point.

cricket

it's not cricket (*British, old-fashioned*) said to mean that someone's behaviour is unfair or unreasonable ○ *The bank puts thousands of pounds a year into cricket – yet their treatment of staff is definitely not cricket.*

Cricket is traditionally associated with the values of fairness and respect for other players.

crisp

burned to a crisp badly burned ○ *Customers who insist on having their food burnt to a crisp should get it that way.*

critical

go critical to reach a stage of development where a project or organization can operate smoothly and successfully ○ *The programme confirmed its initial impact in week two, and really 'went critical' with the third edition on 8 December.*

crocodile

shed crocodile tears to pretend to be sad or to sympathize with someone without really caring about them ○ *He shed a lot of crocodile tears. He described the wrecking of the coal industry as 'a dreadful thing to have to do'.*

There was an ancient belief that crocodiles sighed and groaned to attract their prey, and wept while they were eating it.

cropper

★ **come a cropper** (mainly British)
1 to suffer a sudden and embarrassing failure ○ *Scott must concentrate on learning his new trade. He will come a cropper if he thinks he knows it all before he starts.*
2 to accidentally fall and hurt yourself ○ *Marco nearly came a cropper just before the finish when he just pulled his bike clear of a policeman by a crash barrier.*

'Cropper' may come from the expression 'to fall neck and crop', meaning to fall heavily. A bird's 'crop' is a pouch in its throat where it keeps food before digesting it.

cross

a cross to bear a responsibility or an unpleasant situation which you must live with, because you cannot change it ○ *'My children are much cleverer than me, it is a cross I have to bear,' he quips at one point in the interview.*

The reference here is to Jesus being made to carry the cross on which He was to die to the place of execution.

crossfire

caught in the crossfire suffering the unpleasant effects of a disagreement between other people even though you are not involved in it yourself ○ *Teachers say they are caught in the crossfire between the education establishment and the Government.*

This expression is more commonly used literally to talk about a situation where someone is in the way of two sets of people who are firing guns, and so is likely to be shot by mistake.

crow

as the crow flies in a straight line ○ *Although not distant as the crow flies from Tehran, this mountainous area has always been and still is remote.*

It used to be believed that crows always travelled to their destination by the most direct route possible. 'Make a beeline' is based on a similar idea.

eat crow (mainly American) to admit that you have been wrong and apologize, especially in a situation where this makes you feel ashamed. The usual British expression is to **eat humble pie**. ○ *But by the end of the year, Safire showed he was willing to eat crow. His first judgments of Watergate, he wrote, had been 'really wrong'.*

This expression is said to relate to an incident during the Anglo-American War of 1812-14. An American soldier who had accidentally entered an area occupied by the British was tricked into handing over his gun. He was then forced by a British officer to take a bite out of a crow which he had shot down. When his gun was returned to him, he forced the British officer to eat the rest of the bird.

crunch

★ **when it comes to the crunch** when a situation reaches a very important or difficult point and you must make a decision on how to progress ○ *If it comes to the crunch, I'll resign over this.*

'Crunch' is the sound used to imitate the sound of something hard being crushed, broken or eaten.

crust

earn a crust (British) to earn enough money to live on ○ *In his early days, he would do almost anything to earn a crust from the sport.*

A crust is a piece of bread, especially a piece consisting mainly of the hard outer part of the loaf.

cry

★ **a far cry from something** very different from something mentioned or experienced earlier ○ *It isn't a perfect democracy, but it's a far cry from the authoritarian rule of only a few years ago.*

in full cry (mainly British) at the highest or most intense level of activity ○ *We had left four or five people back in the bar where a Sunday lunchtime jazz band was in full cry.*

This expression refers to the noise made by a pack of hounds when they see the animal they are hunting.

cudgels

take up the cudgels to speak up or fight in support of someone ○ *The trade unions took up the cudgels for the 367 staff who were made redundant.*

A cudgel was a short, thick stick that was used as a weapon in the past.

cuff

★ **off-the-cuff** not prepared or carefully

thought out ○ *The singer offered an apology last night, saying: 'I'm sorry. I didn't mean any offence. It was a flippant, off-the-cuff remark.'*

One explanation for this expression is that after-dinner speakers used to write notes on the cuffs of their shirts, to remind them of what to say. Another explanation is that in the early days of cinema, directors sometimes wrote notes on their cuffs during the filming of a scene, to remind them of what they wanted to say to the actors.

cup

★ **something is not your cup of tea** said to mean that you are not very interested in something ○ *It's no secret that I've never been the greatest traveller. Sitting for hours on motorways is not my cup of tea.*

cupboard

cupboard love (British) the insincere affection shown by children or animals towards someone who they think will give them something that they want ○ *'Cupboard love,' she accused, freeing her ankles of the cat. 'You'd agree with anyone who could open the fridge or cooker.'*

The idea here is that cupboards often contain food or something else that a child or animal might want to have.

curate

a curate's egg (British) something that has both good and bad parts ○ *Wasserman's collection of duets with famous friends is something of a curate's egg.*

A curate is a clergyman in the Church of England who helps the vicar or rector of a parish. A well-known Victorian cartoon published in the British magazine 'Punch' shows a curate having breakfast with a senior clergyman. The curate has been given a bad egg but he is anxious not to offend anyone, so he says that it is 'good in parts'.

curiosity

curiosity killed the cat said to warn someone that they will suffer harm or damage if they try to find out about other people's private affairs ○ *'Where are we going?' Calder asked. 'Curiosity killed the cat, dear. You'll find out soon enough.'*

curtain

★ **bring the curtain down on something** to cause or mark the end of an event or situation ○ *Richardson brings the curtain down on one of the most amazing managerial careers of all-time this weekend.*

In theatres, it is traditional for a curtain to come down in front of the stage at the end of each act and at the end of the play.

curtains

it's curtains said to mean that it is the end of something ○ *If the vote is yes, it's curtains for us. A way of life will disappear.*

The curtains referred to here are the curtains at the front of the stage in a theatre.

curve

throw someone a curve ball (*mainly American*) to surprise someone by doing something unexpected, sometimes putting them at a disadvantage ○ *Our plan is to go into the winter with our reservoirs full, just in case Mother Nature throws us a curve ball next spring.*

In baseball, a 'curve ball' is a ball that curves through the air rather than travelling in a straight line.

cut

★ **a cut above the rest** much better than other similar people or things ○ *Smith's detective stories are generally agreed to be a cut above the rest.*

★ **cut and dried** clear and definite

○ *Now, this situation is not as cut-and-dried as it may seem.*

One explanation for this expression is that it refers to wood which has been cut and dried and is ready to use. Alternatively, it may refer to herbs that have been harvested and dried, to be used for cooking and medicine.

cut and run to escape from a difficult situation quickly, rather than dealing with it in a responsible way ○ *He had an unfortunate tendency to cut and run when things didn't go his way.*

In the past, ships' anchors were attached to ropes. If a warship was attacked, rather than causing delay by pulling up the anchor, the sailors would sometimes cut the rope.

★ **the cut and thrust** (*British*) the aspects of a particular activity or society that make it exciting and challenging ○ *Why does he want to go back into the cut and thrust of business at an age when most men are happily retired?*

This expression comes from sword fighting.

not be cut out for something to lack the right qualities or character for a particular lifestyle or job ○ *As you'll have gathered, I left medicine anyway. I wasn't really cut out for it.*

someone cannot cut it said to mean that someone is not good enough at doing something ○ *Many managers can't cut it at the highest level.*

cylinders

★ **fire on all cylinders** to do a task with great enthusiasm and energy ○ *I saw her a few weeks ago and she was firing on all cylinders. I don't think she would know what to do with herself if she didn't work.*

This expression refers to the cylinders in an engine. There are usually four of them.

Dd

dab

★ **a dab hand at something** (British) very good at doing something ○ She's an avid reader and a dab hand at solving difficult crossword puzzles.

> In the late 17th century, 'dab' meant clever or skilful.

daft

daft as a brush (British) very silly or stupid ○ She was as daft as a brush, and never said anything sensible.

> This expression may have come from 'as soft as a brush', as both 'soft' and 'daft' can mean stupid. Alternatively, it could have come from a fuller version, 'as daft as a brush without bristles'.

daggers

at daggers drawn (British) if two people are at daggers drawn, they are very angry with each other after an argument ○ The couple have been at daggers drawn since they separated six months ago.

look daggers at someone (literary) to stare at someone in a very angry way ○ He looked daggers at Mary as if it had all been her fault.

daisies

pushing up the daisies dead. This expression is used to refer to someone's death in a light-hearted or humorous way. ○ That was the last time I saw the old rogue. I can only assume he's either in prison or pushing up the daisies.

damper

★ **put a damper on something** to stop something being as successful or as enjoyable as it might be ○ The cold weather put a damper on our picnic.

> This expression may refer to either of two meanings of 'damper'. In a piano, a damper is a device which presses the strings and stops them vibrating, so stopping the sound. In a chimney or flue, a damper is a movable metal plate which controls the amount of air getting to the fire, and so controls how fiercely the fire burns.

dance

lead someone a merry dance (British) to deliberately make a lot of difficulties for someone who is trying to achieve something ○ When I tried to find out who was in charge, they led me a merry dance, sending me from one department to another before I found the right person to talk to.

dark

★ **be in the dark about something** to know nothing about something ○ The sooner we can find out what has happened, the better for all of us. But at the moment I'm in the dark.

keep something dark to keep something a secret ○ She took pleasure in keeping dark the identity of her new boyfriend.

a leap in the dark (British) a situation in which you do not know what the results of an action will be, usually when you feel you have no other choice but to take this course of action ○ The couple have taken a leap in the dark, selling their home in London and buying 10 acres of land in the country.

a shot in the dark a complete guess about something ○ It was just a shot in the dark but it was the right answer.

whistle in the dark to try not to show that you are afraid, or to try to believe that a situation is not as bad as it seems ○ *Maggie started telling jokes, trying to keep up everyone's spirits, but we all knew she was just whistling in the dark.*

dash

cut a dash (mainly British) to have a very stylish appearance that attracts attention ○ *The handsome bridegroom cut a dash in an elegant suit with a patterned waistcoat.*

date

★ **past your sell-by date** (British) no longer useful, successful, or relevant ○ *This type of TV programme is well past its sell-by date.*

> Most food has a date stamped on its packaging: this is its sell-by date. After this date it is no longer fresh enough to sell.

dawn

★ **a false dawn** (mainly British, journalism) a situation in which you think that something is finally going to improve but it does not ○ *National elections are scheduled for next year, but this country has seen many false dawns before. Is it really heading for democracy and peace this time?*

day

at the end of the day (spoken) said to mean that something is the most important aspect of a situation ○ *At the end of the day, it's the Germans who will decide.*

★ **call it a day**
1 to decide to stop doing something, usually because you are tired or are bored with it ○ *I searched for the cat for hours but I had to call it a day when darkness fell.*
2 to retire from your job ○ *It's no secret I want his job when he calls it a day.*

★ **carry the day** (journalism) if a person or their opinion carries the day in a contest or debate, they win it ○ *Dr Mead's argument carried the day.*

> This expression was originally used to say which army had won a battle.

the day of reckoning the time when people are forced to deal with an unpleasant situation which they have avoided until now ○ *The president has broken many laws, and his day of reckoning is approaching.*

> According to the Bible, when the world ends, there will be a day of reckoning or day of judgment, when God will judge everyone's actions and send them either to heaven or hell.

don't give up the day job said to someone to mean that they should continue to do their normal job rather than trying something new which they may not be good at, or which is not as secure and which they might fail at. This expression is usually used humorously. ○ *I started my business in the middle of a recession. People thought I was mad and said: 'Don't give up the day job.'*

★ **late in the day** at the very last moment or in the final stages of a situation, with the result that action may no longer be effective ○ *She feels that it is too late in the day for him to start behaving like a loving husband.*

make my day said when you want to challenge another person to compete or argue with you, so that you can prove that you are stronger and better than they are ○ *"Do you want a fight?" – "Go ahead. Make my day."*

> In the film 'Sudden Impact' (1983), Clint Eastwood, playing a detective called Harry, uses this expression to challenge a criminal who is threatening to shoot him.

★ **make someone's day** to do something that makes someone feel very happy ○ *Make your Mum a special card and tell her that you love her. It will make her day.*

put off the evil day (British) to delay doing something unpleasant for as long as possible ○ *You're putting off the evil day when the patient's going to die.*

save for a rainy day to save some of your money in case there are serious problems in the future ○ *Saving for a rainy day and paying off debts is now a top priority for families.*

seize the day said when you are advising someone to do what they want straight away, and not to worry about the future ○ *Don't waste your life. Seize the day.*

This is a translation of the Latin phrase 'carpe diem', which is also sometimes used.

★ **someone has had their day** said to mean that the period during which someone was most successful has now passed ○ *He's done well but, at 60, he has had his day.*

something is all in a day's work said to mean that something that most people would consider difficult, unusual, or exciting is easy or normal because it is part of your job, or because you often experience this kind of thing ○ *For war reporters, dodging snipers' bullets is all in a day's work.*

daylight

★ **do something in broad daylight** to do something illegal or bad openly in the daytime, when people can see it. This expression is often used to emphasize behaviour that is surprising or shocking. ○ *The paintings – valued at $20 million – were stolen in broad daylight by armed men, as some forty visitors looked on.*

daylights

beat the living daylights out of someone
1 to attack someone physically, hitting them many times ○ *The two men were beating the living daylights out of each other.*
2 to defeat someone totally in a competition or contest ○ *He enjoys the money and the fame but his true pleasure*

comes from walking on to a golf course and beating the living daylights out of everyone else.

The word 'daylights' in this expression may be related to an old threat to 'make daylight shine through' someone by stabbing them or shooting them. Alternatively, it may be related to an old meaning of 'daylights' referring to someone's eyes or internal organs. If they were badly beaten, their 'daylights' would stop working.

scare the living daylights out of someone to frighten someone very much ○ *You scared the living daylights out of me last night. All that screaming.*

days

★ **it's early days** (British) said to mean that it is too soon to be sure about what will happen in a particular situation in the future ○ *Maybe in time they will be friends again, but it's very early days.*

★ **someone's days are numbered** said to mean that someone is not likely to survive or be successful for much longer ○ *As rebels advanced on the capital it became clear that the President's days in power were numbered.*

something has seen better days said to mean that something is old and in poor condition ○ *There was an old brass double bed with a mattress that had seen better days.*

dead

come back from the dead to become active or successful again after a period of being inactive or unsuccessful ○ *I could not believe I had done it. I had come back from the dead and my career had survived the ultimate test.*

cut someone dead (British) to deliberately ignore someone, or refuse to speak to them, for example because you are angry with them ○ *I said 'Good morning' to my neighbour but she just cut me dead, and walked past me as though I did not exist.*

dead as a dodo (British) no longer active or popular ○ *The floppy disk is an invention that is now as dead as a dodo.*

> The dodo was a large flightless bird that lived on the islands of Mauritius and Réunion. It became extinct in the late 17th century as a result of hunting and the destruction of its nests by settlers on the islands.

dead as a doornail dead, or no longer active or popular ○ *In 1964, people said the Republican Party was dead as a doornail.*

> It is not certain what 'doornail' actually refers to. In medieval times, it may have been the plate or knob on a door which was hit by the knocker. It was thought that anything that was struck so often must have been dead. Alternatively, doornails may have been the thick nails which were set into outer doors. It is not clear why these nails should be described as 'dead'.

drop dead said to someone when you are telling them to go away and leave you alone because you are very angry or annoyed with them ○ *Richard told me to drop dead.*

★ **drop-dead gorgeous** (informal) very attractive or beautiful ○ *She's funny, kind, clever – and drop-dead gorgeous.*

knock 'em dead (informal) said to someone to increase their confidence before they appear or do something in public, especially something formal such as giving a speech in front of a crowd ○ *Just look 'em in the eye and knock 'em dead!*

> The word 'em' is a form of 'them' which is used in informal or non-standard English.

★ **someone wouldn't be seen dead** said to mean that someone strongly dislikes or disapproves of something ○ *Vincent wouldn't be seen dead in a pair of trainers and a baseball cap.*

deaf

deaf as a post (old-fashioned) very deaf ○ *My father is deaf as a post.*

deal

a done deal a plan or project that has been completed or arranged and that cannot now be changed ○ *The takeover proposal, however, is not a done deal as the company's shareholders must first approve the plan.*

★ **get a raw deal** to be treated unfairly or badly ○ *We must ask why bank customers get such a raw deal. And then find ways to make sure they get treated fairly in future.*

> This may refer to someone being dealt a bad hand in a game of cards.

death

at death's door seriously ill and likely to die very soon ○ *He has won five golf competitions in three months, a year after being at death's door.*

a death blow an act or event that causes a process, a situation, or an organization to come to an end ○ *They warned that the incidents would be a death blow to the Middle East peace process.*

dice with death (British) to do something very dangerous that could kill you ○ *In their daily lives, fishermen are constantly dicing with death.*

> To dice means to play dice, or to gamble.

★ **fight to the death to do something** to try very hard to achieve something or to keep hold of something, refusing to give up ○ *I will fight to the death to win – whatever it takes.*

hold onto something like grim death (mainly British) to hold onto something very tightly ○ *I clung to the chain like grim death.*

a living death an extremely poor quality of life, for example when someone is so ill that they are unlikely to recover ○ *For nearly four years he has been in a coma, kept alive by medical equipment, but trapped in* *what one doctor described as a 'living death'.*

look like death warmed up *(British)* or **look like death warmed over**
(American) to look very ill, pale, and tired ○ *You were looking like death warmed up, but you seem a lot better now.*

★ **sign someone's or something's death warrant** to cause the death or end of someone or something ○ *The company's flawed business strategy has signed the death warrants for thousands of jobs.*

> A death warrant is an official document which orders that someone is to be executed as a punishment for a crime.

★ **to death** used after adjectives such as 'scared', 'worried', and 'bored' to mean 'very' ○ *She was scared to death that he would leave her.*

deck

all hands on deck *(mainly British)* said to mean that a particular situation requires everyone to work hard in order to achieve an aim ○ *We had less than three weeks to organize the wedding, so it was all hands on deck*

> Members of a ship's crew are sometimes called hands and 'deck' refers to the floor of a ship.

hit the deck to suddenly fall to the ground ○ *When we heard the sound of gunfire, we hit the deck and covered our heads with our hands.*

> 'Deck' normally means the floor of a ship or, in American English, a raised platform outside a house. Here it means the floor or ground.

not play with a full deck to not be completely honest in a contest or discussion, and therefore have an unfair advantage over other people ○ *This guy is either very clever or he's not playing with a full deck.*

> A stacked or loaded deck of cards is one that has been altered before a game in order to give one player an advantage.

decks

★ **clear the decks** to make sure that everything that you have been doing is completely finished, so that you are ready to start a more important task ○ *Clear the decks before you think of taking on any more responsibilities.*

> In the past, all unnecessary objects were cleared off the decks or floors of a warship before a battle, so that the crew could move around more easily.

deep

★ **run deep** if a feeling or a problem runs deep, it is very serious or strong, often because it has existed for a long time ○ *My allegiance to Kendall and his company ran deep.*

degree

give someone the third degree *(informal)* to ask someone a lot of questions in an aggressive way in order to find out information ○ *My girlfriend gives me the third degree every time I go out without her. She wants to know where I've been and who I've spoken to.*

demolition

★ **do a demolition job on someone** *(British, journalism)* to attack someone very strongly, or to defeat them completely ○ *In his speech, Cook did a demolition job on the prime minister's strategy.*

dent

★ **make a dent in something** to reduce the amount or level of something ○ *The average family in Britain spends £100 a week on food, which makes a big dent in the household budget.*

department

something is not your department said to mean that you are not responsible for a particular task, or that you do not know much about a particular subject ○ *The political issues are something else, but that's not really my department.*

depth

★ **out of your depth** feeling anxious and inadequate because you have to deal with a situation or subject which you know very little about ○ *When I first started my new job, I felt out of my depth, but now I love it.*

This expression refers to someone who is in deep water but cannot swim very well, or cannot swim at all.

depths

plumb the depths

1 to be an example of extremely bad behaviour ○ *'This crime plumbs the very depths of the abyss into which it is possible for the human spirit to sink,' the judge said.*

2 to find out everything you can about something, including things that are normally secret or hidden ○ *In his writings Shakespeare plumbed the depths of human psychology.*

3 to experience an unpleasant or difficult situation to an extreme degree ○ *They frequently plumb the depths of loneliness, humiliation and despair.*

The above expressions relate to sailing in former times. When a ship was in shallow water one of the sailors would find out how deep the water was by dropping a piece of lead on a string, called a 'plumb', over the side of the ship. 'Swing the lead' is also based on this practice.

deserts

The noun 'deserts' is related to the verb 'deserve', and it is pronounced with stress on its second syllable.

★ **get your just deserts** to deserve the unpleasant things that have happened to you, because you have done something bad ○ *Some people felt sympathy for the humbled superstar. Others felt she was getting her just deserts for years of outrageous behaviour.*

'Deserts' is an old-fashioned word meaning a reward or punishment which is deserved.

designs

have designs on someone to want to have a relationship with another person, although the second person is not interested, or is already in a relationship with someone else ○ *He had a feeling that Francine had designs on him.*

have designs on something to want something and to plan to get it, sometimes in a dishonest way ○ *He has designs on the top job at the company.*

devices

★ **be left to your own devices** to be left to do what you want, or to look after yourself without any help from other people ○ *If left to my own devices, I would eat a chocolate dessert every night.*

An old meaning of 'device' was desire or will.

devil

be between the devil and the deep blue sea (*mainly British*) to be in a difficult situation where the two possible courses of action or choices that you can take are equally bad ○ *We are between the devil and the deep blue sea: if we pay our rent, we won't have any money for food.*

The origin of this expression is in shipping, not religion. It is unclear exactly what the 'devil' was, but it is thought to have been some kind of seam or plank that was awkward and dangerous to reach, so a sailor who had to make it waterproof was in a very unsafe position, and risked falling into the water.

better the devil you know

(*mainly British*) said to mean that it is better to deal with someone you already know, even if you do not like them, than to deal with someone that you know

dime 73

nothing about, because they may be even worse ○ *It is becoming clearer to them that he is no angel; but better the devil you know.*

have a devil of a job or

have the devil's own job to manage to do something, but only after a lot of difficulty ○ *We got there just in time, but we had a devil of a job finding her in that place.*

speak of the devil or

talk of the devil (*spoken*) said when someone you have just been talking about arrives unexpectedly ○ *'Speak of the devil,' she greeted Tom, smiling.*

≡ This expression comes from the saying 'talk of the devil and he will appear'.

diamond

> A rough diamond is a diamond that has not yet been cut and polished.

a rough diamond (*mainly British*) or

a diamond in the rough (*American*)

1 someone, especially a man, that you like and admire because of their good qualities, even though they are not sophisticated or well-mannered ○ *Marden was the rough diamond of the three men, feared for his ruthlessness but respected for his First World War Military Cross.*

2 someone or something that has a lot of talent or potential but which needs hard work before this talent or potential can be revealed ○ *First novels are usually rough diamonds, with flashes of inspiration.*

dice

the dice are loaded against someone said to refer to a situation where everything seems to work to your disadvantage, so that you are unlikely ever to have success ○ *I survived that night on the mountain when all the dice were loaded against me.*

≡ Players who wanted to cheat at dice games sometimes 'loaded' or weighted the dice so that they tended to fall in a particular way.

no dice

1 said to mean that you are trying to achieve something but that you are having no luck or success with it ○ *I spent part of that time calling everyone I knew to see if I could find another job for him. No dice.*

2 said when you are refusing to do what someone has asked you to do ○ *Nope, sorry, we're not interested, no dice.*

≡ This expression comes from the game of craps, and means that the player's last throw is disqualified and not counted.

die

the die is cast said to mean that you have made an important decision about the future and that it is impossible to change it, even if things go wrong ○ *I have made this decision to get a puppy. In fact, the die is cast: I have already paid for it.*

≡ 'Die' is an old singular form of the word 'dice'. Once you have thrown the dice, you cannot do anything to change the way they fall.

★ **to die for** (*informal*) very good or attractive ○ *The food here is to die for, it's heaven on a plate.*

dime

> A dime is an American coin worth ten cents.

a dime a dozen (*American*) existing in large numbers and therefore not especially valuable or interesting. In British English, use **two a penny**. ○ *Action movies are a dime a dozen these days.*

turn on a dime (*mainly American*) to suddenly do something completely different from what you were doing before ○ *Nowadays businesses need to be flexible and to change, and sometimes to turn on a dime in order to stay competitive.*

The idea is of being able to manoeuvre quickly and easily in a small space, like stopping and changing direction with your foot still on the coin. The expression is also used of cars.

dinner

be done like a dinner (mainly Australian) to be completely defeated, often unfairly, in a contest or competitive situation ○ The fact is, you were done like a dinner by a superior team.

dinners

have done something more than someone has had hot dinners (British) to have done something a great number of times ○ Robin and Lizzie Hamer of First Ascent activity holidays have climbed more mountains than you and I have had hot dinners.

dirt

★ **dig up dirt on someone** or **dig the dirt** (British) to search for any information about someone that may damage their reputation ○ They hired a detective firm to dig up dirt on their rival.

dish the dirt on someone to spread stories about someone, especially things that may embarrass or upset them, or damage their reputation ○ Many politicians, who protest that their private lives are their own, are quite happy to dish the dirt on a fellow politician.

do someone dirt or **do the dirt on someone** (American) to betray someone or treat them very badly ○ They tell me you have done me dirt. Tell me it ain't true.

dirty

do the dirty on someone (British) to betray someone or treat them very badly ○ Lots of people make use of a situation like this to do the dirty on somebody they don't like.

★ **wash your dirty linen in public** (British) or

air your dirty laundry in public (American) to talk about unpleasant or personal matters in front of other people, when most people consider that such things should be kept private. ○ We shouldn't wash our dirty laundry in public and if I was in his position, I'd say nothing at all.

distance

★ **go the distance** to complete what you are doing and reach your goal ○ Dave Hilton failed to go the distance when he was forced off the pitch in the second half with a leg injury.

A boxer who succeeds in fighting until the end of the match is said to 'go the distance'.

within spitting distance
1 very close to a particular place ○ Most of the world's biggest financial firms are already established within spitting distance of the Bank of England.
2 very close to achieving an amount, a level, or a goal ○ We are now within spitting distance of our goal. We've raised $9542.55. Just $457.45 to go.

★ **within striking distance**
1 very close to a particular place ○ Ironbridge is well signposted from the motorway and within easy striking distance of both Birmingham and Manchester.
2 very close to achieving an amount, a level, or a place ○ He is within striking distance of victory in the election.

distraction

drive someone to distraction to annoy someone very much ○ Nothing I said or did would get them to tidy up their bedrooms. It drove me to distraction.

Distraction is an old word for madness.

ditch

★ **a last ditch attempt** an action performed when everything else has failed, as a final attempt to avoid disaster, although it too seems likely to fail ○ The

President has been making a last ditch attempt to prevent the rebels taking over the city.

> In this expression, 'ditch' means a trench which has been dug in order to defend a military position. The expression refers to soldiers who are prepared to die in a final effort to defend the position rather than surrender.

divide

★ **divide and conquer** or **divide and rule** (British) a strategy by which someone remains in power by making sure that the people under their control quarrel among themselves and so cannot unite to achieve their aims and overthrow their leader ○ *Trade unions are concerned that management may be tempted into a policy of divide and rule.*

> This expression has its origin in the Latin phrase 'divide et impera'. It describes one of the tactics which the Romans used to rule their empire.

dividends

★ **pay dividends** to bring a lot of advantages at a later date ○ *Taking time out to get fit is time well spent and will pay dividends in the long run.*

> A dividend is a payment of profits that is divided among all the shareholders of a company.

Dixie

someone is not just whistling Dixie (American) said to mean that someone is being honest or realistic in what they are saying and that they should therefore not be ignored ○ *'Is that a threat?' 'I'm not just whistling Dixie.'*

> Dixie was the name given to the region of the southern and eastern United States which formed the Confederate side in the Civil War. The area gave its name to several songs which were popular as Confederate war songs.

doctor

just what the doctor ordered extremely pleasant or useful and helping to make you feel better or to improve a situation ○ *'Meatballs in tomato sauce!' Max exclaimed happily. 'Just what the doctor ordered.'*

dog

a dog and pony show (American) an event with a lot of exciting things happening that has been organized in order to impress someone ○ *We bombarded the management team with charts, graphs, facts, and figures. Our boss responded by dozing off during most of our dog and pony show.*

> This expression refers to circus acts involving dogs and horses.

the dog days

1 the hottest days of the year, which occur in July and August in the northern hemisphere ○ *We spent the dog days of summer in the mountains of Arizona.*

> The ancient Romans named these days 'dies caniculares' or 'dog days' because the Dog Star, Sirius, could be seen in the morning sky at this time of year. They believed that the combination of Sirius and the sun produced very hot weather.

2 a period in someone's life or career when they are not having much success or are not making any progress ○ *Those were the dog days of the Conservative government.*

dog eat dog used for describing a situation in which everyone wants to succeed and is willing to harm other people or to use dishonest methods in order to do this ○ *In the 1992 campaign, he said that if it was going to be 'dog eat dog' he would do anything it took to get himself re-elected.*

dog-in-the-manger wanting to prevent other people from using or enjoying something simply because you cannot use or enjoy it yourself ○ *On the one hand the council has a high regard for the carnival's tourist benefits, but on the other it does not want it to have too high a profile. It's a dog-in-the-manger attitude which has taken the fun out of a great event.*

One of Aesop's fables tells of a dog which prevented an ox from eating the hay in its manger, even though the dog could not eat the hay itself.

a dog's dinner (British) a situation, event, or piece of work that is chaotic, badly organized, or very untidy ○ *The government's latest proposals are a dog's dinner.*

every dog has its day said to mean that everyone will be successful or lucky at some time in their life. This expression is sometimes used to encourage someone at a time when they are not having any success or luck. ○ *I've been waiting a long time for success – four years – but every dog has its day.*

This proverb has been known in English since at least the 16th century. Shakespeare quotes it in 'Hamlet': 'Let Hercules himself do what he may, The cat will mew and dog will have his day.' (Act 5, Scene 1).

it's a dog's life said to mean that a job or situation is unpleasant or boring ○ *It's a dog's life being a football manager.*

you can't teach an old dog new tricks said to mean that it is often difficult to get people to try new ways of doing things, especially if these people have been doing something in a particular way for a long time ○ *I'm 65 and you can't teach an old dog new tricks.*

doghouse

be in the doghouse to have made people very annoyed with you because of something you have done ○ *Four ministers have landed themselves in the*

dog house after failing to turn up to a meeting at the White House.

In American English, a 'doghouse' is a kennel.

dogs

call off the dogs to tell someone to stop criticizing, attacking, or damaging another person ○ *After years of persecution, it's time to call off the dogs. He's been punished enough.*

The dogs referred to here are dogs used for hunting.

go to the dogs if a country, organization, or business is going to the dogs, it is becoming less powerful or successful than it has been in the past ○ *If you ask me, the whole country is going to the dogs.*

let sleeping dogs lie said to warn someone not to disturb or interfere with a situation, because they are likely to cause trouble and problems ○ *Why does she come over here stirring everything up? Why can't she let sleeping dogs lie?*

throw someone to the dogs to allow someone to be criticized severely or treated badly, for example in order to protect yourself from criticism or harm, or because you no longer need them ○ *He will trick you, use you, and throw you to the dogs. He'll do anything to save his own skin.*

The dogs referred to here are dogs used for hunting.

doldrums

★ **be in the doldrums**

1 if an economy or business is in the doldrums, nothing new is happening and it is not doing well ○ *Property prices remain in the doldrums.*

2 to be sad and have no energy or enthusiasm ○ *At that time Freddie had just lost his job and was in the doldrums.*

come out of the doldrums

1 if an economy or business comes out of

the doldrums, it improves and becomes stronger after a period of inactivity ○ *Let's hope that the economy may finally be coming out of the doldrums.*
2 to stop being sad and start to feel happier ○ *With the help of my family and friends, I eventually came out of the doldrums.*

> The above expressions relate to the Doldrums, which is an area of sea near the equator where there is often little or no wind. This meant that sailing ships could be stuck there for long periods.

dollar

the 64,000 dollar question a very important question that is very difficult to answer ○ *They asked the 64,000 dollar question: 'So what makes a good marriage?' Faithfulness comes out top of the list on that.*

> In the United States in the 1940s, there was a radio quiz show called 'Take It or Leave It'. Contestants had to answer questions for prizes ranging from two dollars for an easy question to $64 for the hardest. A similar television quiz show in the 1950s increased the prize to $64,000.

you can bet your bottom dollar said to emphasize that you are absolutely certain that something will happen or that something is true ○ *A police insider was quoted as saying of the crime: 'You can bet your bottom dollar Sinclair was involved.'*

> This expression refers to the piles of coins on a poker table. A confident player would bet by pushing a pile of coins to the centre of the table using the bottom dollar, on which all the others were resting.

dollars

feel a million dollars to feel very healthy and happy ○ *After all my recent problems, I now feel a million dollars.*

it's dollars to doughnuts *(mainly American)* said to show that you are certain that something will happen ○ *It's dollars to doughnuts that, in the future, banks will charge more for their services.*

look a million dollars to look extremely attractive and well-dressed ○ *She looked a million dollars when she got off the plane.*

domino

★ **a domino effect** a situation in which one event causes another similar event, which in turn causes a further event, and so on ○ *The accident created a domino effect, causing about 10 other cars to crash and injuring 14 other people.*

> This expression was first used in the 1950s by an American political commentator to describe what some people thought would happen if one country in a region became Communist: they believed that the other countries in that area would also 'fall' to the Communists. The image is of a row of upright dominoes; if one falls, it knocks the next one over and so on, until all of them have fallen over.

done

done and dusted *(mainly British)* finished or decided, with nothing more to be said or done ○ *The investigation should be done and dusted by the end of next month.*

donkey

do the donkey work *(British)* to do all the most physically tiring or boring parts of a job or a piece of work ○ *The boss sent for Andy and got him to do the donkey work.*

for donkey's years *(British)* for a very long time ○ *I've been a vegetarian for donkey's years.*

> This expression was originally 'as long as donkey's ears', which are very long. The change to 'donkey's years' may have come about because the expression is used to talk about time.

door

be knocking at someone's door to be likely to happen soon, or to be starting to happen ○ *Mike was in terrible trouble but it wasn't long before help was knocking at his door.*

closing the stable door after the horse has bolted (British) or

closing the barn door after the horse has gone (American) acting too late, because the problem that the action would have prevented has already occurred ○ *It is good to see the government taking positive action, even though it might look like closing the stable door after the horse has bolted.*

★ **do something by the back door** (mainly British) to do something secretly and unofficially ○ *He said the government would not allow anyone to sneak in by the back door and seize power by force.*

knock on the door of something to try to join a club or a group, or to try to become part of it ○ *These two players will, I'm sure, soon be knocking on the door of the national team.*

★ **lay something at someone's door** to blame someone for something unpleasant that has happened ○ *We have no doubt about who is responsible for the riot. The blame must be laid at the door of the government.*

one door closes and another one opens said to mean that if one thing you do fails, you will soon have an opportunity to try to succeed at something else. This expression is often used to encourage someone to keep trying after they have had a disappointment or failure. ○ *Robert was philosophical after losing his job. 'Obviously, I am disappointed,' he explained. 'But one door closes and another one opens.'*

push at an open door (British) to find it very easy to achieve your aims ○ *Persuading companies to invest in green technology today is like pushing at an open door.*

the revolving door

1 a situation in which the people working in a particular organization do not stay there for very long, and so it is difficult for anything effective to be achieved ○ *The revolving door on the boardroom has continued to turn, with Victoria Jones becoming the sixth chief executive to leave in the past ten years.*

2 a situation in politics in which someone moves from an important position in government to a position in a private company, especially where this may give them an unfair advantage. ○ *Bill Clinton ran a campaign that included a strong pledge to stop the revolving door between public service and the private sector.*

3 a situation where solutions to problems last for only a short time, and then the same problems occur again ○ *These young people are caught in the revolving door of the justice system, ending up back on the streets after serving time in prison.*

doors

★ **do something behind closed doors** (journalism) to do something in private because you want it to be kept secret ○ *The summer I was fourteen and Rita was twelve, our parents started having long talks behind closed doors.*

dos

★ **the dos and don'ts of something** the things that you should and should not do in a particular situation ○ *The publisher produces a detailed booklet full of dos and don'ts for aspiring authors of romantic fiction, stressing that the story must always have a happy ending.*

dot

do something on the dot to do something at exactly the time you are supposed to do it ○ *They have breakfast at nine o'clock on the dot.*

The minutes on a clock face are often marked by dots.

since the year dot *(British)* for a very long time ○ *Most of these people have lived here since the year dot.*

double

at the double or
on the double *(British)* very quickly or immediately ○ *Michael reached for his phone. 'Jill? My office, please, at the double.'*

> 'At the double' is a military expression meaning at twice the normal marching pace.

down

★ **be going down the drain** or
be going down the tubes or
be going down the pan to be getting worse or to be being destroyed, with little hope of recovery ○ *Small businesses are going down the drain because of the failed economic policies of this government.*

down and dirty *(mainly American)* bold, direct, and sometimes rude ○ *The film portrays the rock band at their most down and dirty.*

★ **down and out**
1 having nowhere to live, no job, and no real hope of improving your situation ○ *Having been down and out himself, Barry understands the problems, and he's helped many people to find homes and jobs.* ○ *There are hundreds of down and outs living just a few yards from his palace.*
2 having been beaten, or having lost badly, in a competition or contest ○ *From this newspaper article, you will see that Ted appears to be down and out as candidate for governor.*

> If boxers are down and out, they have been knocked down and have failed to get up before the referee counted to ten, and have therefore lost the contest.

★ **down-at-heel** *(mainly British)* or
down-at-the-heels *(mainly American)* untidy and not cared for ○ *The flight to Kathmandu is always full of scruffy, down-at-heel people like Hyde.*

> The image here is of a person wearing shoes with worn-down heels because they do not have the money to repair or replace them.

get down and dirty *(mainly American)* to act in an unfair or dishonest way in order to gain an advantage ○ *If the President gets down and dirty, the Governor will give as good as he gets.*

★ **go down the drain** or
go down the tubes or
go down the pan to be lost or wasted ○ *You have ruined everything – my plans for the future, my business. All those years of work have gone down the drain.*

downer

have a downer on someone *(British)* to not like someone, or to disapprove of them ○ *Her dad has a downer on every guy she meets.*

drag

★ **drag your feet** or
drag your heels to deliberately delay making a decision about something that is important to you ○ *There's been substantial criticism of the United States for dragging its feet on measures to protect the environment.*

drain

be going down the drain or
go down the drain → see **down**
laugh like a drain *(British)* to laugh a lot ○ *I've watched this comedy series over and over again but I still laugh like a drain every time.*

> The idea is of loud unrestrained laughter sounding like water disappearing down a drain, and perhaps also of the open mouth resembling the drain.

drawer

★ **out of the top drawer** *(mainly British)*
1 among the best of a particular kind

○ *The Grange Hotel may be out of the top drawer, but it's not pretentious.* ○ *The play has a top-drawer cast including Maria Aitken and Tim Piggot-Smith.*

2 having had a privileged social background ○ *Betty Boothroyd is hardly out of the top drawer. She used to work in showbusiness as a dancer.*

dream

★ **do something like a dream** to do something very well ○ *She had noticed, from across the dance floor, that he danced like a dream.*

★ **a dream ticket** (*mainly British, journalism*) two well-known people, for example politicians or actors, who are expected to work well together and to have a great deal of success ○ *It should have been Hollywood's dream ticket: husband and wife starring together in a romantic blockbuster movie.*

> In the United States, a ticket is a list of candidates that a political party has nominated for election. A 'dream ticket' is a pair of candidates that seem to be perfectly matched and who will attract a lot of support.

dreams

★ **beyond your wildest dreams** better than you could have imagined or hoped for ○ *The response of viewers to our charity appeal was beyond our wildest dreams. The money just kept pouring in.*

never in your wildest dreams said to emphasize that you think that something is extremely strange or unlikely ○ *We were told that we had won a lot of money but never in my wildest dreams could I have thought it would be more than £1 million.*

★ **the person or thing of someone's dreams** the person or the thing that someone prefers to all others ○ *It was in Tunisia that they saw the house of their dreams, the most beautiful dwelling imaginable.*

dressed

all dressed up with nowhere to go prepared for something, but with no opportunity to do it ○ *The team were left all dressed up with nowhere to go after their match was called off because of a frozen pitch.*

dressed to kill wearing very stylish clothes which are intended to attract attention and impress people ○ *She was dressed to kill in a red strapless gown.*

driver

in the driver's seat → see **seat**

drop

★ **at the drop of a hat** willingly and without hesitation. This expression is often used to suggest that someone does not think carefully enough about their actions. ○ *People should sort out their own minor problems and not just call the police at the drop of a hat.*

> In the early 19th century, boxing matches were often started by someone dropping a hat.

★ **a drop in the ocean** (*British*) or **a drop in the bucket** (*mainly American*) something, especially an amount of money, that is very small in comparison with the amount which is needed or expected, so that its effect is insignificant ○ *Unfortunately, this tax won't raise a lot of money. It's a drop in the ocean, really.*

> This expression may come from a line in the Bible in which nations are described as being insignificant, or 'a drop of a bucket'. (Isaiah 40:15)

drop something or someone like a hot potato or
drop something or someone like a hot brick to get rid of something or someone as quickly as possible because they are difficult to deal with, or because you do not want them any more ○ *It is a rule of the tourism business that clients must*

feel happy on holiday. If a place gains a reputation for being unwelcoming, the trade drops it like a hot potato.

drum

★ **bang the drum for something or someone** to support something or someone strongly and publicly ○ *The trade secretary is banging the drum for British industry.*

drummer

march to a different drummer (*journalism*) to act in accordance with beliefs or expectations which are different from those of your colleagues or friends ○ *The state-supported school marches to a different drummer, and I will permit it to continue to do so.*

drunk

drunk as a skunk very drunk ○ *When John arrived here last night, he was drunk as a skunk.*

dry

dry as a bone very dry ○ *By the end of June the pond was as dry as a bone.*

dry as dust
1 very dry ○ *The fields were dry as dust.*
2 very boring ○ *His book is badly written, poorly edited and dry as dust.*

duck

a dead duck someone or something that is a failure ○ *The government is a dead duck.*

★ **a lame duck**
1 someone or something with little real power, for example a politician or a government when their period of office is coming to an end ○ *The government is headed by a president who looks like a lame duck.*
2 someone who is in a very weak position and who needs support ○ *Elizabeth often invites lame ducks to spend Christmas with us.*

a sitting duck someone who is an

obvious target, and whom it is very easy to attack or criticize ○ *They heard the sound of gunfire. 'It's a trap,' Joe whispered. 'And we're sitting ducks! We've got to find somewhere to hide.'*

A duck is an easy target for hunters when it is sitting on the water or on the ground.

take to something like a duck to water to discover that you are naturally good at something and that you find it very easy to do ○ *Gilbey became a salesman for BMW. He took to it like a duck to water, quickly becoming Car Salesman of the Year.*

ducks

get your ducks in a row (*mainly American*) to get everything properly organized and under control ○ *The government needs to get its ducks in a row.*

The 'ducks' in this expression are duckpins. The game of duckpins is a variation of bowling, with ten smaller pins and a smaller ball with no finger holes. The literal meaning of 'to get your ducks in a row' is to get your duckpins set up for the next game.

play ducks and drakes with someone (*British*) to treat someone badly, by being dishonest with them or not taking them seriously ○ *Politicians are playing ducks and drakes with the poorest and most disadvantaged people in the country.*

'Ducks and drakes' is the game of skimming flat stones across the surface of a stretch of water to see how many times you can make the stones bounce. Here, the person's attitude to others is perhaps being compared to someone idly and thoughtlessly skimming stones.

dudgeon

in high dudgeon (*literary*) unreasonably angry or annoyed about something ○ *She left the meeting in high dudgeon after learning that the only perk was free coffee.*

dull

dull as ditchwater or
dull as dishwater extremely boring ○ *He's a dull writer and that's a fact. Dull as ditchwater.*

> The expression 'dull as ditchwater' is over 200 years old, whereas 'dull as dishwater' is a more recent variant. The reference is to the dull dirty colour of the water in ditches or in washing-up bowls.

dummy

spit out the dummy *(mainly Australian)* to behave in a bad-tempered and childish way ○ *He spat out the dummy when his wife said that she wanted to go on holiday without him.*

> The image here is of a bad-tempered baby spitting out its dummy.

dumps

down in the dumps feeling sad, with no hope ○ *Tom's a bit down in the dumps. Let's try to cheer him up.*

dust

be eating someone's dust to be completely defeated by another person in a competitive situation ○ *We were all eating his dust. I didn't know he could run so fast.*

> If you are riding behind another horse in a race, you have the dust kicked up by the other horse in your face.

★ **bite the dust**
1 to fail or to stop existing ○ *There are thousands of restaurants in and around London. Some make big money. Most break even, and quite a few have bitten the dust.*

2 to die. This expression is used to refer to someone's death in a humorous way. ○ *The climax of most Westerns comes when the villain bites the dust.*

> In stories about the Wild West, cowboys were said to 'bite the dust' when they were shot and fell off their horses.

★ **the dust has settled** said to mean that a situation has become calmer and steadier after a series of confusing or chaotic events ○ *Now that the dust has settled, it is clear that nothing much has changed.*

★ **gather dust** to not be dealt with for a very long time ○ *This project has been gathering dust on the shelves of the Ministry of the Environment for the last five years.*

shake the dust from your feet *(British)* to leave a place or a situation, with the intention that you will never return to it ○ *Our job here is done. It's time to shake the dust from our feet and move on.*

> This expression occurs in the Bible (Matthew 10:14), where people are advised that if no one welcomes them or listens to their words as they leave a particular place, then they should shake its dust off their feet (= never go back there again).

you couldn't see someone for dust *(British)* said to mean that someone has left a place or a difficult situation, very quickly and run away ○ *As soon as Maria told her boyfriend she was pregnant, he was off. You couldn't see him for dust.*

> The image here is of someone galloping away on a horse, so that all you see is the cloud of dust kicked up by the horse's feet.

Ee

eagle

an eagle eye an ability to find or notice things ○ *No antiques shop, market or junk shop escapes her eagle eye.*

> Eagles have very good eyesight, and are able to see small animals or objects from a great height.

keep an eagle eye on someone or something to watch a person or thing very carefully ○ *Mr Grogan kept an eagle eye on everything that was going on in the factory.*

ear

bend someone's ear to keep talking to someone about something, usually in an annoying way ○ *You can't go on bending everyone's ear with this problem.*

go in one ear and out the other if a piece of information goes in one ear and out the other, you pay no attention to it, or forget about it immediately ○ *I'd said it so many times before that it just went in one ear and out the other as far as he was concerned.*

★ **grin from ear to ear** to look very happy ○ *McCarthy was grinning from ear to ear. He absolutely radiated warmth and pride.*

have an ear for something to have the ability to learn and understand the structure of a language or piece of music quickly, and to be able to reproduce the sounds of the language or music easily and accurately. Compare **have a tin ear for** something; see **tin**. ○ *He had an ear for languages, which he enjoyed, and by this time he spoke five fluently.*

have someone's ear to have the attention of a person in power, who listens carefully to your opinions and often follows your advice on important issues ○ *He has been one of Italy's most influential figures, a man who is said to have had the ear of every Italian prime minister.*

keep your ear to the ground (mainly British) to make sure that you find out about all the things that people are doing or talking about ○ *Watch and learn. While you do this, keep your ear to the ground. Know who is coming, who is going: a new vacancy could be an opportunity for you.*

> In films, Native Americans are often shown tracking people or animals by listening carefully to the ground for the sound of their footsteps.

lend an ear to someone to listen carefully and sympathetically to a person who has a problem ○ *Slowly your status at work will improve, and your boss and colleagues will lend a sympathetic ear to your gripes and grievances.*

listen with half an ear to not give your full attention to something ○ *She was listening to the news on the radio with half an ear when she suddenly heard his name mentioned.*

out on your ear (informal) suddenly dismissed from a course, job, or group ○ *I'd failed the first year exam in the History of Art. I had to pass the re-sit or I'd be out on my ear.*

play it by ear to deal with things as they happen, rather than following a plan or previous arrangement ○ *'Where will we stay in Gloucestershire?' 'Oh, I guess a bed-and-breakfast place. We'll have to play it by ear.'*

> If someone plays a piece of music by ear, they play it without looking at printed music.

turn a deaf ear to something to refuse to consider a request or an opinion and not pay any attention to it ○ *The Mayor of Paris has long turned a deaf ear to Parisians who want tougher laws to protect the cleanliness of their pavements.*

ears

be all ears to be ready and eager to listen to what someone is saying ○ *'That's a very good question. May I answer it frankly?' 'I'm all ears.'*

★ **fall on deaf ears** if something you say to someone falls on deaf ears, they take no notice of what you have said ○ *The mayor spoke privately to Gibson yesterday and asked him to resign, but said that his plea fell on deaf ears.*

have nothing between your ears to be stupid ○ *He's good-looking but he has nothing between his ears.*

have something coming out of your ears to have so much of something that you do not want or need any more of it ○ *Everyone who wants to talk to me is talking about football. I've had football coming out of my ears. I can't get away from it.*

have steam coming out of your ears to be very angry about something ○ *Not that Labour's front-benchers quite see it that way; indeed, they have steam coming out of their ears at the suggestion.*

pin back your ears

1 (British, old-fashioned) to listen carefully to what someone is saying ○ *Right, pin back your ears, everyone.*

2 (mainly British) in sport, to run very quickly in an attempt to score and help your team win ○ *The Newport back division dropped the ball 30 metres out and Hughes pinned back his ears and raced to the line.*

pin someone's ears back (American) to tell someone off for having done something wrong ○ *Dad was furious about what I'd done and pinned my ears back.*

prick up your ears to start listening eagerly, because you suddenly hear an interesting sound or piece of information ○ *She stopped talking to prick up her ears – and Kenworthy had heard the same sound.*

When some animals hear a sudden or unfamiliar noise, they literally prick up their ears; that is, their ears become more erect so that they can hear the sound better.

someone's ears are burning said about someone who other people are talking about ○ *Howard's ears must have been burning as he was referred to as the 'little man in the big house'.*

up to your ears very busy with work, or deeply involved in an unpleasant situation ○ *'Why don't you come to the cinema with us?' 'I can't. I'm up to my ears in reports.'*

wet behind the ears new to a situation and therefore inexperienced or naive ○ *Terry was just out of university, with a shapely haircut of medium length that failed to hide the fact that he was wet behind the ears.*

There are two possible origins for this expression. It may refer to a young animal being washed by its mother. Alternatively, it may refer to children forgetting to dry behind their ears after washing.

earth

★ **come down to earth** or
come down to earth with a bump to have to face the reality of everyday life after a period of great excitement ○ *When something good does happen, it's important that it is celebrated. Next day something will happen and you'll come back down to earth.*

★ **down to earth** very realistic and practical. Compare **have your head in the clouds**; see **head**. ○ *They think she's too glamorous and won't want to speak to them. But that's just not true at all. She's very friendly and very down to earth. ○ Everyone* liked her *down-to-earth approach to life.*

go to earth (British) to hide from someone or something ○ *The girl who had supplied the gun and plastic explosive device stayed put for a couple of weeks before she, too, went to earth.*

> A fox's hole is called an earth. In hunting, this expression is used to refer to a fox hiding in its earth.

promise the earth to promise to give people things that you cannot in fact possibly give them ○ *One voter summed up the mood: 'Politicians have lost credibility,' he complained. 'They promise the earth and don't deliver.'*

run someone to earth (British) to find someone after a long search ○ *I must admit I thought I had run my man to earth, for although a great many people live there now, there could not be many that would match my description.*

> A fox's hole is called an earth. In hunting, this expression is used to refer to a fox being chased back to its earth.

easier

★ **easier said than done** said to mean that something is simple to achieve in theory, but difficult to do in practice ○ *The alternative option is to scrap the unwanted machines, and use the metal for some other purpose. But this, too, is easier said than done.*

easy

> In the first idiom below, **ABC** is pronounced 'a b c', as if you are spelling it out.

easy as pie or
easy as ABC or
easy as falling off a log very easy to do. Compare **a piece of cake**; see **piece**. ○ *Michael understood at once. 'Why, that's easy as pie,' he said as the rest of us scratched our heads.*

easy come, easy go said to mean that something does not require a lot of effort and is therefore not worth worrying about ○ *My attitude to money is easy come, easy go. That is to say, I earn a lot, but I also give quite a lot away in different ways.*

go easy on someone to punish or treat someone less severely than might be expected or deserved ○ *They had to go easy on him because he was only thirteen and it was also his first offence.*

go easy on something to not have or use too much of something because you think that it is bad for you ○ *Small meals at regular times are important. Go easy on the salt. Don't add extra sugar.*

★ **take it easy** or
take things easy
1 (British) to relax and not worry, hurry, or do anything that needs a lot of energy ○ *The seven astronauts aboard the space shuttle Columbia are taking it easy today, following six full days of medical research.*
2 (mainly American) an informal way of saying 'goodbye' ○ *'Thanks. See you later.' 'Take it easy. Don't do anything I wouldn't do.'*

ebb

★ **at a low ebb** very sad or unsuccessful ○ *When I have been at a low ebb I have found the friendship and Christian love of my fellow churchgoers to be a great strength.*

> The ebb tide is one of the regular periods, usually two per day, when the sea gradually falls to a lower level, as the tide moves away from the land.

echo

cheer someone to the echo (British, old-fashioned) to applaud someone loudly for a long time ○ *Supporters turned out in their thousands to watch some of the best squash played in their country. They cheered Jansher to the echo.*

eclipse

in eclipse (formal) much less successful and important than before ○ *Even when*

her career was temporarily in eclipse she
had no financial worries.

> An eclipse of the sun is an occasion
> when the moon is between the earth
> and the sun, so that for a short time
> you cannot see part or all of the sun.

edge

★ **at the cutting edge** or
on the cutting edge involved in the
most important, exciting, or advanced
developments of a particular subject or
activity ○ *Telluride has always prided itself
on being on the cutting edge of computer
technology.* ○ *These were the men and
women doing the cutting-edge research.*

a cutting edge the ability to be more
successful than your opponents ○ *We
need a cutting edge and hopefully this
product can provide it.*

**give someone the rough edge of
your tongue** → see **tongue**

★ **lose your edge** to no longer have all
the advantages and special skills that you
had in the past ○ *Its staff disagrees with
criticisms that their magazine is out of date
or has lost its edge.*

> If a sword or knife has lost its edge,
> it is blunt.

★ **on edge** anxious and unable to relax
○ *Brenda had every right to be on edge. Ever
since I had left on the Saturday morning, she
had been bombarded with telephone calls.*

on the edge of your seat very
interested and eager to know what
happens next, especially in a film, book or
sports match ○ *Saturday night's final had
the spectators on the edge of their seats.*

★ **take the edge off something**
to weaken the effect or intensity of
something, especially pain ○ *My head
never seemed to clear completely, and the
painkillers only took the edge off the pain.*

> If something takes the edge off a
> blade, it makes it blunt.

edges

fray at the edges to become weaker,
or less certain or stable, to the point of
being damaged or destroyed ○ *The
government's army has begun to fray at the
edges.*

> If a piece of cloth or rope frays, its
> threads or fibres start to come apart.

rough edges
1 small faults in a person's character that
affect their behaviour towards other
people ○ *He had the reputation of
sometimes taking himself a little seriously.
Those rough edges have long since worn off.*
2 technical problems in an otherwise
good performance or piece of
entertainment ○ *The show, despite some
rough edges, was an instant success.*

egg

★ **get egg on your face** to feel
embarrassed or ashamed because of
something you have done or said ○ *Steve
didn't expect to win. He just didn't want to
get egg on his face.*

> People in crowds sometimes throw
> eggs at someone such as a politician or
> performer, to show their anger or
> dislike for them.

lay an egg (*American*) if something lays
an egg, it fails because people are not
interested in it or do not want it
○ *Independent studies showed the ad laid
an egg.*

> This expression is probably derived
> from the idea of an egg being round
> and therefore resembling a zero. A
> 'duck' (duck's egg) is a score of zero in
> British sport, and the equivalent in
> American sport is a 'goose egg'.

eggs

★ **put all your eggs in one basket** to
put all your efforts or resources into one
course of action with the result that you
will have no alternatives left if this fails

○ *Don't put your eggs in one basket; study hard at school and always keep an alternative job in mind.*

eggshells

walk on eggshells to be very careful about what you say or do to someone because they are easily upset or offended ○ *Healthy or sick, good days or bad, I felt I was always walking on eggshells around him.*

elbow

elbow grease the energy and strength you need for doing physical work such as cleaning something ○ *Plenty of elbow grease soon moves all the dirt.*

elbow room

1 the freedom to do what you need or want to do in a particular situation ○ *His overall message to governors, though, was that he intends to give them more elbow room to encourage innovation at the state level.*

2 enough space to move freely or feel comfortable, without feeling crowded or cramped ○ *There was not much elbow room in the cockpit.*

elbows

rub elbows with someone (American) to spend time with an important or famous person. The usual British expression is **rub shoulders with someone** ○ *At his famous parties, writers, artists, and celebrities rubbed elbows with the ultra-rich and the socially élite.*

element

★ **in your element** doing something that you enjoy or do well ○ *My stepmother was in her element, organizing everything.*

Ancient and medieval philosophers believed that all substances were composed from the four elements: earth, air, fire, and water. To be 'in your element' is to be in your natural surroundings, like a bird in air or a fish in water.

elephant

the elephant in the room an obvious truth that is deliberately ignored by everyone in a situation ○ *We both know that we can't carry on like this – it's the elephant in the room.*

★ **a white elephant** something, such as a new building, plan, or project that is a waste of money and completely useless ○ *Will the complex, constructed at some expense but never used, be regarded as a monumental folly, a great white elephant?*

There is a story that the Kings of Siam used to give white elephants, which are very rare, to courtiers who they did not like. The animals cost so much to keep that their owners spent all their money on them and became very poor.

embarrassment

an embarrassment of riches (literary) so many good things that you cannot choose between them, or that become a problem for you in some other way ○ *Football fans have an embarrassment of riches to choose from next week when three matches will be screened live simultaneously.*

empty

run on empty

1 to no longer be as exciting or successful as you once were because you have run out of new ideas or resources ○ *The band's 2008 appearance is widely agreed to be their finest two hours. Certainly, events after this suggest a band running on empty.*

2 to feel tired, confused, and unable to think or work properly because you have not eaten for a long time ○ *If you don't feed your body daily nutrients, you are running on empty – something you can only do for a short time.*

In this expression, the idea is of a car or other vehicle that is still running but has very little fuel left, so the needle of the fuel gauge is pointing to 'empty'.

end

★ **at the sharp end** (*mainly British*) actually involved in an activity or situation and therefore aware of the reality of the situation, rather than having only a theoretical understanding of it ○ *These men are at the sharp end of law enforcement and when a man is waving a gun, they have to act decisively.*

> In sailors' slang, the bow or front end of a ship is known as 'the sharp end'.

be at a loose end to have some spare time but feel rather bored because you do not have anything particular to do. Compare **loose ends**; see **ends**. ○ *Brenda had agreed to see her at 4.30, so Mrs Dambar was at a loose end for two and a half hours.*

> This expression may refer to the ropes on a sailing ship. The ends of the ropes had to be tightly bound to stop them fraying, and sailors were often given this job to do when there was nothing more urgent to be done. Alternatively, the expression may refer to a working horse being untied at the end of the day and released into a field.

★ **be thrown in at the deep end** to start by doing the most difficult part of a job or task, before you have tried to do the easier parts, or to start a job or task without any preparation ○ *Journalist Susan Hocking is being thrown straight in at the deep end when she anchors the evening news next week.*

> The deep end is the end of a swimming pool where the water is deepest.

come to a sticky end to die in an unpleasant or violent way ○ *Hassan comes to a sticky end, but so does almost everyone else in the book.*

★ **a dead end** something such as a plan, a project, or a course of action that has no future and will not develop any further ○ *Do you feel you have reached a dead end at work?*

★ **dead-end** boring and unlikely to lead to anything more interesting or successful ○ *He was a dull, nondescript man in a dull, dead-end job.*

> A dead end is a street which is closed at one end.

★ **do something to the bitter end** to continue doing something in a determined way and finish it, even though this becomes increasingly difficult ○ *Despite another crushing defeat, he is determined to see the job through to the bitter end.*

> Sailors used to refer to the end of a rope or chain that was securely tied as 'the bitter end'. Bitts were posts on the ship's deck and ropes would be tied to these to secure the ship in a harbour.

end it all to kill yourself ○ *I desperately wanted to end it all, but I had an adorable little boy who was totally dependent upon me.*

★ **the end of the road**
1 the point where someone or something can no longer continue or survive in a situation ○ *The administration realizes now that they've come to the end of the road of their policy.*
2 the results of someone's actions that cannot be avoided ○ *If she doesn't stop stealing, there's only jail at the end of the road.*

go off the deep end
1 (*mainly American*) to go mad, or to behave in a strange or extreme manner ○ *At first they thought that I'd gone off the deep end and had lost my mind.*
2 (*British*) to become very angry ○ *Dad didn't go off the deep end at all. He just said it wasn't fair to make my mother worry like that.*

> The deep end is the end of a swimming pool where the water is deepest.

★ **it's not the end of the world** said to mean that the consequences of an event are not as bad as they might seem at first ○ *If I make a mistake, it's not the end of the world. I can always go back and correct it.*

keep your end up to do what you have said you will do or what you are expected to do in spite of difficult circumstances ○ *The fact of the matter is that we signed a contract and we've worked hard to keep up our end, and they must keep up their end.*

on the wrong end of something unsuccessful in an activity or situation or at some disadvantage because of it ○ *A goal from Shaun Goater, a Bermudan international, left Howard Kendall's team on the wrong end of a 1–0 scoreline.*

ends

★ **loose ends** small details or parts of something that have not been sorted out satisfactorily. Compare **be at a loose end**; see **end**. ○ *The overall impact of the story is weakened by too many loose ends being left inadequately resolved.*

This expression may refer to the ropes on a sailing ship. The ends of the ropes had to be tightly bound to stop them fraying, and sailors were often given this job to do when there was nothing more urgent to be done.

★ **make ends meet** to be able to pay for the things you need in life, often with very little money ○ *Many people are struggling to make ends meet because wages are failing to keep pace with rising prices.*

Originally, this expression was 'make both ends of the year meet', which meant to spend only as much money as you received as income.

play both ends against the middle to pretend to support or favour two opposing people or ideas in order to gain an advantage from a situation ○ *The Irish queen was adept at playing both ends against the middle, sometimes confronting the English, and sometimes co-operating with them.*

Englishman

an Englishman's home is his castle (British) said to mean that people have the right to do what they want in their own home, and that other people or the state have no right to interfere in people's private lives ○ *An Englishman's home is his castle. Everyone has a right to defend their home.*

envelope

push the envelope to do something to a greater degree or in a more extreme way than it has ever been done before ○ *Each time they flew faster or higher, they regarded that as pushing the envelope.*

Rather than referring to stationery, the sense of envelope here is probably the one used to refer to the shape of a wave in electronics or a curve in mathematics. Pushing or stretching the envelope suggests changing the properties of the wave or curve.

envy

green with envy → see **green**

error

★ **see the error of your ways** to realize or admit that you have made a mistake or behaved badly ○ *I wanted an opportunity to talk some sense into him and try to make him see the error of his ways.*

even

don't get mad, get even → see **mad**

★ **get even** to get your revenge on someone who has hurt or injured you in some way. ○ *He is so incensed by what he considers shabby treatment that he's determined to get even.*

evils

★ **the lesser of two evils** the less unpleasant of two unpleasant options that someone has to choose between ○ *Should she choose the misery of life on the streets or the unhappiness at home? In the end it seemed the street was the lesser of two evils.*

exception

something is the exception that proves the rule said to mean that, although something you have said does not support an earlier statement, in most cases, the earlier statement is true ○ *To succeed, you must be big and powerful. Osman is neither of these. He is the exception that proves the rule.*

> 'Prove' here means 'to test by experiment or analysis' rather than 'to establish as true'. So, the meaning is that an exception tests a rule, not that it establishes the rule as true in all other situations.

expense

★ **laugh at someone's expense** to make someone seem foolish by laughing at them ○ *Being fat and bald has ruined my life. I'll never forget the people who laughed at my expense.*

eye

★ **an eye for an eye** or
an eye for an eye and a tooth for a tooth said to mean that the punishment for a crime is either the same as the crime or equivalent to it ○ *Why do we put people in jail? As an eye for an eye, or to make them realize they did wrong?*

> Expressions like this can be found in several parts of the Old Testament of the Bible, which advises that people who do wrong to others should suffer the same punishment as the one that they tried to carry out themselves: 'Life shall go for life, eye for eye, tooth for tooth, hand for hand, foot for foot.' (Deuteronomy 19:21)

★ **an eye for something** skill at dealing with something or a good understanding of it ○ *With his unerring eye for light, line and colour, Greenaway has mounted one of the most beautiful drawing exhibitions ever seen.*

★ **be in the public eye** to be famous and often mentioned or seen on television or in the newspapers ○ *Increasingly, people in the public eye are voicing concern about the effects of their lifestyle on their family life.*

cast an eye on something to examine something carefully and give your opinion about it ○ *'Before the elections I was pessimistic,' says Jassem Saddoun, a leading economist who casts a critical eye on domestic affairs.*

★ **cast your eye over something** to look at, consider, or read something very quickly ○ *He cast his eye over the bookcases. She was obviously an avid reader.*

★ **catch someone's eye** if something or someone catches your eye, you notice them because they are very attractive or unusual ○ *He turned the page. The picture caught his eye instantly.* ○ *My mother and my sister love stylish, eye-catching designer hats but cannot afford to buy them.*

get your eye in (British) to become more skilful or experienced in doing a particular thing because you have been practising it or doing it for a long time ○ *We're going to shoot some clay pigeons later. We want to get our eye in for the hunting season.*

> This refers to games such as cricket, golf or snooker, where it might take a while for a player to get used to the conditions of play before being able to estimate the distance and speed of the ball accurately.

give someone a black eye to punish someone severely, but without causing them permanent harm, for something they have done ○ *Whenever the Liberal Democratic Party gets too cocky or corrupt, voters tend to give it a black eye.*

> A black eye is a dark-coloured bruise around a person's eye.

a gleam in someone's eye a plan or project that is only at the earliest planning stage ○ *At present, the plans seem to be no more than a gleam in a developer's eye.*

> Words such as gleam, glint and twinkle can be used to describe the way people's eyes shine or reflect the light. They often suggest hidden energy, emotion, or mischievousness and refer to the initial excitement of having a particular idea before putting it into practice.

have an eye for the main chance (British) to be aware all the time of the best opportunities that are available ○ *New York has always been a place where individuals with an eye for the main chance could make their fortunes.*

in the eye of the storm deeply involved in a difficult or controversial situation which affects or interests a lot of people ○ *He was often in the eye of the storm of congressional debates related to U.S. troop withdrawals from Vietnam.*

> This expression refers to the centre or middle part of a storm. However, in wind storms, such as cyclones and tornados, the eye is in reality a relatively calm area of low pressure in the centre.

keep your eye on the ball to continue to pay close attention to what you are doing. Compare **take your eye off the ball**. ○ *She won widespread praise for her innovation, her tough negotiating skills and her ability to keep things moving, keep her eye on the ball.*

★ **look someone in the eye** to look at someone directly in order to convince them that what you are saying is true, even though you may be lying. ○ *He looked me straight in the eye and said 'Paul, I will never lie to you.'*

not bat an eye (American)
1 to not be shocked or offended by something that would shock or offend most people ○ *I was totally independent.*

My mother never batted an eye about the length of time I stayed out at night.
2 to not be nervous or worried about something that would normally worry most people ○ *Would you believe he ordered them to fill half a tin mug with that stuff and guzzled it without batting an eye, as if it was water?*

> Bat is from a French word meaning to beat or flutter and is used of a bird's wings. The idea is that people who do not blink a lot in a given situation appear calm rather than nervous or surprised.

★ **not see eye to eye with someone** to not agree with someone about something ○ *The Prime Minister did not see eye to eye with him on this issue.*

someone would give their eye teeth for something said to mean that someone wants something very much, and that they would do almost anything to get it ○ *He's the most exciting man I've ever worked with, and I'd give my eye teeth to do something with him again.*

> A person's eye teeth are their canine teeth, the pointed teeth near the front of their mouth.

something is one in the eye for someone (British) said to mean that something that has been done or achieved will annoy a particular person ○ *His Nobel prize will be seen in Mexico as one in the eye for the novelist, Carlos Fuentes, who is regarded as his great left-wing rival.*

spit in someone's eye to deliberately upset or annoy someone ○ *The minister for Trade and Industry spat in the eye of small businesses yesterday when he said: 'I won't support the weak at the expense of the strong.'*

take your eye off the ball to stop paying attention for a moment, with the result that things go wrong for you. Compare **keep your eye on the ball**. ○ *Any reorganization is disruptive. It makes* key management take their eye off the only ball.

★ **there's more to something than meets the eye** said to mean that something is more complicated or more involved than it appears to be at first ○ *'She is convinced there is more to your friendship than meets the eye.' 'Well there isn't.'*

★ **turn a blind eye to something** to deliberately ignore something because you do not want to take any action over it, even though you know you should ○ *The authorities were turning a blind eye to human rights abuses.*

> This expression was first used to describe the action of Admiral Nelson at the Battle of the Nile in 1798. When told that he was being ordered to withdraw, he put a telescope to his blind eye and said that he could not see the signal. He went on to win the battle.

★ **with the naked eye** with only the eyes, and without the help of instruments such as a telescopes or microscopes ○ *Enough light gets through space for us to see thousands of stars with the naked eye, and millions with an optical telescope.*

eyeball

be eyeball to eyeball if two people who are disagreeing with each other are eyeball to eyeball, they are physically close together, and it seems likely that they will start arguing or fighting ○ *The two of us sat eyeball to eyeball. 'Why do you hate me?' she asked, without any apparent emotion.*

eyeballs

up to your eyeballs in something very deeply involved in an unpleasant situation ○ *The one-time media tycoon is down on his luck, out of a job, and up to his eyeballs in debt.*

eyebrows

★ **raise eyebrows** to surprise, shock, or offend people ○ *The BBC opera 'The Vampyr' raised eyebrows when it was shown but the public loved it.*

eyelid

★ **not bat an eyelid** (British)
  1 to not be shocked or offended by something that would shock or offend most people ○ *I thought Sarah and David would be acutely embarrassed. But they didn't bat an eyelid.*
  2 to not be nervous or worried about something that would worry most people ○ *It is a popular myth that modern couples have affairs without batting an eyelid and believe marriage is for bores. In reality, the opposite is true.*

eyes

★ **all eyes are on someone or something** said to mean that everyone is carefully watching a particular person or thing, often because they are expecting something to happen or develop ○ *All eyes will be on the Chancellor tomorrow when he gives his Budget speech.*

★ **before your eyes** or **in front of your eyes** if something happens before your eyes, it happens directly in front of you, and you cannot do anything to stop it or change it ○ *With a wrenching crack the stone statue collapsed before my eyes and crumbled to pieces at the bottom of the fountain.*

★ **can't take your eyes off someone or something** if you can't take your eyes off someone or something, you very much want to keep looking at them, often because they are attractive ○ *Anne looked so beautiful no one could take their eyes off her.*

cry your eyes out to cry a lot for a long time ○ *It was a lovely school; I cried my eyes out when I left.*

do something with your eyes closed
to do something very easily
○ He reassembled the gun quickly and expertly. It was something he could do with his eyes closed.

feast your eyes on something
to look at something with a great deal of enjoyment ○ Billy licked his lips and feasted his eyes on the chocolate cake.

≡ The idea is of allowing your eyes to appreciate something visually in the same way that your mouth allows you to enjoy the quantity and quality of food at a feast or large meal.

have eyes in the back of your head
to be very good at noticing everything that is happening around you ○ She has eyes in the back of her head and is always alert to the slightest sign of trouble.

★ **keep your eyes open** to be aware of things that you can do in a particular situation ○ Take up any opportunity to increase your knowledge and broaden your horizons. Keep your eyes open for any interesting study courses.

keep your eyes peeled to watch very carefully for something ○ They drove there in Charlie's car, so Michael kept his eyes peeled for parking places.

≡ This expression refers to not blinking and so not missing anything that happens, however quick. The skin or peel of the eyes are the eyelids.

make eyes at someone (old-fashioned)
to try to get someone to notice you because you are attracted to them
○ He was making eyes at one of the nurses.

★ **meet someone's eyes** (literary)
to look directly into someone's eyes
○ An uneasy moment of frozen silence passed as Steve looked down and then finally up at me, meeting my eyes with an intense glare.

only have eyes for someone to only be attracted to one particular person ○ The 26 year-old model is adored by thousands but only has eyes for one man – her husband.

only have eyes for something to be determined to have one particular thing ○ The president came seeking investment in Mexico, but found Western Europe only had eyes for the new democracies to its east.

★ **open someone's eyes** to cause someone to become aware of a particular situation or fact for the first time ○ The need for female labour created during two world wars opened many women's eyes to better paid lives in factories and offices.

up to your eyes in something very busy with work or deeply involved in an unpleasant situation ○ I'm afraid I shall be late getting back. I'm up to my eyes in work.

with your eyes glued to something
watching something with all your attention ○ He sat, eyes glued to the TV set with a look usually reserved for a good suspense film.

Ff

face

★ **blow up in your face** if a situation blows up in your face, it unexpectedly goes wrong and destroys your plans or your chances of something ○ *He must have known that having no evidence, this would blow up in his face.*

★ **come face to face with someone** or **meet someone face to face** to meet someone and talk to them directly ○ *When I first heard of his death I didn't want to call her or meet her face to face. I didn't know what to say or how to act.* ○ *The three major vice-presidential candidates took the stage tonight in Atlanta in their only face-to-face confrontation of the campaign.*

★ **come face to face with something** to be forced to experience a problem or the reality of a situation, and have to deal with it or accept it ○ *Before the deal was fully closed, however, Beaverbrook came face to face with a serious problem.*

fall flat on your face to fail or make an embarrassing mistake when you try to do something ○ *I may fall flat on my face or it may be a glorious end to my career.*

★ **fly in the face of something** to be completely against accepted ideas, rules, or practices ○ *The plan to sell rhino horn flies in the face of the international ban.*

get in someone's face (mainly American, informal) to annoy or upset someone by behaving in a very direct or aggressive way ○ *He pretty much got in my face and told me not to leave or I'd get fired.*

get out of someone's face (informal) to leave someone alone and to stop annoying them or interfering with them ○ *Get out of my face or else I'm going to call the police.*

have a face like thunder (British) to look extremely angry ○ *The Arsenal striker had a face like thunder after ending his international career in a humiliating fashion.*

have a long face to look very serious or unhappy ○ *He came to me with a very long face and admitted there had been an error.*

★ **in-your-face** (informal) unconventional and provocative, and likely to upset or offend some people ○ *Christina James plays Perry's widow, a vivacious, in-your-face woman who is sometimes too honest for her own good.*

★ **keep a straight face** to manage to look serious, even though you really want to laugh or smile ○ *His laugh was hard for Nancy to resist, but she managed to keep a straight face.* ○ *It's the way he tells a joke. He is completely straight-faced and I just fall about laughing.*

look someone in the face to look at someone directly in order to convince them that what you are saying is true, even though you may be lying ○ *He looked me in the face again and repeated, 'I swear to you that it wasn't me.'*

lose face to be made to look foolish or to do something which damages your reputation ○ *Perhaps the FDA did not want to lose face by reversing its position.*

> This is a Chinese expression and refers to the covering of one's face with a fan as a sign of disgrace after revealing one's emotions. 'Face' here means the face when wearing an expression of calm.

not have the face (British) to be too nervous or embarrassed to do something

○ *You wouldn't lend me a couple of quid,
would you? I mean, I'm dying for a smoke,
and I haven't the face to borrow off Michael.*

★ **pull a face** (British) or
make a face to show a feeling such as
dislike or disgust by twisting your face
into an ugly expression, or by sticking out
your tongue ○ *She made a face at the musty
smell, and hurried to open the windows.*

★ **put a brave face on something** or
put on a brave face to try not to let
anyone see how upset or disappointed
you are with a difficult situation
○ *Dwight was upset by the news, but he
put a brave face on it and wrote a note of
congratulations.*

★ **save face** to do something so that
people continue to respect you and your
reputation is not damaged ○ *Most
children have an almost obsessive need to
save face in front of their peers.* ○ *The change
of heart on aid seems to show that officials
are looking for a face-saving way to back
down.*

This comes from a Chinese expression
which refers to keeping a calm
expression and managing to avoid the
disgrace of revealing one's emotions.
An English equivalent of this might be
'to keep a straight face'.

★ **say something to someone's face**
to say something openly in someone's
presence, especially something critical or
unpleasant ○ *At school it was hard when
people talked about me. No-one would ever
say anything to my face because they were
scared of me.*

set your face against something
(mainly British) to oppose something in a
determined way ○ *Both the government
and the major rebel groups appear to have set
their faces against a negotiated settlement to
the conflict.*

This expression is used several times
in the Bible. When God 'set His face
against' someone who had done

something wrong, He showed that
He was angry with them.

show your face

1 if you do not want to show your face
somewhere, you do not want to go there,
for example because you are embarrassed
or ashamed about something you have
done ○ *Louis skulked in his Harlem
apartment for three days after his defeat,
too ashamed to show his face.*

2 to go somewhere briefly, for example
because you have been invited there and
you feel you should go for a short time
○ *I felt I ought to show my face at her father's
funeral.*

**someone can do something until
they are blue in the face** said to
mean that however long someone does
something or however hard they try,
they will still fail ○ *You can speculate till
you're blue in the face, but you can't prove a
thing.*

**someone cannot look someone in
the face** said to mean that someone is
too ashamed or embarrassed by
something that they have done to look at
someone else directly ○ *Why did I do that?
I can't ever look her in the face again.*

**someone will be laughing on
the other side of their face** (British)
said to mean that although someone is
happy or successful at the moment,
things are likely to go wrong for them in
the future. The American expression is
**someone will be laughing out of the
other side of their mouth**. ○ *The league
leaders will be laughing on the other side of
their faces if they lose tomorrow.*

stare someone in the face to be very
obvious, although someone may not yet
have realized this ○ *Even when the evidence
is staring them in the face, they deliberately
misread it.*

★ **stare something in the face** to have
to deal with a bad situation that is very
likely to occur, or is about to occur
○ *Some of my patients are actually staring*

death in the face. They've suffered a heart attack, maybe two.

take someone at face value to accept the impression that someone gives of themselves, even though this may be completely false ○ *For a time I took him at face value. At that time, I had no reason to suspect him.*

> The face value of a coin or banknote is the amount that is printed on it, although it may in fact be worth more or less than that amount, for example because it is very old.

★ **take something at face value** to accept what someone says and believe it without thinking about it very much, even though it may be incorrect or untrue ○ *Clients should know better than to take the advice of a wholesaler at face value.*

throw something back in someone's face to reject something that someone has said or done for you in a way that seems very ungrateful or rude ○ *We extended the hand of friendship and you have thrown it back in our faces.*

written all over your face if an emotion such as relief or misery is written all over your face, it is very obvious to people that you are relieved or miserable, because of your expression ○ *Utter jubilation and relief were written all over the faces of the freed hostages.*

fair

fair and square honestly and without cheating or lying ○ *This might start further accusations, but we don't care any more. We won fair and square.*

fairies

be away with the fairies to behave in a strange way that seems to be out of touch with reality ○ *She's a sweet enough girl but she's away with the fairies.*

fall

be heading for a fall to be doing something which is likely to have unpleasant consequences for you ○ *The Tory Party is heading for a fall.*

> This expression was probably first used in fox-hunting to refer to someone who was riding dangerously.

familiarity

familiarity breeds contempt said to mean that if you know someone or something very well, you can easily become bored with them and stop treating them with respect or stop paying attention to them ○ *Of course, it's often true that familiarity breeds contempt, that we're attracted to those who seem so different from those we know at home.*

farm

buy the farm (*American, informal*) to die ○ *The plane nosedived into the ground and exploded. He bought the farm.*

> A possible explanation for this expression is that, in wartime, American Air Force pilots sometimes said that they wanted to stop flying, buy a farm or ranch, and lead a peaceful life. 'Buy the farm' then came to be used when a pilot was killed in a crash.

fashion

after a fashion not very well, or not completely ○ *She was educated, after a fashion, by a governess at home.*

fast

play fast and loose with something to treat something important without enough care or respect ○ *The banks claim high interest rates are necessary because the government is playing fast and loose with public spending.*

pull a fast one to succeed in tricking someone in order to get an advantage ○ *Someone had pulled a fast one on her over a procedural matter and she was not going to let them get away with it.*

fat

chew the fat to speak with someone in an informal and friendly way about things that interest you ○ *We lounged around, chewing the fat for a couple of hours.*

> This may refer to sailors in the past talking to each other while they chewed the fat in the dried meat which they were given to eat.

the fat is in the fire said to mean that someone has said or done something which is going to upset other people and cause a lot of trouble ○ *Immediately the fat was in the fire, for the minister had broken all the rules.*

> When food is being cooked over a fire, if fat or oil falls into the fire, the flames suddenly burn very fiercely.

someone is living off the fat of the land said to mean that someone has a rich and comfortable lifestyle without having to work hard for it ○ *He was pretty fed up with these bloated royalists who were living off the fat of the land while the rest of the country was starving, literally.*

> This is from the story of Joseph in the Bible. During the famine in Israel, Pharaoh invited Joseph's father and brothers to come to Egypt, where there was plenty of food. He told them that they would be able to eat 'the fat of the land' (Genesis 45:18).

fate

★ **seal someone's fate** to make it certain that someone will fail or that something unpleasant will happen to them ○ *The plan removes power from the government, sealing the fate of the unpopular Prime Minister, and transfers it to the President.*

★ **tempt fate** to take unnecessary risks when doing something, or act in a way that may bring you bad luck ○ *Indeed, many experienced yachtsmen charge the organizers with tempting fate in sending so*

many ill-prepared crews into such dangerous waters.

fault

★ **to a fault** more than is usual or necessary ○ *She was generous to a fault and tried to see that we had everything we needed.*

feast

enough is as good as a feast (British, old-fashioned) said to mean that there is no point in having more of something than you need or want ○ *'Enough is as good as a feast,' my great aunt Daisy used to say to me, as I reached an ever-chubbier hand towards the chocolate biscuits.*

> This was first used by the Greek writer Euripides in the 5th century BC to explain that it is wrong to be greedy.

it's feast or famine said to mean that sometimes you have too much of something such as money, while at other times you do not have enough ○ *While her life is rich in memories, funds are a problem. 'It's feast or famine with me,' she says.*

feather

a feather in someone's cap something that someone has done very well, which deserves admiration ○ *Hauptmann's arrest and conviction had been hailed as a triumph for justice and a feather in the cap of the New Jersey police.*

> Traditionally, Native American warriors added feathers to their headdresses as a sign of bravery in battle. Medieval knights in England also wore feathers in their helmets as a sign of their bravery.

you could have knocked me down with a feather (old-fashioned) said to mean that you were extremely surprised or shocked by something ○ *I won 54 votes to 48. I was completely overwhelmed; you could have knocked me down with a feather.*

feathers

> If a bird's feathers are ruffled, they stand out from its body, for example because it is frightened or angry, and they need to be smoothed back into place.

★ **ruffle someone's feathers** to say or do something which upsets or annoys someone ○ *I'm not surprised Rangers and chief executive of six months, Bob Brannan, have parted company. His management style ruffled a few feathers.*

smooth ruffled feathers to make people who are angry or offended by what someone has said feel calmer and happier ○ *Members of the exchange objected to Mr Rawlins's confrontational style. Mindful of this, Mr Lawrence has been smoothing ruffled feathers.*

feelers

put out feelers to carefully try to find out about other people's feelings or plans, so that you will know what to do next ○ *'I'm looking to play in Britain at the end of the next Australian season,' he said last night. 'I've put out feelers for one or two clubs already.'*

≡ Feelers are the long thin sense organs on the heads of insects and certain other creatures such as snails.

feet

be under someone's feet to keep getting in someone's way when they are trying to do something ○ *When you're in the house, your parents moan about you being under their feet. When you're out, they moan because you're not there.*

dead on your feet extremely tired ○ *I'm usually dead on my feet at the end of the game.*

drag your feet → see **drag**

★ **fall on your feet** (British) or
land on your feet to find yourself in a good situation, which you think is the result of luck and not your own efforts ○ *He has fallen on his feet with a new career set to earn him a fortune.*

≡ This may refer to the belief that when a cat falls, it always lands on its feet without hurting itself.

find your feet to become more confident and learn what to do in a new situation ○ *It takes a while for people to find their feet at this level and gain the necessary confidence.*

≡ The idea is of finding your sense of balance so you can move about without falling over or needing to support yourself.

★ **get cold feet** or
have cold feet to be unsure whether you want to do something, or to become too nervous and worried to do it ○ *I feel your boyfriend got cold feet about being in a committed relationship. He may even have fallen out of love.*

get itchy feet to become bored with the place or situation that you are in, and want to move somewhere new or start doing something new ○ *I hated living in London, and I started getting itchy feet. Last year, I decided I really wanted to come out to the States.*

get your feet on the ground (mainly American) to become established in a new situation, or become re-established in an old one ○ *They have modest two-room apartments, and until they get their feet on the ground, they take most meals at the institute's cafeteria.*

get your feet under the table (British) to establish yourself firmly in a new job or situation ○ *Mr MacGregor will wait for the new Transportation Secretary to get his feet under the table.*

get your feet wet or
have your feet wet (mainly American) to get involved in something or experience something for the first time ○ *Charlton thinks it's time for me to get my*

feet wet. He says I'll be able to help the department a lot more if I learn how police actually solve crimes.

★ **keep your feet on the ground** to continue to act in a sensible and practical way even when new or exciting things are happening or even when you become successful or powerful ○ *He says he keeps his feet on the ground by keeping childhood friends around him.*

★ **put your feet up** to have a rest from your work and relax, for example by lying down or sitting in a comfortable chair ○ *All these dishes can be oven-baked from frozen, while you put your feet up and relax.*

rushed off your feet (British) very busy, often because you are not getting any help or support in your work ○ *Now we have a cut-back in staff in this department, and I'm rushed off my feet.*

someone has feet of clay said to mean that someone who is greatly admired or respected has serious faults or weaknesses which people generally do not know about ○ *When those idols are found to have feet of clay, the pain of disenchantment can be profound.*

> According to the Bible (Daniel 2:33), King Nebuchadnezzar asked Daniel to help him to understand a dream he had had about a giant statue. This statue was made of gold, silver, brass, and iron, but it had feet made partly from clay. Daniel told the king that the clay feet were a sign of weakness.

★ **stand on your own two feet** or **stand on your own feet** to show that you are independent and do not need anyone to help you or support you ○ *It now seems clear that foreign aid levels of the 1980s will never be seen again and that these countries will have to stand on their own two feet.*

★ **sweep someone off their feet**
1 to be so attractive, romantic, and exciting that someone falls in love with you almost as soon as they meet you ○ *He is a good fifteen years older than Felicity. He swept her off her feet, though. And I suppose it seemed very romantic.*
2 to be extremely attractive or appealing to someone ○ *Ten British chefs plan to cook a feast they hope will sweep the French off their feet.*

think on your feet to make good decisions and achieve things without having to think about them or plan them first ○ *Being a parent means thinking on your feet and adapting as you go along.*

★ **vote with your feet** to show what you want through your actions, for example showing your dislike of a place or situation by leaving it ○ *It seems thousands of people are already voting with their feet, and leaving the country in the hope of a better life.*

fence

★ **sit on the fence** to refuse to state a definite opinion about something or to say who you support in a conflict ○ *The commission has chosen, extraordinarily, to sit on the fence, murmuring that schools must decide for themselves.*

> The fence referred to is one that separates two properties or territories and someone sitting on it is unable or unwilling to make a decision about which side to stand on.

fences

★ **mend fences** to do something to try to improve a difficult relationship that you have with someone ○ *Yesterday he was publicly criticized for not doing enough to mend fences with his big political rival.*

fever

★ **reach fever pitch** to become very intense and exciting, or very desperate ○ *In the past year, the civil conflict has reached fever pitch.*

fiddle

be on the fiddle (British) to be getting money dishonestly, for example by cheating with the accounts at work ○ *A postman earning only £136 a week drove around in a Porsche for six months before his bosses realized he was on the fiddle.*

★ **play second fiddle** to have to accept that you are less important than someone else ○ *The 44-year-old senator will play second fiddle to a man who has been his junior in the Democrat hierarchy.*

> A fiddle is a violin. The expression here refers to the first and second violins in an orchestra.

field

come out of left field to be completely unexpected ○ *All the firms we've talked to have indicated that they don't know. This has really come out of left field to most people.*

> In baseball, left field is part of the outfield. A ball is said to come out of left field when the pitcher throws it in such a way that it seems to come out of nowhere.

★ **have a field day** to take advantage of a situation, especially one which other people find upsetting or difficult ○ *Debt collectors are having a field day in the recession.*

★ **lead the field** to be the best or most successful person in an activity or competition ○ *The Americans continue to lead the field when it comes to child actors.*

left-field (mainly British, journalism) used for describing an unusual and unconventional performer or piece of entertainment ○ *Over the last few years, the most left-field films in world cinema have come from Japan.*

> In baseball, left field is the part of the outfield where the sun and the wind can cause problems with the ball. In addition, the spectators often shout at the fielder in left field, and so players consider it to be a difficult position to play.

out in left field or
out of left field unusual and unconventional ○ *Most of the business tips are common sense, but others are right out of left field.*

play the field to have many different romantic relationships rather than staying with one person ○ *He gave up playing the field and married a year ago.*

> If gamblers play the field, they bet on all the horses in a race except the one that is considered most likely to win.

fig

a fig leaf something which is intended to hide an embarrassing or awkward situation ○ *It seems that the pledge to rejoin the ERM was a fig leaf, designed to indicate that the government's economic strategy was not dead but merely sleeping.*

> According to the Bible (Genesis 3:7), when Adam and Eve ate the apple in the Garden of Eden, they realized that they were naked and felt ashamed, so they covered their genitals with fig leaves.

fight

a knock-down drag-out fight (American) a very emotional, angry, or even violent argument or fight ○ *Nobody had much of a stomach this year for another knock-down drag-out fight over the state budget.*

> This expression refers to a type of boxing match in which a fighter who had been knocked down was dragged out of the ring and replaced by another contestant.

fill

★ **have had your fill of something** to have had as much of something bad as you can manage ○ *They have had their fill of war, poverty, and repression.*

finders

finders keepers said to mean that you have a right to keep something that you have found ○ *Obviously, someone picked up my umbrella and has made no effort to find the owner. Finders, keepers.*

fine

cut it fine or

cut it close to not leave much time to get somewhere or do something and so to be nearly late ○ *They didn't plan to get here until six o' clock, and that's cutting it a little close.*

finger

have a finger in every pie to be involved in many different activities, often in a way that is disapproved of ○ *He has a finger in every pie and is never short of ideas for making the next buck.*

> The most likely explanation for this expression is that it refers to someone who is involved in making a pie.

★ **have your finger on the pulse** or **keep your finger on the pulse** to know all the latest information about something or have a good understanding of how it works ○ *Although I'm Scottish, after all these years in America I think my editors and I have our finger on the pulse of America.*

> Someone's pulse is the speed and force with which their blood vessels expand and contract as their heart beats. A doctor might feel a patient's pulse by pressing a finger lightly against the large artery in their wrist.

not lay a finger on someone to not hurt someone in any way ○ *One of the men accused of attacking trucker Reginald Denny at the start of the Los Angeles riots says he never laid a finger on him.*

★ **not lift a finger** to not do something or not help someone at all ○ *I'm the one who has to clean it all up. She wouldn't lift a finger if I didn't beg her.*

★ **point the finger at someone** to blame someone for a mistake they have made or accuse them of doing something wrong ○ *One socialist blamed the press for his suicide, but some commentators pointed a finger at the political establishment.*

pull your finger out or

get your finger out (British) to start working harder or to start dealing with something ○ *If anything violent happens, it happens here first. If Bexley Council had any sense they would pull their finger out and shut the place down.*

put the finger on someone (literary) to tell a person in authority that someone has done something wrong or illegal ○ *It's not like we put the finger on anyone, Janie. Nobody is suffering because of what we told that detective.*

★ **put your finger on something** to understand or say exactly what the cause of a problem or the answer to a question is ○ *He had thought that Houston would have arrived at that solution first; but, no, it was Dr. Stockton who had put his finger on the truth.*

twist someone around your little finger or

wrap someone around your little finger to make someone do anything you want them to ○ *A child who is spoilt is able to wrap her parents around her little finger.*

fingers

be all fingers and thumbs → see **thumbs**

get itchy fingers (mainly British) to be very keen to get involved in a particular activity ○ *After a few days of watching other people play, I started getting itchy fingers, and I made a chess set for myself out of cardboard.*

★ **have green fingers** (British) to be very good at gardening. The American expression is **have a green thumb**. ○ *I've never had green fingers; it was as much as I could do to keep the grass mown.*

★ **keep your fingers crossed** or **cross your fingers** to hope for luck or success in something ○ *I will be keeping my fingers crossed that everything goes well.*

> People sometimes actually cross their middle finger over their index finger when they use this expression or are wishing someone good luck.

★ **let something slip through your fingers** to fail to get or keep something, especially something good ○ *If your income is greater than your expenses, count yourself lucky – and don't let it slip through your fingers!*

someone can count something on the fingers of one hand said to mean that there are surprisingly few of the things mentioned ○ *I could count the jobs advertised each year on the fingers of one hand.*

★ **someone gets their fingers burned** or **someone burns their fingers** said to mean that when someone tries to do something, it goes wrong, and there are very unpleasant consequences for them, so that they feel nervous about trying again ○ *The government, after getting its fingers burned so badly, will surely not want to make the same mistake again.*

work your fingers to the bone to work extremely hard ○ *I have washed, cooked, fetched and carried all my life. I worked my fingers to the bone in this house.*

fingertips

★ **at your fingertips**
1 readily available for you to use or reach ○ *All basic controls are at your fingertips for straightforward, no fuss operation.*
2 if you have facts or information at your fingertips, you know them thoroughly and can refer to them quickly ○ *He wanted to know all about his latest projects, so that the correct answers were at his fingertips when he was questioned by the right people.*

someone is hanging on by their fingertips → see **hang**

fingernails

someone is hanging on by their fingernails → see **hang**

fire

breathe fire to be very angry about something ○ *One Democratic legislator who was breathing fire over the Weinberger indictment yesterday was Brooks.*

catch fire to become exciting or entertaining ○ *The play only really catches fire once Aschenbach falls in love.*

★ **come under fire** or **be under fire** to be strongly criticized ○ *The president's plan first came under fire from critics who said he didn't include enough spending cuts.*

do something with fire in your belly to do something in a very enthusiastic, energetic, and passionate way ○ *Some people claim he has changed his style, but Ian has played with fire in his belly throughout his career.*

draw someone's fire to do or say something which makes someone strongly criticize you ○ *Their first substantial work was the flats at Ham Common in 1957. This immediately drew the fire of the architectural establishment.*

> 'Fire' here means gunfire.

fight fire with fire to use the same methods of fighting and the same amount of force as your opponent ○ *The chancellor answered by fighting fire with fire. He attacked Mr Brown for wasting so much time and energy on the issue.*

hang fire to wait and not do anything for a while ○ *Banks and building societies are hanging fire on interest rates to see how the French vote in their referendum.*

> This expression dates from the time when firearms used gunpowder rather than bullets. If a gun hung fire, it did not fire properly because the gunpowder had not caught light. 'Flash in the pan' has a similar origin.

hold fire or
hold your fire to delay doing
something, for example attacking or
criticizing someone, because you are
waiting to see what will happen ○ *The
administration will hold its fire until it sees
the detail of the bill, but is likely then to
oppose it.*

light a fire under someone
(*mainly American*) to force someone to
take action or to start behaving in the
way you want ○ *They need to crank up their
technical research and light a fire under their
marketing force.*

There is a story that some American
farmers in the early part of the 20th
century used to light fires under
particularly stubborn mules that were
refusing to move, in order to make
them do so.

★ **play with fire** to behave in a very risky
way that means that you are likely to
have problems ○ *Schulte warned
government and industrial leaders that those
who even venture to think about mass layoffs
are playing with fire.*

fish

be like a fish out of water to feel
awkward and not relaxed because you
are in a situation or surroundings that
you are not used to ○ *He thought of
himself as a country gentleman; he was like
a fish out of water in Birmingham.*

be neither fish nor fowl to seem partly
one thing and partly another,
and be difficult to identify, classify, or
understand ○ *By the mid-1980s, Canada
had a constitution that was neither fish nor
fowl in terms of political philosophy.*

'Fowl' is an old-fashioned word for a
hen or other bird.

★ **a big fish** an important or powerful
person ○ *The four who were arrested here
last September were described as really big
fish by the U.S. Drug Enforcement Agency.*

a big fish in a small pond one of the
most important and influential people in
a small organization or social group. In
American English, you can also talk
about **a big frog in a small pond**. ○ *In
Rhodesia I was a big fish in a small pond. But
here there'd be many lean years before I built
up a reputation.*

a cold fish a person who seems
unemotional, which makes them appear
unfriendly or unsympathetic ○ *He didn't
really show much emotion – he's a bit of a
cold fish.*

drink like a fish to regularly drink a lot of
alcohol ○ *Her father drank like a fish.*

People used to believe that fish drank
constantly because they breathe
through open mouths.

have other fish to fry or
have bigger fish to fry to not be
interested in something because you
have more important, interesting, or
profitable things to do ○ *I didn't pursue it
in detail because I'm afraid I had other fish to
fry at the time.*

**something is like shooting fish in a
barrel** said to mean that one side in a
battle or contest is so much stronger
than the other that the weaker side has
no chance at all of winning ○ *I heard one
case where some of the enemy soldiers had
come out and they were saying it was like
shooting fish in a barrel.*

there are plenty more fish in the sea
said to mean that there are still many
other people who you might have a
successful relationship with in the future,
even though your romance or love affair
has ended ○ *If your daughter is upset because
her boyfriend left her, telling her that 'there are
plenty more fish in the sea' won't help.*

fishing

be on a fishing expedition (*mainly
American*) to be trying to find out the
truth or the facts about something, often
in a secretive way ○ *You know why you're*

here. You're on a fishing expedition. You're hunting for material.

fit

In the first two idioms here, 'fit' means healthy and full of energy.

fighting fit (British) very healthy and feeling very well and in the right condition to deal with a difficult task ○ *Nathan is now fighting fit and ready to tackle school again after his three-month battle for life.*

fit as a fiddle very fit and healthy ○ *I'm as fit as a fiddle, I'm never ill, I have an iron constitution.*

This expression may originally have applied to a violin player, or fiddler, rather than to a violin, or fiddle. The fiddler had to be fit in order to play all evening at a festival or party. Alternatively, 'fit' could mean 'suitable' rather than 'healthy', so the original meaning may have been 'as suitable for its purpose as a fiddle is for making music'.

fit to be tied (mainly American) very angry ○ *Douglas was fit to be tied. He almost killed Harry. He made Harry pay back every last penny.*

'Fit' here means ready or suitable for a particular purpose.

fits

★ **in fits and starts** not continuously, but regularly stopping and then starting again ○ *Denise's career plans can only proceed in fits and starts.*

A fit is a sudden outburst or attack of a particular emotion.

fix

★ **get a fix on someone or something** to have a clear idea or understanding of someone or something ○ *It's difficult to get a fix on what brokers earn. Their commissions depend on the number and cost of the properties they sell.*

★ **there is no quick fix** said to mean that there are no simple ways of solving a problem ○ *There can be no quick fix for public spending. If the recovery fails to cut the deficit sharply, a rise in taxes will be needed.* ○ *He warned Congress against any quick fix solutions to get the economy moving.*

flag

★ **fly the flag** to represent your country or a group to which you belong at a sporting event or at some other special occasion, or to do something to show your support for it ○ *It doesn't matter whether you are flying the flag for your country, or the Horse Trials Group, or your sponsor, the image you present is all-important.*

keep the flag flying to do something to show your support for a group to which you belong, or to show your support for something that you agree with ○ *I would ask members to keep the flag flying by entering some of their plants in both shows.*

a red flag (mainly American) something that gives a warning of a bad or dangerous situation or event ○ *Anyone who raises a red flag could be met by officials when the ship or plane arrives in this country.*

a red flag before a bull → see **bull**

wrap yourself in the flag (mainly American) to try to do something for your own advantage while pretending to do it for the good of your country ○ *Politicians always try to wrap themselves in the flag on Independence Day, but I think most people can see through that.*

flagpole

run something up the flagpole to suggest a new idea to people in order to find out what they think of it ○ *The President should consider running the capital-gains cut back up the flagpole.*

If you run a flag up a flagpole, you pull it to the top using the rope attached to the side of the flagpole.

flags

put the flags out (British) to celebrate something special that has happened ○ *Birthdays and christenings, or just a spell of good weather, are all the excuse you need to put the flags out and celebrate summer in the garden.*

flame

★ **an old flame** someone who you had a romantic relationship with in the past ○ *Last week Alec was seen dining with his old flame, Janine Turner, in New York.*

An old meaning of 'flame' was the person that someone was in love with.

flames

be shot down in flames to be criticized strongly or rejected completely ○ *Just six months ago his idea would have been shot down in flames for its sheer lunacy.*

★ **fan the flames** to make a bad situation worse ○ *Extremist organizations in the west were actively fanning the flames in the east, he said.*

To fan flames means to make them burn more strongly by waving a fan or other flat object next to them.

go up in flames to fail, come to an end, or be destroyed completely ○ *The Hollywood she'd known had gone up in flames the day she left. A new Hollywood and a new Washington had grown up.*

flash

★ **a flash in the pan** an achievement or success that is unlikely to be repeated or to last ○ *In the days following Beckon's victory, the British establishment has gone out of its way to try and dismiss the result as a flash in the pan.*

This expression has its origins in the way that an old-fashioned flintlock gun worked. Pulling the trigger produced a spark which set light to a small amount of gunpowder held in the 'pan'. This in turn lit the rest of the

gunpowder. However, if it failed to do so there was just a 'flash in the pan' and the gun did not fire properly. 'Hang fire' has a similar origin.

in a flash very quickly or suddenly ○ *Sam was out of his hiding place in a flash and crossed the space between him and the cliff-foot in a couple of leaps.*

flat

★ **fall flat**

1 if an event or an attempt to do something falls flat, it is completely unsuccessful ○ *The champagne opening of a new art gallery fell flat when the boss's wife fired a cork straight through the most expensive painting on show.*

2 if a joke falls flat, nobody thinks it is funny ○ *He then started trying to tell jokes to the assembled gathering. These too fell flat.*

flat as a pancake very flat ○ *There was barely a breeze and the water was as flat as a pancake.*

flat-footed

be caught flat-footed or **be left flat-footed** to be put at a disadvantage when something happens which you do not expect, with the result that you do not know what to do next and often look foolish ○ *'The people around were caught flat-footed,' said Mr. Enko. 'Nobody expected floods of such magnitude.'*

flavour

'Flavour' is spelled 'flavor' in American English.

★ **flavour of the month** (mainly British) someone or something that is very popular at the time ○ *Most stars are likely to declare an unprecedented interest in whatever cause is the latest flavour of the month in celebrity circles.*

American ice cream parlours used to select a particular flavour of the month in order to encourage people to try different flavours of ice cream.

flea

send someone away with a flea in their ear (British) to angrily reject someone's suggestions or attempts to do something ○ *I was prepared to be met with hostility as another nosy outsider, even to be sent away with a flea in my ear. But Moira was happy to chat.*

A flea is a small jumping insect that lives on the bodies of humans or animals and feeds on their blood.

flesh

flesh and blood real and actually existing, rather than being part of someone's imagination ○ *He was the first writer since Shakespeare to show his readers that the past was peopled by flesh and blood human beings very like themselves.*

make your flesh creep to make you frightened, distressed, or uncomfortable ○ *I didn't like him the first time I set eyes on him and now I know why. He made my flesh creep.*

★ **meet someone in the flesh** or **see someone in the flesh** to actually meet or see someone, rather than, for example, seeing them in a film or on television ○ *But what does Jamie think of his hero now, having met him in the flesh?*

★ **press the flesh** (journalism) to talk to people in a crowd and shake their hands. This expression is often used about politicians, who do this when they are trying to get elected. ○ *Royalty's function in the sports arena is generally confined to pressing the flesh and presenting trophies.*

put flesh on something or **put flesh on the bones of something** to add more detailed information or more substance to something ○ *What would a Middle East at peace actually look like? Somebody needs to start putting flesh on those bones.*

someone is flesh and blood said to mean that someone has human feelings or weaknesses, and that they are not perfect ○ *I'm flesh and blood like everyone else and I, too, can be damaged.*

★ **someone is your own flesh and blood** said to mean that someone is a member of your family, and so you must help them when they are in trouble ○ *He's my own flesh and blood; I'll stick by him whatever he does.*

flick

give someone or something the flick (mainly Australian, informal) to reject someone or something or get rid of them ○ *Nikki has given Brandon the flick.*

In Australian football, a flick pass is a pass made by hitting the ball with an open hand. Flick passes are against the rules, which state that the ball should be passed by hitting it with the fist.

flies

be dropping like flies
1 be dying in large numbers within a short period of time ○ *Meanwhile Burketown was left without a police officer while people were dropping like flies.*
2 be failing in large numbers within a short period of time ○ *While other retailers are dropping like flies, supermarkets are making fat profits.*

there are no flies on someone said to mean that someone is quick to understand a situation and is not easily deceived ○ *You have to establish that you are an officer with good and tried soldiers: there are no flies on the enemy.*

flight

★ **a flight of fancy** an imaginative idea or plan that is pleasant to think about but not at all practical ○ *This is no flight of fancy. The prototype is already flying, and production is to begin next year.*

flip

flip your lid (informal) to become extremely angry or upset about something, and lose control of yourself

○ 'Boy, you are brave,' she said, bathing the bleeding cut. 'A lot of grownups flip their lids when you clean a cut like this.'

floodgates

★ **open the floodgates to something** to make it possible or likely that a particular thing will be done by many people, perhaps in a way that seems undesirable ○ *Giving in to the strikers' demands, government ministers said, would open the floodgates to demands by workers in other large state-owned industries.*

floor

fall through the floor to suddenly decrease to a very low level ○ *On the fateful day, Oct. 19, the value of those stocks fell through the floor.*

wipe the floor with someone to prove that you are much better than someone else at doing something, or to defeat them totally in a competition, fight, or discussion ○ *When you play against people whose technique is superior and who can match your courage and commitment, they're going to wipe the floor with you.*

flow

★ **be in full flow** (British)
1 if an activity, or the person who is performing the activity, is in full flow, the activity has started and is being done with a great deal of energy and enthusiasm. The American expression is **be in full flood**. ○ *By 1944-45 he was in full flow, scoring in twelve successive matches and totalling twenty-seven goals in this sequence.*
2 to be talking fluently and easily, and to seem likely to continue for some time ○ *Mark Mueller was already in full flow, telling me how he had been the first to know the movie men were back in town.*

★ **go with the flow** to let things happen to you or let other people tell you what to do, rather than trying to control what

happens yourself ○ *This year I'm going to take a deep breath, leave my troubles and tension in the departure lounge and go with the flow.*

fly

do something on the fly to do something quickly and automatically, without thinking about it or planning it in advance ○ *This gives architects and designers the power to build an environment, explore it and maybe do some designing on the fly.*

the fly in the ointment the person or thing that prevents a situation from being as successful or enjoyable as it otherwise would be ○ *The only fly in the ointment is the enormous debt portfolios of Marine Midland in Latin America.*

> This expression probably comes from the Bible (Ecclesiastes 10:1), which says that in the same way that dead flies give perfume or ointment a bad smell, a little foolishness spoils great wisdom and honour.

★ **someone would love to be a fly on the wall** said to mean that someone would like to be present when a particular thing happens, and hear what is said or see what happens, although this is actually impossible because it will take place in private ○ *I'd love to be a fly on the wall at their team meetings.* ○ *I'd love to work as the personal photographer of a rock star for a year, documenting their life on the road from a fly-on-the-wall perspective.*

someone wouldn't hurt a fly or **someone wouldn't harm a fly** said to mean that someone is very kind and gentle ○ *He is, he insists, a pacifist, who would not hurt a fly.*

food

★ **give someone food for thought** to make someone think very hard about an issue ○ *I am not a religious person, but knowing what a good and faithful servant my* friend has been, it has certainly given me food for thought.

fool

a fool and his money are soon parted said to mean that it is easy to persuade someone who is not sensible to spend their money on worthless things ○ *The sad truth is that a fool and his money are soon parted, and even more so, a fool who is in love.*

★ **fool's gold** a plan for making money that is foolish and sure to fail ○ *The Chancellor dismissed as 'pure fool's gold' the idea that devaluing the pound could assist the British economy.*

> Fool's gold is another name for iron pyrite, a gold-coloured mineral that is found in rock and that people sometimes mistake for gold.

live in a fool's paradise to believe wrongly and stupidly that your situation is good, when really it is not ○ *English economists have been living in a fool's paradise. The recession has started.*

fools

fools rush in where angels fear to tread or
fools rush in said to criticize a person who did something too quickly without thinking clearly about the likely consequences ○ *Sometimes I stop and think, how did I get into this? Fools rush in where angels fear to tread.*

> This proverb comes from Alexander Pope's 'An Essay on Criticism' (1711).

foot

be caught on the wrong foot to be surprised by something that happens quickly and unexpectedly, because you are not ready for it ○ *The supermarket chain seems to have been caught on the wrong foot, still trying to escape its 'cheap' past just as it should be capitalizing on that record.* ○ *Again and again European and UN*

diplomacy has been wrong-footed by events in the Balkans.

the boot is on the other foot (British) or **the shoe is on the other foot**
(American) said to mean that a situation has been changed completely, so that the people who were previously in a better position are now in a worse one, while the people who were previously in a worse position are now in a better one ○ *I'm in the job. You may have assisted along the way, but as far as I know you're not in a position to remove me. The boot is now on the other foot.*

> Until the end of the 18th century, shoes could be worn on either foot, as cobblers did not make 'right' and 'left' shoes. If a person found that one of their shoes hurt their foot, they could try wearing it on their other foot to see if it felt better that way.

foot-in-the-door done in an aggressive or forceful way, in order to persuade someone to agree to do something which they probably do not want to do ○ *Double glazing salesmen have become a bit of a national joke, what with their foot-in-the-door methods.*

> If someone manages to put their foot in a doorway, they can prevent another person from closing the door and keeping them out.

★ **get a foot in the door** to make a small but successful start at something, for example doing business in a new area, and to be likely to do well in the future ○ *The only reason I took the job was because I thought it might help me get a foot in the door.*

get off on the wrong foot to start a relationship or situation badly ○ *Every time I come home on leave, we seem to get off on the wrong foot. We argue a lot.*

> The 'wrong foot' refers to the left foot. There is an ancient superstition that the left side of the body is connected

with bad luck and evil. The Romans sometimes placed guards at the entrances to public buildings to ensure that people entered them with their right foot first. 'Get out of bed on the wrong side' is based on a similar belief.

have a foot in both camps to support or belong to two different groups, without making a firm commitment to either of them ○ *With an Indian father and an English mother, she had a foot in both camps – or perhaps in neither.*

In this expression, a camp is a place where an army has put up its tents during part of a war or battle.

★ **not put a foot wrong** (British) to not make any mistakes ○ *John Walker has said that all great athletes have a season in which they don't put a foot wrong.*

★ **put your best foot forward** to work hard and energetically to make sure that something that you are doing is a success ○ *Sir David said that the commission should have put its best foot forward and produced something independent.*

★ **put your foot down**
1 to use your authority in order to stop something from happening ○ *He had planned to go on holiday with his friends, but his father had put his foot down.*
2 (British) to start to drive as fast as you can ○ *Once out of the park and finding a clear stretch of the Bayswater Road, he put his foot down.*

★ **put your foot in it** to say something which embarrasses or offends the person you are with ○ *I put my foot in it straight away, referring to folk music. Tom sat forward and glared. 'It's not folk music, man. It's heritage music.'*

★ **shoot yourself in the foot** to do or say something stupid which causes problems for you or harms your chances of success ○ *Unless he shoots himself in the foot, in all probability he will become President.*

someone has one foot in the grave said to mean that someone is very ill or very old and is likely to die soon. You use this expression when you are talking about illness and death in a light-hearted way. ○ *The guard and warder are taken in, they're convinced De Fiore's got one foot in the grave.*

start off on the right foot to immediately have success when you begin to do something ○ *To me this was a man who was prepared to start off on the right foot; he was mature with some common sense.*

footloose

footloose and fancy-free (old-fashioned) not married or in a long-term relationship, and having very few responsibilities ○ *A divorced man is footloose and fancy-free. He can go to parties and pubs on his own, and come and go as he pleases.*

This term refers to a sail that could move about freely and unpredictably because the ropes holding it at the foot or bottom were loose.

footsteps

★ **follow in someone's footsteps** to do the same thing that someone else did ○ *Rudolph Garvin was a college student, the son of a physician, who wanted to follow in his father's footsteps.*

forelock

tug your forelock or
touch your forelock (British) to show too much respect to another person and make yourself seem very humble and inferior ○ *A lot of people seem to think we're supposed to go round touching our forelock and scraping our heads against the floor. We're not.*

A forelock is a lock of hair that falls over a person's forehead. In the past, it was customary for lower class people to remove their hats in front of upper class people. If they were not wearing a hat, they touched their forelock instead.

forest

someone cannot see the wood for the trees → see **trees**

forewarned

forewarned is forearmed said to mean that if you know about something which is going to happen in the future, you can be ready to deal with it ○ *The authors' idea is that forewarned is forearmed: if we know how persuasion works, perhaps we can resist some of it.*

fort

hold down the fort (*American*) or **hold the fort** to look after things for someone while they are somewhere else or while they are busy doing something else ○ *Since she entered Parliament five years ago, her husband has held the fort at their Norfolk home during the week.*

fortune

★ **a small fortune** a very large amount of money ○ *For almost two years, Hawkins made a small fortune running a drugstore.*

foundations

shake the foundations of something to cause great uncertainty and make people question their most deeply held beliefs ○ *The crisis shook the foundations of the world economy.*

frame

★ **in the frame for something** (*British*)
1 if you are in the frame for promotion or success, you are very likely to get a promotion or to be successful ○ *Darren Bicknell put himself firmly in the frame for an England call-up at Lord's yesterday.*
2 thought to be responsible for a crime or an unpleasant situation, even though this might be untrue ○ *The fact is, there's only ever been one guy in the frame for this killing, and that's the husband.*

The 'frame' referred to here is probably one of the frames, or images, in a reel of film.

frazzle

wear yourself to a frazzle to feel mentally and physically exhausted because you have been working too hard or because you have been constantly worrying about something ○ *Why should I wear myself to a frazzle, trying to save your skin for you?*

free

free as a bird completely free, with no worries or troubles ○ *I have been island-hopping in the Pacific for the past two and a half years, free as a bird.*

freefall

★ **go into freefall** (*journalism*) if the value or level of something goes into freefall, it starts to fall very quickly ○ *Fears are now widespread that shares could go into freefall before Christmas.*

In parachuting, freefall is the part of the jump before the parachute opens.

frenzy

★ **a feeding frenzy** a situation in which a lot of people become very excited about something, often in a destructive or negative way ○ *His statement was unnecessary, and merely served to start a media feeding frenzy.*

This expression was first used to describe the behaviour of groups of sharks when there is blood in the water but not enough food for them all. In this situation the sharks will attack anything that they see, even each other.

fresh

fresh as a daisy very fresh, bright, or alert ○ *She can sleep through anything and emerge fresh as a daisy at the end of it.*

frighteners

put the frighteners on someone
(British) to threaten someone and try to
scare them into doing what you want
○ *He and his chums tried to put the
frighteners on Kelley before she had written a
single word.*

> 'Frighteners' used to be a name for
> members of criminal gangs who were
> sent to frighten people into doing
> something.

fritz

on the fritz (American) a piece of
machinery that is on the fritz is not
working properly. The British equivalent
is **on the blink**. ○ *My mother's toaster
went on the fritz.*

frog

have a frog in your throat to find it
difficult to speak clearly because you
have a cough or a sore throat ○ *Even
when I was little, other kids would ask if I had
a frog in my throat. I just have a raspy voice.*

> In medieval times, there was a belief
> that if you drank water containing
> frogspawn, the frogs would grow
> inside your body. People believed that
> sore throats and coughing could be
> caused by the frogs trying to escape
> from your stomach through your
> throat.

fruit

★ **bear fruit** to produce good results
○ *People see material conditions getting
worse. They don't see the economic reforms
championed by the President as bearing fruit.*
forbidden fruit something that you
want very much but are not allowed to
have ○ *Knowing that from now on you can't
eat chocolate or have sugar in your tea can
make you want those forbidden fruits even
more.*

> This expression refers to the story in
> the Bible in which Eve tempts Adam to

> eat the fruit of the tree of knowledge,
> which God had forbidden them to
> touch.

frying pan

out of the frying pan into the fire
from a bad situation to an even worse
one ○ *I was hoping to get my career back on
track at Everton, after a bad time at Villa. But
as it turned out, I'd gone out of the frying pan
into the fire.*

fuel

★ **add fuel to the fire** to make a bad
situation worse ○ *You must not take the route
of trying to borrow your way out of trouble.
This really would be adding fuel to the fire.*

funeral

it's your funeral said to mean that you
think someone is wrong by insisting on
doing something in a particular way, but
that they will be affected by the bad
consequences resulting from it, and you
will not ○ *Have it your own way. You'll be
sorry. It's your funeral.*

full

be full of yourself to be very proud
or conceited, and think only of yourself
○ *I tired of him quite quickly – he's so full of
himself.*

fur

the fur is flying said to mean that
people are arguing very angrily about
something ○ *The world's oldest major
championship does not start until tomorrow,
yet already the fur is flying thick and fast.*

> The image here is of animals tearing
> out each other's fur during a fight.

furniture

part of the furniture someone or
something that has been present
somewhere for such a long time that
everyone accepts their presence without
questioning it or noticing them ○ *In ten
years he has become part of the furniture of*

English life, his place on the stage firmly fixed and universally respected.

furrow

plough a lonely furrow or
plough a lone furrow (British, literary) to do something by yourself and in your own way, without any help or support from other people ○ *It seems that Shattock was something of an original thinker, ploughing a lonely furrow.*

≣ A furrow is a long narrow trench made in the ground by a plough.

fuse

be on a short fuse or
have a short fuse to lose your temper very easily and be quick to react angrily when something goes wrong ○ *Perhaps he's irritable and has a short fuse, letting you know when he's not pleased.*

≣ See the explanation at 'light the fuse'.

blow a fuse to suddenly lose your temper and not be able to control your anger ○ *For all my experience, I blew a fuse in the quarter-final and could have been sent off.*

≣ A fuse is a safety device found in electrical equipment. If the equipment becomes too hot, the fuse blows, or burns. This breaks the electrical circuit, so that the equipment will stop working.

light the fuse to do something which starts off a new and exciting development, or which makes a situation become dangerous ○ *Ghana's independence in 1957 lit the fuse which led to the rapid freeing of colonial Africa.*

≣ The fuse referred to here is the type that is used to set off a firework or explosive device.

Gg

gaff

blow the gaff (British) to tell people something which was supposed to be kept secret ○ *I said 'I've blown the gaff ... revealed the truth and told stories about what really went on.'*

'Blow' here means 'reveal'. In the 19th century, 'gaff' was a slang word used to refer to dishonest behaviour which was intended to deceive people.

gag

★ **be gagging for something** (British, informal) to want something very much ○ *'Girls everywhere are gagging for a car like this,' announced a spokesperson at the launch.*

gallery

play to the gallery to try to impress the public and make yourself popular, instead of dealing seriously with important matters ○ *It took more than 20 years for the House of Commons to allow TV cameras there, because some members were frightened that others would play to the gallery.*

The gallery in a theatre is a raised area like a large balcony, that usually contains the cheapest seats. In the past, the poorest and least educated people sat there. Actors and other performers found it easier to get applause from them than from the other members of the audience.

game

★ **ahead of the game** well prepared to deal with any change that happens in the activity that you are involved in ○ *We're always looking at new technologies to keep ahead of the game.*

★ **beat someone at their own game** to do something more successfully than someone else, although they have a reputation for doing it very well ○ *The Cats beat Brisbane at their own game: they were more aggressive and equally skilled.*

★ **the game is up** said to mean that someone can no longer continue to do something wrong or illegal because people have found out what they are doing ○ *He narrowed his eyes as the blue lights of the police car filled the cab. Sensing the game was up, he pulled over.*

a game of cat and mouse → see **cat**

★ **a game plan** the things that someone intends to do in order to achieve a particular aim ○ *So few people stick to their game plan. I stuck to mine. I had always wanted to be a millionaire from a very early age.*

In American football, a game plan is a strategy which the players and coach develop before a match.

★ **give the game away** to reveal something which someone had been trying to keep secret ○ *Johnson had intended to make his announcement in a forthcoming feature in The Times but the paper gave the game away.*

new to the game having no previous experience of an activity that you are taking part in ○ *Don't forget that she's new to this game and will take a while to complete the task, so you need to be very patient.*

not play the game (mainly British, old-fashioned) to behave in an unfair and unacceptable way ○ *Labour chancellors really aren't supposed to do this sort of thing. It is not playing the game.*

This is a quotation from the Olympic Creed written by Pierre de Coubertin, founder of the modern Olympics, in 1896. The expression was then used by Sir Henry Newbolt in his poem 'Vita Lampada' (1898): 'But the voice of the schoolboy rallies the ranks: "Play up! Play up! and play the game!"'

on the game (British, informal) working as a prostitute ○ How can anyone with kids think of going on the game?

the only game in town the only option worth considering ○ He's the only game in town, and I am hoping that he can show some real leadership strength.

This expression may refer to someone being prepared to take part in a game of poker, even if it was dishonest, because it was the only one going on at the time.

★ **play the game** to do things in the accepted way or in the way that you are told to in order to keep your job or to achieve success ○ In order to survive in the political system, they have to play the game.

play someone at their own game to behave towards someone in the same unfair or unpleasant way that they have been behaving towards you ○ I never used to get introduced to their clients. So I've started playing them at their own game. When I have clients to come and see me, I don't introduce them either.

★ **play a waiting game** to delay making any decisions or taking any action, because you think that it is better to wait and see how things develop ○ I propose to play a waiting game, and hope that a few of the pieces of this puzzle will soon begin to fit together.

games

★ **play games** to not be serious enough about a difficult situation ○ The company says it needs about a week to make a decision on staffing. One employee says he thinks the company is playing games with them.

gangbusters

like gangbusters (mainly American) very energetically and sometimes aggressively ○ The Lakers, who struggled early, came on like gangbusters at precisely the right time, which is to say, when the playoffs started.

A gangbuster is someone, especially a police officer, whose job is to break up criminal gangs.

garbage

garbage in, garbage out said to mean that if you produce something using poor quality materials, the thing you produce will also be of poor quality ○ A computer expert, he said he'd learned from computer programming that if you put garbage in, you get garbage out.

This expression comes from computing. If the wrong information is put into the computer, the output will be useless.

garden

★ **common-or-garden** (British) very ordinary. In American English, the usual expression is **garden-variety**. ○ Whether you're looking for specialist equipment or a common-or-garden mixing bowl, it's worth making a trip to the Harrods Cookshop.

These expressions were originally used to describe the most ordinary variety of a species of plant.

lead someone up the garden path (mainly British) or

lead someone down the garden path (American) to deceive someone by making them believe something which is not true ○ He may have led me up the garden path. He said everything was over with Penny but now he seems to be seeing her again.

gas

run out of gas (mainly American) to suddenly feel very tired or lose interest in what you are doing ○ *Miller, who missed second place by four seconds, said she 'ran out of gas' close to the finish.*

> The image here is of a car stopping because it has run out of gas, or, in British English, petrol.

gasp

★ **last gasp**

1 (*journalism*) achieved at the last possible moment ○ *Last gasp negotiations by the National Museum of Photography could ensure major new shows by legendary photographers Richard Avedon and Sebastiño Salgado.*

2 the very last stage of a long process or period of time ○ *Eleven thousand years ago, at the last gasp of the ice age, the area was covered with rich, semi-deciduous forest, not dry grassland.*

> These phrases come from 2 Maccabes 7.9 in the Apocrypha. Seven brothers and their mother were tortured by King Antiochus, and one of the brothers spoke out defiantly 'when he was at his last gasp', or when he was dying.

gauntlet

> Gauntlets are long thick gloves which protect your hands, wrists, and forearms.

★ **run the gauntlet**

1 to have to go through a place where people are trying to harm or humiliate you, for example by attacking you or shouting insults at you ○ *President-elect Chamorro also had to run the gauntlet as bags of water rained down from the Sandinista section of the stadium.*

2 to suffer bad treatment from people because of something you are trying to achieve ○ *He has run the gauntlet of arrest, police investigation, spells in prison and house detention in connection with his ties to radical groups.*

> 'Gatlopp' is a Swedish word meaning 'lane run'. The 'gatlopp' was a Swedish military punishment that came into common use in England during the Thirty Years' War (1618-48). The victim had to run between two rows of soldiers who would whip or beat them. In England, the unfamiliar Swedish word 'gatlopp' was replaced by the more familiar English word 'gauntlet'.

take up the gauntlet to respond to a challenge by showing that you accept it ○ *We received many letters on the subject, and several said we should ask our readers for nominations. We are taking up the gauntlet. Write to us with your suggestions.*

★ **throw down the gauntlet** to do or say something that challenges someone to take action or to compete against you ○ *The truckers threw down their gauntlet to the government after an all-night meeting of their strike committee*

> In medieval times, a knight would throw one of his gauntlets to the ground as a challenge to another knight to fight. If the second knight picked it up, he accepted the challenge.

gear

> The image in this idiom is of driving a car.

★ **get into gear** to start to deal with something in an effective way ○ *The town itself has got into gear with a campaign to improve the environment.*

genie

the genie is out of the bottle said to mean that something has been done or created which has made a great and permanent change in people's lives, especially a change which people regret ○ *The genie is out of the bottle and all attempts to stop the tide of GM crops are in vain.*

In Arabian mythology, a genie is a mischievous spirit with magical powers. This expression may refer to the story of Aladdin, who rubs a lamp and releases a genie from it. There is a pantomime based on this story.

gentle

gentle as a lamb very kind and calm ○ *Brian was as gentle as a lamb and wouldn't hurt anyone.*

get

from the get-go *(informal)* from the beginning of an activity ○ *Borrowing to make distributions was part of the plan from the get-go because of the seasonal nature of the business.*

ghost

give up the ghost
1 to stop trying to do something, because you no longer believe that you can succeed ○ *In Manhattan there was no Memorial Day parade this year. The organizers said they've given up the ghost after so few people turned out last year.*
2 if a machine gives up the ghost, it stops working ○ *A short way off the return ferry, Danny's car gave up the ghost again.*

This expression originally meant 'to die', and people still occasionally use it with this meaning.

lay the ghost of something to do something which stops you being upset or affected by something bad in your past ○ *Jockey Adrian Maguire laid the ghost of a ghastly week with a comprehensive win in the Irish Champion Hurdle yesterday.*

gift

the gift of the gab or
the gift of gab *(American)* the ability to speak confidently, clearly and in a persuasive way ○ *He was entertaining company and certainly had the gift of the gab.*

This expression may be related to the Irish and Gaelic word 'gab', which means mouth.

gift horse

look a gift horse in the mouth to find faults or difficulties when someone offers you a gift or opportunity ○ *When you're an entrepreneur, you don't look a gift horse in the mouth.*

This expression refers to the fact that you can judge the age of a horse by looking at its teeth.

gills

green around the gills looking as if you are going to be sick ○ *Kenny stumbled out from the washroom. 'I'm all right now.' He still looked quite green around the gills.*

The gills of a fish are the organs it uses to breathe instead of lungs. This is being used as a humorous term for the mouth.

gilt

take the gilt off the gingerbread *(British)* to spoil something or make it seem less good ○ *Knowing that Jim didn't want to be there rather took the gilt off the gingerbread.*

In the past, gingerbread was sometimes decorated with gilt, which is a very thin layer of gold.

girl

a big girl's blouse *(British)* a man whose behaviour is weak and not like a man's should be ○ *We'll get that soppy big girl's blouse with the dodgy knee who cries all the time.*

A blouse is a shirt worn by girls or women. This expression perhaps refers to what a timid or weak man would be assumed to wear instead of a proper shirt, for example when playing football or rugby.

give

★ **give and take** a situation in which two

people or groups do things to help or please each other ○ *I'm in a happy relationship where there's a lot of give and take.*

give it up for someone (informal) to cheer or applaud someone ○ *'As a mark of our gratitude for all her unstinting effort over the last year' - to no one's surprise, he produced a mid-size bunch of sprayed carnations from behind his back - 'let's give it up for Kath.'*

★ **give or take something**

1 said to mean that a number, especially a large number, is approximate ○ *There is a buried crater 35 kilometres across, in North America. It dates back 66 million years, give or take a million.*

2 said to mean 'apart from'. It is often used humorously. ○ *We are not in Sydney; this is Manchester. The two do have a similar feel to them, give or take the odd beach, bridge, harbour and opera house.*

glance

★ **at first glance** said when you are describing your first impression of someone or something, especially when you know that this first impression was wrong or incomplete ○ *The difficulty comes when two people, who appeared at first glance to have so much in common, discover that they have simply grown apart.*

glass

★ **the glass ceiling** the attitudes and traditions which sometimes prevent women, or people from ethnic or religious minorities, from getting the most important jobs ○ *A woman judge has at last succeeded in breaking through the glass ceiling into the Court of Appeal, the second highest court in the land.*

people who live in glass houses shouldn't throw stones said to mean that you have faults and so you should not criticize other people for their faults ○ *When will they learn? People in glass houses really shouldn't throw stones.*

gloss

put a gloss on something to try to convince people that things are better than they really are ○ *Garland could see no harm in putting an optimistic gloss on what the specialist had actually said.*

A gloss is an explanation that is added to a book or other text in order to explain an unfamiliar term. The idea here is that the explanation being given is a misleading one.

glove

fit like a glove to be exactly the right shape or size, or to be exactly right or appropriate in some other way ○ *Surprisingly, she has not sung Leonora for a long time, yet, as I reminded her, she used to say the part fitted her voice like a glove.*

gloves

the gloves are off (journalism) said to mean that people have decided to compete aggressively with each other ○ *In the software price war, the gloves are off.*

The reference here is to boxers fighting with bare fists, which is more dangerous than fighting with gloves on.

glutton

a glutton for punishment a person who keeps on doing something which is unpleasant or difficult for them ○ *What I want to know is why on earth you want anything to do with this confused and angry man. Obviously you're a glutton for punishment.*

A glutton is a greedy person.

gnat

strain at a gnat (literary) to concern yourself with something unimportant, perhaps neglecting something that really is important ○ *When it comes down to distinguishing 1 percent growth from a mild recession, you'd be straining at gnats to tell the difference.*

This expression comes from the Bible (Matthew 23:24). Jesus used it when He was criticizing the scribes and the Pharisees for being too concerned with unimportant areas of the Jewish law.

go

don't even go there (informal) said to mean that a topic is considered to be too unpleasant or controversial to be mentioned ○ *Bloom is romantically linked to Kate Bosworth, but don't even go there. Keeping his private life private is one of the ways he copes with his celebrity status.*

go figure (mainly American, informal) said to mean that you cannot explain something surprising, stupid, or hard to understand, as there seems to be a contradiction ○ *'It was certainly unexpected,' said Mickelson, who hadn't touched a club for two weeks before the tournament. 'I didn't hit it great today and somehow I shot 59. So go figure.'*

go off on one (British, informal) to suddenly become very angry ○ *I've never seen him go off on one before but I saw a very different side to him then.*

★ **have a go at someone** (mainly British) **1** to criticize someone strongly, often without good reason ○ *Finally I felt angry, because I figured she was just having a go at me for the sake of it.*
2 to attack someone physically ○ *A mob had a go at him with stones.*

what goes around comes around said to mean that people's actions will eventually have consequences which they will have to deal with, even though this may not happen for a long time ○ *What goes around comes around. If you ignore the other guy when he asks for help, you might just be setting yourself up for a little of the same later on.*

goal

★ **an own goal** (British) a failure to achieve something which results in damage to your own interests ○ *He said that the Government must get its act together and stop scoring economic own goals.*

In sports such as football and hockey, if someone scores an own goal, they accidentally score a goal for the team they are playing against by knocking the ball into their own net.

goalposts

move the goalposts to change the rules or aims in a situation or activity, in order to gain an advantage and to make things more difficult for the other people involved ○ *They seem to move the goalposts every time I meet the conditions which are required.*

goat

act the goat (British) to behave in a silly way ○ *Betty had a little yellow umbrella up. I acted the goat a bit, turning and waving umpteen times till she was laughing.*

Goats are often associated with unpredictable behaviour.

get someone's goat to annoy someone ○ *It was a bad result and a bad performance, but what really got the media's goat was the manager's refusal to take all the blame.*

This expression may be connected with the early 20th-century practice in America of putting goats in the same stable as racehorses, since the goats seemed to have a calming effect. If someone stole the goat, the horse would be upset and its performance would be affected.

God

God's gift exactly what a particular group of people like or need ○ *I can't stand him – he thinks he's God's gift to women.*

★ **play God** to behave as if you have complete power and can do anything that you want ○ *He insisted that the* government should not play God: the market alone should decide what industries should be set up.

take God's name in vain → see **name**

gold

all that glitters is not gold (British) said to mean that someone or something may not be as good or as valuable as they first appear ○ *All that glitters is not gold and it's a good idea to delay finalizing any important agreements, otherwise you may jeopardize a valuable relationship.*

gold dust (British) something that is very difficult to get ○ *Leg make-up was essential during the War when stockings were like gold dust.*

★ **a pot of gold** a lot of money that someone hopes to get in the future ○ *When he went to Hamburg, he should have said he was going to make his pot of gold. Instead, he said he was going to improve his football.*

strike gold to find, do or produce something that brings you a lot of money or success ○ *The company has struck gold with its new holiday development.*

good

★ **as good as new** in very good condition and looking new ○ *Manufacturers recommend that carpets should be washed regularly to prolong their life and keep them looking as good as new.*

★ **give as good as you get** to argue, fight or compete as strongly and fiercely as your opponent ○ *Always give as good as you get in discussions and meetings.*

good as gold behaving very well ○ *They were both in the playroom as good as gold.*

good-for-nothing lazy or irresponsible or behaving in a way which is likely to harm or upset other people ○ *Ruth's father was a rich, charming, but good-for-nothing man.*

you can't keep a good man down said to mean that if people are able and determined, they will recover from any

difficulties or problems and be successful. You can replace 'man' with 'woman' or with another word referring to a person. ○ *Rios hit a winning smash from a sitting position before toppling over. You can't keep a good man down, although there are those who would like to try.*

goodbye

★ **kiss goodbye to something** to accept the fact that you are going to lose something or that you will not be able to have it ○ *After the accident, I felt sure I'd have to kiss my dancing career goodbye.*

goods

★ **deliver the goods** to achieve what is expected or required of you ○ *Is the leadership in a position to deliver the goods in two years?*

have the goods on someone (American) to know things about someone which could harm them if these things were made public ○ *He was offering services and materials for about 20 years internationally before anyone had the goods on him and could prove that he was doing it.*

goose

cook your goose to do something which gets you into trouble or spoils your chances of success ○ *By trying to steal my girlfriend he cooked his goose. After that I just had to sack him.*

There is a story that King Eric XIV of Sweden once arrived at a town to find that the people had hung a goose from a tree. This was intended as an insult, perhaps because geese were associated with stupidity. The King announced that he would 'cook their goose', and his soldiers invaded the town and set fire to its main buildings. An alternative theory is that the expression refers to Aesop's fable of the goose which laid golden eggs: see the explanation at 'kill the goose that lays the golden egg'.

kill the goose that lays the golden egg to result in an important source of income being destroyed or seriously reduced ○ *It's a classic case of too many tourists loving a place to death. 'They're killing the goose that laid the golden egg,' said the park manager.*

This expression comes from Aesop's fable about a peasant who owned a goose which laid golden eggs. The peasant was so eager to become rich that he cut the bird open, hoping that he would be able to get all the eggs at once.

someone wouldn't say boo to a goose said to mean that someone is very quiet, shy or nervous ○ *'If you remember, at college I wouldn't say boo to a goose.' 'That's right, you were very quiet.'*

a wild goose chase a search for something that you have little chance of finding because you have been given wrong information ○ *Every time I've gone to Rome to try to find out if the story could be true, it has turned out to be a wild-goose chase.*

In medieval times, a wild goose chase was an unusual kind of horse race. It started with an ordinary horse race. The winner then rode in any direction they chose and the other riders had to follow. The race may have been called 'a wild goose chase' because the movements of wild geese are often irregular and unpredictable, which makes them difficult to hunt.

gooseberry

play gooseberry (*British*) to be present somewhere with two other people who are having a romantic relationship and who want to be alone together

The origin of this expression is not known, although it may refer to the third person picking gooseberries to pass the time while the other two are busy being romantic.

gospel

take something as gospel to accept something as being completely true ○ *You will read much advice in books and magazines but you should not take it all as gospel.*

In the Christian religion, the gospel is the message and teachings of Jesus Christ. The four books of the Bible which describe His life and teachings are called the Gospels.

grabs

★ **something is up for grabs** said to mean that something is available for anyone who is willing or able to compete for it ○ *Thirty-five Senate seats are up for grabs in tomorrow's election.*

grace

★ **fall from grace** to have made a mistake or done something wrong or immoral, and as a result, to have lost power or influence and spoiled your good reputation ○ *The band later fell from grace when it was discovered that they never sang on their own records.*

★ **a saving grace** a good quality or feature in someone or something that prevents them from being completely bad or worthless ○ *She definitely outshone the so-called 'stars' and is one of the film's few saving graces.*

grade

★ **make the grade** to succeed at something, usually by reaching a particular standard ○ *Top public schools failed to make the grade in a new league table of academic results.*

In American English, a 'grade' is a slope. This expression was originally used in connection with United States railways to refer to a train which succeeded in climbing a steep section of track.

grain

★ **go against the grain** to be the opposite of your ideas, beliefs or principles ○ *He would have to take this work, although it went against the grain of everything he believed in and hoped for.*

≡ The grain of a piece of wood is the direction of its fibres. It is easier to cut or plane wood along the direction of the grain, rather than across it.

grandmother

teach your grandmother to suck eggs (British) to give advice about something to someone who actually knows more about it than you do ○ *'It's a sarcophagus. Dig it good and wide,' he said. 'Go teach your grandmother to suck eggs,' said Leshka, and waved him away with a show of irritation.*

grapes

★ **sour grapes** a situation where someone criticizes another person or accuses them of using unfair methods because they are jealous of their success ○ *These accusations have been going on for some time now, but it is just sour grapes.*

≡ In one of Aesop's fables, a fox tries several times unsuccessfully to reach a bunch of delicious-looking grapes. In the end he gives up, telling himself that they are probably sour and inedible anyway.

grapevine

★ **hear something through the grapevine** or
hear something on the grapevine (British) to hear about something informally, from the people you know ○ *I hear through the grapevine that you are getting ready to sue us. If that's true, I want to hear it from you.*

≡ One of the early telegraph systems in America was given the nickname 'the grapevine telegraph' because the wires often became tangled, so that they reminded people of grapevines. During the American Civil War, the telegraph

system was used to communicate propaganda and false information, as well as real news about the progress of battles, so that anything heard on the 'grapevine' was likely to be unreliable.

grass

the grass is always greener on the other side of the fence said to mean that other people may appear to be in a better or more attractive situation than you, but in reality their situation may not be as good as it seems ○ *The old saying goes that, to many people, the grass is always greener on the other side of the fence, and the majority of Britain's young people are no exception.*

★ **the grass roots** the ordinary people who form the main part of an organization or movement, rather than its leaders ○ *The revolution is actually coming from the grass roots and I think eventually the authorities will follow.*

kick something into the long grass (British, journalism) to refuse to deal with something immediately, often because it will create problems ○ *There were suggestions this week that the Government intends to kick the proposals into the long grass.*

like watching grass grow extremely boring ○ *Some people say that watching a cricket match is like watching grass grow.*

put someone out to grass to make someone retire from their job, or to move them to an unimportant job, usually because people think that they are too old to be useful. ○ *The Prime Minister refused to be put out to grass. Asked if he would quit, he replied 'The answer is no.'*

≡ When horses have reached the end of their working lives, they are sometimes released into fields to graze.

grave

dig your own grave to put yourself in a difficult situation by doing something wrong or making foolish mistakes ○ *If you go ahead with a private investigation, you'll be digging your own grave professionally.*

★ **turn in your grave** (British) or **turn over in your grave** (American) if someone who is dead would turn in their grave, they would be very angry or upset about something that is happening now if they knew about it ○ *Churchill and Bevan would turn in their graves if they could hear the pathetic attempts at public speaking made by members of all parties in the past three weeks.*

gravy

★ **a gravy train** a secure and easy way of earning money over a long period, especially by having a job that is easy and well-paid ○ *I keep his salary down because I don't want anyone to think he's riding into work on a gravy train.*

In the United States, 'gravy' was slang for money or profit. Railway workers invented this expression in the early 1920s to describe a regular journey which provided good pay for little work.

Greek

be Greek to someone or **be all Greek to someone** (British) to be impossible for someone to understand ○ *Her explanations were Greek to us, and we were left with the feeling that we still had a lot to learn.*

The idea behind this expression is that Greek is very difficult to learn and understand, especially because it uses a different alphabet from most other European languages.

green

green as grass (British) completely inexperienced or naive ○ *The job we had to do was wholly new, and we were all as green as grass.*

green with envy extremely envious of something that another person has or

does ○ *This is the most unexpected discovery I have made in 20 years of digging. Archaeologists in other parts of the world will be green with envy.*

A greenish-coloured complexion was traditionally believed to indicate jealousy.

grin

grin and bear it to have to accept a difficult situation because there is nothing that you can do about it ○ *Severe abdominal pain should always be checked. Don't just grin and bear it.*

grip

★ **get a grip on something** to take control of a situation so that you can deal with it successfully ○ *So far the country has failed to get a grip on its inflation rate.*

get a grip on yourself or **get a grip** to control yourself, so that you can deal with things successfully ○ *A bit of me was very frightened and I consciously had to get a grip on myself.*

★ **lose your grip** **1** to lose control over a situation ○ *The opposition feel that the president has lost his grip on the country.* **2** to become less efficient and less confident, and less able to deal with things ○ *He wondered if perhaps he was getting old and losing his grip.*

grips

★ **get to grips with something** to start dealing with a situation seriously, for example by getting a proper understanding of it ○ *In the front of the van, Julie's still getting to grips with the gears and the brakes and the steering.*

grist

★ **grist for the mill** or **grist to the mill** (British) something that can be put to good use in a particular situation ○ *You are, of course,* *much better at writing songs when you are completely miserable – it gives you so much more grist for the mill.*

'Grist' was grain that was brought to a windmill or watermill to be ground. Millers needed regular supplies of grain to keep their businesses in operation.

groove

★ **in the groove** having a continuous series of successes ○ *Nick is in the groove, as he showed with seven goals last weekend.*

This expression may refer to the way the needle fits neatly into the groove on a record.

ground

be thick on the ground (British) to be plentiful ○ *Jobs are not exactly thick on the ground.*

★ **be thin on the ground** (British) to be rare ○ *Ideas are thin on the ground in the British film industry.*

break ground (American) to start building something ○ *Simpson and Hurt hope to break ground on a planned outdoor theater at Ten Chimneys next August.*

★ **break new ground** to do something completely different, or to do something in a completely different way. You use this expression to show approval of what is being done. ○ *The programme broke new ground in giving to women roles traditionally assigned to men.*

cut the ground from under someone to seriously weaken someone's argument or position, often by doing something unexpected ○ *The scenario is this – you overspend on credit cards; and then a downturn in business cuts the ground from under you.*

fall on stony ground (British) to be ignored ○ *Warnings about the effects on public services fell on stony ground.*

This expression comes from Jesus's story in the Bible (Mark 4:5-6) about a man sowing seed which falls on different kinds of ground. The seed that falls on stony ground dies because the roots cannot grow properly. In the story, the seed represents Christ's teachings and the stony ground represents the people who soon forget or ignore what He has said.

★ **find common ground** to come to an agreement on something ○ *The participants seem unable to find common ground on the issue of agriculture.*

★ **gain ground** to make progress and become more important or more powerful ○ *The idea that Britain ought to change its constitution has been gaining ground for years.*

get in on the ground floor to get involved from the very beginning with something, especially something that is likely to be profitable for you ○ *These smaller companies are getting in on the ground floor of what will be a gigantic industry.*

get something off the ground to put something into operation, often after a lot of hard work getting it organized ○ *Councillor Riley spoke of the dedication and enthusiasm of staff and volunteers in getting the schemes off the ground.*

go to ground (British) to hide from someone or something ○ *He left the hotel and went to ground in the station waiting-room. It was a safe place.*

In hunting, this expression is used to refer to a fox escaping into its hole.

hit the ground running to start a new activity with a lot of energy and enthusiasm, and not to waste any time ○ *She is in excellent shape and in good spirits. She will hit the ground running when she gets back.*

The image here may be of soldiers landing by parachute or helicopter in a battle area and moving off quickly as soon as they reach the ground.

★ **lose ground** to lose some of the power or advantage that you had previously ○ *The United States lost more ground in its trade balance with other countries during the third quarter, running up the biggest trade deficit so far this year.*

★ **the moral high ground** the belief that your policies and actions are morally superior to the policies and actions of your rivals ○ *The party now held the moral high ground and he, as President, could defend it in every country in the world.*

> In a battle, the army which is on higher ground has the advantage.

★ **prepare the ground** to do things which will make it easier for something to happen ○ *The talks prepared the ground for the meeting of finance ministers and central bankers in Washington.*

run someone into the ground to make someone work so hard and continuously at something that they become exhausted ○ *Well-trained horses had been starved to death or run into the ground.*

run someone to ground (British) to find someone after a long search ○ *Truman eventually ran him to ground, asleep and rather the worse for wear in a hotel.*

> In hunting, this expression is used to refer to a fox being chased back to its hole.

run something into the ground to use something continuously without repairing or replacing it, so that eventually it is destroyed or useless ○ *They're quite good bikes, you can run them into the ground for quite a long time, then just get a new one.*

stamping ground a place where someone works or goes regularly ○ *Former pals found her much changed at Christmas when she returned to her old stamping ground, the Blue Anchor pub in Croydon, South London.*

> This expression may refer to the way that stallions stamp while mating. Alternatively, it may come from the dances of male prairie chickens when they gather in spring in order to mate.

suit someone down to the ground (British) to completely meet your needs or requirements ○ *Helen has finally found a method of exercise that suits her outgoing character down to the ground.*

guard

> Your guard is the position that you adopt when you are ready to defend yourself in sports such as boxing or fencing.

★ **catch someone off guard** to completely surprise someone ○ *There was a bright flash, followed a few moments later by a thunderous roar that caught us all off guard.*

★ **lower your guard** to relax when you should be careful or alert, often with unpleasant consequences ○ *The U-boat's crew had made the mistake of relaxing, of lowering their guard just when their sense of danger should have been at its keenest.*

off your guard not prepared for something when it happens so that you do not react normally ○ *Taken off his guard, he toppled backwards into the arms of his attacker.*

★ **the old guard** a group of people who have worked in an organization or system for a very long time ○ *The company's old guard is stepping aside, making way for a new, more youthful team.*

> The original 'Old Guard' consisted of the most experienced regiments of Napoleon Bonaparte's Imperial Guard. These soldiers were considered to be the best in the French army.

★ **on your guard** alert and prepared for any attack against you ○ *When Hilton came, he would have to be on his guard each second, for the man was dangerous.*

guest

be my guest said to someone to mean that you are giving them permission to do something, or inviting them to do something ○ *'Dad,' she said. 'Tomorrow, I want to go swimming.' I indicated the cool, clear water before us. 'Be my guest,' I said.*

guinea pig

★ **a guinea pig** a person on whom new ideas or methods are tested ○ *I got the impression they weren't sure of the possible outcome and that I was being used as a guinea pig.*

gum tree

up a gum tree (British, old-fashioned) in a very difficult situation ○ *It's a good job we started when we did or we really would be up a gum tree now.*

> This expression may be based on the fact that opossums often hide in gum trees when they are being hunted.

gun

hold a gun to someone's head or **put a gun to someone's head** to force someone to do something by threatening to take extreme action against them if they do not do it ○ *Not a man to have a gun put to his head, Mr Riordan was soon tearing up the offer and cancelling future meetings with the union.*

★ **jump the gun** to do something before the right, proper or expected time ○ *The book wasn't due to be released until September 10, but some booksellers have jumped the gun and decided to sell it early.*

> If a runner jumps the gun, they begin running before the pistol is fired to start the race.

★ **a smoking gun** (mainly American) evidence which proves that a particular person is responsible for a crime ○ *First of all, there's no smoking gun. In the course of our investigation we did not find a single piece of evidence.*

under the gun (mainly American) under great pressure and in danger of failing completely ○ *Society, in many ways, is under the gun. We have a multitude of problems – medical, health problems, crime problems, educational, literacy.*

guns

be going great guns said to mean that someone is being very successful at something ○ *The firm's chairman and managing director is going great guns with his expansion plans.*

★ **the big guns** the most important and powerful people in an organization ○ *She is in great demand by the film industry's big guns.*

> Cannons used to be referred to as 'big guns' or 'great guns', while rifles or muskets were called 'small guns'.

spike someone's guns (British) to prevent someone from carrying out their plans, or to do something to make their actions ineffective ○ *She was agreeable and competent and spiked the guns of the critics who were out to demolish her.*

> In the past, when soldiers captured a large enemy gun which they could not move, they hammered a nail or spike into the hole where the gunpowder was put. This meant that the gunpowder could not be lit and so the gun would not work.

★ **stick to your guns** to refuse to change your decision or opinion about something, even though other people are trying to tell you that you are wrong ○ *He should have stuck to his guns and refused to meet her.*

> The image here is of soldiers remaining in position, even though they are being attacked by the enemy.

with all guns blazing with a lot of enthusiasm and energy ○ *Manchester United stormed into the European Cup with all guns blazing.*

> Here, blazing means firing
> continuously.

gut

bust a gut *(informal)* to work very hard at something ○ *I was busting a gut doing horrible jobs – toilet cleaning among other things – to support us.*

guts

spill your guts *(informal)* to tell someone everything about something secret or private ○ *Vincent has spilled his guts.*

Everything. We got a signed confession from him.

> Your guts are your intestines or
> internal organs. The idea is of
> dramatically revealing something
> hidden.

work your guts out *(informal)* to work very hard ○ *These women were amazing. They worked their guts out from 7.30 to 4.30 every day, often all evening and weekend too if they had families.*

Hh

habits

★ **old habits die hard** said to mean that people are often reluctant to change their way of doing something, especially something which they have been doing for a long time ○ *Despite ideas of equality, old habits die hard and women still carry the main burden of looking after home and family.* ○ *The band broke up in 1970 and die-hard fans have been waiting for a reunion ever since.*

hackles

★ **raise someone's hackles** to make someone angry or annoyed ○ *The taxes will presumably be designed not to raise voters' hackles too much.*

> 'Hackles' are feathers on the necks of cockerels and some other birds. They rise up when the bird becomes aggressive.

hair

come within a hair's breadth of doing something to very nearly do something ○ *The parliament came within a hair's breadth of forcing immediate political union between the two countries.*

get in someone's hair to annoy someone and be a nuisance to them ○ *They were very busy and had little time to get in one another's hair.*

get out of someone's hair to stop being a nuisance to someone ○ *Would you like me to get out of your hair and leave you alone?*

a hair of the dog (*spoken*) an alcoholic drink that someone has, usually the day after drinking too much alcohol, because they think it will make them feel less ill ○ *I need a drink, chum. A large hair of the dog.*

keep someone out of your hair to succeed in arranging things so that you are no longer involved with someone who is a nuisance ○ *Just do me a favor, will you? Keep her out of my hair from now on.*

keep your hair on (*British*) to calm down and not be angry or impatient. The usual American expression is **keep your shirt on**. ○ *His annoyance evaporated in a grin. 'You're right. She's got a tough job. I'll try to keep my hair on in future.'*

★ **let your hair down** to relax and enjoy yourself, without worrying about behaving politely ○ *It is only with friends that most people feel they can let their hair down and be themselves.*

make someone's hair stand on end to make someone very frightened or shocked ○ *The first ten minutes of the film made my hair stand on end.*

make your hair curl to make you very shocked or worried ○ *I could tell you stories that would make your hair curl.*

not a hair out of place used for describing someone whose appearance is very neat and tidy ○ *Not a hair out of place, dressed in navy and white for our photograph, she is clearly a perfectionist.*

not turn a hair to be very calm in an unpleasant or difficult situation, and not show any sign of being afraid or anxious ○ *She started off by accusing him of blackmail but he didn't turn a hair: in fact he more or less ignored her.*

pull your hair out, tear your hair out to be very angry, upset, or anxious about something ○ *The nation is tearing its hair out over what to do with these child criminals.*

wear a hair shirt to deliberately make your own life unpleasant or uncomfortable in a way that is not necessary ○ *No one is asking you to wear a hair shirt and give up all your luxuries.*

≣ In the past, hair shirts were very rough, uncomfortable shirts made from horsehair. People sometimes wore them for religious reasons, to show that they were truly sorry for their sins.

within a hair's breadth of something very close to something ○ *Sumpa allowed the van to slip to within a hair's breadth of the precipice, then gave the engine full throttle.*

hairs

have someone by the short hairs to have someone completely in your power ○ *The hard fact is that they have got us by the short hairs. We can't do anything without material support from them.*

≣ 'Short hairs' in this expression may refer to a person's pubic hair, to hair on the back of their neck, or to the hair in a beard.

something will put hairs on your chest said to mean that an alcoholic drink is very strong ○ *Some of the concoctions would put hairs on your chest and indeed those brave enough to sample some left very early on in the evening.*

split hairs to make distinctions in a situation where the differences between things are actually very small and unimportant ○ *But once you start splitting hairs like that, where are you going to stop?*

halcyon

halcyon days (*literary*) a time in the past when something was especially successful ○ *When we ask him whether the wool industry will ever see those halcyon days again, he turns away and shakes his head.*

≣ The seven days before and after the shortest day of the year are sometimes called halcyon days. 'Halcyon' comes from the Greek word for kingfisher. According to Greek legend, Halcyone and her husband were turned into kingfishers by the gods. It was believed that these birds built their nests on the sea during the seven days before the shortest day of the year and then sat on their eggs for the next seven days, and that the gods always ensured calm weather during this period.

half

go off half-cocked to be unsuccessful in what you are trying to do, because you have not taken enough care or prepared properly ○ *Remember, don't go off half-cocked when we get there. Stick to the plan.* ○ *In-store guest appearances are usually embarrassing, half-cocked events.*

≣ If a gun goes off at half-cock, it does not fire properly and so the shot is wasted. This is because the firing mechanism has not been raised high enough to connect with the trigger.

how the other half lives used for describing the lives of people who are very different from you, for example very rich or very poor, or living in a different country ○ *He clearly has little idea how the other half lives, though, carrying a 1,000-dollar note in his pocket to flourish in small shops which cannot give him change.*

★ **your other half** or **your better half** your husband, wife, or partner ○ *They invited us out to dinner after the election because they said it was high time they met my other half.*

halfway

★ **meet someone halfway** to accept some of a person's opinions or wishes, so that you can come to an agreement with them or have a better relationship with them ○ *Senator Gray said Democrats are willing to meet the president halfway on measures to stimulate the economy.*

halves

not do things by halves to always do everything very well and very thoroughly ○ *In Italy they rarely do things by halves. When designers latch on to a theme, they work it through thoroughly, producing the world's most wearable clothes in the most beautiful fabrics.*

hammer

go at it hammer and tongs
1 (British) to do something with great energy and enthusiasm ○ *'He loved gardening,' sniffed Mrs Gascoigne. 'He went at it hammer and tongs as soon as he got back from work.'*
2 (mainly British) to have a noisy argument ○ *'They were going at it hammer and tongs.' 'What about?' 'I'm not very sure, but they were arguing.'*

The image here is of a blacksmith holding a piece of heated iron with a pair of tongs, and striking the iron repeatedly with a hammer.

★ **go under the hammer** (British) to be offered for sale at auction. The American expression is **go on the block**. ○ *The first half of the collection goes under the hammer on Friday and there are some real treasures.*

In an auction, the auctioneer shows that a sale has been made by banging a hammer on a table.

hand

be bound hand and foot by something to not be able to act freely or do what you want because something prevents you ○ *These people are still bound hand and foot by tradition.*

be hand in glove with someone or something to be working very closely with another person or organization, often in order to do something dishonest or immoral ○ *Employment on the building sites is controlled by more than 40 gangs, who are believed to be hand in glove with the police.*

The original form of the expression was 'hand and glove'. It was used to say that there was a strong connection or similarity between two things.

★ **be waited on hand and foot** to be looked after by someone else who takes care of you in every way and makes you very comfortable ○ *If you are incapable of lying on a beach and being waited on hand and foot, then La Samanna, on the Caribbean island of St Martin, is not for you.*

★ **bite the hand that feeds you** to be ungrateful and behave badly towards the person who has helped or supported you ○ *She may be cynical about the film industry, but ultimately she has no intention of biting the hand that feeds her.*

the dead hand of someone or something (mainly British) used for describing a very negative influence that someone or something has on a situation, for example by preventing change or progress ○ *For too long we have lived under the dead hand of the dieticians and the nutritionists. We have become a society where feasting is frowned on and food faddism is the fashion.*

do something to keep your hand in to do something in order to use the skills which you have developed in the past, so that you do not lose them ○ *I had to wait two years before I was offered another part, and just to keep my hand in, I went on tour with a play that wasn't very good.*

★ **force someone's hand** to force someone to do something that they are not ready to do or do not want to do ○ *Today's move may be a tactical manoeuvre designed to force the hand of the Prime Minister.*

In card games, to force an opponent's hand means to force them to play a card earlier than they want to.

give someone a big hand to clap a performer ○ *I'm Hal Morgan and these are the Praise Him Singers from Muncie, Indiana, so let's give them a big hand.*

give with one hand and take away with the other to help someone in one way, but also do something which has the opposite effect, for example harming them or preventing them from achieving what they want ○ *My parents were very supportive, but they gave with one hand and took away with the other, because I never really learned to be independent.*

★ **go hand in hand** if two things go hand in hand, they are closely connected and cannot be considered separately from each other ○ *The principle of the playgroup movement is that play and learning go hand in hand: your child masters new skills and absorbs knowledge while having fun.*

hand-to-mouth if someone is acting in a hand-to-mouth way, they do not plan ahead, but decide what to do from day to day ○ *Unless a government sets its course from the start, it is doomed to spend the rest of its term in hand-to-mouth improvising.*

★ **have a free hand** to have the freedom to make your own decisions on how something should be done ○ *I shall have a free hand and be able to train the squadron as I like.*

★ **have a hand in something** to be one of the people involved in doing or creating something ○ *Peter is a very experienced yachtsman, and had a hand in the design himself.*

have someone eating out of your hand to have a situation where someone does whatever you want because they admire or love you so much ○ *No one can handle the press as she can and she usually has them eating out of her hand by the time they leave.*

> The image here is of an animal which is tame and will take food from a person's hand.

have someone in the palm of your hand

1 to have a group of people, especially an audience, giving you their full attention

and responding enthusiastically to everything you say or do ○ *A cursory look at the audience shows that she's got them in the palm of her hand.*

2 to have complete control over someone so that they will do whatever you want ○ *Boris shrugged off a warning that he is 'playing with fire'. Barbara's ex-boyfriend said: 'She has Boris in the palm of her hand.'*

have to do something with one hand tied behind your back to have a disadvantage which makes it difficult for you to succeed in doing something ○ *The club is having to improve the team with one hand tied behind its back because it has no money to spend on new players.*

have the upper hand to have more power in a competitive situation than the other side and to be able to control things ○ *The changes are by no means revolutionary, but they do suggest that for the first time economic reformers now have the upper hand in the party hierarchy.*

have your hand in the till (*mainly British*) to be caught stealing or doing something wrong. The usual American expression is **be caught with your hand in the cookie jar**. ○ *He had his hand in the till, and was sacked from his job at the supermarket.*

a heavy hand a way of dealing with people that is very harsh or severe, and often unfair ○ *The heavy hand of the military has not prevented their economies from doing very well.*

hold someone's hand to help and support someone in a new or difficult situation ○ *I will support him up to a point but I can't hold his hand forever and there comes a time when John has to take responsibility himself.*

know something like the back of your hand to know something very well ○ *He knows the city like the back of his hand.*

★ **lend a hand** or
lend someone a hand to help

someone to do something ○ *If I'd known, I'd have been glad to lend a hand – you should have rung me up.*

★ **live from hand to mouth** or **live hand to mouth** to not have enough money to live comfortably, and to have no money left after you have paid for basic necessities ○ *I have a wife and two children and we live from hand to mouth on what I earn.* ○ *The village of Cuestecita is typical of the desperate hand-to-mouth economy that exists on the fringes of Cerrejon.*

★ **an old hand** someone who is very skilled at something because they have been doing it for a long time ○ *An old hand at photography, 34-year-old Tim has been shooting British landscapes and wildlife as a hobby for the last 13 years.*

overplay your hand to act more confidently that you should, because you believe you are in a stronger position than you really are ○ *He said the police had overplayed their hand in not accepting the 'generous' offer.*

≡ 'Hand' in this expression refers to the cards dealt to you in a card game.

★ **reject something out of hand** to reject an idea or suggestion without hesitating and without discussing it first ○ *He has rejected out of hand any suggestion that there can be any compromise over the proposals.*

the right hand doesn't know what the left hand is doing said to mean that the people in one part of an organization do not know what the people in another part are doing and this is causing confusion or difficulties ○ *The right hand doesn't know what the left is doing. One company digs up roads and fills them in, and then another service does the same a few days later.*

≡ This expression comes from the Bible. (Matthew 6:3), when Jesus says that if people give money to charity, they

should do it without boasting or telling anyone about it. (They should do it so secretly that even their left hand would not know what their right hand is doing.)

show your hand to let other people see what your position is in a competitive situation, and what you intend to do ○ *On domestic politics he seemed unwilling to show his hand too clearly.*

≡ If you show your hand in a card game, you reveal your cards to another player.

someone can do something with one hand tied behind their back said to mean that someone can do something very easily ○ *The Explorer camcorder is so neat and nifty you can operate it with one hand tied behind your back.*

★ **someone or something gets out of hand** said to mean that a situation or person cannot be controlled any longer ○ *We heard a man being abusive. It was getting out of hand so we rang the police.*

a steady hand on the tiller a situation in which someone is keeping good control of a situation ○ *'If ever there was an urgent need for a steady hand on the tiller, it is now,' said one European diplomat.*

≡ In a boat, the tiller is the handle with which you steer.

★ **take someone or something in hand** to take control of someone or something, in order to improve them ○ *The feeling is growing that the present government only reacts to events rather than taking the situation in hand.*

throw in your hand to give up trying to do something ○ *After a brief bounce, Wall Street crashed again, and the financier had to throw in his hand.*

≡ In card games such as poker, if you throw in your hand, you put your cards on the table to show that you accept that you have lost.

★ **try your hand at something** to try doing something in order to see whether you like it or whether you are good at it ○ *In his latest book, he tries his hand at fiction.*

★ **turn your hand to something** to start doing something and do it well, even though you may not be trained to do it ○ *Judy is one of those women who can turn her hand to most things.*

work hand in hand if two people or organizations work hand in hand, they work closely together, often with a single aim ○ *Steelmakers are working hand in hand with auto makers to slash the cost of producing automotive parts.*

you have to hand it to someone (spoken) said to acknowledge how well someone has done something or how good they are at it, even though you do not like the person or do not approve of their actions ○ *Whatever you thought of his act, you had to hand it to him – he knew how to make money.*

handle

fly off the handle to suddenly become very angry about something and behave in an uncontrolled and irrational way ○ *Unless some decision was reached, they might fly off the handle and do something foolish.*

≣ The reference here is to an axe head which has become loose, and so when someone swings the axe, the axe head flies off.

hands

★ **at the hands of someone** if someone experiences a particular kind of treatment, especially unpleasant treatment, at the hands of a person or organization, they receive it from them ○ *She spoke of the humiliation she endured at the hands of the police.*

be rubbing your hands with glee (mainly British) to be very pleased about

something, often something bad which has happened to an enemy or opponent ○ *Some of the cereal producers are rubbing their hands with glee. Lower prices for grain will help them win back a bigger slice of the market in France.*

★ **be wringing your hands** to be expressing sadness or regret about a bad situation, but not taking any action to deal with it ○ *Mr Ashdown had accused the Government of wringing its hands and doing nothing as the country's jobless figures spiralled.*

≣ If you wring something, you squeeze or twist it.

★ **change hands** if something changes hands, one person or organization gets it from another, usually by buying it ○ *The property has changed hands several times recently.*

★ **fall into someone's hands** or **fall into the wrong hands** to be taken or caught by an opponent or enemy ○ *There is a real fear that food supplies could fall into the hands of the Mafia, thus increasing the misery of ordinary citizens.*

★ **get your hands dirty** to get involved with all aspects of your job, including routine, practical, or more junior work, or dealing with people directly. This expression is usually used showing approval. ○ *Getting their hands dirty keeps top managers in touch with the problems of customers, and it shows everybody that serving customers is important.*

★ **get your hands on someone** or **lay your hands on someone** to catch someone who has done something wrong and usually punish them ○ *That's the most likely explanation, they say, but we can't be sure until we lay our hands on the culprits.*

★ **get your hands on something** or **lay your hands on something** to succeed in obtaining something you want or need ○ *First of all, how was he able to get his hands on that money so easily?*

★ **have your hands full** to be very busy ○ *The federal government will obviously have its hands full trying to enforce environmental laws while keeping residents happy.*

★ **in safe hands** being cared for by a competent person or organization and therefore not likely to be harmed or damaged ○ *They could get on with their own lives, knowing their girls were in safe hands.*

★ **in someone's hands** in someone's possession or under their control ○ *Some delegates have criticized the move, saying it will leave too much power in the hands of the party leadership.*

★ **off your hands** if someone or something is off your hands, you are no longer responsible for them, because another person has taken responsibility for them instead of you ○ *I can always take the children off your hands for a while, if you've nothing much else for me to do.*

★ **on your hands**
1 if you have a problem or task on your hands, you have to deal with it ○ *What is already clear though is that the local police now have yet another problem on their hands.*
2 if you have a person on your hands, you are responsible for caring for them or dealing with them, especially when this is difficult or demanding ○ *Those parents who took a lax attitude to family discipline now have hooligan children on their hands.*

★ **out of your hands** if something is out of your hands you are no longer responsible for it ○ *Things were out of our hands now. We could only wait.*

★ **play into someone's hands** to make a foolish mistake or act in the way that someone wants you to act, so that they gain an advantage over you or defeat you ○ *The main opposition parties played into his hands by boycotting the election.*

a safe pair of hands (*mainly British*) someone, especially a politician, who is

good at their job and unlikely to make any serious mistakes ○ *The mayoral office will be defined by the first incumbent, so he must be a safe pair of hands.*

shake hands on something to conclude a deal or an agreement successfully ○ *So keen were the Russians to shake hands on the deal that they offered to accept palm oil in part payment.*

★ **sit on your hands** to not do something which you should be doing ○ *The pace of development in Formula One is so fast that if you sit on your hands you quickly regret it.*

someone does not dirty their hands said to mean that someone avoids doing physical work or the parts of a job that they consider unpleasant or distasteful ○ *These are people who live in the commuter belt around the capital with more secure jobs and who have never had to dirty their hands to earn a living.*

★ **someone's hands are tied** said to mean that something such as a law is preventing someone from acting in the way that they want to ○ *He would like to help but he is powerless because his hands are tied by regulations approved by the council of ministers.*

sully your hands (*formal*) to do something that you find unpleasant or distasteful to do ○ *He had no intention of sullying his hands by playing politics.*

★ **wash your hands of something or someone** to refuse to be involved with a problem or a person who causes problems or to take responsibility for them any longer ○ *The Macclesfield MP said: 'We cannot wash our hands of responsibility for the state of the economy.'*

According to the Bible (Matthew 27:24), Pontius Pilate washed his hands in a bowl to show that he would not take responsibility for the death sentence which the public demanded he should pass on Jesus.

★ **win hands down**

1 to win a contest easily ○ *We have been beaten in some games which we should have won hands down.*

2 to be clearly the best in a comparison between things ○ *The New Winter Palace Hotel wins hands down for both comfort and evocative location, situated a few steps away from the banks of the Nile.*

> This expression was originally used in horse racing to describe jockeys who won their races very easily and could cross the winning line with their hands lowered and the reins loose.

★ **with your bare hands** without using any weapons or tools ○ *Rescue workers and residents were digging through tonnes of mud with shovels and their bare hands yesterday in search of survivors.*

handsome

handsome is as handsome does

(old-fashioned) said to mean that you should judge someone by their actions and not by their appearance ○ *Handsome is as handsome does, my mother and grandmother always said, in order to counter self-admiration.*

hang

be hung out to dry to be in a very difficult situation where you have been abandoned by the people who previously supported you ○ *Once again, the CIA – apparently unable to resist political manipulation by the administration – is in danger of being hung out to dry.*

★ **get the hang of something** to learn how to do an activity ○ *Once one gets the hang of it, reading a good play can be a delightful and challenging experience.*

★ **hang tough** (mainly American, journalism) to continue to fight or compete strongly for something and refuse to accept defeat ○ *The White House is hanging tough for a good agreement.*

hang up your boots (British) to stop playing a sport, especially football, and retire ○ *I want a few triumphs and medals to reflect on when I eventually hang up my boots.*

let it all hang out to behave in a very informal and relaxed way, without worrying about hiding your emotions or behaving politely ○ *The defence most frequently claimed for the baring of the more dreadful revelations is that of 'unburdening'; let it all hang out and you will feel better.*

someone is hanging on by their fingertips or

someone is hanging on by their fingernails said to mean that someone is managing to survive in a difficult situation or to stay in the position they want to, but they are always in danger of failing ○ *Real Madrid's poor start to the season has left coach Benito Floro hanging on to his job by his fingernails.*

happy

happy as a clam (mainly American) very happy ○ *Join the other kids. Do that, and before you know it you'll be happy as a clam.*

happy as a lark very happy ○ *Look at me – eighty-two years old and happy as a lark!*

happy as Larry (British, informal) very happy ○ *I gave her a police badge to wear on her sleeve and she's as happy as Larry.*

> 'Larry' may refer to the successful Australian boxer Larry Foley (1847–1917). Alternatively, 'Larry' may come from 'larrikin', a 19th century word for a hooligan or ruffian, used mainly in Australia.

happy as a pig in muck (British, informal) very happy ○ *From day one I adored it. I was as happy as a pig in muck.*

hard

hard as nails very unsympathetic towards other people ○ *He's a shrewd businessman and hard as nails.*

★ **hard done by** (British) feeling that you have been treated unfairly ○ *Those who* *felt hard done by* made their dissatisfaction clear.

play hard to get to deliberately make it difficult for someone to obtain something that they need from you, such as your agreement or permission ○ *Only a few days ago, the Social Democrats were playing hard to get as the CDU tried to woo them into coalition talks.*

hardball

play hardball *(mainly American)* to do anything that is necessary to achieve or obtain what you want, even if this involves being harsh or unfair ○ *The White House decided to retaliate by taking jobs away from his state, showing they were tough guys who could play hardball.*

> Hardball is the same as baseball, and is here being contrasted with softball, in which a larger, softer ball is used and pitches are thrown underarm.

hare

run with the hare and hunt with the hounds *(British)* to try to support both sides in an argument or conflict, in order to make your own life easier ○ *They learn very quickly to run with the hare and hunt with the hounds; to side with whoever is nearest in a relentless quest to avoid rows.*

> A hound is a dog that has been bred for hunting.

start a hare *(British)* to introduce a new idea or topic which other people become interested in ○ *Some work needs to be done before the connection is proved. But Mr Birchall has started a hare that many researchers will be watching.*

> To 'start' a hare means to disturb it and cause it to leave its hiding place, so that the hounds start chasing it.

harness

> A harness is a set of straps like the one that is fitted to a horse when it pulls a cart.

in harness
1 *(mainly British)* actually doing a job which you have been appointed to do ○ *They hope to have the Australian Test forward Troy Coker back in harness before the end of the season.*
2 *(British)* if two or more people work in harness, they work together or produce something together ○ *Experts in production statistics and computing may work in harness on a single project.*

harvest

reap the harvest → see **reap**

hat

go hat in hand to someone *(mainly American)* to ask someone very humbly and respectfully for money or help. The usual British expression is **go cap in hand to someone**. ○ *He won't go hat in hand to the White House to ask that sanctions be lifted against his country.*

> In the past, it was customary for lower-class people to remove their hats in front of upper-class people. The expression may also refer to the fact that people sometimes hold out their hats when they are begging, for other people to put money in.

keep something under your hat to not mention to anyone else something that someone has told you ○ *Look, if I tell you something will you promise to keep it under your hat? Promise now, not a word to anyone.*

> This was a slogan used to promote security in Britain during the Second World War.

knock something into a cocked hat *(mainly British)* to be much better or more successful than something else ○ *I am writing a novel which is going to knock Proust into a cocked hat.*

> One explanation for this expression is that it refers to the cocked hats of the

18th century, which were made by folding the edge of a round hat into three corners or points. According to this explanation, the expression originally meant to change something completely. Alternatively, the expression may refer to an American game of skittles where only three pins were set up, in the triangular shape of a cocked hat.

★ **old hat** unoriginal or out of date ○ *I think that's a bit old hat now, isn't it? I wanted to do something quite different.*

This expression may have developed because in the times when it was customary for women to wear hats, the fashions in hats used to change very quickly.

pass the hat or
pass the hat around to collect money for someone or something ○ *Airbus will soon be passing the hat around again for an enormous 700-seat aeroplane.*

The image here is of people using a hat to collect money in.

someone will eat their hat if something happens (old-fashioned) said to mean that someone does not believe that a particular thing will happen ○ *I will eat my hat if the Liberal Democrats improve their parliamentary representation at the next general election.*

★ **take your hat off to someone** to express admiration for something that someone has done ○ *You have to take your hat off to whoever thought this one up.* ○ *Hats off to them for supporting the homeless.*

People sometimes remove their hats as a sign of respect when they meet someone.

talk through your hat to say something that is ridiculous or totally incorrect ○ *He is talking through his hat*

when he attributes the overcrowding and over-use of parts of the Lake District to its designation as a national park.

throw your hat into the ring or
throw your cap into the ring to become one of the people taking part in a competition or contest ○ *He said straightaway that he would play. I am delighted that he has decided to throw his hat into the ring.*

In the past, prize fighters at showgrounds used to challenge people to fight them. Someone who was willing to accept the challenge would throw their hat into the ring.

hatch

go down the hatch to be eaten or drunk, usually quickly or greedily ○ *A record £4.4 billion worth of confectionery went down the hatch last year.*

In the 18th century, this expression was used as a toast in the navy. A hatch is an opening in the deck of a ship, through which people and goods can pass.

hatches

batten down the hatches to prepare for a difficult situation by doing everything you can to protect yourself ○ *While most companies are battening down the hatches, fearing recession, Blenheim is leading an assault on the US market.*

Battens are strips of wood used for fastening things down. Hatches are openings in the deck of a ship, or the wooden flaps which cover the openings.

hatchet

A hatchet is a small axe.

bury the hatchet to agree to forget a quarrel and become friends again ○ *One employee said the two men had finally buried the hatchet after their falling-out.*

In the past, when Native American tribes made peace after fighting each other, it was traditional for each tribe to bury a tomahawk or small axe, as a sign of peace.

do a hatchet job on someone or something to say or write a lot of bad things about someone or something in order to harm their reputation ○ *Reporter Malcolm, he says, set out to do a hatchet job on him and succeeded.*

This expression may relate to violent gang warfare in the United States during the early part of the 20th century. See explanation at 'a hatchet man'.

a hatchet man a man whose job is to destroy things or do unpleasant tasks, often on behalf of someone else ○ *He had to play the hatchet man and it was not pleasant for the many he laid off.*

This expression may relate to violent gang warfare in the United States during the early part of the 20th century. Gangs often hired an assassin or 'hatchet man' to hack an important member of a rival gang to death with a hatchet. This work was known as a 'hatchet job'.

haul

A haul in the following expressions means a journey.

be in something for the long haul (*mainly American*) to intend to continue doing something until it is finished, even if it is difficult or unpleasant ○ *Impatience is not our problem. We're in it for the long haul. Five years is the minimum.*

★ **a long haul** a task or course of action that will be very difficult to deal with and will need a great deal of effort and time ○ *Revitalizing the economy will be a long haul.*

★ **over the long haul** (*mainly American*) over a long period of time in the future

○ *The smart economic message for the nation is that prudent leadership, coupled with patience, will accomplish more over the long haul.*

hawk

watch someone like a hawk to pay close attention to everything that someone does, usually to make sure that they do not do anything wrong ○ *Some guys just sit there and watch her like a hawk, dead sure she's trying to cheat.*

Hawks have very good eyesight, and are able to see small animals or objects from a great height.

hay

make hay while the sun shines to take advantage of a good situation which is not likely to last ○ *Making hay while the sun shines, the Egyptian government has taken radical measures to liberalize the economy.*

head

be banging your head against a brick wall (*mainly British*) or

be banging your head against a wall to feel frustrated because someone is stopping you from making progress in what you are trying to do ○ *It is a waste of valuable energy banging your head against a brick wall, wishing things were different.*

★ **be hanging over someone's head** if something difficult or unpleasant is hanging over someone's head, it worries them because it may cause something bad to happen to them in the future ○ *If the post fell vacant, it is unlikely that the Home Office would want to appoint him if an inquiry was hanging over his head.*

This expression may relate to the story of the Sword of Damocles; see explanation at 'sword'.

★ **be head and shoulders above someone** to be much better than other people or things of the same kind

○ Richards, according to Imran Khan, was head and shoulders above any other player at his peak.

bite someone's head off to speak to someone in an unpleasant, angry way, because you are annoyed about something ○ And don't bite my head off just because you're in a bad mood!

build up a head of steam to gradually become more and more angry, anxious, or emotional about something until you can no longer hide your feelings ○ Bob was the most angry, as if in waiting for the other items to be cleared he had built up a greater head of steam.

★ **bury your head in the sand** to deliberately refuse to accept the truth about something unpleasant ○ Don't be an ostrich and bury your head in the sand, hoping your problems will disappear.

≡ People used to think that ostriches buried their heads in the sand when they were in danger.

★ **come to a head** or
bring something to a head if a problem or disagreement comes to a head, it reaches a state where you have to take action to deal with it. You can also say that a particular event or factor brings a problem or disagreement to a head. ○ These problems came to a head in September when five of the station's journalists were sacked. ○ The issue that brought things to a head over the weekend was the sudden dip in late demand for summer holidays across the industry.

≡ This expression may refer to farmers waiting for cabbage leaves to grow together and form a head. Alternatively, the reference may be to a boil on a person's body forming a head just before it bursts.

do someone's head in (mainly British, spoken) to make someone very unhappy, upset, confused, or ill, and make them feel as if they cannot cope or are going

mad ○ During her year off she worked at a boutique in Bromley, doing things like cleaning coat hangers. 'It did my head in,' she laughs.

★ **fall head over heels** to fall suddenly and deeply in love with someone ○ It was obvious that Alan had fallen head over heels in love with Veronica.

≡ Until the late 18th century this expression was 'heels over head', which refers to someone doing a somersault.

★ **from head to toe** or
from head to foot over the whole of someone's body ○ She was covered from head to toe with bruises.

get in over your head or
be in over your head to become or be deeply involved in a situation which is too difficult for you to deal with ○ He realized that he was in over his head, and that only his family could help him.

≡ Here, the reference is to getting into water that is too deep to stand up in.

get your head around something to succeed in understanding or accepting something such as a new idea ○ He can't get his head around the fact that the children born in this country are not 'immigrants'.

★ **give someone their head** to allow someone to do what they want to do, without trying to advise them or stop them ○ He was a nice, decent man who treated people properly and he recognized ability and gave people their heads.

≡ This expression is from horse riding and refers to when the rider loosens the reins, allowing the horse to move more freely.

★ **go head-to-head** to compete directly with another person or organization, especially in business and sport ○ General Motors and Ford are expected to go head-to-head in the markets to buy up rival 15% stakes in Jaguar. ○ As top athletes, we should be *running against each other whenever possible. Head-to-head competition makes our sport what it is.*

★ **go over someone's head**

1 to appeal to a higher authority than someone in an attempt to get what you want ○ *He was reprimanded for trying to go over the heads of senior officers.*

2 if something that someone says or writes goes over someone's head, they do not understand it because it is too difficult for them ○ *The few books that exist today either come from abroad, having been written for pre-school native speakers, or introduce grammar that goes over young heads.*

★ **go to your head**

1 if someone lets success go to their head, they start to think that they are better or cleverer than other people, and they begin to behave in an arrogant or silly way ○ *Ford is definitely not a man to let a little success go to his head. He knows he still has a lot to learn.*

2 if alcohol goes to your head, it makes you slightly drunk and perhaps affects your judgement so that you do silly things ○ *He was not accustomed to strong liquor and it went to his head.*

have your head in the clouds to be out of touch with reality and perhaps have impractical ideas about achieving success ○ *Whether some of them still have their heads in the clouds after our FA Cup win over Spurs, I don't know.*

have your head screwed on to be sensible and realistic ○ *Good girl! I always knew you had your head screwed on properly.*

a head of steam a lot of support for something such as a plan or cause ○ *While most senior Conservative MPs still believe an election next year is more likely, there's an increasing head of steam behind going to the polls this November.*

≣ A steam engine can only work when the steam has reached a particular pressure level.

head-to-head if two people or groups who are in conflict have head-to-head talks, they meet to discuss the subjects they disagree about ○ *They have just begun a third session of head-to-head talks which are expected to last until late afternoon.* ○ *Next time you have a head-to-head with someone in authority, watch your language.*

★ **keep a cool head** to remain calm in a difficult situation ○ *I have to keep a cool head and try not to let my anger show.*

★ **keep your head** to remain calm in a difficult situation ○ *The most important thing is to keep your head and look to the future.*

★ **keep your head above water** to struggle to survive, for example by keeping out of debt ○ *Thousands of other small businesses like mine are, at best, struggling to keep their heads above water or, at worst, have gone bust.*

★ **keep your head down**

1 to try to avoid trouble or involvement in a difficult or dangerous situation by behaving in a quiet way, so that people will not notice you ○ *After unity, he had little time for Christian Democrats who had kept their heads down under the old regime.*

2 to continue to concentrate and work hard at something ○ *When he gets a chance of winning, he keeps his head down and really goes for it.*

knock something on the head (British)

1 to show that a story or an idea is not true or correct ○ *It's time to knock on the head the idea that we are not fully human, not fully alive, unless we have that special somebody in our lives.*

2 to decide to stop an activity , or not to start it ○ *I remember us in the early days saying: 'When we stop enjoying ourselves, we'll knock it on the head.'*

★ **laugh your head off** or **shout your head off** to laugh or shout a great deal ○ *They were probably laughing their heads off.*

★ **lose your head** to panic and not remain calm in a difficult situation ○ *He warned the party not to lose its head, saying that it was not a 'time for panic'.*

not right in the head (spoken) strange, foolish, or crazy ○ *'According to Great-Aunt Louise,' I said, 'the grandmother wasn't quite right in the head. Maybe Mrs Issler was ashamed of that too.'*

off the top of your head

1 (spoken) if you comment on something off the top of your head, what you say is an immediate reaction and is not a carefully considered opinion, and so it might not be correct ○ *Last year the amount of money we put into development and support was, off the top of my head, about twenty-eight thousand pounds.*

2 if you know something off the top of your head, you know it well and can remember it easily ○ *OK, off the top of your head, do you know the capital of South Korea?*

off your head (British, informal) very strange, foolish, or dangerous ○ *It's like working in a war zone. You must be off your head to live in that area.*

on your head be it or

on your own head be it (mainly British) said to warn someone that they are responsible for something that they intend to do or something that happens as a consequence ○ *If you choose to ignore my generous offer, then on your own heads be it.*

out of your head (informal) very strange, foolish, or dangerous ○ *If he didn't kill anybody, it was only by luck because he was out of his head and screaming like a maniac.*

put your head above the parapet (British) to do or say something in public that has previously been kept private, and risk being criticized or attacked ○ *This is a policy option which cannot be ignored – although no-one is prepared to put their head above the parapet to say so.*

Parapets are banks of earth or walls which soldiers build for protection against enemy attacks.

put your head in a noose or
stick your head in a noose to deliberately do something which will put you in danger or in a difficult situation ○ *If I have to be caught, OK, but I am damned if I will put my head in a noose and walk into that hotel!*

A noose is a loop and knot that is tied in rope in order to hang someone.

put your head into the lion's mouth to deliberately place yourself in a dangerous or difficult situation ○ *Put your head into the lion's mouth and just say 'I don't know what the hell is going on.'*

This expression refers to the traditional circus act where a lion-tamer puts their head in a lion's mouth.

put your head on the block → see **block**

★ **scratch your head** to be puzzled and unsure about what to do about a problem or question, or to be unsure what the solution is ○ *A lot of people are scratching their heads and saying, 'What are we doing? Are we getting our money's worth?'*

someone can do something standing on their head said to mean that someone can do something very easily ○ *Tom, the cameraman, had won five Oscars during his long working life, and could have directed the whole picture standing on his head while playing a game of cards.*

someone cannot make head or tail of something or
someone cannot make head nor tail of something said to mean that someone cannot understand something at all ○ *I couldn't make head or tail of it myself, but it sounded like part of some sort of hymn or prayer.*

★ **something rears its head** or
something rears its ugly head said to mean that something bad starts to

appear or be active ○ *Now the same ugly forces of racial hatred are beginning to rear their heads again.*

★ **turn something on its head** or **stand something on its head** to use the same facts of an argument or theory to produce a different or opposite conclusion ○ *Instead of pleading for women's rights, they should turn the argument on its head and point out the cost of denying women the right to earn.*

heads

★ **heads roll** said to mean that the people responsible or in positions of power when something goes wrong are punished, usually by losing their job or position ○ *The widely-held view is that heads should roll over the losses.*

> In the past, people in important positions were sometimes beheaded if they were considered responsible for a mistake or problem.

knock people's heads together (mainly British) to force people who are disagreeing to reach an agreement ○ *If he's unable to knock everybody's heads together, then questions are going to be raised about his own ability to continue in office.*

put your heads together to try to solve a problem together with other people ○ *If there's a problem, there's no sense of floundering around. We all just sit down, put our heads together and figure it out.*

★ **turn heads** to be so beautiful, unusual, or impressive that people are attracted to you and cannot help looking at you or paying attention to you ○ *At the age of 20, the dark-haired actress was already turning heads in the right places.*

headway

★ **make headway** to make progress in the thing that you are trying to achieve ○ *A spokesman said the two sides have agreed* on a timetable for the rest of the talks and have also made headway on some security issues.

heap

at the bottom of the heap low down in society or in an organization ○ *At the bottom of the heap live at least 1 million people – the rural poor.*

at the top of the heap high up in society or in an organization ○ *While the executive salaries should put Suncorp at the top of the heap in Queensland, they would barely rate in Sydney and Melbourne.*

heart

> The heart is traditionally regarded as the centre of the emotions.

★ **a bleeding heart** someone who is too sympathetic towards people who claim to be poor or suffering ○ *This huge leap in crime and the misery it causes can't be blamed on poverty, as the bleeding hearts always insist: we are much richer now than we were then.* ○ *This was precisely the sort of bleeding-heart sentimentality that Charles Lindbergh deplored.*

★ **break someone's heart**
1 to make someone feel extremely upset and unhappy, because you end a love affair or close relationship with them ○ *When he left his wife for me I was appalled. What I'd wanted was a good time, but in the end I broke his heart.*
2 if something breaks someone's heart, the fact that it is happening makes them feel sad and depressed, because they believe that it is bad or wrong ○ *It broke my heart to see this woman break down the way she did.*

a broken heart if someone has a broken heart, they feel very sad because a love affair or close relationship has ended ○ *We have all read in fiction of people dying of a broken heart, but can this happen in reality?* ○ *Mary is broken-hearted and has spent many nights crying.*

cross my heart (*spoken*) said when you want to assure someone that you are telling the truth. This expression is used mainly by children. ○ *And I won't tell any of the other girls anything you tell me about it. I promise, cross my heart.*

> This expression refers to the Christian practice of moving your hand across your chest in the shape of a cross.

★ **cry your heart out** to cry a great deal ○ *I threw myself on to the bed and cried my heart out. It took me a good while to get over the emotional damage of that encounter.*

★ **eat your heart out** when you want to draw attention to something you have done, you can say 'eat your heart out' and mention the name of a person who is famous for doing the same kind of thing. In the following example, James Bond is a fictional spy. ○ *We just managed to overtake the bus, and smashed through the gate just as it was being closed. James Bond, eat your heart out, I say.*

> This idea is an old one - the Greek philosopher Pythagoras is reputed to have used the saying 'do not eat your heart out', meaning 'do not waste your life worrying'.

from the bottom of your heart if you mean something from the bottom of your heart, you mean it very sincerely ○ *I want to thank everyone from the bottom of my heart. So many people have helped me.*

harden your heart against someone or something to force yourself to feel unfriendly or unsympathetic towards someone or something, even if you do not want to ○ *The most important things for Nicholas now are mobility and Braille lessons. You will have to harden your heart against doing everything for him.*

★ **in your heart of hearts** if you believe, know, or feel something in your heart of hearts, you believe, know, or feel that it is true, even though you are very reluctant to accept it ○ *But in your heart of hearts, you must know that you're not going to save some of these children?*

★ **lose heart** to start to feel discouraged or to lose interest in something, usually because things are not progressing in the way that you hoped ○ *I suppose I'm less optimistic than I was at first. This disease seems to recur so often you begin to lose heart.*

lose your heart to someone (*literary*) to fall in love with someone ○ *Don't lose your heart to him too soon because he could just be filling in time with you.*

★ **open your heart** or
pour out your heart to tell someone your most private thoughts or feelings ○ *At first my boyfriend was incredibly supportive. I'd phone him up and pour out my heart in a way I couldn't to anyone else.*

★ **set your heart on something** to decide that you want something very much and aim to achieve or obtain it ○ *She decided not to try for university. Instead she set her heart on a career in catering.*

★ **someone has a heart of gold** said to mean that someone is kind and generous, and enjoys helping other people ○ *He helped all the local sporting organizations – bowls, hockey, rugby and tennis. He had a heart of gold.*

someone's heart bleeds for someone said to mean that someone feels a lot of sympathy for someone else because they are suffering ○ *You looked so sad when you walked up the aisle at the funeral. My heart bled for you when I saw you.*

someone's heart hardens against someone or something said to mean that someone starts to feel unfriendly or unsympathetic towards someone or something ○ *All of a sudden my heart hardened against my beautiful mother and her desire for fun and a rich, handsome husband.*

someone's heart is in the right place said to mean that someone is kind, considerate, and generous, although they may lack other qualities which you consider to be important ○ *Whether Johnson's professional judgement was good or not, I decided that his heart was in the right place.*

someone's heart is in their mouth said to mean that someone feels extremely anxious or nervous, because they think something bad may be about to happen ○ *My heart was in my mouth when I walked into her office.*

someone's heart isn't in something said to mean that someone is doing something that they are unenthusiastic about and which they are not enjoying ○ *Playing was no longer fun. I lost my competitiveness and my heart wasn't in it.*

someone's heart sinks said to mean that someone suddenly feels very worried or disappointed ○ *There was a police car outside the house. My heart sank.* ○ *I'll never forget that heart-sinking moment when they told me the news.*

★ **something is close to your heart** said to mean that a subject is very important to you and that you are concerned about it or interested in it ○ *For presenter Manjeet K. Sandhu the position of Asian women in society is an issue very close to her heart.*

★ **take something to heart** to pay a lot of attention to someone's advice or criticism, and be greatly influenced or upset by it ○ *He could have taken this criticism to heart since he built his reputation on being a good manager.*

wear your heart on your sleeve to allow your feelings to be obvious to everyone around you ○ *She simply doesn't wear her heart on her sleeve so it's sometimes difficult to know what she's feeling.*

heartstrings

★ **tug at the heartstrings** to cause someone to feel a great deal of pity or sadness for someone or something

○ *Miss Cookson knows exactly how to tug at readers' heartstrings.*

In medieval times, it was believed that 'heartstrings' were tendons which supported the heart.

heat

the heat is on said to mean that you are under a lot of pressure to do or achieve something ○ *To perform well when the heat is on, all you have to do is let it happen.*

if you can't stand the heat, get out of the kitchen said to mean that someone should either learn to tolerate the difficulty or unpleasantness of an activity, or stop being involved in it ○ *If you are a manager of a top football club and you don't like the heat you should get out of the kitchen.*

This expression became very widely known when the American President Harry S. Truman used it in 1952 to announce that he would not stand again for president.

in the heat of the moment without stopping to think about what you are doing or saying, because you are angry or excited ○ *He said that his comments were made in the heat of the moment and were not supposed to be a personal attack.*

★ **turn up the heat on someone** to put pressure on a person or situation in order to get what you want ○ *The firm will be turning up the heat on its rivals in a highly competitive industry now scrapping for a share of the domestic market.*

heather

set the heather on fire (mainly Scottish) to be very exciting and successful ○ *Their results have not set the heather on fire.*

heaven

in seventh heaven extremely happy ○ *After I was given my first camera I was in seventh heaven.*

According to Islam, there are seven heavens. The seventh is the most glorious and is governed by Abraham. In the Jewish religion, the seventh heaven is the dwelling place of God and his angels.

move heaven and earth to do everything you possibly can to make sure that something happens ○ *He had been moving heaven and earth for six weeks in order to prevent the film being made; and he had failed.*

heavens

the heavens opened (*mainly British, literary*) said to mean that it began to rain very heavily ○ *As we sat down to eat, the heavens opened for a few minutes and we all crouched under our blue awning holding our plates.*

heel

★ **bring someone to heel** or
call someone to heel to force or order someone to obey you ○ *In practice it's still not clear how the president will use his power to bring the republics to heel.*

heels

★ **at your heels**
1 following close behind you ○ *They led the girls away, their mother at their heels.*
2 (*journalism, written*) threatening or challenging you in some way ○ *Intel and Motorola may dominate the market for microprocessors but scores of firms are snapping at their heels.*

★ **dig in your heels** or
dig your heels in to refuse to do something such as change your opinions or plans, especially when someone is trying very hard to make you do so ○ *He could dig in his heels and fight stubbornly for what he believed to be right.*

drag your heels → see **drag**

★ **hard on the heels of something** or
hot on the heels of something
if one event follows hard on the heels of another or hot on the heels of another, one happens very quickly or immediately after another ○ *The news comes hard on the heels of the appointment of new chief executive Cedric Walker.*

★ **hard on someone's heels** or
hot on someone's heels
1 doing nearly as well as someone else in a competitive situation, and likely soon to be doing better than them ○ *The next generation of British athletes is pressing hard on the heels of today's champions.*
2 close behind someone, often chasing them ○ *But the law was hard on their heels. Within two weeks gang leader Michael McAvoy and Brian Robinson were behind bars.*

kick up your heels to enjoy yourself a lot, for example at a party ○ *Combine music, culture and good food in Jersey this month. Kick up your heels at the annual Jersey Jazz Festival.*

This refers to a horse that has been released into a field, as horses commonly do this as they gallop off.

★ **kick your heels** (*mainly British*) or
cool your heels (*mainly American*)
to wait somewhere and feel bored or impatient because you have nothing to do, or because someone is deliberately keeping you waiting ○ *The Tunisian authorities wouldn't grant us permission to fly all the way down to Sfax, so I had to kick my heels at Tunis Airport.*

set someone back on their heels or
rock someone back on their heels to surprise or shock someone, and often put them at a disadvantage ○ *Ireland started brightly, only to be rocked back on their heels by the first error just 10 minutes into the match.*

show someone a clean pair of heels (*mainly British*)
1 to win a sporting contest clearly and decisively ○ *Lum Kon showed everyone a clean pair of heels in the 100m and 200m.*
2 to be clearly better than the rest of the

people or organizations in a competitive situation ○ *Only one point stands: Japan has shown all the other rich countries a clean pair of heels.*

take to your heels (*literary*) to run away. ○ *He took to his heels and rushed out of the room.*

heights

★ **dizzying heights** (*American*) or **the dizzy heights** a very high level of success in a particular field ○ *Turner had first known such dizzy heights in the 1960s when she became one of the top exponents of black American music.*

hell

★ **all hell breaks loose** said to mean that there is a lot of fuss, arguing, or fighting ○ *In 'Jungle Fever', a happily-married black architect begins an affair with his Italian-American secretary, but all hell breaks loose when his wife finds out.*

> This expression first appeared in John Milton's 'Paradise Lost' (1667), book 4, line 917, when the Archangel Gabriel addresses Satan: 'Wherefore with thee Came not all hell broke loose?' (ie why did all hell not break loose and come with you?). Here, 'broke' means 'broken', but the meaning of this expression has since changed.

come hell or high water said to mean that someone is determined to do something, in spite of the difficulties involved ○ *The chairman of the Senate Judiciary Committee says the all-male panel will have two female members this year, come hell or high water.*

★ **from hell** used after a noun to refer humorously to something or someone extremely unpleasant, or as bad as they can possibly be ○ *A cute family puppy turns into the pet from hell in this comedy starring Charles Grodin.*

give someone hell

1 to make someone's life very unpleasant

by behaving badly towards them ○ *She gets teased at school. The children give her hell, particularly the older boys.*

2 to shout at someone or speak to them angrily because they have done something wrong ○ *When she didn't get off the train at Euston, I phoned the police and they found her in a sleeping compartment. She gave me hell for embarrassing her!*

3 to be very painful ○ *My back's giving me hell, let me tell you! But I'm going to dig the garden up.*

go hell for leather to move or do something very quickly, often without care ○ *The Dutch boys are confident from all their skating and go hell for leather.*

> This expression may originally have related to horse riding. 'Leather' would refer to a saddle.

★ **go through hell** to have a very difficult or unpleasant time ○ *After the case he made no comment, but his solicitor said that he had gone through 10 months of hell.*

go to hell to be destroyed ○ *This government has to wake up. The country is going to hell and they're just sitting on their backsides.*

hell freezes over if something will not happen until hell freezes over, it will never happen ○ *'Tell them you'll get married when hell freezes over,' she says.*

hell hath no fury like a woman scorned said to mean that women often react to something which hurts or upsets them by behaving very angrily and viciously ○ *Faithless husbands who doubt that hell hath no fury like a woman scorned should read Tolleck Winner's novel 'Love With Vengeance' and beware.*

> This comes from William Congreve's 'The Mourning Bride' (1697): 'Heav'n has no rage, like love to hatred turn'd, Nor Hell a fury, like a woman scorn'd.'

hell on earth a place or a situation that is extremely unpleasant or that causes great suffering ○ *Organizing it all has been* hell on earth, but it's worked absolutely brilliantly.

★ **just for the hell of it** for fun or for no particular reason ○ *On the same street, David, aged 10, has been arrested for burglary. Another boy has been caught putting sugar in petrol tanks, just for the hell of it.*

★ **a living hell** a situation or a place that is extremely unpleasant or that causes great suffering. ○ *School is a living hell for some children.*

play hell or

play merry hell to cause trouble by behaving badly or to protest strongly or angrily about something ○ *She played merry hell and stormed out in a rage.*

play merry hell with something (British) or

play hell with something to have a bad effect on something or to cause great confusion ○ *Divorce and remarriage play hell with property and inheritance law.*

put someone through hell to give someone a very difficult or unpleasant time ○ *Her family say the girl has put them through hell since the incident.*

★ **raise hell**

1 to cause trouble by behaving badly in public, for example by making a lot of noise and breaking things or upsetting other people ○ *Are they the type that first thing they want to do is go out and raise hell, or are they here to play football?* ○ *He has had a reputation as a hell-raiser but claims to have now settled down.*

2 to protest strongly and angrily about a situation in order to persuade other people to correct it or improve it ○ *She came in and raised hell. Her son's sports bag was missing. It had everything in it – trainers, track suit, hundreds of pounds' worth.*

the road to hell is paved with good intentions said to mean that it is not enough for someone to make plans or promises, but they must also do those things ○ *The road to hell is paved with good intentions, and there are many, many pots of*

vitamin tablets which have been started but never finished.

> To pave a path or road means to cover it using flat stones called paving stones. The word 'pavement' is derived from this word. This expression was used by the writer Samuel Johnson and is mentioned in his biography in an entry dated 16 April 1775, in the form 'hell is paved with good intentions'. The idea is that good intentions do not guarantee a good outcome.

there'll be hell to pay said to warn someone that there will be serious trouble if a particular thing happens or if it does not happen ○ *If I try to get through the kitchen with these muddy boots, there'll be hell to pay. You know what she's like.*

to hell and back if someone has been to hell and back, they have had a terrible experience, although it is now finished ○ *We have been to hell and back but the love of this little boy has kept us going.*

herd

ride herd on someone (American) to supervise other people or their actions or watch them closely ○ *His departure would undermine state efforts to ride herd on the oil companies.*

> Originally, 'riding herd' involved patrolling on horseback around a herd of animals, in order to make sure none of them wandered away.

here

★ **neither here nor there** (spoken) completely unimportant or irrelevant, and not affecting a situation in any way ○ *'You know John doesn't believe in marriage, mum.' 'What John believes is neither here nor there.'*

herring

★ **a red herring** a piece of information, a suggestion, or an action that is irrelevant and, often deliberately, is taking people's attention away from the main subject or problem that they should be considering ○ *This is a total political red herring and an attempt to divert from the main issues in the campaign.*

A red herring is a herring that has been soaked in salt water for several days, and then dried by smoke. Red herrings were sometimes used when training dogs to follow a scent. They were also sometimes used to distract dogs from the scent they were following during a hunt.

hide

someone hasn't seen hide nor hair of someone said to mean that someone has not seen someone else, although they expected to ○ *They never found her. It was a bad business. The wrong she did, it's never left me, but I haven't seen hide nor hair of her since.*

A hide is the skin of an animal, especially the tough skin of a large animal.

be on a hiding to nothing (British) to have absolutely no chance of being successful at what you are trying to do ○ *A car manufacturer capable of making only 50,000 cars a year is on a hiding to nothing.*

A hiding is a flogging or beating, but the origin of this expression is unknown.

high

high as a kite very excited ○ *When I had finished the course I felt as high as a kite. But when my wife asked me what I had learnt I could not be specific.*

★ **leave someone high and dry** to leave someone in a difficult situation which they are unable to do anything about ○ *Schools with better reputations will be flooded with applications while poorer schools will be left high and dry.*

The image here is of a boat which is left on a beach after the tide has gone out.

★ **ride high** to be very popular or successful at the present time ○ *The elections came at a time when Labour was riding high, while support for the Conservatives had slumped.*

The image here is of a horse rider who sits very straight in their saddle and seems very proud and confident.

search high and low for something or **hunt high and low for something** to look for something very carefully and thoroughly, looking in every possible place that it could be ○ *I've hunted high and low for the photos, but I've moved since then and I can't find them.*

highway

highway robbery → see **robbery**

hill

★ **over the hill** no longer young, and too old to do a particular thing ○ *It's true some people regard you as probably over the hill at fifty.*

The image is of the top of a hill as the middle of life, so passing over the top of the hill leads downwards to old age and death.

hilt

★ **to the hilt** or **up to the hilt** used to emphasize that someone does something to the greatest possible extent ○ *He'll be a good candidate. We'll back him up to the hilt.*

The hilt of a sword or knife is its handle. The image here is of a knife or sword being pushed in all the way to the handle.

hip

joined at the hip if two people are joined at the hip, they are very close to each other emotionally and they spend a great deal of time together ○ *Though we often work together, we're not joined at the hip, so we see things differently.*

shoot from the hip or
fire from the hip to give your opinion or react to situations very quickly, without stopping to think it through properly ○ *She specifically declared that she did not shoot from the hip. She liked to think hard and long before taking decisions.*

> The image here is of a cowboy removing his gun from its holster and firing immediately, without raising it to take aim.

history

★ **be history** (*spoken*) to be no longer important, relevant, or interesting ○ *He sometimes wonders if he made the right choice when he decided to give up football. 'I might have made it in football, but that's all history now.'*

★ **the rest is history** said to mean that you do not need to say any more about an event because you are sure that everyone is familiar with what happened next ○ *A job with the company was advertised in The Daily Telegraph. I applied and the rest is history.*

hit

★ **hit and miss** done carelessly or without proper planning, so equally likely to fail or succeed ○ *The acting, however, is hit and miss: it ranges from the highly stylish to the appallingly gauche.*

★ **hit it off** if two people hit it off when they first meet, they find that they like each other or get on well together and have many things in common ○ *After their extended two hour talk yesterday, the two leaders actually seem to have hit it off.*

★ **a hit list**
   1 a group of people or things that someone intends to take action about, for example by punishing them or getting rid of them ○ *They published a hit list of countries guilty of unfair trade practices, and called for bilateral negotiations with the offending countries.*

   2 a list containing the names of important people who a terrorist or criminal organization intend to kill ○ *The letter, which said the family is on a hit list, has been passed to police for further investigation.*

make a hit if you make a hit with someone, they like you or are impressed by you when they meet you ○ *Eleanor and Sara made a hit with the whole delegation.*

Hobson

Hobson's choice (*mainly British*) a decision which forces you to choose between two things which are both bad, and so you cannot possibly be happy ○ *They want rid of him, he is irreplaceable. It really is Hobson's choice for them. Hell with him, or Hell without him.*

> This expression may refer to a man called Thomas Hobson, who earned money by hiring out horses at the end of the 16th century. He had a particular system for using each horse in turn, so a customer was given no choice, even if there were many horses available.

hog

> A hog is a pig.

go hog wild (*British*) to behave in an uncontrolled and excited way ○ *That doesn't mean you should go hog wild and double the recipe's sugar content. Just keep the word 'moderation' in mind.*

> Hogs can sometimes become uncontrolled and aggressive.

★ **go whole hog** (*American*) or
   go the whole hog to do something to the fullest extent possible ○ *Dixons sells a range of hi-fi speakers costing from £10.99 to £72.99. Or you can go the whole hog and buy a dedicated sound output system for £299.*

live high on the hog (*mainly American*) to have a good life, with plenty of money ○ *He and Austen were living high on the hog in a flat with three servants.*

hold

hold up your hands to admit something or confess that you have made a mistake or done something wrong ○ *If we had lost by big margins to better teams then we would hold up our hands and admit we're not good enough. But that's not the case.*

★ **put something on hold** to decide not to do, change, or deal with something now, but to leave it until later ○ *Some observers suggest that, as a result of this, he'll just put the project on hold until the political climate changes.*

This expression is probably from the term used when someone making a telephone call waits for the operator to connect them.

holds

★ **no-holds-barred** used for describing a way of behaving when people act very forcefully or enthusiastically, without paying attention to any limits that may exist ○ *At left-back, Jones became something of a cult figure with his no-holds-barred approach to the game.*

This expression refers to a wrestling match in which many of the usual rules do not apply, and so competitors can hold their opponent in any way they like.

hole

be in the hole (*American*) to owe money to someone else ○ *The Federal Housing Administration has just been discovered to be $4 billion in the hole.*

The 'hole' referred to here may have been a slot which was cut in the surface of a poker table in a gambling house. The money which the house charged was placed in the slot, and fell into a locked drawer. Gamblers who owed money to the house were said to be 'in the hole'.

blow a hole in something

1 to spoil something such as a plan or make it less effective ○ *If schools opted out of local authority control, would it blow a hole in the new system?*

2 to reduce an amount of money considerably ○ *A major natural disaster such as an earthquake or hurricane could blow a hole in the fund.*

burn a hole in your pocket if money is burning a hole in your pocket, you are very eager to spend it as soon as possible, especially on something you do not really need but would like to have ○ *Money always tends to burn a hole in my pocket.*

a hole card (*mainly American*) something that you keep secret or hidden until you are ready to use it to gain an advantage over other people ○ *The fact that I knew where she was and had in my possession a boxful of evidence were my only two remaining hole cards.*

In five card 'stud' poker, the 'hole' card is the only card which is dealt to you face down so that the other players cannot see it.

in a hole (*mainly British*) in a difficult or embarrassing situation ○ *The Tories are now in a dreadful hole after last Thursday's election results.*

someone needs something like a hole in the head said to mean that someone does not want something at all, and that it would only add to the problems that they already have ○ *We need an interest rate rise like we need a hole in the head.*

This is said to be a translation of a Yiddish expression. It became more widely known following the play 'A Hole in the Head' (1957) by Arnold Schulman, and a film of the same name starring Frank Sinatra (1959).

holes

pick holes in something to find weak points in something such as an argument or theory which show that it is wrong ○ *They say that the great science of the 21st century will be biology. Thus we do not need so many physicists as in the past. It is easy to pick holes in this argument.*

something has more holes than Swiss cheese (*mainly American*) said to mean that something, such as an argument or theory, has so many flaws that it cannot be taken seriously ○ *'The current laws,' he says, 'have more holes than Swiss cheese.'*

≡ 'Swiss cheese' is an American term for cheese such as Emmenthal, which has round holes in it.

hollow

beat someone hollow (*British*) to defeat someone completely ○ *Waterman was the first independent operator to take on the big boys at the pop game and beat them hollow.*

★ **ring hollow** if a statement or promise rings hollow, it seems false, or insincere ○ *Details of his 27-year affair have been revealed to all. His speeches on family values and the stability of marriage ring hollow now.*

≡ The idea is of an object that is meant to be solid making a loud noise when struck, indicating that it is weaker or cheaper than it was believed to be.

holy

the holy of holies something that people think is the most special or important thing of its kind ○ *Last year, his work was performed for the first time at the Aldeburgh Festival, the holy of holies in the contemporary British music scene.*

≡ In a Jewish synagogue, the holy of holies is the inner room which only the chief rabbi may enter.

home

★ **at home**

1 if you feel at home in a particular situation, you feel relaxed, comfortable,

and happy ○ *Melanie is equally at home singing oratorio, spirituals, jazz or performing in musical theatre.*

2 if someone or something looks at home somewhere, they look as if it is normal, natural, or appropriate for them to be there ○ *The 16-year-old's huge shoulder and arm muscles would look more at home on a male hammer thrower.*

★ **be home and dry** (*mainly British*) or **be home and hosed** (*mainly Australian*) to have achieved victory or success in a contest or other activity, or to be certain to achieve it ○ *There are still three weeks to polling day and the Labour candidate is not yet home and dry.*

≡ These expressions may refer to a long-distance runner who wins comfortably and has already washed by the time the others reach the finishing line.

be nothing to write home about to be not very interesting, exciting, or special ○ *Yes, there is cheese, bread and meat in the local market and shops, but it's nothing to write home about.*

★ **be on home ground** to feel confident and secure because you are in the area where you work or live, or are doing something that is very familiar to you ○ *This is a play where Godber is on home ground, writing about the mining communities of his childhood.*

bring home the bacon

1 to be the person in a family who goes out to work and earns enough money for the family to live on ○ *The question 'Who brings up the baby and who brings home the bacon?' has become one of the most important of all political questions.*

2 (*journalism*) to win or do very well in sport ○ *But Reid and Duffield showed that, given the right horsepower, they are capable of bringing home the bacon in style.*

★ **bring something home to someone** to make someone fully aware of how serious or important something such as a problem, danger, or situation is ○ *This new TV advert really brings home to people how badly some children are treated.*

close to home if a remark is close to home, it makes people feel uncomfortable or upset because it is about a sensitive or very personal subject ○ *The message the film conveyed struck so hard and so close to home that it moved me to tears.*

★ **hit home** or
strike home if a situation or what someone says hits home or strikes home, people realize that it is real or true, even though it may be painful for them to accept it ○ *In many cases the reality of war doesn't hit home with reservists until they're actually called upon to fight.*

hit a home run (American) to do something that is very successful ○ *Bartlett Giamatti hits a home run here with his memoir of encounters with W.H. Auden over many years.*

≡ In baseball, when a batter hits a home run, they hit the ball a very long way, so that they are able to run round all the bases and score a run before the other team gets the ball back.

the home stretch or
the home straight the last part or stage of a long or difficult activity ○ *This month, Wales take on the Czech Republic in the home straight of the qualifying competition.*

≡ The home stretch or home straight is the final part of a horse race.

★ **make yourself at home** to relax and feel comfortable somewhere as if you were in your own home or in a very familiar situation ○ *Arnold and Gwen had found the hidden key, let themselves in and made themselves at home.* ○ *'Sit down,' Anne said. 'Make yourself at home.'*

honest

honest as the day is long (old-fashioned) very honest ○ *This boy's hard-working, ambitious, smart, and honest as the day is long. They don't come any better than Russell here.*

hoof

★ **do something on the hoof**
1 (British) to do something in response to things that happen, rather than as part of a carefully considered plan ○ *They expressed their disquiet at the disarray over the government's handling of its economic policy and their fears that policy was being made on the hoof.*
2 to do something while you are doing something else, or without stopping to sit down ○ *We know the character: his shirt is always undone, he is rude, consumes junk food on the hoof and is always complaining.*

≡ To do something 'on the hoof' literally means to do it while on horseback without stopping to get off.

hook

do something by hook or by crook to do something even if it is very difficult for you, or you have to use dishonest means ○ *If a man took Antonia's fancy, she would go out of her way to get him by hook or by crook.*

≡ The hook in this expression is a billhook, which is a cutting tool with a hooked blade. A shepherd's crook is a long stick with a curve at the top. This expression may refer to a medieval law which allowed ordinary people to collect firewood from forests belonging to the King or a lord, so long as they took only dead wood which they could reach with crooks and billhooks.

★ **get off the hook** to manage to get out of the awkward situation you are in without being punished or blamed ○ *We cannot let the government get off the hook for what it has done.*

hook, line, and sinker very intensely,

deeply, or fully ○ *I fell for her hook, line and sinker.*

> When fish are caught, they sometimes swallow part of the fishing line and the 'sinker' or weight, as well as the hook.

on your own hook (*American*) alone, without any help ○ *St. Mary's Hospital does not meet incoming flights with its own vehicle. Patients come on their own hook.*

> The reference here is to someone catching a fish using their own equipment and without help from others.

ring off the hook (*mainly American*) if your telephone is ringing off the hook, so many people are trying to call you that it is ringing all the time ○ *His phone started ringing off the hook as banks and financial institutions begged for his help.*

sling your hook (*British*) to go away ○ *The team is entering a new era and if Richardson doesn't want to be part of it then he should sling his hook.*

> The 'hook' in this expression may be a ship's anchor, which had to be taken up and tied up with ropes or chains, which were called a sling, before the ship could move on.

swallow something hook, line, and sinker to be fooled into believing something completely and being deceived by it ○ *Our president is one heck of a salesman, and people are just swallowing this thing hook, line, and sinker, without knowing what it's all about.*

hooks

get your hooks into someone to control or influence someone very strongly, often in a way that is not good for them ○ *The big industries like to get their hooks into the bright young people, to subsidize them through their education and then reap the benefit.*

hoops

make someone jump through hoops or

make someone go through the hoops to make someone prove their ability and willingness to obtain something that they want by forcing them to do a lot of difficult things first ○ *The academic staff still wanted the rigour so they basically put a four-year course into three years and made us jump through hoops.*

> Circus animals are sometimes trained to jump through hoops which are hung or held above the ground and sometimes set on fire.

hoot

not give a hoot or

not give two hoots to not care about something or someone at all ○ *I'm really disgusted with our politicians. They don't give two hoots about their constituents.*

hop

★ **be caught on the hop** (*British*) to be unprepared for something that happens and so be unable to respond quickly or appropriately ○ *In both cases the West was caught on the hop when a brutal dictator decided that it was safe to use force to resolve a long-standing territorial dispute.*

hopping mad extremely angry ○ *Apparently, the family is hopping mad that she left them nothing in her will.*

a hop, skip, and a jump if one thing is only a hop, skip, and a jump away from another, they are very close together or very closely linked ○ *Of course, the Romanian language is just a hop, skip, and a jump from Italian.*

horizon

★ **on the horizon** almost certainly going to happen or be done quite soon ○ *With breast cancer, as with many common diseases, there is no obvious breakthrough on the horizon.*

horn

blow your own horn (American) to boast about yourself. The British expression is **blow your own trumpet**. ○ Maybe I am a superstar right now, but I don't go around blowing my own horn; this is a game which kicks you right back in the face.

> In the past, the arrival of important people in a place was announced by the playing of trumpets.

hornet

stir up a hornet's nest to do something which causes a lot of controversy or produces a situation which is extremely difficult to deal with ○ According to my brother Paul, this Lonnie Norton was asking a lot of questions and stirring up a hornet's nest around town.

> A hornet is a large wasp with a powerful sting.

horns

lock horns to argue or fight with someone ○ During his six years in office, Seidman has often locked horns with lawmakers as well as the administration.

> The reference here is to two male animals, such as deer, fighting over a female and getting their horns caught together or 'locked'.

on the horns of a dilemma having to choose between two or more alternatives, which seem to be equally good or equally bad ○ I was often caught on the horns of a dilemma. Do I work late in the air-conditioned cool darkness of the office, or retreat to the cafe for a cold lemonade?

> In logic, a dilemma is a situation where an argument leads to two choices which are both undesirable. In the Middle Ages, a dilemma was traditionally represented as an animal with two horns such as a bull.

pull in your horns or
draw in your horns to start behaving more cautiously than you did before, especially by spending less money ○ The world's big spenders have pulled in their horns during the recession and the top designers have felt the pinch.

> When snails sense danger, they pull in their 'horns', which are the stalks that their eyes are on.

horse

back the wrong horse to support the wrong person, for example the loser in a contest or election ○ We think they're backing the wrong horse if they support the Mengistu government.

come down off your high horse or
get down off your high horse to stop acting in a superior way ○ It is time for the intellectuals to get down off their high horses and to really take the struggle into the ghettoes.

> In the past, very large horses were a sign of high rank because they were owned and ridden only by knights.

eat like a horse to eat a lot because you have a large appetite ○ When Kelly is on medication, he eats like a horse and when he is off, he has almost no appetite at all.

flog a dead horse (British) or
beat a dead horse (American) to waste your time trying to achieve something that cannot be done ○ They're exhausted. You're flogging a dead horse. You have some talented boys but they're playing like run-down machines.

from the horse's mouth if a piece of information comes from the horse's mouth, it comes directly from the person who knows best or knows most about it, and so you are sure it is true ○ Most of the book is completely true; it comes from the horse's mouth.

> This expression may refer to the fact that you can tell a horse's age by looking at its teeth. Alternatively, it may simply refer to a racing tip which

is so reliable that it is as if the horse itself has told you how well it is going to perform.

get on your high horse to behave as if you are better than other people, and refuse to accept any criticism of yourself ○ *When Kuwait was occupied, President Bush and Prime Minister John Major lost no time in getting on their high horses.*

a one-horse race *(mainly British)* a contest in which it is obvious even before it starts that one person or team is much better than the others and will win ○ *Marseille are threatening to turn the French championship into a one-horse race.*

a one-horse town a town that is very small and uninteresting ○ *Lumut is something of a one-horse town, but you can always take a boat across to Pangkor island and look at Dutch ruins.*

★ **someone is a dark horse** said to mean that very little is known about someone, although they may have recently had success or may be about to have success ○ *To many people, Atkinson is a dark horse who worked away for many years behind the scenes at British Airways.*

This expression may refer to a horse which people do not know very much about, so that it is difficult to predict how well it will do in a race.

a stalking horse
1 something that is being used to obtain a temporary advantage so that someone can get what they really want at a later date. This expression is usually used to show disapproval. ○ *The development will act as a stalking horse for further exploitation of the surrounding countryside.*
2 someone in politics who stands against the leader of a party to test the strength of any opposition to them. They then withdraw in favour of a stronger challenger, if it looks likely that the leader can be defeated. ○ *There was even talk of*

one of them putting up for the leadership as a 'stalking horse' for the real contender.

Stalking horses were horses that were used by hunters. They were trained to allow their rider to hide behind them, and so get closer to the birds they were hunting.

★ **a Trojan horse** a policy or activity that seems harmless, but is likely to damage or destroy something important ○ *The Chancellor did not tax child benefit, but he has created a Trojan Horse enabling him to tax this benefit in the future.*

This refers to an ancient Greek story. The city of Troy was under siege from the Greeks. The Greeks built a large hollow wooden horse and left it secretly as a gift for the Trojans, who took it into the city. However, Greek soldiers were hiding inside the horse, and they were able to cause the destruction of the city.

you can lead a horse to water but you can't make it drink said to mean that you can give someone the opportunity to do something, but you cannot force them to do it if they do not want to ○ *You can't educate kids who aren't interested. You can lead a horse to water but you can't make it drink.*

horses

change horses in midstream to stop using one system and start using another one, or to stop supporting one person and start supporting someone else. ○ *I think we were very wise not to change horses in midstream.*

The American President Abraham Lincoln used this expression in 1864, 'I am reminded of the story of an old Dutch farmer, who remarked to a companion that it was best not to swap horses when crossing streams.'

hold your horses *(spoken)* said to tell someone to wait, slow down, or stop for a moment, often when you think that they are going to do something silly ○ *Hold your horses a minute, will you, and just take another look at this badge.*

horses for courses *(British)* said to mean that different people are suitable for different things or kinds of situation, and this ought to be taken into account when making choices in particular cases ○ *We know the selection for the matches will be a case of horses for courses, and so, like anyone else, I'll just be happy to be playing, whatever position.*

≣ Some horses are especially suited to particular kinds of races or conditions.

ride two horses at the same time or **ride two horses at once** *(British, journalism)* to try to follow two conflicting sets of ideas at the same time ○ *He is not doing his popular appeal much good by continuing to ride two horses at the same time.*

wild horses wouldn't make someone do something said to mean that someone will not do something even if other people try to force them to ○ *Wild horses wouldn't make Nicola sell the yard if she found out it would make me rich.*

hostage

a hostage to fortune *(mainly British)* someone who cannot control how a situation develops, and so has to accept any bad things that happen ○ *Charles, then nearly 33, had already made himself a hostage to fortune by declaring that 30 was a suitable age to settle down.*

≣ This expression comes from an essay by Francis Bacon, 'Of Marriage and Single Life' (1625): 'He that hath wife and children hath given hostages to fortune.'

hot

hot and bothered very upset or worried about something ○ *Sir Terence was astonished that everybody had got so hot and bothered about the affair.*

hot and cold *(British)* extremely worried or nervous, so that you feel as if your body is both hot and cold at the same time ○ *When she realized what she was reading she grew hot and cold all over.*

someone blows hot and cold

1 said to mean that someone's attitude to something keeps changing, so that sometimes they seem enthusiastic or interested, and sometimes they do not ○ *The media, meanwhile, has blown hot and cold on the affair.*

2 said to mean that sometimes someone's work or performance is good, and sometimes it is not ○ *They seem to have blown hot and cold in their early matches.*

too hot to handle if someone or something is too hot to handle, you mean that they are so dangerous, difficult, or extreme that people do not want to be involved with them ○ *Even for someone of Mr Hurd's skill and experience, the situation proved too hot to handle.*

hot cakes

sell like hotcakes *(mainly American)* or **sell like hot cakes** or **go like hot cakes** to be very popular and sell in large numbers very quickly ○ *Their jam was selling like hot cakes.*

≣ 'Hotcakes' is the usual form in American English, and it is also occasionally used in British English. In American English, 'hotcakes' are pancakes, while in British English 'hot cakes' are cakes which have just been baked.

hour

★ **at the eleventh hour** very late or at the last possible moment ○ *The concert, scheduled for last Saturday, was cancelled at the eleventh hour, after the star Peter Gabriel pulled out on Thursday.* ○ *The eleventh hour decision came as the President made it clear he was prepared to gamble his political career if it came to conflict.*

In the Bible, Jesus uses this expression in the story of the labourers in the vineyard (Matthew 20:1-16). In Jesus's time the hours were counted from dawn until dusk, with the twelfth hour bringing darkness, and so the eleventh hour was the last hour before dark.

hours

at all hours at any time of the day or night ○ *In Hollywood, you can shop at all hours, and get almost anything you want.*

house

bring the house down if a person or their performance brings the house down, the audience claps and cheers loudly for a long time because they liked the performance so much ○ *We had just one rehearsal and I was petrified but, as Lenny predicted, the sketch brought the house down.*

In this expression, the 'house' means a theatre.

eat someone out of house and home to eat so much food that it costs someone a lot of money to feed you ○ *They eat everybody out of house and home but nobody minds because they provide such first-rate entertainment.*

This expression was used in Shakespeare's play 'Henry IV Part II', act 2 scene 1 (1597). When asked why she wants her lodger Sir John Falstaff arrested, the landlady Mistress Quickly replies: 'He hath eaten me out of house and home; he hath put all my substance into that fat belly of his.'

get on like a house on fire if two people get on like a house on fire, they quickly become close friends, for example because they have similar interests ○ *I went over and struck up a conversation, and we got on like a house on fire.*

This expression suggests suddenness and intensity, like an old wooden house with a thatched or straw roof that would catch fire and burn easily and quickly.

a halfway house (British) a compromise between two things, or a combination of two things ○ *A halfway house between the theatre and cinema is possible.*

A halfway house was an inn located halfway between two neighbouring towns or villages and would have been used by coach passengers in former times. The name is still seen on signs for pubs and inns.

★ **a house of cards** a system, organization, or plan that is likely to fail or collapse ○ *This government could fall apart like a house of cards during the first policy discussion.*

This refers to the building of an elaborate but unstable pyramid structure using playing cards.

★ **put your house in order** or **get your house in order** to make sure that all your affairs are arranged properly and there is nothing wrong with them ○ *The government gives the newspaper industry a twelve-month deadline to put its house in order or face tough statutory controls.*

someone would not give someone or something house room (British) said when someone strongly dislikes or disapproves of someone or something and wants to have nothing to do with them ○ *I feel that some of the paintings that people pay thousands of pounds for are absolute rubbish. I wouldn't give them house room.*

houses

round the houses (British) if someone is going round the houses, they keep talking about unimportant things, rather than concentrating on what they are supposed to be discussing ○ *Although in many cases we talk round the houses, we get to the important issues as well.*

hue

a hue and cry a loud protest about something or opposition to it ○ *There probably will be a hue and cry about my suggestion of more power to the police.*

Until the 19th century, 'hue and cry' was the legal name for the cries of someone who had been robbed and who was calling for others to help. It was an offence for anyone to refuse to join the chase, once they heard the cry. 'Hue' comes from the Old French 'huer', meaning 'to shout'.

huff

★ **in a huff** behaving in an irritable, bad-tempered, and childish way, because you could not get something you wanted ○ *He stormed off in a huff because he didn't win.*

hump

get the hump (British) to get annoyed or irritated by something ○ *Dad used to coach me in the back garden when I was about 10, but he tried to drum too much into me and I used to get the hump with him.*

over the hump past the worst part of an unpleasant or difficult situation ○ *I think we're basically over the hump in this instance. We've got an economy now that's likely to grow.*

i

dot the i's and cross the t's to add the final minor details to a piece of work, plan or arrangement ○ *Unless all the i's are dotted and the t's are crossed, a contract is not likely to be valid.*

In old-fashioned styles of handwriting, you write a word with one movement of your pen, and then go back and add the dot to any i's and the cross-stroke to any t's.

ice

★ **break the ice** to say or do something to make people feel relaxed and comfortable at a party or a meeting ○ *Break the ice with tea or coffee and get to know your client a little better.*

This refers to the need to break the ice around a ship before it is able to sail.

★ **put something on ice** to postpone something ○ *Plans have been put on ice for a meeting in London of the five permanent members of the United Nations Security Council.*

This expression refers to the use of ice to preserve food and prevent it from decaying.

★ **skate on thin ice** to get into a difficult situation which may have serious or unpleasant consequences ○ *All through my career I had skated on thin ice and somehow had, so far, got away with it.*

★ **something cuts no ice** said to mean that something does not impress you ○ *Flying is dreadful. Statistics cut no ice with anyone scared of going up in the air in a plane.*

This expression refers to ice-skating. In order for the skater to move easily, the blades must be sharp so that they cut into the ice.

icing

★ **the icing on the cake** an extra good thing that happens and makes a situation or activity even better. In American English, you can also talk about **the frosting on the cake**. ○ *I was proud to be a member of the Mercedes-Benz Grand Prix team, but to drive their fantastic sports cars as well really was the icing on the cake.*

inch

come within an inch of doing something to very nearly do something ○ *A driver who comes within an inch of smashing into a tree will nonetheless claim that there is nothing wrong with his eyesight.*

give someone an inch and they'll take a mile said to mean that if you do a small favour for someone, they will become greedy and ask you to do bigger and bigger favours for them and make you regret doing the first favour ○ *Be tough and uncompromising – if you give colleagues an inch, they will take a mile.*

to within an inch of your life very severely ○ *His fists were clenched as if he were going to beat Smythe to within an inch of his life.*

information

too much information (*informal*) said to mean that you do not want to hear any more about something, because it is private or embarrassing ○ *'I've been to the toilet twice already.' 'Too much information!'*

ink

bleed red ink (*journalism*) to have severe financial problems ○ *Even large companies are bleeding red ink. But they are quickly closing plants and axing thousands of jobs to boost performance.*

> This expression comes from the practice in the past of using red ink to fill in entries on the debit side of a book of accounts.

innings

> An innings is a period in a game of cricket during which a particular team or player is batting.

have a good innings (*British, old-fashioned*)
1 to be successful for a long time ○ *His career ended when his horse fell and he was left with permanent loss of vision in his left eye. 'I had a good innings,' he says.*
2 to live for a long time and have a good life ○ *He himself had had a good innings, he said, but he was sorry for younger victims in desolate circumstances.*

ins

★ **the ins and outs** all the complicated details or facts about a situation or system ○ *There are many helpful books now available written by cookery and dietary experts who can advise on the ins and outs of dieting in great detail.*

insult

★ **add insult to injury** to make a bad situation worse by doing something that upsets or harms someone, after you have already done something bad to them ○ *The Council of State opposed the president's suggestion and added insult to injury by leaking its hostile and secret comments to the press.*

iron

cast iron or
cast-iron (*British*) absolutely certain and to be believed ○ *Even if one could visualize her as a murderer, she has a cast-iron alibi.*

strike while the iron is hot to act immediately, while you have the best chance of succeeding at something ○ *This is the week to get plans off the ground. It's time to strike while the iron is hot.*

> A blacksmith can only bend or work iron when it is hot.

★ **with an iron fist** with great force and often violence ○ *The Generals have ruled the nation with an iron fist for more than half of its independent existence.*

irons

have a lot of irons in the fire to be involved in several different activities or have several different plans at the same time, so that it is likely that something will succeed even if other things fail ○ *'I will be earning a lot more money,' he says, declining to say how much more. 'I also have a number of other irons in the fire.'*

ivory

★ **someone lives in an ivory tower** said to mean that someone's lifestyle or their work prevents them from experiencing the problems experienced by ordinary people, and so they remain generally unaware of these problems ○ *They're all out of touch – they live up in a little ivory tower, and they don't see what's going on down here.*

> This is a translation of a French expression 'tour d'ivoire', which was used by the critic Saint-Beuve to describe the way in which the writer Alfred de Vigny isolated himself from the rest of society.

Jj

jack

a jack-of-all-trades

1 someone who has many different skills ○ *He soon caught the theatre bug, and became a jack-of-all-trades at the local amateur theatre.*

2 someone who can do a lot of different things but who is not very good at doing any of them ○ *His critics sometimes described him as a jack-of-all-trades.*

> The name Jack was used to refer to any man or workman.

Jack

★ before you could say Jack Robinson

said to mean that something happened very suddenly and quickly ○ *The pair of them were out of the door and down the steps before you could say Jack Robinson.*

> The identity of Jack Robinson is unknown and the name might have become popular because both elements were once extremely common. The phrase appears in the novel 'Evelina' (1778) by Fanny Burnley: 'I'll do it as soon as say Jack Robinson'.

jackpot

★ hit the jackpot

1 to suddenly be very successful and earn a lot of money ○ *The National Theatre hit the jackpot with its first musical, Guys And Dolls.*

2 to suddenly succeed in getting or finding something that you have been trying to get or find ○ *I went through all the people called Lasalles in the Sydney phone book until I hit the jackpot.*

> This expression was originally used in poker. A 'jackpot' was a sum of money which increased until someone could start the betting with a pair of jacks or higher.

jail

★ get out of jail

(British, journalism) to narrowly succeed in avoiding defeat or a difficult situation ○ *Chelsea got out of jail because Everton made the fundamental mistake of trying to defend a one-goal lead.*

> This expression comes from the game 'Monopoly', where players can use a special card in order to leave jail early.

jam

jam tomorrow

(mainly British) said to mean that people are being promised that they will have something in the future, although they cannot have it now ○ *The City simply does not believe it. It has been promised jam tomorrow too many times before by the company.*

> This expression comes from the children's story 'Through the Looking Glass', by Lewis Carroll, where the Red Queen says, 'The rule is jam tomorrow and jam yesterday, but never jam today.' As Alice points out, this means that nobody will ever get any jam.

Jell-O

like trying to nail Jell-O to the wall

(American) extremely difficult or impossible. **Jell-O** is a trademark. ○ *Right now, it's just about like trying to nail five pounds of Jell-O to the wall.*

> Jell-O is a dessert that resembles ready-made jelly. This expression was first used by the American President

Theodore Roosevelt in a letter to William Roscoe Thayer in 1915. He was describing the difficulty of negotiating with Colombia over the Panama Canal.

jewel

★ **the jewel in someone's crown** the best thing that someone has, or the achievement that they can be most proud of ○ *His achievement is astonishing and this book is the jewel in his crown.*

This expression was known in Victorian times, but is probably most well known as the title of a novel by Paul Scott, published in 1966, that formed part of a series set in the Raj, or Victorian India. In this title, India is seen as the 'jewel', and the 'crown' is the British Empire.

job

do a job on someone (*informal*) to defeat or harm someone in some way ○ *Coetzer is a difficult opponent. But I'm equally sure I can do a job on him.*

a full-time job a task that takes a great deal of time and effort ○ *Maintaining a happy home in which a family can thrive is a full-time job, and for many women it becomes their career for life.*

jobs

jobs for the boys (*British*) a situation where well-paid or important jobs in a particular organization are given to people who are the friends, relatives or supporters of someone in that organization, rather than to the people who are best qualified to do the jobs ○ *The council has faced a string of allegations over 'jobs for the boys'.*

Johnny

Johnny-come-lately a person who becomes involved in an activity or organization after it has already started, and who is therefore less reliable or experienced than the people who have been involved since the beginning ○ *The basic trouble was that, in the eyes of the left, Benn was always something of a Johnny-come-lately.*

This name used to be given to new or inexperienced sailors in the American navy.

joker

the joker in the pack (*mainly British*) someone or something that is different from the other things or people in a situation and does not seem to fit in, or may cause problems ○ *Ray enjoys long walks and the occasional game of golf. He is probably best known as the quiet one who is the joker in the pack.*

The joker in a pack of playing cards is the card which does not belong to any of the four suits.

Joneses

keep up with the Joneses to try to have or do the same things as other people that you know, even if you do not really have enough money to do this, or are not really interested in these things ○ *Her mother was very keen on keeping up with the Joneses, and through much of her teens Linda accepted what she now calls 'these false values'.*

This expression comes from the title of a comic strip by Arthur Momand, which was first published in the New York 'Globe' in 1913.

judgment

'Judgment' is often spelled 'judgement' in British English.

sit in judgment to criticize other people ○ *I think people should work hard to keep a marriage alive. I don't want to sit in judgment on other people, but if there's anything that's good, try to hold on to it.*

jugular

★ **go for the jugular** to attack an opponent or enemy very decisively at the point where you can cause the greatest damage ○ *If England go for the jugular in tonight's game, we won't have to worry about scraping a draw.*

> The jugular vein is a large vein in the neck and supplies blood to the neck and face.

jump

★ **get a jump on someone** (*mainly American*) to do something before someone else does and so gain an advantage over them ○ *This year, many stores did try to get a jump on the shopping season by holding promotional sales even before Thanksgiving.*

> This expression refers to a competitor in a running race leaving the starting blocks ahead of the other competitors.

★ **jump up and down** to be very excited, angry or upset about something ○ *He is not someone who jumps up and down. He is a man of quiet determination and firm principles.*

someone is for the high jump (*British*) said to mean that it is certain that someone will be punished for something they have done wrong ○ *God help anyone who was sneaking a cup of tea when they shouldn't have been. They'll be for the high jump.*

> This expression may refer to criminals in the past being sentenced to death by hanging.

take a running jump (*mainly British*) to mind your own business and not interfere ○ *'My dad reckons your stories are all made up.' 'Well you can tell your dad to take a running jump because we don't make up the letters – ever.'*

jury

★ **the jury is still out** said to mean that people have not yet formed an opinion about something or reached a decision ○ *The jury's still out on what are the long-term effects of air pollution.*

> This refers to the time when the jury in a court case retires from the court room to decide on a verdict.

kangaroos

have kangaroos in your top paddock (mainly Australian, informal) to have strange ideas or be crazy ○ *Some attribute my attitude to having a few kangaroos loose in the top paddock.*

> A paddock is a small field next to a farm or stable. The idea is that wild animals have displaced the farm animals.

keel

★ **on an even keel** calm or progressing steadily, especially during or after a period of troubles or difficulties ○ *She sees it as her role to keep the family on an even keel through its time of hardship.*

> The image here is of a ship moving along smoothly and steadily, because it is balanced and not leaning to either side.

keen

keen as mustard (mainly British, old-fashioned) very eager or alert ○ *I have an adult pupil who scored very low in assessments but is keen as mustard.*

> 'Keen' means enthusiastic, but also used to mean sharp when referring to the blade or cutting edge of a tool or weapon. An acidic or sour taste can also be referred to as sharp, so enthusiasm is being likened to the sharp taste or 'edge' given to food by mustard.

keep

something earns its keep said to mean that something is good value and justifies the amount of money that it costs or the space that it takes up ○ *In Bob's garden everything must earn its keep, with fruits and vegetables given priority over flowers.*

keeper

I am not someone's keeper said to mean that you do not know where someone is and that you cannot be expected to know ○ *'I don't know where he is,' Hughes replied, 'I'm not his keeper.' 'No, simply his employer.'*

not your brother's keeper not responsible for other people in any way ○ *Part of me wants to help him, but part of me realizes I can't be my brother's keeper.*

> These expressions come from a story in the Bible (Genesis 4:9). Cain has killed his brother, Abel, but he tries to deny it. When he is asked where his brother is, he replies, 'I know not: Am I my brother's keeper?'

ken

something is beyond your ken said to mean that you do not have much knowledge, understanding or experience of something ○ *The subject matter is beyond the ken of the average layman.*

> 'Ken' here means the full range of someone's knowledge or understanding. The Scottish verb 'ken' means 'know'.

kettle

★ **a different kettle of fish** something that is completely unlike another thing that you have mentioned ○ *Artistic integrity? Who needs it? Money? Now that's a completely different kettle of fish.*

kibosh

put the kibosh on something to prevent something from happening, continuing or being successful ○ *The company gave its subscribers access to software that puts the kibosh on pop-up ads if a user doesn't want them.*

≣ The origin of this expression is uncertain, but some people think that 'kibosh' may come from Yiddish.

kick

kick someone upstairs ➜ see **upstairs**

kick someone when they are down to hurt, upset or criticize someone when they are already in a weak position or at a disadvantage ○ *It (expulsion) would be regarded by many people, including many in the party, as going too far in kicking a man when he's down.*

kick-off

for a kick-off said to mean that you are mentioning just one of many things, points or reasons ○ *Is it not in fact the opinion of the public that most dentists earn far too much for a kick-off?*

≣ The kick-off is the beginning of a football match.

kid

like a kid in a candy store *(mainly American)* enjoying yourself far too much and not controlling your behaviour in any way. The usual British expression is **like a child in a sweet shop**. ○ *A money manager in Chicago, he went on a buying binge and 'felt like a kid in a candy store,' he recalls.*

treat someone with kid gloves to treat someone very carefully, for example because they are very important or because they are easily upset ○ *Mr Sarbutts was treated as a VIP. Everybody was treating him with kid gloves.*

≣ Kid is very soft leather.

kill

in at the kill *(British)* present and either watching or taking part when a contest or struggle comes to an end and one side is completely defeated ○ *Burns was one of the happiest men at the finish. He was in at the kill 106 miles and four-and-a-quarter hours after the start of the race.*

★ **move in for the kill** to act decisively to defeat your enemy or opponent ○ *Nick and I appeared almost unstoppable and we moved in for the kill.*

killing

★ **make a killing** to make a large profit very quickly and easily ○ *The boss of Britain's top pizza concern made a killing on the market yesterday by selling off most of his shares.*

kindness

kill someone with kindness to treat someone very kindly even though this is not what they need or want ○ *'He is killing me with kindness,' Sallie says. 'He's just too attentive.'*

king

a king's ransom *(mainly British)* a very large sum of money ○ *Roberts is asking a king's ransom for her next film role.*

live like a king to have a luxurious and very comfortable lifestyle ○ *Company executives lived like kings. The top thirty-one executives were paid a total of 14.2 million dollars, or an average of 458,000 dollars.*

kingdom

blow someone to kingdom come to destroy someone, especially in a very violent way ○ *One false move could blow us all to kingdom come.*

≣ This comes from the line 'Thy kingdom come' in the Lord's Prayer in the Bible. (Matthew 6:10)

kiss

kiss and make up to sort out a disagreement and end a conflict ○ *They argue constantly and publicly but always manage to kiss and make up.*

★ **kiss-and-tell** referring to the public story someone tells after they have had a love affair with a famous person ○ *On many occasions we discussed selling details of kiss-and-tell stories.*

▤ This expression appears in the play 'Love for Love' by William Congreve (1695): 'Oh, fie, Miss, you must not kiss and tell'.

★ **the kiss of death** something that is certain to cause failure or ruin ○ *Relying on clichés is the kiss of death for a decent writer.*

▤ This expression refers to the Bible story of how Judas betrayed Jesus by kissing him. This identified Jesus to the Romans, and led to his arrest and crucifixion.

kit
the whole kit and caboodle → see **caboodle**

kitchen
everything but the kitchen sink very many things, many of which are unnecessary ○ *When she goes on a picnic, she always wants to take everything but the kitchen sink.*

kite
fly a kite (*mainly British*) to suggest ideas or possibilities in order to see how people react to them before deciding whether or not to put them into practice ○ *The committee has paid a good deal of attention to what might be politically possible. It is consciously flying a kite.*

kittens
have kittens (*mainly British*) to be extremely worried or upset by something ○ *The boss will have kittens if I don't get that dress back inside the hour.*

▤ In the Middle Ages it was said that if a pregnant woman was having stomach pains she had kittens clawing inside her womb.

knee
knee-high to a grasshopper (*old-fashioned*) very young ○ *I've lived here since I was knee-high to a grasshopper.*

knees
be on your knees to be extremely weak or tired ○ *Several times this afternoon he had sounded as if he were on his knees.*

★ **bring something to its knees** to cause a country or organization to be in an extremely weak condition ○ *Britain was brought to its knees after a wave of paralysing strikes.*

go down on your knees to beg desperately for something ○ *They won't take the manager back, even if he gets down on his knees and apologises.*

knell
★ **sound the death knell** to be likely to cause the end or failure of an activity or organization ○ *The announcement that the mine would close in March with the loss of more than 980 jobs sounded the death knell for the village.*

▤ A death knell is the ringing of a church bell at a funeral or to announce someone's death.

knickers
get your knickers in a twist (*British, informal*) to become extremely upset or worried about something ○ *Let's not get our knickers in a twist until we see the outcome of those games.*

knife
like a knife through butter quickly and without any problems ○ *Think about the women who have gone through life like a knife through butter, slicing through every kind of setback and discouragement.*

★ **on a knife-edge** (*mainly British*) in a situation in which nobody knows what is going to happen next ○ *Our finances are on a knife-edge at the moment.*

stick the knife in to deliberately do or

say things which will upset another person or cause problems for them ○ *Her colleagues, often eager to stick the knife in, defended her yesterday.*

twist the knife to deliberately do or say things which make a situation even worse for someone who is already upset or experiencing problems ○ *Jones then twisted the knife with another goal.*

knight

> 'Armour' is spelled 'armor' in American English.

a knight in shining armour a man who rescues you from a difficult situation ○ *I just felt dizzy and then I collapsed. I am very, very grateful to Tom and I always will be – he really was my knight in shining armour.*

≡ In stories written or set in the Middle Ages, a knight in shining armour traditionally came to the rescue of a 'damsel (or young woman) in distress'.

knitting

stick to your knitting to continue to do something that you are experienced at and not try to do something which you know very little about ○ *It failed because we did not understand the plumbing business, and it taught us a lesson about sticking to our knitting!*

knives

★ **the knives are out** (*mainly British*) said to mean that people are feeling very angry or resentful towards someone, and are trying to cause problems for them ○ *His book has hit the shops and the knives are out.*

knock

knock someone sideways (*British*) to make someone feel amazed, confused or very upset ○ *Something like this, a huge shock, completely knocks you sideways.*

knock something sideways (*British*) to severely damage something so that it

may not recover ○ *Confidence in the British legal system has been knocked sideways, hasn't it?*

knot

cut the Gordian knot (*literary*) to succeed in solving a very complicated and difficult situation or problem ○ *Scott decided to close the inquiry last year when he concluded that it would be possible to go on for ever. 'You have to cut the Gordian knot.'*

≡ According to an ancient legend, Gordius, the king of Phrygia, tied a knot that nobody could untie. It was said that if anyone untied it, they would become the next ruler of Asia. When Alexander the Great heard this, he solved the problem by cutting through the knot with a sword.

★ **tie the knot** (*informal*) to get married ○ *The couple tied the knot last year after a 13-year romance.*

≡ Tying knots in items of clothing or ribbons worn by the bride and groom is a traditional feature of many wedding ceremonies, symbolizing their unity.

knots

tie someone in knots to confuse someone by using clever arguments, so that they cannot argue or think clearly any longer ○ *He could tie her in knots in an argument and never once missed an opportunity to prove his intellectual superiority.*

tie yourself in knots to make yourself confused or anxious, and so you are not able to think clearly about things ○ *He was tying himself in knots, trying to sound at once supportive of the Government, yet somehow disapproving of the 'damage' to Britain's 'reputation'.*

know

★ **know someone or something inside out** to know someone or something extremely well ○ *Liam has played for and against some of the greatest clubs in Europe and knows the game inside out.*

not know whether you are coming or going (*spoken*) to feel very confused and unable to think clearly ○ *The truth is I'm so excited that I hardly know whether I'm coming or going.*

knuckle

near the knuckle (*British*) close to the limits of what people find acceptable ○ *There are important people who fear the public will be outraged. This kind of material is very near the knuckle.*

knuckles

★ **rap someone on the knuckles** to criticize or blame someone for doing something that you consider to be wrong ○ *If we find the bank made a mistake or was negligent, we will rap them on the knuckles.*

In the past, teachers sometimes punished pupils who behaved badly by hitting them on the knuckles with a ruler or stick.

labour

'Labour' is spelled 'labor' in American English.

★ **a labour of love** a job or task that you do for pleasure or out of duty without expecting a large reward or payment for it ○ *They concentrated on restoring outbuildings such as the Victorian greenhouse, an expensive labour of love.*

This expression appears in the Bible (1 Thessalonians 1:3), which refers to people's 'labour of love' (= the work that they do prompted by love), and the strength of people's confidence in Jesus.

lads

one of the lads *(British)* a man who is accepted as being part of a group of men who behave in ways which are considered typically masculine ○ *He likes being one of the lads, you know, having pints down the pub.*

lady

it isn't over until the fat lady sings said to encourage someone not to give up hope because nothing is certain and there is still time for the situation to change ○ *'Who knows, Michael might fall off and break a leg,' he joked. 'As they say, it isn't over until the fat lady sings.'*

The origin of this expression is uncertain but it may refer humorously to the fact that in the final part of an opera there is often a piece sung by the heroine before her death, a part often played by a large soprano singer.

lam

on the lam *(mainly American)* trying to escape or hide from someone, for example the police or an enemy ○ *He was arrested on Friday, after living on the lam since 1999.*

'Lam' is an American slang word meaning running away.

lamb

like a lamb gentle, quiet, and obedient ○ *She'd followed him like a lamb. She hadn't asked him why he was taking her to a medical research laboratory rather than to a normal hospital or clinic.*

lambs

like lambs to the slaughter if people go somewhere like lambs to the slaughter, they behave quietly and obediently without resisting because they have not realized that it will be dangerous or unpleasant, or because they realize that they are powerless ○ *The record companies have an easy life. We grovel and follow their every word like lambs to the slaughter.*

land

get the lay of the land or
get the lie of the land to find out the details of a situation or problem ○ *I'm not sure what's going to happen. That's why I'm coming in early. I want to get the lay of the land.*

land-office

do a land-office business *(American, old-fashioned)* to be very successful ○ *The Paradiso, one of the capital's newest and most luxurious clubs, was doing a land-office business.*

In the United States before the Civil War, the government opened up land offices which sold rights to pieces of land in the West. So many people wanted to buy land to settle on that there were often long queues outside the offices before they opened in the morning.

lane

★ **the fast lane** a way of living which seems full of activity and excitement but which often involves a lot of pressure as well ○ *Tired of life in the fast lane, Jack, a fifty-ish American businessman, decides to give it all up to fulfil a dream of becoming a painter.*

'Fast lane' and 'slow lane' refer to the speed of traffic in the different lanes of a motorway.

lap

Your lap is the area at the top of your thighs when you are sitting down, where a child would sit.

fall into someone's lap if something good falls into someone's lap, it happens to them without any effort on their part ○ *It would not be safe to assume that victory will fall into our lap at the next election.*

in the lap of the gods if something is in the lap of the gods, it will be decided or affected by luck or chance, rather than anything you can do ○ *Once they had repaired my lung they had to stop the operation. The liver is self-healing anyway, so at that stage, my life was in the lap of the gods.*

The idea here is that nobody knows what blessings will fall from the lap of the gods until they actually appear on earth.

in the lap of luxury in conditions of great comfort and wealth ○ *We don't live in the lap of luxury, but we're comfortable.*

The image is probably of luxury personified as a woman with a small child sitting on her lap whose every need is attended to by her.

land in your lap if a problem lands in someone's lap, they are forced to deal with it although it is not really their responsibility ○ *These problems have landed in the lap of Donald Jackson, an unassuming manager with little international experience.*

large

large as life (British) said to mean that you have found someone in a place, especially a place where they are not supposed to be. The usual expression in American English is **big as life**. ○ *I called on him one Friday night on some pretext or other and there they all were, large as life.*

larger

★ **larger than life** used for describing someone who seems more interesting or exciting than other people, for example because they are very talented, or because they behave in an unusual or interesting way. In American English, you can also describe them as **bigger than life**. ○ *John Huston was a larger-than-life character, whose temperament was as dramatic as any of the fictional figures in his own films.*

lark

up with the lark (mainly British, old-fashioned) up very early in the morning ○ *Most bakers are up with the lark, but Neville Wilkins is in action hours before the rest.*

A lark is a British bird that is well-known for its tuneful early morning song.

last

stick to your last (old-fashioned) to continue doing what you know about and not try to do new things, at which you are likely to fail ○ *Looking back, I* *should have stuck to my last and gone on to get a research job in one of the studios.*

This expression comes from the proverb 'let the cobbler stick to his last'. A last is a foot-shaped object which a cobbler uses as a model or mould to make shoes the right shape and size.

lather

in a lather very worried and upset about something ○ *The truth of the matter is that you have spent the past six months working yourself up into a lather over situations which are really none of your business.*

When horses get very hot, the sweat on their coats sometimes forms a foamy substance called lather.

laugh

★ **have the last laugh** to make your critics or opponents look foolish or wrong, by becoming successful when they said that you would fail ○ *Singer Des O'Connor is expecting to have the last laugh on his critics by soaring to the top of the Christmas hit parade.*

laundry

★ **a laundry list** *(mainly American)* a large number or long list of things ○ *This document is expected to set out a laundry list of reasons why shareholders should reject the bid.*

wash your dirty laundry in public → see **dirty**

laurels

In ancient Greece, the laurel or bay tree was associated with the god Apollo. The winning competitors in the Pythian games, which were held in honour of Apollo, were given crowns or wreaths of laurel.

look to your laurels to work hard or think seriously about what you are doing,

in order to make sure that you continue to be successful ○ *The City of London maintains a dominant role, but it must now look to its laurels.*

★ **not rest on your laurels** to not rely on previous successes, but to continue working hard to make sure that you have continued success ○ *The trouble with all successful restaurants, however, is the tendency to rest on their laurels and stagnate.*

law

★ **be a law unto yourself** to behave in an independent way, ignoring laws, rules, or conventional ways of doing things ○ *Most athletic departments are pretty much a law unto themselves – unaccountable in terms of where this money goes.*

the law of the jungle a situation where the normal rules and values of civilized life do not exist, and so, for example, strength, power, and aggressiveness have more effect than moral values and legal rights ○ *The streets are subject to the law of the jungle and policing has been entrusted to private law enforcement agencies.*

This phrase became popular from 'The Jungle Book' by Rudyard Kipling (1894). 'The law of the Jungle, which never orders anything without a reason, forbids every beast to eat Man, except when he is killing to show his children how to'. Instead of encouraging aggression, this law actually places limits on the use of violence in the animal kingdom.

★ **lay down the law** to tell people very forcefully and firmly what to do ○ *They were traditional parents, who believed in laying down the law for their children.*

★ **take the law into your own hands** to punish someone who you believe has done something wrong, even though you have no right to, and even if this means that you yourself break the law ○ *Could* *we have taken the law into our own hands and thrown the unwanted visitors out?*

lay

get the lay of the land → see **land**

lead

> In these expressions, 'lead' is pronounced with the same vowel sound as the word 'red'.
>
> Lead is a very heavy metal.

go down like a lead balloon to be completely unsuccessful and unpopular ○ *A senior source said the memo had gone down like a lead balloon.*

swing the lead *(British)* to pretend to be ill and not do something you should be doing, such as going to work ○ *There is no question of taking money away from those who are genuinely sick. We simply want to stop anyone swinging the lead.*

> In the past, when a ship was in shallow water, one of the sailors would drop a piece of lead on a string, called a plumbline, over the side of the ship to find out how deep the water was. Sometimes sailors would just swing the plumbline, because they were too lazy to do the work properly. 'Plumb the depths' is also based on this practice.

leaf

shake like a leaf → see **shake**

> The 'leaf' in these expressions is a page of a book.

★ **take a leaf out of someone's book** to copy someone and behave or do something in the same way as them, usually because they were successful when they acted in that way ○ *If he wants a better rapport with the British public, it's high time he took a leaf out of Bruno's book and started doing game shows, even pantomimes.*

★ **turn over a new leaf** to start to behave in a better or more acceptable way than previously ○ *The military leader said he and the king have agreed to turn over a new leaf in their relations with one another.*

leaps

★ **in leaps and bounds** or
by leaps and bounds
rapidly ○ *The U.S. population grew by leaps and bounds.*

lease

★ **a new lease of life** *(British)* or
a new lease on life *(American)*
If someone or something is given a new lease of life, something makes them successful once again or improves their condition ○ *The old oak table was picked up for just £4 and subsequently given a new lease of life by Kim's mother.*

> A lease is a contract by which you can rent property for a fixed period of time.

leash

> A 'leash' is a long thin piece of leather or chain, which you attach to a dog's collar so that you can keep the dog under control.

give someone a longer leash to allow someone a lot of freedom to do what they want, rather than controlling them very strictly ○ *At the beginning of the 1992 campaign, Dan Quayle was given a longer leash than ever before.*

keep someone on a short leash or
keep someone on a tight leash
to control someone carefully and only allow them a small amount of freedom to do what they want ○ *The government strove to impress the country with its calm reasonableness and kept its troops on a tight leash.*

strain at the leash to be very eager to do something ○ *The players had better realise that we have enough youngsters straining at the leash to take their places if they don't do their jobs.*

least

least said, soonest mended (British, old-fashioned) said to mean that it is a good idea to say very little, because you might upset someone or make a situation worse if you say too much ○ *Say nothing. Least said, soonest mended is what I always say. Especially in court.*

leave

be left in the dust (American) to be outdone or left far behind by someone or something ○ *The Canadian economy was left in the dust by the torrid pace of expansion in the U. S. economy in the third quarter.*

When a vehicle moves off, or a person runs off, the moving wheels or feet cause dust on the road to rise up behind them.

left

left, right, and centre (British) or **left and right** (American) used to emphasize that something is happening or being done a great deal ○ *They're all expecting the state to pay out money left right and centre.*

leg

break a leg said to a performer who is about to go on stage as a way of wishing them good luck ○ *Jason sent Phillip a fax from the airport before Monday's show, with the greeting: 'Break a leg and enjoy yourself.'*

There are many superstitions associated with the theatre. For example, many performers consider that it is unlucky to say 'good luck' directly to anyone. Instead, they pretend to wish them bad luck.

★ **give someone a leg up** to help someone to achieve something and become successful, especially by giving them an advantage that other people do not have ○ *The mother seemed to think that her name had given her boy a leg up on the competition.*

To give a rider a leg up means to help them get on to the horse.

not have a leg to stand on to be in a very weak position, for example because you are unable to prove a claim or statement you have made ○ *I haven't got a leg to stand on. I had no witnesses.*

pull someone's leg to tease someone about something, for example by telling them something which is not true ○ *Is he serious or just pulling our legs?*

There are two possible explanations for this expression, although there is no proof for either. One suggestion is that in the past, when someone was being hanged, their friends or family sometimes pulled their legs hard so that they died more quickly and suffered less. Alternatively, the expression may refer to thieves tripping people up before they robbed them.

talk the hind leg off a donkey (British) to talk a lot ○ *He could talk the hind leg off a donkey. It took real perseverance to get through to him on the telephone.*

legs

have legs if an idea, plan, or story has legs, it is likely to work or be true ○ *Mr Blucher was confident that his concept had legs, so he persisted and pressed Mr Cooper for a meeting.*

on its last legs no longer as useful, successful, or strong as before, and about to fail altogether ○ *By the mid-1980s, the copper industry in the US was on its last legs.*

leopard

a leopard does not change its spots (mainly British) said to mean that it is not possible for someone bad or unpleasant to change and become good and pleasant ○ *Women who believe they have tamed a 'wild' man are usually wrong. The cliché that a leopard doesn't change its spots still happens to be true.*

A form of this proverb is used in the Bible (Jeremiah 13:23), by the prophet Jeremiah, to say that wicked people never change. He asks: 'Can Ethiopians change the colour of their skin or leopards change their spots?' He concludes that people who have been taught to do wrong, or who have always done wrong will find it difficult to become good.

letter

a dead letter a law or agreement that people do not pay any attention to, although it still exists ○ *In this conflict, international humanitarian law is a dead letter. Unacceptable practices are going on.*

A dead letter is a letter that the post office is unable either to deliver or to return to the sender, because it does not have the right addresses.

★ **follow something to the letter** to carry out instructions, rules, or advice exactly in every detail ○ *Even if that international agreement is followed to the letter, the ozone layer won't recover fully until the year 2060.*

★ **the letter of the law** what is actually written in the law, rather than the moral principles on which it is based. You usually use this expression to show disapproval. ○ *The Home Office stuck to the letter of the law over the definition of dependants.*

level

on the level honest and truthful ○ *Wait a minute, is this guy on the level or not?*

licence

The noun 'licence' is spelled 'license' in American English.

a licence to print money (*mainly British*) a commercial activity that allows people to get a lot of money with little effort or responsibility ○ *Under this Government the privatised utilities have* become a licence to print money at the expense of the consumer.

lid

blow the lid off something or **take the lid off something** (*journalism*) to reveal the true nature of a difficult or dangerous situation or problem which has previously been hidden ○ *'The Knowledge' is a new documentary series blowing the lid off music business scandals.*

★ **keep the lid on something** to keep the true nature of a particular situation or problem hidden, or to control it and stop it becoming worse ○ *But I understand that Murray was desperately trying to keep the lid on a potential scandal.*

lie

get the lie of the land → see **land**

★ **live a lie** to live in a way which you feel to be dishonest and false ○ *My mother never told my father the truth about me. We've been living a lie all this time, and now she has taken me from him.*

nail a lie (*British, journalism*) to show that something is definitely not true ○ *Top designer Calvin Klein is one of those helping to finally nail the lie that young is best. He has just appointed 40-year-old Lisa Taylor as his new top model.*

a white lie something which is untrue, that is often said in order to protect someone or to avoid hurting someone's feelings ○ *I believe that this is a case where a little white lie is really more appropriate than the truth.*

life

★ **fight for your life** to be very seriously ill or injured and be in danger of dying ○ *A boy aged 15 was fighting for his life last night but two younger children were said to be out of danger.*

frighten the life out of someone or **scare the life out of someone** to frighten someone a great deal

○ *Further tests revealed that three of my veins had furred up and I needed triple bypass surgery. It scared the life out of me.*

get a life said to someone to express criticism, or ridicule of them, for example because they never do anything interesting, or because they are being unrealistic and stupid ○ *It was six o'clock in the evening. I was still in my pajamas. Nicole looked at me, said she thought I was deteriorating, and suggested I get a life.*

hold someone's life in your hands to have complete control over what happens to someone ○ *You feel a responsibility to people because sometimes you're holding their life in your hands.*

larger than life → see **larger**

★ **the life and soul of the party** (British) or **the life of the party** (American) someone who is very lively and entertaining on social occasions, and is good at mixing with people ○ *She was having a very enjoyable time and was clearly the life and soul of the party.*

life is a bowl of cherries said to mean that life is full of pleasure and enjoyment. This expression is often used negatively to comment on an unpleasant or difficult situation. ○ *Life's not exactly a bowl of cherries when you're an international champ.*

live the life of Riley to have a very enjoyable time because you have no worries about money or work ○ *He was living the life of Riley, enjoying holidays in Italy and trips to the theatre, while we had barely enough to eat.*

> This expression probably comes from a song 'Is That Mr Reilly', which was popular in America in the 1880's and described what Reilly's life would be like if he was rich.

put your life in someone's hands to put yourself in a situation where someone has complete control over what happens to you ○ *After all these years, do you take me for a fool? What makes you think*

I would put my life in your hands?

risk life and limb to do something very dangerous that may cause you to die or be seriously injured ○ *He is not prepared to risk life and limb on this dangerous track to clinch the title.*

someone can't do something to save their life (spoken) said to mean that someone cannot do something at all ○ *He can't sing to save his life but he is a good guitarist.*

take your life in your hands to take a lot of risks when you do something ○ *A rider who does not know the road takes his life in his hands by cycling in the dark.*

light

★ **be given the green light** if a plan or action is given the green light, someone in authority says that it can be carried out ○ *Despite local planning opposition he has finally been given the green light to develop a terrace of 11 derelict houses he owns in South Kensington.*

in the cold light of day if you think about a problem, feeling, or event in the cold light of day, you think about it some time later and in a calmer or more practical way than was possible at the time it happened ○ *He has to sit down in the cold light of day and analyse what needs to be done to prevent the club from being relegated.*

★ **a leading light** (mainly British) someone who is considered to be one of the most important, active, and successful people in an organization or campaign ○ *He is a leading light in the just launched campaign to rid football of racism.*

> A leading light was a light which was placed at the entrance to a harbour or shallow channel of water, as a guide for ships.

light as a feather weighing very little ○ *It was a monstrous machine as large as the Albert Hall and as light as a feather.*

★ **the light at the end of the tunnel**

something which gives you hope about the future and for the end of a difficult or unpleasant situation ○ *After horrific times we are seeing light at the end of the tunnel.*

light dawns said to mean that someone suddenly realizes or understands something that they should have realized or understood before ○ *'Oh!' she said, as if the light had finally dawned on her. 'I'm on the wrong floor, huh?'*

out like a light very deeply asleep ○ *Dad gently closed the door again. 'She's out like a light,' I heard him whisper to my anxious mother.*

★ **see the light** to start to understand or agree with something, especially after a long period when you have not understood or agreed with it
○ *Christianity taught him values which the West preached but largely ignored in practice. But he had seen the light and urged everyone to share it with him.*

★ **see the light of day**
1 to become known by or available to a large number of people ○ *This book might never have seen the light of day without the enthusiasm, support, and friendship of my editor, Daniel Bial.*
2 to be born ○ *Tens of millions of new souls are seeing the light of day in Africa alone each year.*

lightning

lightning does not strike twice said to mean that someone who has been exceptionally lucky or unlucky is unlikely to have the same good or bad luck again ○ *Observers reckon he will be very lucky to repeat the performance. Lightning does not strike twice, particularly in big business.*

a lightning rod for something (mainly American) a person who is naturally blamed or criticized by people, although there are other people who are responsible ○ *He told the Palermo court he was an innocent lightning rod for Italy's many crime problems.*

A lightning rod is a long metal strip, one end of which is fixed on the roof of a building, with the other end in the ground to protect the building from being damaged by lightning.

like lightning extremely quickly or very suddenly and unexpectedly ○ *I ran across that room like lightning and pushed back the curtain.*

lights

the lights are on but nobody is at home said to mean that although someone seems to be normal or satisfactory, they are in fact very stupid or useless ○ *According to Harrington, many projects are not properly thought through: 'You get the feeling that the lights are on but no one's at home.'*

lily

gild the lily to act unnecessarily by trying to improve something which is already very good ○ *Here in Europe I'm gilding the lily. There they really need advice.*

This expression may be based on lines in Shakespeare's 'King John' (1595): 'To gild refined gold, to paint the lily... Is wasteful and ridiculous excess.' (Act 4, Scene 2)

limb

go out on a limb to do something risky or extreme, which puts you in a position of weakness ○ *It seems to me that you would prefer to stay in your present situation rather than go out on a limb and try something completely new.*

In this expression, a limb is a branch of a tree. The image here is of someone who climbs out along a limb, away from the main trunk.

★ **out on a limb** in a position of weakness without any help or support ○ *No company wants to be the first to put its rates up. The companies who have tried have found themselves out on a limb.*

tear someone limb from limb

if someone threatens to tear you limb from limb, they are extremely angry with you and threaten you with violence ○ *Police were lucky they found him before I did because they would have been arresting me. I would have torn him limb from limb.*

limits

★ **off limits** if an area is off limits, you are not allowed to go there. If a thing is off limits, you are not allowed to use it or do it ○ *The area was kept off limits to foreign journalists until early this year.*

line

all the way down the line at every stage of a situation or activity, or including all the people or things involved in a situation or activity ○ *It is the British government that has fought for reform all the way down the line.*

★ **along the line** or

down the line during the course of a situation or activity, often at a point that cannot be exactly identified ○ *And then somewhere along the line I looked at what was really happening.*

be out of line (*spoken*) to be completely wrong to say or do a particular thing ○ *Addressing a fellow officer like that is out of line, and I won't stand for it, hear me?*

> The line referred to here is a line of soldiers, who are expected to act as a unit.

★ **the bottom line** the most important and basic part of what you are discussing ○ *The bottom line is that the great majority of our kids are physically unfit.*

> This expression refers to the last line in a set of accounts, which states how much money has been made.

★ **cross the line** to start behaving in an unacceptable way, for example by getting involved in something extreme or anti-social ○ *The show's pretty outrageous, but I don't think it crosses the line.*

> The 'line' in this expression may refer to boxing matches in the past, when a line was drawn on the ground which neither boxer could cross. 'Draw the line' may be based on a similar idea.

★ **down the line**

1 at a later date ○ *Whether that happens further down the line we cannot say.*

2 if something happens a particular number of years or months down the line, it happens after that amount of time ○ *So 25 years down the line, you look back and there's a sense that it was all better back then.*

★ **draw the line**

1 to know at what point an activity or situation stops being reasonable and starts to be unacceptable ○ *It is difficult for charities to know where to draw the line between acceptable and unacceptable sources of finance.*

2 to not do a particular activity, because you disapprove of it or because it is so extreme ○ *I'll do virtually anything – although I think I'd draw the line at running naked across the set!*

> There are several theories about the origin of this expression. It may come from early versions of tennis, in which the court had no fixed size: players agreed their own limits and drew lines accordingly. Alternatively, it may be connected with the 16th century practice of using a plough to cut a line across a field to indicate a boundary between two plots of land. A third possibility is that it refers to boxing matches in the past, when a line was drawn in the ring which neither boxer could cross. 'Cross the line' may be based on a similar idea.

draw a line in the sand to put a stop to or a limit on something ○ *It was time to draw a line in the sand, forget the past, and work together.*

draw a line under something to enable a bad situation to be considered as over, so that people can start again or continue with things more productively ○ *He said the document draws a line under the painful chapters of our past and clears the way for a new beginning.*

★ **a fine line** a point at which it is difficult to distinguish between two different activities or situations, especially when one is acceptable, and the other is not ○ *There is a fine line between being nicely looked after and being fussed over too much – so don't overdo it.*

get a line on someone (mainly American) to get some information about someone ○ *We've been trying to get a line on you, and the more we try, the less we find.*

★ **in the firing line** in a position where you are likely to be criticized or attacked ○ *There comes a time in their lives when your children begin to test the influence they have over others and, as parents, you are first in the firing line.*

★ **in the front line** or
on the front line with a very important part to play in achieving or defending something ○ *Those in the front line of the British economy are united in believing that Britain must remain a full playing member of the EU.*

⧉ The image here is of soldiers in the front line during a battle.

in the line of fire in a position where you are likely to be criticized or attacked ○ *All very well to say that, when you're not in the line of fire like me.*

★ **on line** (mainly American) operating fully. The usual British expression is **on stream**. ○ *We expect to be on line as export numbers build up with a capacity to produce tens of thousands of tonnes of feed.*

★ **put something on the line** or
lay something on the line
1 to do something which causes you to risk losing something such as your reputation or your job ○ *He had put his career on the line and I wasn't prepared to allow what he had done to be diminished in significance.*
2 to speak truthfully and directly about your feelings ○ *You have to put your emotions on the line with love, but he cannot do this.*

⧉ Originally, 'lay it on the line' may have been connected with gambling. It meant to lay a bet on the sideline in the game of craps, or on the counter of a betting window at a racecourse.

shoot a line (British) to say something that is exaggerated, untrue, or difficult to believe ○ *He'd been looking for new blood for his office in Vienna. That was the line he shot, though knowing him, I'm sure he had an ulterior motive.*

★ **sign on the dotted line** to formally agree to something by signing an official document. This expression is often used to mean simply that you make a firm commitment about something. ○ *Once you sign on the dotted line you are committed to that property.*

★ **step out of line** to do something that you should not do or to behave in an unacceptable way ○ *Values and traditions were accepted and agreed by everyone. If you stepped out of line, you knew what to expect.*

⧉ The line referred to here is a line of soldiers, who are expected to act as a unit.

★ **toe the line** to behave in the way that people in authority expect you to behave ○ *Journalists who refuse to toe the line will have to be sacked.*

⧉ At the start of a race, runners stand in a row with their toe just behind the starting line.

linen

wash your dirty linen in public
→ see **dirty**

lines

on the right lines or
along the right lines (British) behaving in a way which is likely to result in success ○ *Sometimes all you really require is just a friendly voice to tell you that you are on the right lines.*

★ **read between the lines** to understand what someone really means, or what is really happening in a situation, even though it is not stated openly ○ *He was reluctant to go into details, but reading between the lines it appears that the Bank of England has vetoed any idea of a merger between British banks.*

link

★ **a weak link** an unreliable part of a system, which may cause the whole system to fail ○ *It was automatically assumed that Edward would be the weak link in the partnership.*

lion

fight like a lion to fight bravely ○ *She would have fought like a lion to protect her son.*

★ **the lion's share** the largest part of something ○ *Defence has taken the lion's share of this year's budget.*

This refers to Aesop's fable 'The Lion and his Fellow Hunters', in which a lion goes hunting with several other animals and takes everything that they catch for himself, instead of sharing it with them.

★ **walk into the lion's den** to deliberately place yourself in a dangerous or difficult situation ○ *The Minister walked into the lion's den of his press accusers, looked them in the eye, and fought back.*

This expression comes from the story in the Bible of Daniel (Daniel 6), who was thrown into a den of lions because he refused to stop praying to God. However, he was protected by God and the lions did not hurt him.

lions

throw someone to the lions to allow someone to be criticized severely or treated badly, without trying to protect them ○ *Tanya isn't sure exactly why she's been thrown to the lions. She traces it back to quotes she made about the business that were reproduced out of context.*

In Roman times and at other periods in the past, people were sometimes put to death by being thrown into a den of lions.

lip

button your lip to keep silent about something although you would really like to speak ○ *He had the grace and good sense to button his lip, even though this clearly caused him personal pain.*

★ **keep a stiff upper lip** to hide your emotions and not let other people see what you are feeling ○ *I shared my feelings with no one because I had always believed in keeping a stiff upper lip, and putting on my best face for family and friends.*

This is supposed to be a national characteristic of the English.

★ **pay lip service to something** or
give lip service to something to appear to be in favour of an idea without doing anything to support it ○ *These agreements give lip service to money going back to the people. But there is not even a formula for how it would be determined.*

In this expression 'service' means the same as respect. A contrast is being made here between what people say and what they really think, based on an idea expressed in various places in the Bible.

lips

lick your lips to look forward eagerly to a future event ○ *His home supporters licked their lips in anticipation of the first Scottish-born winner since Tommy Armour in 1931.*

★ **on someone's lips**
1 if something is on people's lips, a lot of people are talking about it and seem to be interested in it ○ *The question on most people's lips was not whether there would be war but when it would it break out.*
2 if a question or comment is on someone's lips, they want to ask or say it or are in the process of asking or saying it ○ *He stopped in the dressing room beside their bedroom, hung his coat over the corner chair, his apology already on his lips.*

read my lips said to tell someone to believe and trust what you are saying ○ *Mr Bush won the White House in 1988 thanks, in large part, to his now infamous pledge 'read my lips: no new taxes'.*

someone's lips are sealed said to mean that someone will keep a secret that someone else has told them ○ *As for anything told to me in confidence, well, my lips are sealed.*

litmus

★ **a litmus test** (*journalism*) an effective and conclusive way of proving or measuring the quality or success of a particular thing ○ *The success of wind power represents a litmus test for renewable energy.*

Litmus paper is used to test the acidity of substances. It turns red in acid conditions and blue in alkaline conditions.

live

live and breathe something to be extremely enthusiastic about a particular subject or activity ○ *Williams lived and breathed motor racing.*

lives

have nine lives to keep managing to get out of difficult or dangerous situations without being hurt or harmed ○ *I think this is probably going to be the end, although he has shown he is a political cat with far more than nine lives.*

This expression comes from the saying 'a cat has nine lives', which people use to say that cats seem to survive a lot of very dangerous situations or events.

loaf

half a loaf is better than none said to mean that it is better to take what you can get, even if it is very little, than to risk having nothing at all ○ *I'm very disappointed that all we have in the form of test matches is just one solitary test, but half a loaf is better than no loaf, and we are happy that at least we are getting this test.*

lock

★ **lock, stock, and barrel** completely or including every part of something ○ *It would have been much easier for us to have shut the business down lock, stock and barrel, and to have saved our cash and not paid a dividend.*

The three main parts which make up a complete gun are the lock, the stock, and the barrel.

lockstep

in lockstep (*mainly American*) if two people or things move in lockstep, they are very closely linked and dependent on one another, so that if one changes, the other changes too ○ *Many criminologists argue that support for the death penalty moves in lockstep with the crime rate.*

Lockstep is a way of marching in which the marchers follow as close behind each other as possible.

loggerheads

★ **be at loggerheads** to strongly disagree about something ○ *Social workers and doctors are at loggerheads over how well the new system will work.*

In medieval times, loggerheads were implements with long handles and a round bowl on one end. In battles, the bowl was filled with hot tar, and then thrown at the enemy.

loins

gird your loins or
gird up your loins (journalism, literary) to prepare yourself to deal with a difficult or stressful situation ○ He is girding up his loins for another round of high-level meetings.

> This expression is used several times in the Bible. The Hebrews wore long loose robes which they tied up with a girdle or belt when they were working or travelling.

long

★ **be long on one thing and short on another** to have a lot of one thing but not very much of another ○ The prime minister's speech was long on words but short on solid action.

long as your arm very long ○ The phone's been buzzing non-stop. I've a list of messages as long as my arm.

look

give someone a dirty look or
give someone a filthy look to look at someone in a way that shows that you are very angry about something ○ Tony was being a real pain. Michael gave him a dirty look and walked out of the kitchen.

looked

★ **have never looked back** to have never regretted a decision ○ He became a professional photographer in 1978, and has never looked back.

loop

★ **in the loop** part of a group of people who make decisions about important things, or know about these decisions ○ There are ways that are being worked out to make sure that the Congress is fully in the loop.

out of the loop not part of a group of people who make decisions about important things, or know about these decisions ○ He is out of the inner loop, and it irks him.

throw someone for a loop or
knock someone for a loop (mainly American) to shock or surprise someone very much ○ The banker was surprised to find Johnson in his usual high spirits. If Kravis's offer had thrown him for a loop, Johnson wasn't letting it show.

loose

★ **cut loose** to become free from the influence or authority of other people ○ Italy has not cut loose from the ERM as determinedly as Britain.

hang loose to relax or not to be too serious about something because it is not important ○ Get something to eat and come back to the office. And hang loose.

★ **on the loose**
1 free because you have escaped from somewhere ○ You have to wake up every day knowing that whoever carried out those awful murders is still on the loose.
2 not being controlled or supervised by anyone and free to behave however you want ○ The problem is high-spirited youngsters on the loose in the country's leafy lanes.

Lord

take the Lord's name in vain → see **name**

lose

★ **lose it** (informal)
1 to become extremely angry or upset ○ I completely lost it. I went mad, berserk. I was shouting and swearing.
2 to become unable to do something you are usually able to do ○ He walked on stage, looked out into the audience and just lost it. He forgot the words and started to make up completely different ones.

loss

★ **at a loss** not knowing what to do or say in a particular situation ○ These women also face language barriers and are at a loss to know where to go for help.

at a loss for words → see **words**

a dead loss a completely useless person or thing ○ *Politics is in crisis, and politicians are a dead loss.*

losses

★ **cut your losses** to decide to stop spending time, energy, or money on an activity or situation on which you have already spent a lot without having any success ○ *Only you can decide if you should push on to the end of your degree or cut your losses and get out.*

lot

all over the lot *(American)* spread across a large area or over a wide range of things. The British equivalent of this expression is **all over the shop**. ○ *IBM's investments have been all over the lot – in fiber-optic technology, data-retrieval systems, computer networks and so on.*

> In American English, a lot is an area of land.

★ **throw in your lot with someone** to decide to join someone and to share whatever good or bad things happen to them ○ *That does not mean that France is ready to throw in its lot with other Community states on defence matters.*

> In the past, 'lots' were objects such as pieces of straw or paper which people used when making a decision or choice. Each lot represented, for example, a different piece of property or course of action. All the lots were put together and then chosen at random to decide who would receive the different pieces of property or what action would be taken.

loud

★ **loud and clear** if someone says something loud and clear, they say it openly and forcefully so that it cannot be misunderstood or ignored ○ *The message must come across loud and clear from the manager: No matter how hard I ask you to work, I work as hard or harder.*

love

all's fair in love and war said to mean that under difficult circumstances any kind of behaviour is acceptable ○ *He appears to live by the boorish credo that all is fair in love and war. And being cruel to mistresses and wives isn't wrong.*

for love nor money if you cannot get something for love nor money, it is very difficult to get ○ *You won't get a room here, not for love nor money.*

★ **no love lost** or
little love lost if there is no love lost between two people or groups, they do not like each other at all ○ *There was no love lost between the country's two most powerful politicians.*

> Originally this expression had the opposite meaning to its present one. It used to mean that the two people liked each other a lot.

luck

down on your luck suffering a period of bad luck ○ *Even when people are down on their luck, they deserve the same human courtesy that any of us would expect.*

the luck of the draw something that depends on chance rather than on the efforts or qualities of the people involved ○ *On better acquaintance, you may decide that there's no basis for a real friendship with a colleague. That's just the luck of the draw.*

> This expression refers to the act of drawing a card at random from a pack of playing cards.

lucky

★ **strike lucky** or
strike it lucky *(British)* to suddenly have some good luck ○ *I arrived at 12.30 to give myself time to find a parking meter, but struck lucky immediately.*

> This expression has its origins in mining in the 19th century. It refers to someone finding the minerals or oil

that they were looking for. 'Strike oil' is based on the same idea.

lump

like it or lump it *(informal)* to have to accept a situation even though you do not like it, because you cannot do anything to change it ○ *If you're a shareholder in the club then you have some sort of say in the way things are run. But as a paying customer you like it or lump it.*

★ **a lump in your throat** a tight feeling in your throat because of a strong emotion such as sorrow, nostalgia, or gratitude ○ *Meg felt a lump in her throat. She was going to miss Dot, even though the two of them had never been particularly close.*

lunch

out to lunch not aware of what is happening around you, or not intelligent or capable ○ *He has failed to fulfil his role as the mayor who could take charge. He is seen as a man who is out to lunch.*

★ **there's no such thing as a free lunch** said to mean you cannot expect to get things for nothing, since most things that are worth having need to be paid for or worked for ○ *The government has spent 14 years telling the nation that there is no such thing as a free lunch and*

lecturing us on the virtues of sound economics.

This expression dates back to at least 1840 in the United States. It recently became popular again when the American economist Milton Friedman used it in the 1970s.

lurch

★ **leave someone in the lurch** to put someone in a difficult situation by suddenly going away or abandoning them, without giving them very much notice of your plans ○ *My secretary left me in the lurch on Friday and I haven't found a replacement yet.*

In the card game cribbage, a player is left in a position known as the lurch when an opponent has scored 51 points before the player has managed to either score 31 points or move their peg around the first corner of the board that is used to keep the score.

lying

★ **not take something lying down** to complain about or fight against a bad situation ○ *It is clear that he means to push everyone out who does not agree with him, and I for one am not going to take it lying down.*

Mm

mad

don't get mad, get even said to mean that, if someone harms you, you should not waste your energy on being angry, but you should concentrate on harming them in return ○ *Use these bad feelings that you have. Don't get mad. Get even.*

This expression is believed to have come from the strong-willed Irish-American politician Joseph P Kennedy, father of John F Kennedy. A book by Alan Abel with this title, described as 'a manual for retaliation', was published in 1983.

mad as a hatter *(mainly British)* very strange, foolish, or crazy ○ *Her sister's as mad as a hatter and if you ask me she's not much better herself.*

In the 19th century, 'hatters' or hat-makers used nitrate of mercury to treat fabrics such as felt. This substance is poisonous, and if the hat-makers breathed it in, they often suffered brain damage. As a result, hatters were traditionally thought of as mad.

mad as a hornet *(mainly American)* extremely angry ○ *Bob grinned. 'I'll bet he's as mad as a hornet.' 'He did not sound at all pleased,' Jerry admitted.*

A hornet is a large wasp.

man

the man on the Clapham omnibus *(British)* an ordinary, average person ○ *The wealthy and powerful never liked the man on the Clapham omnibus knowing what they were about.*

Clapham is an area of London, and 'omnibus' is an old-fashioned word for bus.

no use to man or beast or **no good to man or beast** completely useless ○ *Circumstances had compelled him, much against his will, to take no less than six beginners, some of them first-voyagers, of no use to man or beast.*

This is part of the old saying, 'When the wind is in the east, 'tis neither good for man nor beast.'

★ **someone's right-hand man** someone's close assistant and the person they trust to help and support them in everything they do ○ *He was always by her side, and supported her in everything she did. He was her right-hand man, her business manager, and he travelled with her everywhere.*

There are several possible explanations for this expression. One is that the right side of the body is traditionally associated with skill and strength. Another is that it may refer to the soldier who was responsible for the right side of a troop of horses. Also, in the past, the position on the right of the leader at political or social gatherings was the place of honour.

map

★ **put someone or something on the map** to cause someone to become well-known or important ○ *The film which really put Ellen Barkin on the map was The Big Easy.*

marbles

have all your marbles to be completely sane and rational ○ *The producer Mirian Adhtar has found four particularly fearless old ladies; and they have all their marbles.*

lose your marbles *(informal)* to become crazy or senile ○ *At 83 I have not lost my marbles and my memory is, thank God, as clear as it ever was.*

pick up your marbles and go home *(American)* to leave a situation in which you are involved because you are dissatisfied with the way things are going. The use of this expression suggests that you are wrong to do this. ○ *Many people regard a U.S. presence as a desirable counterweight. No one wants the U.S. to pick up its marbles and go home.*

> The reference here is to a player in a game of marbles who is annoyed about losing and therefore stops playing and takes the marbles away so that nobody else can play either.

march

★ **steal a march** to do something before someone else and so gain an advantage over them ○ *Investors from other countries will be annoyed that their Japanese competitors have once again stolen a march on them.*

> If an army steals a march on the enemy, it moves secretly and takes the enemy by surprise.

mark

★ **a black mark** an expression of disapproval for something that you have done ○ *Any complaints, you got a black mark straight away, it didn't matter whether they were valid or not.*

> This expression may refer to a practice in schools in the past. If children misbehaved, the teacher put black marks against their names on a list.

first off the mark acting more quickly than anyone else ○ *The fine art season began yesterday, and Christie's were first off the mark with a collection of seven paintings by Paul Cézanne.*

get off the mark *(mainly British)*
1 to start to do an activity quickly ○ *Don't waste time with small talk; get off the mark right away.*
2 to score or win for the first time in a sporting contest ○ *The goal was Atkinson's second of the season, having got off the mark against Ipswich Town on Saturday.*

> The 'mark' in this expression is the line which runners stand behind at the start of a race.

hit the mark to be very good, and to succeed in pleasing people ○ *As with the rest of the book, the idea is there, but the result doesn't hit the mark.*

> The 'mark' in this expression is the target used in archery or shooting.

★ **leave your mark** or
leave a mark
1 to do something important that has a lasting effect ○ *He now has five more years in office and would still dearly like to leave his mark on the world.*
2 to have an experience that has a lasting effect on you ○ *I lived abroad, in Asia, for four years, and this is an experience that tends to leave its mark.*

★ **make your mark** to do something which causes you to become noticed or famous ○ *The article looks at the new generation of Japanese directors making their mark in world cinema.*

off the mark incorrect or inaccurate ○ *Mussels are sometimes called 'Poor Man's Oysters', but I think that name is way off the mark.*

on the mark correct or accurate ○ *Michael is right on the mark about movies being out of step with American culture.*

overshoot the mark to do something to a greater extent than is necessary or desirable ○ *I quite unwittingly overshot the mark, and I still feel embarrassed about it.*

≣ The 'mark' in this expression is the target used in archery or shooting.

overstep the mark to behave in a way that is considered unacceptable ○ *Sometimes newspapers overstep the mark but overall they do more good than harm.*

≣ The 'mark' in this expression may be the line behind which runners stand before the race. Alternatively, it may refer to boxing matches in the past, when a line was drawn in the ground which neither boxer could cross.

★ **quick off the mark** *(mainly British)* quick to understand or respond to something, or to take advantage of an opportunity. ○ *These price cuts are great news for the holidaymaker who is quick off the mark.*

slow off the mark slow to act or to react to a situation or event ○ *International relief efforts on behalf of the refugees were slow off the mark.*

≣ The 'mark' in this expression is the line which runners stand behind at the start of a race.

up to the mark of a satisfactory standard or quality ○ *They get rid of those whose work is not up to the mark.*

≣ The 'mark' in this expression is a hallmark, which is an official symbol put on gold and silver items that reach a particular standard.

★ **wide of the mark** incorrect or inaccurate ○ *For once, it seems that their figures are not too wide of the mark.*

≣ The 'mark' in this expression is the target used in archery or shooting.

marker

★ **put down a marker** to do something that shows people what you are capable of, or what you intend to do in the future ○ *Having considered carefully his every word,*

I can now put down my marker. I simply do not believe he says what he means.

market

★ **in the market for something** interested in buying or getting something ○ *If you're in the market for expensive skin care products, the following list includes some of the most well known.*

marrow

'Marrow' is the fatty substance inside the bones of a person or animal.

chilled to the marrow *(mainly British)* feeling very cold ○ *An icy wind murmured through the trees. Lenny was chilled to the marrow of his bones.*

to the marrow absolutely; completely ○ *I was thrilled to the marrow when the invitation arrived.*

masters

serve two masters to be loyal to two opposing principles, beliefs, or organizations ○ *But there is something more fundamentally wrong: Sir Nicholas is expected to serve two masters: politics and the law.*

≣ This expression is used in the Bible (Matthew 6:24, Luke 16:13). In the Sermon on the Mount, Jesus says that no man can serve two masters, because he will hate one of them and love the other.

mat

go to the mat *(mainly American)* to fight very fiercely about something ○ *Librarians have gone to the mat for us and I'm determined to do my bit to help them meet the demand for the books.*

≣ This expression refers to a wrestler who fights fiercely and is willing to risk a fall.

match

★ **meet your match** to find that you are competing or fighting with someone who is as good as you or is better than you ○ *When I got into the room with Wesley, it was almost like looking into a mirror for me. I had finally met my match in power and intellect.*

a shouting match an angry debate about something ○ *We didn't want to get into a horrible shouting match with the university.*

This expression is more commonly used to talk about a quarrel in which people shout at one another.

the whole shooting match the whole of something ○ *I filled in my donor card, ticking the whole shooting-match, from kidneys to liver.*

This may be a reference to someone winning all the prizes in a shooting contest.

McCoy

the real McCoy something that is genuine, rather than a fake or a copy ○ *You can buy prosciutto anywhere, but if you want the real McCoy, you need to go to Parma.*

It is possible that 'McCoy' was originally 'Mackay'. There was a 19th century whisky manufacturer called Mackay who advertised his product as 'the real Mackay' to distinguish it from other brands with similar names. Alternatively, the expression may come from a dispute between two branches of the MacKay clan over which was older. Eventually the MacKays of Reay, or the 'Reay MacKays', won the dispute.

meal

make a meal of something (*mainly British*) to spend more time or energy on something than is necessary ○ *Alexander has made such a meal out of a mildly mistaken newspaper report.*

a meal ticket a way of getting money on a regular basis and securing a good

lifestyle ○ *A degree has never been a meal ticket, but the recession is making life for graduates tougher than ever.*

a square meal a large, filling, nutritious meal ○ *The troops are very tired. They haven't had a square meal for four or five days.*

On sailing ships in the past, sailors ate off square wooden plates.

meaning

someone does not know the meaning of the word said to emphasize that someone does not have a particular quality or never had a particular kind of experience ○ *She is an optimist; Ruthie doesn't even know the meaning of the word depression.*

means

by fair means or foul by any possible method, even if it is dishonest or unfair ○ *She never gave up trying to recover her property, by fair means or foul.*

measure

★ **for good measure** in addition to other things in order to make certain that something is successful or complete ○ *This is a fairly conventional love story, with a murder mystery thrown in for good measure.*

★ **have the measure of someone** to understand someone or know what they are like ○ *Lili was the only person I knew who had the measure of her brother.*

meat

be the meat in the sandwich (*British*) to be in a very difficult position because you have been caught between two people or groups who are in conflict with each other ○ *These oil and gas companies are the meat in the sandwich in a fight involving contractors and the provincial government.*

dead meat

1 (*informal*) a person who is in serious trouble which may result in them being injured or killed. This expression is often used in threats. ○ *He's dead meat if he comes back here.*

2 a person who is in serious trouble which will have unpleasant consequences for them, such as losing their job ○ *Anyone who remembered her said she was dead meat.*

meat and drink to someone (mainly British) something you find easy to cope with and enjoy doing ○ *What normal people considered pressure was meat and drink to Robert Maxwell.*

one man's meat is another man's poison said to point out that different people like different things ○ *Art is everywhere. Because it is a question of personal taste, the cliché of one man's meat being another's poison is in this case especially fitting.*

> The Roman author Lucretius said in 'De Rerum Natura': 'What is food to one person may be bitter poison to others.'

medicine

give someone a taste of their own medicine to do the same bad thing to someone that they have done to you ○ *The cowardly thugs who mug old people should be given a taste of their own medicine with the return of corporal punishment.*

melting pot

in the melting pot (mainly British, journalism) constantly changing, so that you do not know what will finally happen ○ *I am very disappointed. The whole business has been put into the melting pot again.*

> A 'melting pot' is a container in which metal is melted down before being made into new objects.

men

dead men tell no tales said to mean that someone who is dead cannot reveal the truth about what caused their death ○ *Hanley told police the gun went off*

accidentally while Mr Khan was playing with it. 'These statements were a cover-up,' Mr Spencer told the jury. 'Hanley killed Mr Khan. He knows that dead men tell no tales.'

★ **the men in suits** (mainly British) the men who are in control of an organization or company and who have a lot of power ○ *A lot of young people feel detached from older politicians – the men in suits.*

separate the men from the boys to show who is strong and capable and who is not ○ *This is the game that will sort out the men from the boys. It is absolutely vital to win the replay and get to the final.*

messenger

shoot the messenger to unfairly blame a person who has given you bad news or information, when you should instead be angry with the people who are really responsible for the situation ○ *I don't make the rules – don't shoot the messenger!*

mickey

★ **take the mickey** (mainly British) to tease someone or make jokes about them in a way that causes them to seem ridiculous ○ *He started taking the mickey out of this poor man just because he was bald.*

middle

★ **in the middle of nowhere** a long way from any other place ○ *When I was 14, my family moved away from Glasgow to a village in the middle of nowhere.*

★ **middle-of-the-road**

1 politically neither very left-wing nor very right-wing ○ *He is a moderate, middle-of-the-road person who understands both sides of the discussion.*

2 very ordinary, rather than unusual, exciting, or extreme ○ *These are, for the most part, ordinary middle-of-the-road people who want the usual things out of life.*

midnight

burn the midnight oil to stay awake very late at night in order to finish a piece of work ○ *Chris is burning the midnight oil trying to finish his article on the Bosnian situation.*

> The image here is of someone working late into the night by the light of an oil lamp.

mile

go the extra mile to be willing to make a special effort to do or achieve something ○ *I discovered that going the extra mile has always been the hallmark of successful people.*

a mile off if you say that you can spot something or someone a mile off, you mean they are very obvious and easy to recognize ○ *You can spot undercover cops a mile off.*

run a mile (*mainly British*) to escape as quickly as possible ○ *He likes the ladies but he'd run a mile if one chased him.*

miles

miles away thinking deeply about something, and not paying attention to what is happening around you ○ *Her mother was pacing up and down and seemed miles away. She hadn't noticed them at all.*

milk

it's no use crying over spilled milk said to mean that it is pointless to worry or be upset about something that has happened and cannot be changed ○ *But a rueful Mr Phelps reflected that, for him, 'it didn't work, did it? But it's no use crying over spilt milk.'*

milk and honey (*literary*) a situation in which you are very contented and have plenty of money ○ *The days of milk and honey are back – at least for US equity salesmen in the City.*

> This expression is used in the Bible to describe the Promised Land of the Israelites. (Exodus 3:8)

milk and water (*mainly British*) weak and ineffectual ○ *Fryer dismissed the report as milk and water.*

mill

go through the mill to experience a very difficult situation ○ *'Oh I've been through the mill,' said Shirley. 'Single parent, no money, and a boyfriend who beat me up.'*

> The reference here is to grain passing through a mill and being made into flour.

★ **run-of-the-mill** ordinary and unexciting ○ *I was just a very average run-of-the-mill kind of student.*

> This expression may be using the image of a watermill making the same movements continuously and regularly so long as the flow of water stays the same. Another suggestion is that it comes from the use of 'run-of-the-mill' in the United States as a term for timber which has been sawn at a sawmill but has not yet been graded.

million

a chance in a million something that is very unlikely to happen ○ *It is amazing really. He had a chance in a million of surviving. We are so relieved he is all right.*

one in a million very special ○ *At 25, Bernstein was a star. One in a million.*

millstone

★ **a millstone around your neck** a very unpleasant problem or responsibility that you cannot escape from ○ *Long-term illness can make you feel like a millstone around your family's necks.*

> A millstone is one of a pair of very heavy round flat stones which are used to grind grain.

mincemeat

make mincemeat of someone to defeat someone completely in a fight, argument, or competition ○ *I remember old Fiona made mincemeat of him at a dinner party without him even realizing.*

> In British English, mincemeat is meat that has been cut into very small

pieces by being forced through the small holes in a machine called a mincer.

mind

★ **blow your mind** (informal) to be extremely exciting, surprising or interesting ○ Oxford really blew his mind. He loved the feeling of the place, he loved the people.

★ **cross your mind**
1 if a thought crosses your mind, you suddenly think of it ○ The thought crossed my mind that she might be lying about her age.
2 if something never crossed your mind, it never occurred to you or you did not consider that it could happen ○ It evidently never crossed his mind to enter politics.

give someone a piece of your mind to tell someone angrily what you think of them ○ The more she thought about it, the more upset she became. She would like to go out and give him a piece of her mind.

have a one-track mind to only ever think or talk about one subject ○ Saunders is the complete modern striker, busy, quick, and with a one-track mind for scoring goals.

This probably refers to a single-track railway, which will only allow trains to move in a single direction.

★ **in your mind's eye** in your imagination or memory ○ I can often see you in my mind's eye, sitting in your flat alone.

★ **in your right mind** rational and behaving sensibly ○ Those places are so dangerous that no one in their right mind would go there unless they had to.

★ **keep something in mind** to be careful to remember something important ○ Go where you like, but keep in mind that some places are more problematic than others for women travelling alone.

★ **the mind boggles** said to mean that something is difficult to imagine or

understand because it is so amazing, strange, or complicated ○ The mind boggles to think what they could eventually achieve.

mind over matter said to describe situations in which someone seems able to control events or solve a physical problem by thinking in a focused way about it ○ Good health is simply a case of mind over matter.

mind your p's and q's → see p

★ **out of your mind**
1 crazy, foolish, or insane ○ When her boss told her she would have to reduce her salary, she snapped, 'Are you out of your mind?'
2 extremely worried, jealous, or afraid ○ I was out of my mind with fear, I didn't know what to do.

slip your mind if something slips your mind, you forget it ○ The reason for my visit had obviously slipped his mind.

a weight off your mind something that you no longer need to worry about ○ Armstrong heaved a sigh of relief, 'That's a weight off my mind.'

minds

★ **in two minds** (British) hesitant and unable to reach a decision about something ○ Roche was in two minds whether to make the trip to Oslo.

miracles

A miracle is a wonderful event that you cannot explain, or that would not normally be considered possible.

work miracles to achieve very impressive results ○ This beauty cream really works miracles and freshens up my face.

misery

put someone out of their misery
1 to end a situation which is causing someone to suffer ○ Almost 1,000 British school leavers awaiting exam results were today put out of their misery.
2 to deliberately kill a person who is

suffering, for example because they have an illness that cannot be cured ○ *There were at least a dozen pills in the bottle, surely enough to put her out of her misery.*

3 to kill an animal because it is very old or sick, or because it is badly injured ○ *I carry medicines to relieve sick and injured animals. Some are in such pain that I'm forced to put them out of their misery.*

miss

★ **miss the boat** to fail to act in time to take advantage of an opportunity ○ *Critics would say that both Congress and the White House have seriously missed the boat on this set of issues over the last few years.*

mockers

put the mockers on something *(mainly British)* to prevent something from happening or from being successful ○ *Paul put the mockers on the whole meal by complaining that everything was under-salted.*

≡ The origin of this expression is uncertain, but some people think that 'mockers' may come from Yiddish.

money

have money to burn to have more money than you need ○ *It's certainly a ridiculous figure. I'd expected something like £30 or £40. They must have money to burn, these people.*

make money hand over fist to make a lot of money very quickly ○ *North Carolina National Bank is making money hand over fist in Texas.*

≡ This is derived from the image of a sailor moving his hands steadily one over the other while pulling in a rope or raising a sail.

money for old rope *(British)* money that you can earn very easily and with very little or no effort ○ *I had always believed that the fashion model's job was money for old rope.*

≡ In former times, sailors would unpick lengths of old rope and sell the strands to shipyards. These pieces of rope would then be hammered into the gaps between the planks on ships' decks and then covered in pitch to seal the decks and make them watertight.

money is the root of all evil said to mean that greed is the cause of a particular problem or the cause of society's problems in general ○ *I believe the amount involved in this project is a substantial sum, and money is the root of all evil, as they say.*

≡ This proverb comes from a letter in the Bible from St. Paul to his disciple Timothy. (1 Timothy 6:10)

★ **money talks** said to mean that people with a lot of money have power and influence and they can get whatever they want ○ *As far as he is concerned, money talks and he can do what he likes.*

★ **put your money where your mouth is** to give practical support to causes or activities that you believe are right, especially by giving money ○ *If the minister is so keen on the school he should put his money where his mouth is and give us more resources.*

right on the money *(mainly American)* completely right ○ *His analysis was right on the money.*

≡ This expression was originally used to describe a bet which turned out to be exactly right.

the smart money if the smart money is on a particular result, then that result is expected by the people who know a lot about it ○ *The smart money is on him losing his seat to the Labour challenger.*

spend money like water to spend a lot of money unnecessarily ○ *She spends money like water to create a luxurious home far beyond her means.*

throw good money after bad to spend a lot of money in an attempt to get back money that you have already lost, for example in a bad investment ○ *We are not offering any more cash; we don't want to throw good money after bad.*

★ **throw money at something** to try to solve or improve a problem by spending a lot of money on it, instead of thinking about it carefully or doing other things ○ *The government's answer to the problem has been to throw money at it.*

monkey

have a monkey on your back (mainly American) to have a serious problem that is making your life difficult or unpleasant ○ *The whole medical system that has become a monkey on the back of people without an adequate income.*

make a monkey out of someone to make someone seem ridiculous or stupid ○ *If it makes any difference, I'm not here to make monkeys out of the police, I'm a cop myself.*

monkey business dishonest or unacceptable behaviour ○ *You try any monkey business and you're in trouble, right?*

not give a monkey's (British, informal) to not care at all ○ *They said they would not injure the child, but they didn't give a monkey's about what they did to me.*

throw a monkey wrench into the works → see **wrench**

month

a month of Sundays
1 a very long time ○ *Torrential rain and jet-black skies can make each day seem like a month of Sundays.*
2 if something will not happen in a month of Sundays, it is very unlikely to happen ○ *'I think I know what you're about,' he growled, 'but it'll never work – not in a month of Sundays.'*

monty

the full monty (British) something that is as complete or extreme as possible ○ *Ron sang 'My Way' right through, from the* simple piano intro to the big orchestral finish, the full monty.

moon

ask for the moon to ask for something that you cannot possibly have ○ *We're not asking for the moon, but we are asking for some help so that we can continue to progress.*

howl at the moon to waste your time and energy trying to do something which is impossible or trying to get something which you cannot have ○ *You need to adjust your expectations and stop howling at the moon.*

once in a blue moon very rarely ○ *I only get over to Cambridge once in a blue moon and I'm never in London.*

> In some places, if there are two full moons in a calendar month, the second is called a 'blue moon'. This is rare.

★ **over the moon** (mainly British) very happy ○ *I'm over the moon about the way this album turned out.*

promise the moon to promise to give people things that you cannot in fact possibly give them ○ *So many banks try to lure customers by promising the moon.*

moth

like a moth to a flame in a way that shows that someone is strongly attracted to something ○ *The bright lights of west London drew Kharin like a moth to a flame.*

motions

★ **go through the motions** to do something that you have to do or are expected to do, but without any real effort or enthusiasm ○ *Many of the students who did attend classes with any regularity were just going through the motions.*

mould

'Mould' is usually spelled 'mold' in American English.

The 'mould' in these expressions is a container that is used to make something into a particular shape. Soft or liquid substances are put into the mould, and when they harden they form objects with the shape or pattern of the mould.

★ **break the mould** to completely change the way something has traditionally been done, and do it in a new way ○ *His stated ambition is to create a third party and break the mould of US two-party politics.*

they broke the mould when they made someone said to mean that a particular person or thing is special or unique, and that there is nobody else or nothing else quite like them ○ *He is a most remarkable man. They broke the mould when they made him.*

mountain

make a mountain out of a molehill to make a small, unimportant problem seem big and important ○ *It's unlikely that Smith will be punished; you are making a mountain out of a molehill.*

the mountain must go to Mohammed said to mean that if someone you want to see does not come to you, then you must go to them ○ *The mountain must go to Mohammed; we'll send a man tomorrow.*

These expressions are based on a story about the prophet Mohammed, who was asked to show his power by making Mount Safa come to him.

a mountain to climb (*mainly British*) something that will be difficult to achieve ○ *We nearly beat Warrington in the Cup last season and although it's a mountain to climb, we can do it.*

mountains

move mountains to do something that seems impossible, particularly when love or a particular belief makes you feel

determined to succeed ○ *We should all repeat five times a day, 'It is possible to change!' With this belief, you can move mountains.*

This expression comes from the proverb 'Faith will move mountains', which is based on the words of Jesus to his followers in the Bible (Matthew 17:20). He tells them that if they believe in God, they can make great things happen.

mouth

all mouth and no trousers (*British*) talking a lot about doing something but never actually doing it ○ *Ms Cunningham said that the First Minister had failed to deal with the matter, and accused him of being "all mouth and no trousers".*

down in the mouth (*British*) unhappy or depressed ○ *As for George, I hear he's rather down in the mouth.*

foam at the mouth

1 to be very angry ○ *Stewart was foaming at the mouth about an incident at the hospital the previous afternoon.*

2 to be very excited about something ○ *At that time the newspaper had foamed at the mouth in favour of agreement with Fascist countries.*

laugh out of the other side of your mouth (*American*) said to warn someone that although they are happy or successful at the moment, things are likely to go wrong for them in the future. The British expression is **laugh on the other side of your face**. ○ *You'll laugh out of the other side of your goddam mouth after this game.*

make your mouth water

1 to look or smell delicious to you ○ *She was bent down getting the casserole from the oven. The fragrant steam made his mouth water.*

2 (*journalism*) to be very attractive or appealing to you ○ *The zoo's site in Regent's Park would make any developer's mouth water.*

shoot your mouth off

1 to talk loudly and boastfully about yourself or your opinions ○ *He'd been shooting his mouth off saying he could sing, when of course, he couldn't.*

2 to talk publicly about something which is secret ○ *What if he decides to try for a little more money, or to shoot his mouth off around town?*

talk out of both sides of your mouth (*American*) to give completely different advice or opinions about something in different situations ○ *One of Larry's problems is that he speaks out of both sides of his mouth. At Harvard he panders to the students with his radical ideas. But then, in the outer world, he has to pull back from these positions.*

move

get a move on to hurry ○ *You'd better get a move on if you're going to make it back in time for the match.*

movers

★ **the movers and shakers** (*journalism*) the people who take an active part in a particular event, organization or movement and who often bring in new developments ○ *She and her husband have become movers and shakers behind the scenes of the Labour Party.*

⫶ This comes from the poem 'Ode' by Arthur O'Shaugnessy (1874): 'We are the music-makers And we are the dreamers of dreams… We are the movers and shakers Of the world for ever, it seems.'

mud

be dragged through the mud to be accused of behaving in an immoral or unacceptable way ○ *One doesn't like to see an admired institution dragged through the mud like this.*

mud sticks (*mainly British*) said to mean that when something bad is said about someone, people will continue to believe it, although it may have been proved to be completely untrue ○ *Whether he's innocent or not, some of the mud has stuck.*

a stick-in-the-mud a person who does not like doing new things or having fun ○ *It was such a shame many of the guests didn't bother to dress up. What stick-in-the-muds!*

★ **throw mud** to try to spoil a person's reputation by saying bad things about them or by telling lies ○ *The newspaper and magazine articles that followed were especially vicious, with supporters of both stars quick to throw mud.*

murder

★ **get away with murder** to be able to do whatever you like without anyone trying to control, punish, or criticize you ○ *His charm and the fact that he is so likeable often allows him to get away with murder.*

scream blue murder (*British*) to make a lot of noise or fuss about something ○ *People are screaming blue murder about the amount of traffic going through their town.*

⫶ The expression 'blue murder' is perhaps derived from the French oath 'morbleu', which is a variation of 'mort Dieu'. 'Bleu' or blue is used in French as a euphemism for 'Dieu' or God, so 'morbleu' literally means 'blue death'.

muscles

★ **flex your muscles** to behave in a way that is intended to show that you have power and that you are considering using it ○ *It's time to flex your muscles and show the world what you are capable of.*

music

★ **face the music** to accept responsibility for something that you have done wrong and to prepare yourself to be criticized or punished for it ○ *The authorities had found us out and we were about to face the music.*

The 'music' in this expression may refer to the orchestra at an opera or musical. The orchestra sits in front of the stage, so when a performer faces the audience, they also face the orchestra, or 'music'. Alternatively, the expression may come from an army practice in which a soldier who had been dismissed for dishonourable behaviour was sent away with drums beating.

★ **music to your ears** a statement that makes you feel very happy when you hear it, for example because you have been hoping or waiting to hear it for a long time ○ *The judge's words were music to the ears of the accused.*

mustard

not cut the mustard to not be as good as you should be ○ *You have to be on form every week and people soon start noticing if you're not cutting the mustard.*

In the United States, 'mustard' used to be slang for 'the best' or 'the genuine article'.

muster

★ **pass muster** to be satisfactory for a particular purpose or job ○ *Only one country has yet to fulfill all the membership requirements, but it is expected to pass muster soon.*

In the army and navy, a 'muster' is an inspection of the soldiers' or sailors' uniforms and equipment.

mutton

mutton dressed as lamb (British) a woman who dresses in a style which is considered suitable only for younger women ○ *This woman is older than me, heavier than me and is mutton dressed as lamb.*

Mutton is the meat of an adult sheep, and lamb is the meat of a young sheep, as well as being the name of the animal itself.

Nn

nail

★ **another nail in the coffin** the latest in a series of events which are seriously harming something or someone ○ *The vote is another nail in the coffin of the one-party system which the country has now largely renounced.*

hit the nail on the head or
hit it on the nail to describe a situation or problem exactly ○ *I agree with Dr Carey, everything he says. I think he's hit the nail right on the head.* ○ *'It sounds as if he almost depended on you as much as you depended on him.' 'You just hit it on the nail.'*

on the nail
1 (British) if you pay cash on the nail for something, you pay for it immediately and in cash. The American expression is **on the barrelhead**. ○ *You have to pay cash on the nail sometimes, and this was one of them.*
2 exactly ○ *'When did Captain Schmidt come to see you?' 'Six o'clock, just about on the nail.'*

⧉ This expression may refer to cylindrical counters called 'nails' that were sometimes used by traders in the Middle Ages. When a price had been agreed, the money was placed on the nail, so that everyone could see that the correct amount was being paid.

name

★ **make a name for yourself** to become famous or well-known as a result of doing a particular thing ○ *Diane Abbott has made a name for herself as a hardworking MP.*

★ **the name of the game** the most important aspect of an activity or situation ○ *In the current economic climate, survival is the name of the game.*

a name to conjure with (mainly British) a person or thing that is very important, influential, or memorable ○ *His partners are serious about his potential as a name to conjure with in the scent market.*

⧉ In this expression, the importance and influence associated with a person or thing are regarded as a kind of magical power which you can call on by using their name.

not have a penny to your name or
not have a cent to your name to have very little money ○ *He didn't have a penny to his name.*

someone's name is mud said to mean that someone has said or done something which has made them very unpopular with a particular group of people ○ *His name has been mud at the Telegraph since he left to work for a rival newspaper.*

⧉ This expression may refer to Dr Samuel Mudd. John Wilkes Booth, the assassin of Abraham Lincoln, broke his leg while trying to escape and was treated by Dr Mudd. Although Mudd did not know what his patient had done and acted in good faith, he was put in prison and he and his family were hated for many years.

take God's name in vain or
take the Lord's name in vain to use God's name disrespectfully, especially by swearing ○ *He persevered, and always gently corrected us when we took the Lord's name in vain.*

take someone's or something's name in vain to use another person's or a thing's name for your own purposes in an inappropriate or disrespectful way ○ *Let's remember that what we do from this point is being done in the name of justice. Let's not take her name in vain.*

This is from the second of the Ten Commandments in the Bible. It says that people should never use the name of God carelessly: 'Thou shalt not take the name of the Lord thy God in vain.' (Exodus 20:7)

names

★ **call someone names** to use insulting words or expressions to describe someone when you are talking to them or about them ○ *At my last school they called me names because I was so slow.*

napping

be caught napping to not be prepared for something that happens, and perhaps lose an advantage as a result ○ *European firms have been caught napping. As a result, they now control barely one-tenth of the world market while Japanese firms control nearly half of it.*

'Napping' means the same as sleeping or dozing.

nature

the nature of the beast something that is an essential part of the character of the person or thing that you are talking about ○ *Baker likes to say that negotiations always get tougher towards the end. That's the nature of the beast.*

navel

navel-gazing thinking only about yourself and your own problems or activities, rather than concerning yourself with the problems or activities of other people ○ *I'm very good at motivating people to do things, so I'm a doer rather than a thinker. I've never really done much navel-gazing!*

Ξ Your navel is your belly button.

near

so near and yet so far said to express regret or sadness when you have got very close to achieving what you wanted, but in the end you just failed ○ *It was a crushing experience to have victory snatched away in such a desperate manner. It's heartbreaking to be so near and yet so far.*

neck

breathe down someone's neck
1 to be close behind someone in a race, contest, or other competitive situation ○ *No doubt Jones and Armstrong maintain a consistently high standard because both have talented rivals breathing down their necks.*
2 to closely watch and check everything that someone does ○ *Most farmers have bank managers breathing down their necks, so everything has to have an economic reason.*

dead from the neck up (British, informal) stupid ○ *If you want my opinion, your lawyer is dead from the neck up.*

get it in the neck (British, informal) to be punished or strongly criticized for something wrong that you have done ○ *This film is an attack on the media, especially the television news media. It's quite nice to see them get it in the neck for once.*

★ **neck and neck** exactly level in a race or contest, so that it is impossible to say who will win ○ *The latest opinion polls show both parties running neck and neck.*

Two horses are said to be neck and neck when they are exactly level and it is impossible to say which one is winning the race.

put your neck on the block → see **block**

put your neck on the line to do something although it is risky and you may lose your reputation or money as a result ○ *Gere put his neck on the line to make Sommersby. It was a gamble, both in terms of his public image and his wallet.*

risk your neck to do something

dangerous which could result in your being killed or injured ○ I won't have him risking his neck on that motorcycle.

someone could wring someone's neck or

someone would like to wring someone's neck said to mean that a person is very angry with someone else ○ That crazy Dot! He could wring her neck for this! She had no right to tell tales to his mother!

≡ To wring something means to twist it and squeeze it.

★ **stick your neck out** (informal) to say or do something which other people are afraid to say or do, even though this may cause trouble or difficulty for you ○ At the risk of sticking my neck out, I doubt whether the compensation fund will be needed.

≡ This expression may come from boxing, where fighters need to keep their necks and chins drawn in or protected in order to avoid being hit by their opponent.

this neck of the woods (informal) the place where you are at the moment ○ What's there to do in this neck of the woods?

★ **up to your neck in something** (informal) very deeply involved in something bad such as debt or corruption ○ The Prime Minister was up to his neck in scandal.

your neck of the woods (informal) the area that you live in ○ I discovered, however, that stone troughs were pretty scarce in my neck of the woods and expensive as well.

≡ This expression originated in the United States. 'Neck' comes from 'naiack' which means 'point' or 'corner' in an Algonquian Native American language.

needle

like looking for a needle in a haystack extremely difficult or even impossible to find ○ Police have told Mrs Barrow that searching for the cat will be like looking for a needle in a haystack. The chances of recovering the animal are slim.

nelly

'Nelly' is sometimes spelled 'nellie'.

not on your nelly (British, old-fashioned) said to mean that there is no chance at all of something happening. ○ They finally become adults, thanks to all your hard work, and do they turn up for mum's birthday? Not on your nellie.

≡ This expression may come from cockney rhyming slang. 'Not on your Nellie Duff' stands for 'not on your puff', which also means 'definitely not'.

nerve

★ **touch a nerve** or

touch a raw nerve to upset someone, by mentioning a subject that they feel strongly about or are very sensitive about ○ Buchanan's speech touched a raw nerve here at the Capitol.

nerves

a bag of nerves (British) or

a bundle of nerves someone who is extremely nervous, worried, or tense ○ What's the matter? You're a bundle of nerves.

★ **get on someone's nerves** to annoy or irritate someone ○ The phone used to get on my nerves – people ringing him at home as if it was an extension of the office.

live on your nerves (British) to be always worried and anxious, because you are in a difficult situation ○ Once this is all over and done with I've told her she's to go into the clinic for a complete rest to get her strength back, because she's living on her nerves.

★ **a war of nerves** or

a battle of nerves a situation in which two opposing people or groups are trying to weaken each other psychologically, for example by frightening each other, in order to get what they want without taking any direct action ○ *In the war of nerves between the two sides, it is becoming more and more difficult to separate their real intentions from their propaganda tactics.*

nest

feather your nest to take advantage of your position in order to get a lot of money, so that you can lead a comfortable life ○ *The politicians seem anxious to feather their nests at the expense of the people.*

Some birds line their nests with soft feathers which they pluck from their own breasts or gather from the ground.

fly the nest or
leave the nest to leave your parents' home to live on your own ○ *When their children had flown the nest, he and his wife moved to a thatched cottage in Dorset.*

foul your own nest (*literary*) to do something which damages your own interests or chances of success ○ *Man has invented a hundred brilliant ways of fouling his own nest – the pollution, the heat, the poisons in the air, the metals in the water.*

★ **a nest egg** a sum of money that you are saving for a particular purpose ○ *All he wanted was a few months decent money to help him retire. He thought this was his last chance to build a nest egg.*

net

★ **cast a wide net** to involve a large number of things or people in what you are doing ○ *The U.S. has cast a wide diplomatic net, asking a variety of other nations to deliver the same message to Iran and to Syria.*

★ **slip through the net**
1 (*British*) if people slip through the net, the system which is supposed to help or deal with them does not do it properly. The American expression is **fall through the cracks**. ○ *It's hard to knock the selection process because the chances of any young talent slipping through the net are so minimal.*

2 (*mainly British*) if someone who is behaving illegally slips through the net, they avoid being caught by the system or trap that is meant to catch them ○ *Government officials fear some of the criminals identified by British police may have slipped through the net.*

nettle

★ **grasp the nettle** (*mainly British*) to deal with a problem or unpleasant task quickly and in a determined way ○ *It's better to grasp the nettle, speak to your superior and make it clear you regret your mistake and are determined it will never happen again.*

If you grasp a nettle firmly, it is less likely to sting you than if you just touch it lightly.

new

...is the new... (*British, informal*) said to mean that something has become the new fashion or has replaced something else. People are creative with this expression: 'brown is the new black/fish is the new meat, etc.' ○ *Forty is the new thirty. Everyone knows that. This is boom time for Middle Youth.*

news

★ **be news to someone** if something someone says is news to you, you did not know about it previously and are surprised by it or think it may not be true ○ *When he was told about the story, the governor said it was news to him.*

no news is good news said to mean that there is no need to worry, because people normally only send information when something bad has happened ○ *I had heard nothing all week. 'Oh well,' I thought. 'No news is good news.'*

nice

nice as pie very kind, friendly, and charming. You usually say this when someone's behaviour is not what you expect, or when it contrasts with their behaviour at other times. ○ *He is nice as pie when you meet him, then you hear he is going around bad-mouthing you.*

niche

★ **carve a niche** or
  carve out a niche to create a secure position for yourself, especially at work ○ *He has carved a niche for himself as an ABC television commentator and is certain to be kept on as long as the network continues to broadcast Saturday matches.*

  ≡ A niche is a hollow area that is made in a wall to display something such as a statue or an ornament.

nick

★ **in the nick of time** at the last possible moment, when it is almost too late ○ *She woke up in the nick of time and raised the alarm.*

nickel

A nickel is a five cent coin and a dime is a ten cent coin.

nickel and dime (American)
  1 not very important or only functioning on a small scale ○ *A lot of American kids run similar nickel and dime ventures, selling sweet, cool drinks outside their parents' home in the long, hot summers.*
  2 to weaken or exhaust someone or something, for example by continually taking small amounts of money away from them, or by continually making small changes or requests ○ *Oakland, like other cities, has been reeling from financial crisis and consequently has been nickel and diming essential services for years.*

a wooden nickel (American) something completely false or worthless ○ *He looked at the card as though it were a wooden nickel. 'That doesn't prove a thing,' he said.*

night

a night owl someone who regularly stays up late at night, or prefers to work late at night ○ *The street noise and late-night parties make this hotel a haven for night owls.*

ninepins

fall like ninepins (British) to be damaged or destroyed quickly in large numbers ○ *Conservative council seats fell like ninepins.*

  ≡ Ninepins are skittles.

nines

dressed to the nines or
  dressed up to the nines wearing very smart or glamorous clothes ○ *Everyone is dressed up to the nines. Huge hats, frills, tight dresses, sequins and high heels.*

  ≡ There have been many explanations offered for the origin of this expression. Most relate to the number nine in some way, but none has been generally accepted.

nineteen

talk nineteen to the dozen (British) to talk very quickly, without pausing ○ *Ms Wallace visited her on February 28th and found her 'vivacious and chatty and talking nineteen to the dozen'.*

  ≡ This expression suggests the idea of using nineteen words where most people would only use twelve. It is unclear why the number nineteen was chosen rather than any other.

nip

nip and tuck describes a situation in which it is impossible to say who will win a competition or contest because both sides are performing equally well ○ *It was nip and tuck throughout as the players struck the ball with equal venom.*

  ≡ One explanation for this expression is that it comes from sword-fighting, where a 'nip' is a light touch and a 'tuck' a heavier blow. Another is that it comes from horse racing, where it means the same as 'neck and neck'.

nits

pick nits to point out small problems or faults with something, often ones which seem relatively unimportant ○ *He then spent the second half of his interview picking nits, particularly about the environmental impact on 'the beautiful' Bluebell Hill.* ○ *And two years into my case, I am relieved to have a solicitor to deal with the enormous quantity of nitpicking and legalistic verbiage.*

> Nits are the sticky eggs laid by the head louse, a small insect that lives and breeds in human hair.

nod

get the nod to receive permission from someone to start something, or be promised their support ○ *We'll hold off interviewing Hythe any further until we get the nod from you.*

★ **give someone the nod** to give someone permission to start something, or promise them your support ○ *Of the 15 members of the committee, all seven Republicans are prepared to give him the nod.*

a nod and a wink (British) a situation in which someone communicates something to you by saying it indirectly or by giving you some kind of signal. This expression is usually used to show disapproval, often because something illegal or dishonest is taking place. ○ *A nod and a wink from the chairman is all it takes to move share prices up or down.*

a nod's as good as a wink said to mean that it is not necessary to explain something further, because you understand what someone has already told you indirectly ○ *Professor Mason was a very shrewd and skilled operator, and if he wanted to get his own way, a nod was as good as a wink.*

> This comes from the saying 'a nod's as good as a wink to a blind horse', which suggests that both the nod and the wink are equally useless, as the horse would not be able to see either.

on the nod (British) without being questioned or argued about ○ *The party cannot be seen to let the treaty through on the nod.*

> One explanation for this expression is that it comes from auctions, where bidders nod as a sign that they want to buy something.

noises

★ **make noises** to talk about something in a vague or indirect way ○ *Your credit card is over the limit and the bank manager is making noises about your overdraft.*

make the right noises to say things that suggest that you will deal with a problem or issue in the way that someone wants you to ○ *The President was making all the right noises about multi-party democracy and human rights.*

nook

every nook and cranny all parts of a place or object ○ *I do love how he knows every nook and cranny of Venice and can speak such good Italian.*

> A nook is a corner or recess in a wall, and a cranny is a narrow opening or gap.

nooks

★ **the nooks and crannies** the smaller or less accessible parts of a place or object which are not normally noticed ○ *In the weeks before Christmas, we would scour the house, searching all the nooks and crannies trying to find our presents.*

nose

cut off your nose to spite your face to do something in order to hurt another person, without realizing or caring that you will hurt yourself just as much or even more ○ *The manager does not want to cut off his nose to spite his face by leaving Neville out of the match, but he does want the player to realise the error of his ways.*

> In this expression, 'to spite' means to deliberately annoy or upset.

follow your nose

1 to make decisions and behave in a particular way because you feel instinctively that this is what you should do, rather than because you are following any guidelines or rules ○ *I'd started a bit of journalism, so I had a source of income. And I've just followed my nose doing that ever since.*
2 to go straight ahead, or to follow the most obvious route ○ *More or less follow your nose till you come to Marks and Spencer's. Bear right there. And it's there.*

★ **get up someone's nose** (mainly British, informal) to irritate someone a great deal ○ *This producer looks as if he's going to get up everybody's nose. He has only been here for a few hours and already he has been babbling about 'discipline' to Annie.*

give someone a bloody nose (British)

1 to defeat someone in a contest or competition in a way that does not cause permanent damage but makes them look foolish or inferior ○ *Most are so fed up with this new tax that they are threatening to give the Government more than a bloody nose in the forthcoming by-election.*
2 to damage the other side in a war or conflict enough to cause it to withdraw, at least for a time ○ *Giving the national army a bloody nose is one thing. Taking on its full might is another.*

keep your nose clean to behave well and avoid trouble ○ *The best advice I can give is tell you to keep your nose clean.*

keep your nose out of something to not interfere in something, because it does not concern you ○ *Nancy realized that this was his way of telling her to keep her nose out of his business.*

keep your nose to the grindstone to concentrate on working hard at your job, and not concern yourself with other things ○ *There is more to life than keeping your nose to the grindstone and saving for a rainy day.*

≣ A grindstone is a revolving stone disc
≣ which is used to sharpen metal tools.

≣ The reference here is to a person
≣ bending over the grindstone while
≣ they are working, so that their nose is
≣ close to it.

lead someone by the nose to control someone completely so that they do whatever you want ○ *The Government has let itself be led by the nose by the timber trade into suppressing the report for the narrow commercial advantage of those involved.*

≣ Bulls and other animals sometimes
≣ have rings through their noses so that
≣ a rope can be tied to the ring in order
≣ to lead them along. This expression is
≣ used in Shakespeare's play Othello,
≣ when Iago says Othello 'will as
≣ tenderly be led by the nose as asses
≣ are.' (Act I, Scene 3)

★ **look down your nose at someone or something** to regard a thing or person as inferior and treat them with scorn or disrespect ○ *The minister and his intellectual friends still look down their noses at Disneyland and the American soap operas such as Santa Barbara.*

★ **a nose for something** a natural talent for finding something ○ *Harry runs his own news agency in the north. He has a well-trained nose for a story.*

not see beyond your nose or
not see beyond the end of your nose to think only about yourself and your immediate needs, rather than about other people or wider and longer-term issues ○ *Time to act your age. You're too busy thinking about you and about everything to do with you that you don't see beyond the end of your nose.*

on the nose exactly ○ *This is Radio One FM. Precisely on the nose seven sixteen.*

≣ The origin of this expression is in
≣ broadcasting. When a show was
≣ running on time, the producer put a
≣ finger on his or her nose to signal this
≣ fact to the performers.

pay through the nose for something *(informal)* to pay more for something than you consider fair or reasonable ○ *It looks as though those taking out new insurance policies on their houses, cars, boats and planes will be paying through the nose.*

★ **poke your nose into something** or **stick your nose into something** to interfere in something that does not concern you ○ *If anyone should be apologizing, it should be me for poking my nose into other people's business.*

put someone's nose out of joint to offend or upset someone, because they think that they have not been treated with the respect that they deserve ○ *Gillian's sons were resentful of their new step-sisters. Barry had his nose put out of joint by Lucy's aloof sophistication, although she was his junior.*

★ **rub someone's nose in it** to embarrass or upset someone by reminding them of something that they do not want to think about, such as a failure or a mistake that they have made ○ *You obviously delight in the defeat of a fellow performer! And proceed to rub his nose in it, don't you?*

★ **thumb your nose at someone or something** to behave in a way that shows disrespect or contempt for someone or something ○ *There is a hard-core of young persistent offenders, and too many of them are simply laughing at authority and thumbing their noses at the court.*

> To thumb your nose at someone literally means to make a rude gesture by placing the end of your thumb on the end of your nose, spreading out your fingers, and wiggling them.

★ **turn up your nose at something** to reject something because you think that it is not good enough for you ○ *Even in the United States top-flight university graduates turned up their noses at business jobs and tried instead to get into government service.*

★ **under your nose** if something, especially a bad thing, happens under your nose, it happens in your presence or very near to you, and you do not or cannot do anything to stop it ○ *Then suddenly I knew what had been going on here all along, right under our noses.*

nowhere

★ **from nowhere** or **out of nowhere** suddenly or unexpectedly ○ *I remember looking both ways before crossing and seeing nothing. The car came from nowhere and hit me.*

nuclear

go nuclear *(mainly British, informal)* to get extremely angry and start behaving in a forceful or irrational way as a result ○ *Since I dropped the pictures off, I've been wearing a crash helmet in case you go nuclear. On a scale of ten, how angry are you at me for them?*

nudge

a nudge and a wink or **nudge-nudge, wink-wink** said to mean that someone is talking about something in a sly, suggestive way, because the subject is embarrassing or because they may get into trouble if they say it openly ○ *The article then listed a series of nudge-nudge, wink-wink rumors that insinuated that the Prime Minister was having an affair.*

> This expression became popular as a result of the 1970s British TV comedy series 'Monty Python's Flying Circus'. One of the characters in a sketch made suggestive remarks and followed them by saying 'nudge-nudge, wink-wink, say no more'. People sometimes nudge each other or wink at each other as a way of hinting at something.

number

a back number someone who is no longer useful or successful ○ *Lester is 55 in November, but I don't think that will make much difference. He's a great jockey and won't be a back number even at that age.*

> A back number of a magazine or newspaper is an edition of it that was published some time ago and is not the most recent.

do a number on someone (*informal*) to harm someone in some way, for example by cheating them or by totally defeating them in a game or match
○ *The Irish team are looking to do a number on England in Dublin tomorrow.*

have someone's number
to understand what kind of person someone is, so you know how to treat them or deal with them ○ *If they have your number from the start, and it is a small hotel, you are bound to get extra attention.*

look after number one or
look out for number one to selfishly put your own needs and interests before everyone else's ○ *My priority is to look after number one – to create a lifestyle I am happy with.*

someone's number is up said to mean that something unpleasant is going to happen to someone, and that there is nothing that they can do about it ○ *'Oh, Nancy, we're safe!' breathed Bess. 'I thought for a while our number was up!'*

> This is derived from army or navy life. A soldier or sailor who had been killed or who had died was said to have lost his mess number, or given up his allotted place in the dining hall.

numbers

★ **play the numbers game**
to use amounts or figures to support an argument, often in a way that confuses or misleads people ○ *Since everyone plays the numbers game differently,* there is hot debate about the real volume of sales.

> In the United States, the 'numbers game' or 'numbers racket' is an illegal lottery. It involves people placing small bets on a series of numbers that appear in particular sections of that day's newspaper, for example the stock market figures.

nut

do your nut (*British, informal*)
to become very angry about something ○ *I wanted to ask Lorraine out and I knew that Wendy would do her nut if she found out.*

a tough nut to crack a problem that is difficult to solve or a person who is difficult to deal with or to defeat in an argument or competition ○ *Despite not having won a title of note, Harrington has taken 17.5 points from a possible 20 in international singles, making him a tough nut to crack.*

nuts

★ **the nuts and bolts of something**
the detailed facts and practical aspects of something, as opposed to abstract ideas about it ○ *Surely you have to work out the nuts and bolts of something before you can commit yourself to it?* ○ *I'm a nuts and bolts politician. I always have been.*

nutshell

★ **in a nutshell** used for summarizing something in a brief way ○ *She wants me to leave the company. I want to stay. That's it in a nutshell.*

nutty

nutty as a fruitcake (*British, informal*)
very strange, foolish, or crazy ○ *Despite his maddening fidgeting, the man is a charmer – intense, funny, and nutty as a fruitcake.*

> 'Nutty' or 'nuts' is an informal word for mad. Nutty can also mean containing a lot of nuts in the way that a fruitcake often does.

Oo

oaks

great oaks from little acorns grow
or
mighty oaks from little acorns grow said to mean that something large and successful began in a small and insignificant way ○ *Henry Ford did not start his operations by opening hundreds of factories in his first year. Remember, mighty oaks from tiny acorns grow.*

Acorns are the nuts that grow on oak trees.

oar

put your oar in (*mainly British*) to give your opinion, even if other people have not asked you for it ○ *He let them say their piece without putting his oar in; he is obviously a good listener.*

This comes from an old expression 'to have an oar in every man's boat', meaning to interfere in other people's business.

odds

★ **at odds with something** not matching or corresponding to another thing ○ *His outlook on life was pessimistic, quite at odds with his wife's out-going personality.*

at odds with the world confused or discontented ○ *We are more inclined to blame a feeling of being at odds with the world on a headache or upset stomach, rather than the other way round.*

★ **be at odds with someone** to disagree with someone about something ○ *The region has reportedly been at odds with the central government both militarily and politically.*

★ **pay over the odds** (*British*) to pay more for something than it is really worth ○ *Over the years, London's home owners have got used to having to pay over the odds for their property.*

This expression refers to someone paying more than the agreed or usual price when they are betting on a horse in a race.

off-chance

★ **on the off-chance** in the hope that something good will happen, although that is unlikely ○ *One American visitor had turned up on the off-chance of catching a glimpse of the princess.*

oil

like oil and water two people who are like oil and water are very different from each other ○ *He and the General did not get along. The two were like oil and water together.*

no oil painting (*British*) unattractive or ugly ○ *I started seeing a guy who was no oil painting but wonderfully bright and interesting.*

pour oil on troubled waters to do or say something to make an angry or tense situation calmer or more peaceful ○ *He is an extremely experienced politician, who some diplomats believe may be able to pour oil on the troubled waters.*

Pouring oil on rough water can calm it. The Greek author Plutarch mentioned it in about 95 AD: 'Why does pouring oil on the sea make it still and calm?'

strike oil to suddenly become successful in finding or doing something ○ *A new generation of high-tech billionaires struck oil in the information industries – computers, microchips and software.*

This expression is more commonly used literally to say that someone discovers oil in the ground as a result of drilling.

old

old as the hills very old, and perhaps old-fashioned or very traditional
○ *Their equipment may be modern, but the techniques remain as old as the hills.*

olive

★ **an olive branch** something that indicates that you want to end a disagreement ○ *'We are holding out an olive branch, inviting the landowners to talk. We are trying to break the deadlock.'*

The story of the Flood in the Bible (Genesis 8:11) tells how Noah sent out a dove to see if there was any sign of land. If the dove found some land, it would mean that God had forgiven man. When the dove returned, it had a fresh olive leaf in its beak, so Noah knew that the floodwaters had almost gone.

omelette

'Omelette' is usually spelled 'omelet' in American English.

you can't make an omelette without breaking eggs said to mean that it is impossible to achieve something without there being bad or unpleasant side-effects ○ *You can't make an omelette without breaking eggs – you just have to break as few as possible. Even so, it seems wrong to put a major road through such beautiful countryside.*

omnibus

the man on the Clapham omnibus
→ see **man**

once-over

give someone the once-over to look at someone or analyse them quickly to get a general impression of their appearance or character ○ *Penny gives me the once-over. I'm wearing a bright jacket that'll go down well with European viewers, she says.*

one

be one up on someone to have an advantage over someone, because you have done something that they have not done or because you know something that they do not know ○ *Just because you met somebody doesn't mean you know anything about them.' 'No, but you're one up on the person who hasn't met them.'*

get it in one *(British)* to make a correct first guess ○ *'Is that a Birmingham accent?' I asked, explaining that all my family were originally from that part of the world. 'You got it in one. I grew up in Birmingham.'*

put one over on someone to gain a victory or advantage over someone ○ *Clark insisted: 'It's nice to put one over on your old boss but I don't hold any grudges.'*

onions

know your onions *(British, old-fashioned)* to know a great deal about a particular subject ○ *It shows she really knows her onions in the historical field too.*

This may derive from the rhyming slang 'onion rings', meaning 'things'.

open

be wide open if a contest or competition is wide open, it is very difficult to say who will win because the competitors are all equally good ○ *The Tories breathed a sigh of relief last night as two polls showed the election race was still wide open.*

blow something wide open
1 to change something completely by doing things in a totally different way
○ *Pamela has blown the old newsreader image wide open.*
2 to reveal something secret that other people have been trying to hide ○ *Has it*

occurred to you that he can blow the operation wide open?

leave yourself wide open or
lay yourself wide open if you leave yourself wide open to criticism or ridicule, you make it very easy for other people to criticize or ridicule you, because you behave in a naive or foolish way ○ *The statement leaves us wide open to attack.*

open-and-shut easily decided or solved because the facts are very clear ○ *The prosecution behaved as if they had an open-and-shut case.*

> In this expression, the word 'and' means 'and then', suggesting that the case being dealt with has been opened and then closed again almost immediately because it was easy to solve or deal with.

order

★ **the order of the day** what usually happens in a particular situation ○ *Wage cuts were the order of the day owing to the government's deflationary policy.*

★ **a tall order** a task that will be very difficult ○ *I've got to beat him by four shots tomorrow, and that's a very tall order.*

> An old meaning of 'tall' is large or excessive.

orders

★ **marching orders**
1 (*British*) an act of telling someone to leave something such as a job or a relationship. The American expression is **walking papers**. ○ *What does it take for a woman to say 'that's enough' and give her man his marching orders?*
2 (*American*) the instructions that you are given in order to carry out a plan or achieve an aim ○ *As one mid-level White House official put it, 'We're still waiting for our marching orders.'*

> The above expressions relate to the army. When soldiers are given marching orders, they are ordered to march to a particular place.

organ

the organ grinder's monkey (*British*) someone who is closely associated with a powerful person and acts on their behalf, but has no real power themselves ○ *'Do you feel that you've been squeezed out?' 'Well, I feel more like the organ grinder's monkey, actually.'*

> In former times, organ grinders were street entertainers who played barrel organs. Sometimes they had a monkey that performed to the music.

out

★ **out-and-out** very clearly and definitely the kind of person or thing mentioned ○ *This was almost certainly an out-and-out lie.*

overdrive

★ **go into overdrive** to begin to work very hard or to perform intensely or very well ○ *When the bodies were discovered, the media went into overdrive.*

> Overdrive is an extra gear on some vehicles, which enables them to go faster than they can with ordinary gears.

overtime

work overtime to work very hard in order to achieve something ○ *This might explain why people sleep longer when the immune mechanisms are working overtime to fight off infections.*

> This expression is more commonly used to say that someone is spending extra time doing the job that they are employed to do.

own

★ **get your own back** (*British*) to take revenge on someone because of something that they have done to you

○ *All you're interested in is in getting your own back on Terence.*

go behind someone's back to do something secretly or without getting someone's permission, often in order to deliberately upset them ○ *Leonard, you haven't been completely open with me. You think I wouldn't know when you go behind my back?*

★ **hold your own** to be able to defend your position against someone who is attacking you or threatening you ○ *Some areas of heavy industry, such as shipbuilding, were able to hold their own in international markets.*

Pp

p

mind your p's and q's to try to speak and behave politely or to act in an acceptable way, so that you do not offend people ○ *She always put on her best act and minded her p's and q's in front of the queen, but their relationship wasn't that close.*

This expression may originally have been a warning to children not to confuse p's and q's when learning the alphabet. Alternatively, 'p's and q's' may stand for 'pleases and thank yous', or expressions of politeness.

pace

★ **set the pace** to do something which is regarded as a good example, so that other people then do the same thing ○ *The consensus is that Versace has got it right this season and has set the pace for mainstream fashion.*

This is derived from the fact that a fast runner determines the speed at which all the other competitors in a race have to run.

someone can't stand the pace or **someone can't take the pace** said to mean that someone does not work or function effectively when they are under pressure, and so cannot compete or do things as well as other people ○ *They were constantly testing me, as if to prove I couldn't take the pace.*

paces

★ **put someone through their paces** to get someone to show you how well they can do something ○ *The eleven boxers on the British team are in the hands of the British coach, Ian Irwin, who is putting them through their paces.*

To put a horse through its paces means to test it to see how well it has been trained.

pack

ahead of the pack more successful than your competitors or rivals ○ *This new management system has kept the company far ahead of the pack in terms of product development.*

A pack here is a group of animals such as hounds or wolves.

page

on the same page (*American*) in agreement about what you are trying to achieve ○ *We're all on the same page in our careers, we all have the same professional needs.*

turn the page to make a new start after a period of difficulties ○ *Shareholders at Fiat's annual meeting will be looking for signs that the troubled company really does mean to turn the page.*

paid

★ **a pain in the neck** (*informal*) someone or something that is very annoying ○ *He was a pain in the neck. I was glad when he left my department.*

★ **put paid to something** (*mainly British*) to completely end or destroy someone's hopes, chances, or plans ○ *Great Britain gave a limp performance here last night that put paid to their chances of reaching the Olympic finals.*

pains

growing pains temporary difficulties and problems in an organization or a relationship as it develops and grows stronger ○ *The country is now facing some troublesome growing pains. The economy is still expanding, but at a slower rate than in the recent past.*

Growing pains are pains that children sometimes get in their muscles and joints. Many people wrongly think that they are caused by the children growing too fast.

paint

something is like watching paint dry said to mean that you find something extremely boring ○ *'We've done one shot since nine this morning,' complains Donna, a student who has taken the day off to be an extra. 'It's like watching paint dry.'*

pale

★ **beyond the pale** completely unacceptable ○ *There will be no more compromises with people whose views are beyond the pale.*

'Pale' comes from the Latin 'palum', meaning 'stake', and in English it came to refer to a territorial boundary marked by a line of stakes. The area inside was regarded as civilized, but the area beyond the pale was seen as barbaric.

palm

grease someone's palm to give money to an official in order to gain an unfair advantage over other people or in order to get something that you want ○ *Files do not move in government offices unless you grease the palms of officials.*

The idea behind this expression is that grease and oil help machines work smoothly. In the same way, bribing people will make it easier to get what you want.

pan

be going down the pan or **go down the pan** → see **down**

Pandora

★ **open a Pandora's box** to do something that unintentionally causes a lot of problems, which you did not know existed before ○ *This latest controversy has opened a Pandora's box of intrigue amongst the coalition government's different factions.*

According to Roman mythology, Prometheus offended the gods and in revenge Jupiter ordered the creation of Pandora, the first woman. Jupiter gave Pandora a box which she was to offer to the man she married. Pandora married Prometheus's brother Epimethius. He opened the box and all the problems and wickedness that now trouble the world flew out and could never be put back.

pants

beat the pants off someone (*informal*) to defeat someone completely in a contest or competition ○ *Devlin indicated the chess table beside the sofa. 'Any excuse to get away from that. He was beating the pants off me.'*

bore the pants off someone or **scare the pants off someone** or **charm the pants off someone** (*informal*) to bore, scare, or charm someone a lot ○ *When I was a kid, circuses bored the pants off me, but I'd always wanted to be a performer.*

someone is caught with their pants down said to mean that something happens that someone is not prepared for and that reveals an embarrassing or shocking fact about them. In British English, you can also say that someone **is caught with their trousers down**.
○ *In 1991, the Department of Transport was caught with its pants down and took seven months to produce the document needed to change legislation.*

wear the pants → see **wear**

paper

not worth the paper it's written on
if a promise, agreement, or guarantee is not worth the paper it's written on, it is in fact worthless, although it appears to be official or definite ○ *If consumers do not know they can get compensation when a service breaks down, these service standards will not be worth the paper they are written on.*

a paper tiger a person, country, or organization that seems to be powerful, but does not really have any power ○ *Unless the assembly has the power to fire the mayor, it will prove to be nothing but a paper tiger.*

a paper trail (*American*) written evidence of someone's activities
○ *The criminal proceedings were raised after investigations found a paper trail of checks that were written on dummy bank accounts.*

someone can't fight their way out of a paper bag said to mean that someone is very bad at fighting ○ *We've already shown you that they are no use to you as allies. They couldn't fight their way out of a paper bag.*

★ **something looks good on paper**
said to mean that something seems to be a good idea, plan, or argument when you read about it, but may not be good in reality ○ *This system looks good on paper but it is expensive and, in my view, still of very limited value.*

papers

get your walking papers or
be given your walking papers
(*American*) to be made to leave something such as a job or a relationship. The British expression is **be given your marching orders**. ○ *It was Vogel's turn to get his walking papers from the board of directors.*

This is derived from the instructions given to infantry soldiers about the length and destination of a march.

par

In golf, 'par' is the number of strokes a good golfer is expected to take for a particular hole or for the whole course.

★ **below par** or
under par
1 below the standard expected ○ *The recession has left sales a little below par in the past two or three years.*
2 tired or ill and unable to perform or work as well as usual ○ *Women who feel below par are unlikely to perform at their best.*

★ **par for the course** normal and to be expected ○ *He said long hours are par for the course. 'I'm up every morning at six, or even earlier.'*

parade

rain on someone's parade
(*journalism*) to do something which spoils someone's plan, usually a plan that is very important to them ○ *It's irritating that he could rain on my parade by stealing the record before me.*

parker

'Nosey' is sometimes spelled 'nosy'.

a nosey parker (*British*) someone who is interested in things that are nothing to do with them ○ *The village's resident nosey parker, Olive, likes to spy on her neighbours with binoculars.*

'Parker' may refer to Matthew Parker, who became Archbishop of Canterbury in 1559, and had a reputation for interfering in people's business.

parrot

learn something parrot fashion
(*British*) to learn something by repeating it many times, without really understanding what it means ○ *There are no books, pens or chairs here, just a*

blackboard and a dirt floor where 150 dusty children sit in rows, learning their words parrot fashion.

> Some parrots are able to imitate human speech, and repeat words and phrases, although they do not really understand what they are saying.

part

★ **look the part**

1 to dress or behave in the way that is characteristic of a particular kind of person ○ *You look the part of an English gentleman, so he is half ready to believe you as soon as you meet.*

> This is probably derived from the idea of an actor wearing a costume that suited the role or part that they were playing.

2 (mainly British) to seem impressive ○ *I don't know what it's like to drive but it certainly looks the part.*

★ **part and parcel** involved or included in something and unable to be separated from it ○ *There comes a time during every player's season when his form dips and the goals don't go in. It's part and parcel of being a professional.*

take someone's part (British, old-fashioned) to support or defend someone, especially in a dispute with other people ○ *It seemed to me that she should have taken my part, should somehow have defended me from my father.*

take something in good part (British) to not be offended or upset by something ○ *One or two comments were made about his clothes but he took it all in good part.*

party

bring something to the party to make a contribution to a particular activity or situation ○ *Johnson asked, 'What do they bring to the party?' 'They bring a lot to the party,' Cohen replied, 'principally $3 billion in capital.'*

past

be past it or

be getting past it (British) to no longer be as good as in the past ○ *My husband Eric could do with another second-hand car. The one we've got at the moment is getting a bit past it.*

I wouldn't put it past someone said to mean that you would not be surprised if someone did something bad ○ *I wouldn't put it past him to double-cross Schrader, especially after the rumour I heard the other day.*

pasture

put someone out to pasture to make someone retire from their job, or move them to an unimportant job, usually because people think that they are too old to be useful ○ *I'm retiring next month. They're putting me out to pasture.*

> When horses have reached the end of their working lives, they are sometimes released into fields to graze.

pastures

greener pastures a new and better situation ○ *There are drawbacks for nurses seeking greener pastures overseas, and many are put off by the lengthy process involved in going to work in the US.*

★ **pastures new** (British) a new situation ○ *If the job doesn't meet my ambitions I'll be off to pastures new. I want to go to the top.*

> This is a quotation from 'Lycidas' (1638) by the English poet Milton: 'At last he rose, and twitch'd his Mantle blew: Tomorrow to fresh Woods, and Pastures new.' This is sometimes wrongly quoted as 'fresh fields and pastures new'.

pat

★ **a pat on the back** congratulations or appreciation for something someone has done ○ *Any mail order shop that gives such* rapid response to a customer's complaint deserves a pat on the back.

stand pat (mainly American) to not change something or refuse to change your mind about something ○ There are certain issues on which Britain would stand pat and insist on unanimity.

In the game of poker, if a player stands pat, they are satisfied with the hand dealt to them and do not exchange any of their cards.

patch

★ **not a patch on someone or something** (British) not nearly as good as someone or something else ○ Of course, the facilities aren't a patch on those of richer schools, but the boys think they're terrific.

This is probably a shortened version of 'not fit to be a patch on', suggesting a piece of cloth that is not good enough to be used as a patch to mend a hole in a good piece of clothing.

path

beat a path to someone's door to be eager to talk to someone or to do business with them ○ Fashion editors now beat a path to Mugler's door and thousands of followers flock to get into one of his events.

This expression has been attributed to the American writer Ralph Waldo Emerson (1803-82), who used similar words in a lecture: 'If a man write a better book, preach a better sermon, or make a better mousetrap than his neighbour, 'tho he build his house in the woods, the world will make a beaten path to his door.'

★ **cross someone's path** to meet someone by chance ○ The book is full of cutting criticisms of the celebrities who crossed her path.

path-breaking (mainly American, journalism) completely different and new and affecting the way in which things are done or considered in the future

○ Russia's Parliament today approved a path-breaking measure that gives individual farmers a right to buy and sell their own land.

pay dirt

'Pay dirt' is often written as 'paydirt'.

hit pay dirt or
strike pay dirt (mainly American) to find or achieve something important and valuable ○ 'Let's not give up on the courts,' Millard says. 'We still might hit pay dirt with one of the issues.'

This expression probably refers to earth which contains enough gold dust to make it financially worthwhile to look for gold in it.

peanuts

if you pay peanuts, you get monkeys (British) said to mean that if an employer pays very low wages, they cannot expect to find good staff ○ The new pay policy will definitely have an effect on quality. The truth of the matter is that if they pay peanuts, they will get monkeys.

pearls

cast pearls before swine (literary) to waste your time by offering something that is helpful or valuable to someone who does not appreciate or understand it ○ I have wonderful costumes, with feathers and top hats, but it's like casting pearls before swine, they don't care what you wear.

This expression comes from the Bible, from the Sermon on the Mount (Matthew 7:6), when Jesus is giving His followers advice on how they should live. He tells them not to waste things that are holy on the unholy, and not to throw precious things (such as pearls) to the pigs.

pearls of wisdom something that sounds very wise or helpful. People usually use this expression ironically, to suggest that in fact they think the person is saying something very obvious or boring. ○ *I'm sure we're all very grateful for the pearls of wisdom that fall from Mr. Greenberg's lips.*

pear-shaped

★ **go pear-shaped** if a situation goes pear-shaped, things start to go wrong, and bad things start happening ○ *We started well, top of the table, but it all went pear-shaped and we lost five matches in a row.*

peas

like two peas in a pod very similar in appearance or character ○ *She is convinced the men are brothers. She said: 'It was uncanny. They were like two peas in a pod.'*

pebble

not the only pebble on the beach (mainly British) not the only person who is important or should be considered in a particular situation, although they may think they are ○ *You should encourage him to understand that he is very definitely not the only pebble on the beach.*

pecker

keep your pecker up (British) to remain cheerful in a difficult situation ○ *'I'll give you a ring later because I must go now.' 'Fine. Well, keep your pecker up.' 'I'll try.'*

'Pecker' was a slang term for the nose, comparing it to a bird's beak. If someone is unhappy, they tend to look downwards so that their nose points towards the ground.

pecking

★ **the pecking order** the order of importance of the people or things within a group ○ *Offices came in 29 sizes, which varied in accordance with the occupant's place in the corporate pecking order.*

When groups of hens are kept together, a 'pecking order' tends to form. This means that a stronger bird can peck a weaker bird without being pecked in return.

pedestal

A pedestal is a base on which something such as a statue stands.

knock someone off their pedestal to show that someone is not as good or talented as people generally think ○ *The tabloids had been trying for several years to knock Jackson off his pedestal.*

★ **put someone on a pedestal** to think someone is extremely good, talented or perfect ○ *I put my own parents on a pedestal. I felt they could do no wrong.*

peg

a peg on which to hang something a way of introducing or drawing attention to your ideas or opinions
○ *He rarely discusses the book, using it as a peg on which to hang his opinions – and not necessarily those related to the book.*

a square peg in a round hole someone who is in a situation or is doing a task that does not suit them at all ○ *Taylor is clearly the wrong man for the job – a square peg in a round hole.*

take someone down a peg or two or **bring someone down a peg or two** to make someone who is behaving in an arrogant and unpleasant way realize that they are not as important or talented as they think ○ *I do think he needed taking down a peg or two.*

This expression may refer to the tuning of musical instruments such as guitars or violins, where pegs are used to keep the strings tight. Alternatively, it may refer to the game of cribbage, where pegs are used to keep the score.

pegged

have someone pegged to understand completely the way someone is or who they are ○ *Those who have her pegged as fragile singer-songwriter should hear her touring band at full tilt blasting out the Na Na Song.*

pennies

not have two pennies to rub together to have very little money ○ *And from all those interviews her family gave to the Press they sounded as if they hadn't two pennies to rub together.*

pinch pennies to try to spend as little money as possible ○ *States and the federal government are pinching pennies everywhere they can and often cutting arts programs first.*

penn'orth

your two penn'orth (*British*) your opinion about something, which may not have been asked for. The American expression is your **two cents' worth**. ○ *I'm just putting my two penn'orth in, that's all. The same as you are.*

≡ 'Two penn'orth' means 'two pennies' worth'.

penny

in for a penny, in for a pound (*mainly British*) said to mean that you are firmly committed to a particular course of action, even though it will probably cost a lot of money or use a lot of resources if you continue ○ *In for a penny, in for a pound. I took the jacket to the counter.*

not have a penny to your name → see **name**

★ **the penny drops** (*mainly British*) said to mean that someone finally understands or realizes something ○ *It seems the penny has finally dropped – house prices won't budge until first-time buyers are tempted into the market.*

≡ This expression probably refers to slot machines, which only operate when you put in a coin.

penny-wise and pound-foolish (*mainly British, old-fashioned*) careful in small matters but careless in more important ones ○ *If we had auditors to go out and check on this, we would have saved billions of dollars. In other words, we have been penny-wise and pound-foolish here.*

turn up like a bad penny (*British, old-fashioned*) to appear again in a place where you are not welcome or wanted ○ *Her husband was able to trace her, to turn up again on her doorstep like the proverbial bad penny.*

two a penny or
ten a penny (*British*) used for describing things or people that are not especially valuable or interesting because there are a lot of them. The American expression is **a dime a dozen**. ○ *Gloomy economic forecasts are ten-a-penny in Europe.*

perch

A perch is a pole, branch or other place where a bird sits to rest.

fall off the perch (*British, old-fashioned*) to die ○ *He fell off the perch years ago.*

fall off your perch to fail, or suffer damage to your status or position ○ *There'll be no end of people ready to knock you down or grin with glee when you fall off your perch.*

knock someone off their perch (*British*) to cause someone to fail, or damage their status or position ○ *For the leading regional firms this is an excellent time to knock London firms off their perch and seize the advantages of lower fees and local contacts.*

petard

hoist by your own petard (*formal*) if someone is hoist by their own petard, their plan to benefit themselves or to harm someone else results instead in benefit to the other person or harm to themselves ○ *His plans backfired terribly and in the end he was hoist by his own petard.*

≡ 'Petards' were metal balls filled with gunpowder which were used to blow up walls or gates. The gunpowder was lit by a slow-burning fuse, but there was always a danger that the device would explode too soon and 'hoist' the person lighting it, that is, blow them up in the air.

Peter

rob Peter to pay Paul to use money meant for paying off one debt to pay off a different debt and so still be in debt ○ *His mortgages ran into arrears and he borrowed from loan companies. He started robbing Peter to pay Paul.*

phrase

to coin a phrase said when you are making a pun or using a cliché or colloquial expression, in order to show that you realize people might think that it is a silly or boring thing to say, but you think it is relevant in spite of this ○ *Stunned Jackson was, to coin a phrase, 'sick as a parrot'.*

> To coin a new word means to invent it or use it for the first time. In this expression, the term is being used ironically.

picnic

be no picnic be difficult or unpleasant ○ *'Poor little mites,' she said of the evacuees. 'It's no picnic for them being taken away from their homes.'*

picture

★ **get the picture** to understand what another person is trying to explain or describe to you ○ *They smoke, they play snooker, they do the pools. You get the picture, I'm sure.*

in the picture

1 involved in the situation you are talking about ○ *I was completely in the picture from the beginning.*
2 very likely to get something such as a promotion or success ○ *He told me that Annabella was back in the picture. She was the best one they could find.*

keep someone in the picture (British) to tell someone about any changes or

developments in a situation ○ *He's changed so many things – too many to mention. But he's always kept me in the picture.*

out of the picture

1 no longer involved in the situation you are talking about ○ *Once Derek was out of the picture, however, Malcolm's visits to the Swires became more frequent.*
2 not one of the people who is being considered for a promotion or place on a team ○ *But I've been told I'm fifth-choice striker, so I'm totally out of the picture.*

★ **put someone in the picture** (British) to tell someone about a situation which they need to know about ○ *I believe that I could now produce evidence to prove my case, if you are prepared to listen. I brought you here for that reason, to put you in the picture.*

pie

eat humble pie to admit that you have been wrong and apologize, especially in situations where this is humiliating or embarrassing for you ○ *The Queen's Press secretary resigned over his personal attack on the duchess. He was forced to eat humble pie and publicly apologise to the duchess.*

> 'Umbles' is an old word for the guts and offal of deer. When nobles had venison or deer to eat, the 'umbles' were made into a pie for their servants. As 'umbles' pie was eaten by 'humble' people, the two words gradually became confused. 'Humble pie' came to be used to refer to something humiliating or unpleasant.

★ **pie in the sky** very unlikely to happen ○ *Ideally what I would like to see would be free childcare, but I think that's a bit pie in the sky at the moment.* ○ *Changes are a real possibility. This is not pie-in-the-sky stuff.*

> This expression comes from the song 'The Preacher and the Slave' (1911) by Joe Hill, an American songwriter and workers' organizer: 'You'll get pie in the sky when you die. (That's a lie.)'

piece

all of a piece with each part or aspect consistent with the rest ○ *Thus the biosphere is all of a piece, an immense, integrated, living system.*

★ **a piece of cake** something that is very easy to do ○ *'It's not exactly a stressful job is it?' 'If it's quiet, it's a piece of cake. It's just a bit boring.'*

a piece of the action → see **action**

say your piece to give your opinion about a particular matter, although you are aware that other people may not agree with you, or be interested in what you have to say ○ *Each preacher stood for two minutes on a box, said his piece, and stepped down.*

pieces

★ **go to pieces**

1 to be so upset or distressed by something that you cannot control your emotions or cope with the things that you have to do ○ *Every time he's faced with a problem he goes to pieces.*

2 if your work or a relationship goes to pieces, it is no longer as good as it once was and you cannot stop it getting worse ○ *My work is all going to pieces.*

★ **pick up the pieces** to do what you can to get a situation back to normal again after something bad has happened ○ *People in the high desert communities near Palm Springs, California, are picking up the pieces after last night's earthquake.*

shot to pieces completely ruined ○ *When I came here my confidence was shot to pieces.*

pig

eat like a pig to eat a lot of food, usually in a greedy or disgusting manner ○ *She could hear the part of herself that was self-critical say, 'You eat like a pig. I can't stand looking at you. You're fat.'*

make a pig of yourself (informal) to eat a very large amount at one meal

○ *I'm afraid I made a pig of myself at dinner.*

make a pig's ear of something (British, informal) to do something very badly ○ *I made a pig's ear of it last time and I'm going to make sure that won't happen again.*

move like a greased pig (mainly American) to move very fast so that nobody can catch or stop you ○ *He is a god of rock music – even though rock can be hard and heavy, it can move like a greased pig through a cocktail party, knocking over everything it doesn't slide past.*

squeal like a stuck pig to scream very loudly, as though you are in a lot of pain ○ *Alan tried to calm him while Miller continued to scream like a stuck pig.*

sweat like a pig (informal) to be very hot and to sweat a lot ○ *The two officers standing just out of camera shot were sweating like pigs in the studio lights.*

piggy

the piggy in the middle (British) someone who is involved against their will in a conflict between two other people or groups, which leads to a very unpleasant situation for them ○ *When the men arrived on Doug's cruiser it was not to service his engine. He found himself piggy in the middle of an ivory smuggling outfit and Customs.*

'Piggy in the middle' is a children's game in which two children throw a ball to each other over the head of a third child who tries to catch it.

pigs

pigs might fly (British) said to mean that you think that something that someone has said is very unlikely to happen or be true ○ *'There's a chance he isn't involved in this, of course.' 'And pigs might fly.'*

pike

come down the pike (American) to start to happen or to become available ○ *There may be some new treatments coming* down the pike. There's a new medicine called tacrine or THA that was recently made available.

≣ The reference here is to someone
≣ travelling along a turnpike or toll road.

pile

at the bottom of the pile or **at the top of the pile** low down or high up in society or in an organization ○ *I'm more concerned about the people at the bottom of the pile who don't have jobs and who don't have houses.*

pill

a bitter pill to swallow a difficult or unpleasant fact or situation that has to be accepted ○ *Gordon Hodgson, Cowie's chief executive, said the failure to win was 'a little bit of a bitter pill to swallow'.*

★ **sugar the pill** (British) or **sweeten the pill** (British) or **sugar-coat the pill** (American) to try to make bad news or an unpleasant situation more acceptable for someone by giving them or telling them something good or pleasant at the same time ○ *Ministers may reprieve Harefield hospital to sugar the pill of a further round of hospital cuts and closures in London and the South-east.*

★ **swallow a bitter pill** to accept a difficult or unpleasant fact or situation ○ *Our people have swallowed a bitter pill in accepting this peace agreement.*

pillar

from pillar to post (mainly British) if someone is moved from pillar to post, they are moved repeatedly from one place or position to another, usually in a hurried or disorganized way so that they suffer as a result ○ *I didn't want the children pushed from pillar to post.*

≣ This expression comes from an early
≣ form of tennis that was played
≣ indoors. Players often played shots
≣ back and forth across the court, from

≣ the posts supporting the net to the
≣ pillars at the back of the court.

pillar to post (British, journalism) used for describing a victory in sport, especially in horse racing, in which the winner was in the lead from the start of the race ○ *Sally Prosser held off the best of the Far East to top the Asian circuit, thanks largely to a pillar to post victory in the JAL Malaysian Open.*

≣ This may refer to the posts that mark
≣ the start and finish of a racecourse.

pilot

'Autopilot' is often written as 'auto-pilot' in British English.

★ **on automatic pilot** or **on autopilot** acting without thinking about what you are doing, usually because you have done something many times before or because you are very tired ○ *Steve seemed to be on automatic pilot and able to go on driving without a word of complaint or apparent fatigue.*

≣ In aircraft, automatic pilot is a device
≣ which automatically keeps the plane
≣ on course without the need for the
≣ pilot to do much.

pinch

★ **at a pinch** (British) or **in a pinch** (American) if absolutely necessary. ○ *Six people, and more at a pinch, could be seated comfortably at the table.*

★ **feel the pinch** to not have as much money as you used to have, and so be unable to buy the things you would like to buy ○ *Poor households were still feeling the pinch and the imposition of VAT on fuel made matters worse.*

pink

in the pink (old-fashioned) very fit and healthy ○ *'Hello. Good evening. How are you?' 'Very well. And you?' 'Oh, in the pink.'*

'Pink' here means best, and the word is derived from the flower of this name, which also gave its name to the colour pink.

tickled pink extremely pleased about something ○ *Her dressmaker, Nicole Marnier, would just be tickled pink if we put one of her outfits in the magazine.*

This expression may refer to someone's face becoming pink or redder when they are being tickled.

pins

be on pins and needles or **sit on pins and needles** (*mainly American*) to be very anxious or nervous because you are waiting to see if something happens the way you want it to ○ *I think we all have been sitting on pins and needles and anxious for something to happen.*

pipe

put that in your pipe and smoke it said to tell someone that although they may dislike or disagree with something you have just said, they must accept that it is a fact or true ○ *As for rules, the only person who makes rules in this house is me. So you can tell Miss Underwood from me: she can put that in her pipe and smoke it.*

pipeline

★ **in the pipeline** being planned or in progress. The usual expression in American English is **in the works**. ○ *Over 350 major hospital schemes have been completed. There are nearly 300 more in the pipeline.*

piper

he who pays the piper calls the tune said to mean that the person who pays for something has the right to decide how that thing operates or is organized ○ *The ancient law that he who pays the piper calls the tune has not been repealed even in this permissive democracy.*

This may come from the custom, dating back to the 17th century, of hiring travelling musicians to play at festivals and weddings. The people who paid for the music were able to choose the tunes they wanted to hear.

pitch

★ **make a pitch**
1 to tell people how good something is and try to persuade them to support it or buy it ○ *The president also used his remarks to make a pitch for further space exploration.*
2 to try to obtain something ○ *So far Federal Reserve Chairman Alan Greenspan hasn't made a pitch for the job.*

queer someone's pitch (*mainly British*) to make it very difficult for someone to achieve what they are trying to do ○ *We did everything for you here, and you repay the school by doing your best to queer the pitch for us at a college to which we normally send our best boys.*

In the past, a pitch was the place where a showman set up his tent or stall. If anyone, especially the police, spoiled or interrupted his show, they were said to queer the pitch. There is an old verb 'queer' which means 'cheat' or 'spoil'.

place

★ **fall into place**
1 if you have been trying to understand something, and then everything falls into place, you suddenly understand it and everything becomes clear ○ *Bits of the puzzle fell into place. He knew now who had written the letter summoning Father Benjamin.*
2 if things fall into place, events happen naturally to produce the situation you want ○ *During February everything will start to fall into place, leaving you with a satisfied feeling that you're living life to the full.*

out of place
1 not in the correct place ○ *Everything*

plate 219

was neatly arranged. There was no sign of anything out of place.

2 seeming wrong in a particular situation ○ *The man seemed somehow out of place at a gallery opening. He looked more earnest than elegant.*

a place in the sun a job or situation where someone will be happy and well-off, and have everything that they want ○ *I've done what everybody's done. I've fought my way in. I think I've earned my place in the sun.*

> This phrase was used by Bernard von Bulow, the German Chancellor, in a speech to the German parliament in 1897, referring to his country's desire to play a part in the colonisation of East Asia: 'We do not wish to force anyone into the shade, but demand our own place in the sun'.

★ **put someone in their place** to show someone that they are less important or clever than they think they are ○ *In a few words she had not only put him in his place, but delivered a precise and damning assessment of his movie.*

★ **take second place** to be considered to be less important than another thing or person and be given less attention than them ○ *My personal life has had to take second place to my career.*

places

★ **be going places** to be showing a lot of talent or ability and be likely to become very successful ○ *If we can play like that every week, then this club is going places.*

★ **in high places** used for describing people who have powerful and influential positions in a government, society, or organization ○ *You do not rise so high, so fast, without having a few friends in high places.*

plague

avoid someone or something like the plague to deliberately avoid

someone or something because you dislike them so much ○ *I normally avoid cheap Chianti like the plague.*

> The plague is bubonic plague, a disease which killed over 50 million people in Europe and Asia during the 14th century and was referred to as the Black Death.

plain

plain as day very easy to see, or very obvious and easy to understand ○ *He was lying there plain as day, a starchy sheet covering the lower half of his hospital gown.*

plain as the nose on your face very obvious or easy to understand ○ *It's plain as the nose on your face that this company is wildly undervalued.*

planet

★ **what planet is someone on?** or **what planet does someone come from?** *(British, informal)* said to mean that you think someone has crazy ideas, or behaves in a very strange way, or does not understand something at all ○ *What planet are they on? The Government could easily do something about bank charges, but they won't because that might offend their supporters in the banking industry.*

plank

walk the plank *(journalism)* to accept responsibility for something that has gone wrong and leave your position ○ *If they think that the President is going to lose, they might decide, 'OK, why should I walk the plank for him?'*

> Many people believe that pirates used to kill their prisoners by forcing them to walk along a plank sticking out from the edge of a ship until they fell into the sea.

plate

★ **have enough on your plate** or **have a lot on your plate** to have a lot of work to do or a lot of things to deal with ○ *He's got enough on his plate without worrying about tactics and the performances of others.*

★ **something is handed to someone on a plate** (*mainly British*) said to mean that someone is given something desirable without having to work for it or make an effort to get it ○ *He conveyed the unfortunate impression of never having had to fight for anything in his life: even the presidency was handed to him on a plate.*

step up to the plate (*American*) to come forward and take responsibility for something ○ *He's got to step up to the plate and deal with these accusations.*

≣ When baseball players step up to the plate, they move into batting position.

platter

hand someone something on a silver platter or

hand someone something on a platter to give someone something without them having to work or make an effort to get it ○ *You act like a five-year-old. You expect me to hand you everything on a silver platter, and when you don't get it, you stamp your little foot and cry.*

≣ A platter is a large plate or shallow dish used for serving food.

play

make great play of something (*British*) to put too much emphasis on something or exaggerate its importance ○ *The Conservatives made great play of the defection to them of 20 former members of the SDP.*

make a play for something to try to get something that you want ○ *Analysts say the company could soon be making a play for properties around the world.*

make a play for someone to try to win the attention or admiration of a person who you find attractive ○ *All the girls made a play for him.*

play someone for a fool to deceive someone and use them for your own advantage ○ *John, do not play me for a fool. You owe me better than that.*

playing field

★ **a level playing field** a situation that is fair. You usually use this expression when talking about the fact that a situation is not fair, or when saying that you think it should be fair. ○ *At the moment we are not competing on a level playing field.*

plot

★ **lose the plot** (*journalism*) to become confused and not know what you should do ○ *Vikram's working so many hours as junior doctor he's losing the plot completely and keeps mumbling about the people he's killed by falling asleep on the job.*

the plot thickens said to mean that a complicated situation or series of events starts to become even more complicated or mysterious ○ *At this point the plot thickened further. A link emerged between the attempt to kill the Pope and the kidnapping of the American.*

≣ This phrase was widely used in 19th century melodramas, or popular plays that involved extreme situations and extreme emotions, and is now used humorously

plug

★ **pull the plug on something** to stop supporting a project or activity, usually with money, so that it fails and has to stop ○ *The Government has set out detailed conditions under which it would pull the plug on the sale.*

plum

a plum in your mouth (*British*) an upper-class accent ○ *I heard Mr Downer speaking on the radio on the previous day. I was not conscious of the 'plum in the mouth', but I was aware of his clear diction.*

This is from the idea that the accent used by upper-class speakers of British English makes them sound as though they have a plum in their mouth.

plunge

★ **take the plunge** to do something that you have been thinking of doing for some time, even though it is difficult or risky ○ *Helen decided to take the plunge and turned professional in 1991.*

poacher

poacher turned gamekeeper
(*British*) someone who has changed their job or opinion and now has one which seems the opposite of the one they had before ○ *Gary Mason, boxing's poacher turned gamekeeper, will make his managerial debut tomorrow.*

A poacher is someone who illegally hunts animals such as deer, pheasant or salmon. A gamekeeper is someone employed by a landowner to look after these animals, which are known as game.

pocket

★ **dip into your pocket** or
dig into your pocket to pay for something with your own money ○ *Potential lenders will need to be persuaded that the government is tackling its economic problems before they dig into their pockets again.*

in someone's pocket if you are in someone's pocket, they control you or have power over you and so you do everything that they tell you ○ *The Labour party suffered badly in the election from Conservative claims that it was in the pockets of the unions.*

★ **out of pocket** having less money than you should have or than you intended, for example because something was more expensive than you expected or because of a mistake ○ *The promoter claims he was*

left £36,000 out of pocket.

★ **out-of-pocket** used for describing expenses which someone pays out of their own money, and which are normally paid back later ○ *I charge twenty dollars an hour plus out-of-pocket expenses.*

pockets

★ **line your pockets** to make a lot of money in a dishonest or unfair way ○ *He has been lining his pockets for 27 years while his country has festered in poverty.*

live in each other's pockets
(*mainly British*) to spend a great deal of time together, perhaps too much ○ *Just because you're married doesn't mean you have to live in each other's pockets.*

point

★ **be a sore point with someone** if a particular subject is a sore point with someone, it makes them feel angry, embarrassed, or upset ○ *The continuing presence of foreign troops in their country remains a very sore point with these students.*

★ **boiling point** a situation which has become very tense or dangerous because the people involved are so angry that they are likely to go out of control ○ *Tempers were already close to boiling point as the dispute remained deadlocked for the ninth day.*

not to put too fine a point on it
(*British*) said to mean that what you are about to say may sound unpleasant, unkind, or critical ○ *We didn't meet. In fact, not to put too fine a point on it, I was warned off.*

★ **a sticking point** a problem which stops you from achieving something, especially in a series of negotiations or a discussion ○ *Sources say a Republican call for a cut in the capital gains tax is the main sticking point in budget negotiations.*

points

★ **score points**
1 to gain an advantage over someone,

especially in a discussion or argument ○ They're not remotely concerned about the disabled. They're concerned about trying to score points off Willie Brown, the Democratic speaker of the State Assembly. ○ We can see our leaders looking shifty in close-up every night on television. There is no frankness, only point-scoring.

2 to do something that impresses someone or makes them admire you ○ Again, Laine paused, clearly confident in his arguments. He was scoring points with the judge and the spectators. The judge kept nodding in agreement.

pole

in pole position (mainly British) in a very strong position in a competition or competitive situation, and likely to win or be successful ○ They've been favourites all season and are in pole position now.

someone wouldn't touch something or someone with a barge pole (British) or

someone wouldn't touch something or someone with a ten-foot pole (American) said to mean that someone does not want to have anything to do with someone or something, because they do not trust them or like them ○ The history of the place kept the price down. No one would touch it with a barge pole.

≣ A barge pole is a very long pole that is used to move a barge forward.

up the greasy pole (British) reaching a more successful position as a result of working very hard and dealing with all the difficulties you meet ○ The way has now been eased to allow other women of courage and commitment to follow me up the greasy pole of promotion.

≣ In the past, climbing up or along a greasy pole in order to get a prize at the end of it was a popular fairground competition.

poles

★ **poles apart** very different ○ The East seemed to be poles apart from the capitalist West.

≣ The reference here is to the north and south poles.

poor

poor as a church mouse (old-fashioned) very poor ○ I was as poor as a church mouse, but I bought that wreck of a car.

≣ Mice living in a church are unlikely to find much to eat as there is no kitchen or food cupboard.

pop

take a pop at someone (British, journalism, informal) to hit someone ○ Andy was just having a quiet meal with some of his pals when this guy took a pop at him.

★ **take a pop at someone or something** (British, journalism, informal) to attack or criticize someone or something ○ Sheena couldn't resist taking a pop at the revival of Scots culture abroad.

port

a port in a storm a person, place, or organization where you can get help in a difficult situation ○ She was sweet to take me in the way she did, hardly any notice at all, just told me to come right to her. A port in a storm is a welcome thing.

possum

play possum (literary) to try to make people ignore you by pretending to be dead or asleep ○ 'Playing possum, huh?' said Joe. 'Right,' said Frank. 'I figured it might be interesting to hear what they had to say to each other when they thought I was unconscious.'

≣ The possum or opossum is a North American and Australian animal. If it is threatened by another animal it sometimes lies still, as if it is dead, so that the animal will lose interest.

post

The following expressions refer to the finishing post in a horse race.

first past the post finishing first or achieving something first in a race or competitive situation ○ *First past the post was Kenyan athlete John Mutai, who pipped Irishman Jerry Healy by just 20 seconds.*

This expression is often used in talking about electoral systems. A first-past-the-post electoral system is one in which the candidate who gets the most votes or the party that wins in the most areas wins the election.

pip someone at the post or
pip someone to the post (British) to narrowly beat someone in a competition or race to achieve something ○ *They were concerned that their rivals might pip them to the post.*

postal

go postal (informal) to become extremely angry ○ *When he saw the sign he went postal.*

posted

★ **keep someone posted** to continue giving someone the latest information about a situation that concerns them ○ *She made me promise to keep her posted on developments.*

poster

poster child (journalism) someone who is so typical of a quality, activity, or situation that everyone associates them with it ○ *Eikenberry has led a campaign to make Lowry the poster child for tax increases and everything wrong with government.*

A poster child is literally a young person who appears on a poster advertising something.

pot

go to pot if something is going to pot, its condition is becoming very bad, because

it has not been properly looked after ○ *The neighbourhood really is going to pot.*

keep the pot boiling to make sure that a process does not stop ○ *I threw in a question, just to keep the pot boiling while my brain caught up.*

This expression may refer to meat which is chopped into pieces and cooked in a pot. Alternatively, the 'pot' may have been a melting pot, where metal objects were melted down.

the pot calling the kettle black said to mean that someone with a particular fault accuses someone else of having the same fault ○ *In a prime case of the pot calling the kettle black, 48-year-old Ian, whose recent loves included two 22-year-olds, asked a friend: 'Why must she go for an older man? She should know better than that.'*

In the past, both pots and kettles were hung over fires, and would be burned black.

the pot of gold at the end of the rainbow something that will be very difficult to achieve in reality, although you dream of getting it ○ *I would rather be honest with people than mislead them that there is going to be some pot of gold at the end of the rainbow.*

There is an old legend that a pot of gold is buried at the point where the end of the rainbow meets the ground.

a watched pot never boils (old-fashioned) said to mean that if you wait and watch anxiously to see something happen, it will seem to take a very long time, or it will not happen at all ○ *This strategy is doomed from the start because it is far too public: a watched pot never boils.*

potato

drop something or someone like a hot potato → see **drop**
a hot potato a subject or problem that is very topical and controversial which most

people would rather not have to deal with ○ *When she is confronted with a political hot potato such as abortion or tightening the gun laws, she is not beyond voicing her opinion.*

potatoes

small potatoes something that is not important or significant ○ *While a total tour attendance of around 20,000 is small potatoes by British standards, it is very big in this country.*

pot luck

'Pot luck' is usually written as 'potluck' in American English.

be pot luck if a meal at your house will be pot luck, you have not planned it or prepared any special food ○ *'We'll just be casual and eat in the kitchen. It's just pot luck,' Moira said. 'Hope you don't mind.'*

A potluck is a meal at which different guests bring different parts of the meal.

★ **take pot luck** to make a choice from what is available, although you do not have any knowledge to help you, and so it is a matter of luck whether you get something good ○ *We'd take potluck at whatever restaurants might still be open.* ○ *Travel firms stuck with hundreds of unsold package holidays are offering great breaks on a pot-luck basis.*

pound

your pound of flesh something you are entitled to, even though you might not need it and it will cause problems for the people you are getting it from ○ *Banks are quick enough to demand their pound of flesh from the small businessman and other regular customers when overdrafts run a little over the limit.*

This expression comes from Shakespeare's play 'The Merchant of Venice' (Act 4, Scene 1). Shylock is owed money by Antonio, and attempts to

carry out an agreement which allows him to cut off a pound of Antonio's flesh.

powder

keep your powder dry to be ready to take immediate action in case a situation suddenly gets worse ○ *The only course upon which the government could agree was to move cautiously, keep its powder dry, and await the outcome of events abroad.*

The powder referred to here is gunpowder. The expression comes from a story about the English leader Oliver Cromwell. He is said to have ended a speech to his soldiers, who were about to cross a river and go into battle, by saying: 'Put your trust in God, my boys, and keep your powder dry.'

powder keg

sit on a powder keg to be in a very dangerous situation, in which something could suddenly go seriously wrong at any time ○ *The Prime Minister was all too aware that he was sitting on a powder keg which could explode at any moment.*

A powder keg was a small barrel which was used to store gunpowder.

power

all power to your elbow or **more power to your elbow** (British, old-fashioned) said to wish someone luck and to encourage them to be successful ○ *Bobby Gould is a good man and he's now paving the way for a very good third division campaign. So all power to his elbow.*

This phrase wishes someone the strength to keep raising their glass and keep on drinking.

the power behind the throne a person who has all the power and control in an organization or situation, although someone else may appear to rule ○ *She was the real power behind the throne, a strong and single-minded woman manipulating a weaker husband for her own ends.*

practise

The verb 'practise' is spelled 'practice' in American English.

★ **practise what you preach** to behave in the way that you encourage other people to behave ○ *Blundell practised what he preached; having declared himself to be a Kenyan, he was the first British-born resident to apply for Kenyan citizenship.*

praise

damn with faint praise to say something about someone which sounds nice but which shows that you do not really have a high opinion of them ○ *In recent months he has consistently damned the government with faint praise, but earlier this week he issued an appeal for continuity.*

This expression was first used by the English writer Alexander Pope in his 'Epistle to Dr Arbuthnot' (1735): 'Damn with faint praise, assent with civil leer, And, without sneering, teach the rest to sneer.'

praise someone or something to the skies to praise someone or something a lot ○ *If you are a famous sportsman, you have got to get used to hearing yourself praised to the skies but only minutes later reading about how you are a disaster.*

praises

★ **sing the praises of someone** or **something** to praise someone or something in an enthusiastic way ○ *This may sound like we're singing our own praises here, but I honestly think most people find our music irresistible.*

prawn

come the raw prawn (*mainly Australian*) to try to cheat or trick someone ○ *I'm afraid to say they were caught trying to come the raw prawn, as it were.*

prayer

someone does not have a prayer of doing something said to mean that it is impossible for someone to achieve something ○ *He did not seem to have a prayer of regaining the world title.*

pregnant

you can't be half pregnant said to mean that it is often necessary to commit yourself fully to an idea or project, and you cannot keep changing your mind about it ○ *We did, however, pick up a valuable lesson: you can't be half-pregnant. An entrepreneur must be able to give his enterprise a full commitment.*

press

a full-court press (*American*) a situation in which people are making a lot of effort and putting a lot of pressure on something or someone in order to get a particular result ○ *The administration's full-court press on economic remedies also includes moves by the Treasury Secretary.*

In basketball, a full-court press is where the defending players stay close to the attacking players over the whole area of the court, rather than just in front of their own basket.

★ **get a bad press** to be repeatedly criticized, especially in the newspapers, on television, or on radio ○ *So-called 'arranged marriages', common in many cultures, tend to get a bad press in the West.*

pretty

sit pretty to be in a good, safe, or comfortable situation ○ *When the war started, they thought they were sitting pretty, because they had all that extra surplus grain.*

price

★ **at any price** even if unpleasant things happen as a result of your actions ○ *There's likely to be more violence from rebel groups that are determined to stop the peace process at any price.*

★ **at a price**

1 if something can be obtained at a price, it is very expensive ○ *Guests can always find a meal of sorts in the hotel restaurant, but at a price.*

2 if you get something you want at a price, you get it but you have to accept something unpleasant as well ○ *Fame comes at a price.*

everyone has their price or
every man has his price said to mean that everyone can be persuaded to do something dishonest or immoral, if they are offered a large enough amount of money ○ *While it may not be true that every man has his price, there are always those who have.*

pricks

kick against the pricks *(mainly British, literary, old-fashioned)* to show your opposition to people in authority ○ *Kicking against the pricks when you're 30 or 40 or more strikes me as a better test of one's convictions.*

⸙ This expression occurs in the Bible (Acts 9:5). It refers to cattle kicking out when people try to move them along by poking them with sticks.

pride

★ **swallow your pride** to decide to do something even though it is shameful or embarrassing, and you would prefer not to ○ *However, if political compulsions demand, he can swallow his pride and ally himself with his political enemies.*

print

★ **the small print** or
the fine print the part of a contract, agreement, or advertisement which contains important legal information, often in very small writing ○ *Patients who thought they were fully covered are being hit by huge bills because they did not read the small print on their insurance forms.*

prisoners

take no prisoners *(journalism)* to carry out a plan or an action in a very forceful and determined way, without caring if you harm or upset other people ○ *You will have to fight for what you want and what you believe in and you should assume the attitude that you're taking no prisoners.*

production

make a production of something to do something in a complicated or exaggerated way, when it could be done much more simply ○ *He made a production of brushing his hands clean on his pant legs.*

⸙ A production here is something such as a play or a musical.

profile

★ **a high profile** if someone has a high profile, people notice them and what they do ○ *He will be thinking about his future now that he has such a high profile in the cycling world.* ○ *She works three days a week in a high-profile job as communications director for a top advertising agency.*

★ **keep a low profile** to avoid doing things that will make people notice you ○ *The Home Secretary was keeping a low profile yesterday when the crime figures were announced in the House of Commons.*

proof

the proof of the pudding is in the eating said to mean that something new can only be judged to be good or bad after it has been tried or used ○ *A year after the changes were implemented, perhaps we can now apply the old saying that 'the proof of the pudding is in the eating'.*

⸙ In this expression, 'proof' means the testing of something rather than establishing that it is true. The idea is that the best way to test the quality of a pudding is to taste it rather than admire its appearance.

pudding

over-egg the pudding (mainly British) to try so hard to improve something that you spoil it, for example by making it seem exaggerated or extreme ○ *The movie obviously over-eggs the glowing childhood pudding with lots of cuddles, warm milk and snow pattering against the window panes.*

pull

pull the other one or
pull the other one, it's got bells on it (British) said to mean that you do not believe something someone tells you ○ *'The Duchess gave it to me.' 'Think I'd believe that? Pull the other one, it's got bells on it.'*

≡ 'One' in this expression refers to someone's leg. See the explanation for 'pull someone's leg' at 'leg'.

pulp

beat someone to a pulp or
beat someone to pulp to injure someone very badly by hitting them repeatedly ○ *Motorists were pulled from their cars, beaten and kicked to a pulp, and left to die in the road.*

pump

★ **prime the pump** (journalism) to take action to help something succeed or grow, usually by spending money on it ○ *Spring is the time when the government primes the pump to help farmers prepare their fields.*

≡ To prime a water pump means to pump it until it is full of water and all the air has been forced out, so that it is ready to be used.

punch

★ **pack a punch** to have a very powerful effect ○ *Arthur Miller's classic play 'Death of a Salesman' still packs a punch.*

pleased as punch very pleased ○ *Branfoot announced he was as pleased as punch with his team's performance.*

≡ 'Punch' is a character from traditional 'Punch and Judy' puppet shows, who enjoys making trouble for people. The puppet usually has a big grin.

punches

★ **not pull your punches** or
pull no punches to speak very honestly and directly about something even if it upsets people ○ *He had never lied to me in the past and he didn't pull his punches now. He told me that in his opinion, Robin would be dead in nine months.*

≡ If boxers pull their punches, they do not hit their opponent as hard as they could do.

roll with the punches to not allow difficulties or criticism to discourage you or affect you badly ○ *He has impressed all sides by his ability to negotiate and willingness to roll with the punches.*

≡ If boxers roll with the punches, they move their head and body backwards, away from their opponent's punch.

pup

be sold a pup (British) to buy or accept something and then feel deceived because it is not as good as you thought it would be ○ *No-one is being sold a pup. What you see is what you get.*

≡ A pup is a puppy or young dog, and is probably being contrasted with an animal that is older and does not need to be trained before being put to work.

purposes

at cross purposes if two people are at cross purposes, there is a misunderstanding between them because they think they are talking about or trying to do the same thing as each other, but they are actually talking about or trying to do different things ○ *They had been talking at cross purposes earlier, Enron realized. The Hungarian hadn't been offering him a slice of the deal at all.*

purse

★ **hold the purse strings** to control the way that money is spent in a particular family, organization, or country ○ *Six out of ten women think that financial institutions treat them like simpletons, even though they usually hold the domestic purse strings.*

push

at a push if absolutely necessary
○ *The only thing you didn't get in the village was milk and you could always, at a push, get some from the farm.*

get the push or
be given the push *(British, informal)* to lose your job ○ *The boss has been given the push in favour of his current number two.*

★ **when push comes to shove** or
if push comes to shove when a situation reaches a critical point and you must make a decision on how to progress ○ *They knew they could sit back, and when push came to shove I'd do all the work.*

pusher

★ **a pen pusher** *(mainly British)* or
a pencil pusher *(American)* someone who works in an office in contrast to more active kinds of work ○ *Many of the men who now sit on company boards are pencil pushers with PhDs and MBAs from top schools, but lack operating experience in business.*

putty

putty in your hands someone who will do anything you ask or tell them to do ○ *I was completely in awe of him, I was putty in his hands.*

Putty is a thick paste that is used to fix sheets of glass into window frames.

quantity

★ **an unknown quantity** a thing or person that you know very little about ○ *She had known Max for some years now, but he was still pretty much an unknown quantity.*

quart

a quart into a pint pot *(British)* a large amount of something that will not fit into a small container or space ○ *In putting together the article, I was faced with the problem of fitting a quart into a pint pot, there being so much material available.*

  A quart is a unit of measure for liquids. It is equal to two pints.

quarterback

a Monday morning quarterback *(American)* a person who criticizes or judges something unfairly, because although they now have full knowledge of the way things happened, the people involved could not possibly have had that knowledge and so could not have behaved any differently ○ *Some Monday-morning quarterbacks said the initial lower bid, without junk bonds, was a factor in his losing the company.*

  In American football, the quarterback is usually the player who calls out signals which tell the team which moves to make. In the United States, most professional football games are played on Sunday. A 'Monday morning quarterback' is someone, usually a man, who tells people what the coach should have done to win the game.

question

★ **beg the question**
  1 to make people want to ask a particular question ○ *Hopewell's success begs the question, why aren't more companies doing the same?*
  2 *(formal)* to suggest that another, more important problem has not been dealt with ○ *The New York Times stated that 'the warming of the earth's climate is no longer in dispute', somewhat begging the question of whether or not that warming is a greenhouse effect or, indeed, necessarily part of a continuing long-range trend.*

  This is a rough translation of the Latin expression 'petitio principii', a technical term used in logic to describe a situation in which the truth of something is assumed before it has been proved.

★ **a question mark** doubt or uncertainty ○ *Multi-party democracy has arrived – albeit with many question marks about its eventual form.*

quick

cut someone to the quick to make someone very upset ○ *That tone of hers always cut him to the quick.*

  The quick is the very sensitive flesh under the fingernails or toenails.

quick as a flash very quickly ○ *Harrison responded as quick as a flash.*

quids

quids in *(British, informal)* having made more money than you expected ○ *Workers at a window factory were furious when they found German money in their wage* packets. *But they soon cheered up when they realised it left them quids in.*

A quid is an informal word for a pound sterling.

quiet

quiet as a lamb very quiet, calm or gentle ○ *She's fine, quiet as a lamb. You really mustn't worry.*

quiet as a mouse very quiet or silent ○ *We were quiet as mice, hiding in there.*

quits

call it quits to decide to stop doing something or stop being involved in something ○ *There is a disco called the Club Coqui, which stays open until the last customer is ready to call it quits.*

quote

★ **quote, unquote** said to mean that you do not think that a particular word or phrase that has been used is accurate or suitable ○ *'Even though I'm this big, huge superstar quote unquote, I have family problems, insecurities about my body,' she says.*

Rr

rabbit

★ **pull a rabbit out of the hat**
(*journalism*) to unexpectedly do
something which solves a problem or
helps you to achieve something ○ *I
cannot pull a rabbit out of a hat every time I
go into the boxing ring. All I can do is do my
best.*

> This expression refers to a traditional
> magician's trick, in which a rabbit is
> produced mysteriously out of an
> apparently empty hat.

**someone is like a rabbit caught in
the headlights** said to mean that
someone is so frightened or nervous that
they do not know what to do ○ *He just
sat there, like a rabbit caught in the
headlights.*

> Animals such as rabbits or deer
> sometimes remain still because they
> do not know which way to run when
> the light from a vehicle's headlights
> shines on them at night.

race

★ **a race against time** a situation in
which you have a very short time to finish
a task and have to work very quickly
○ *The paramedics were in a race against time
to treat a six-year-old girl suffering with
breathing difficulties in Crawley, West Sussex.*

rack

on the rack (*mainly British*) in a state of
anxiety, distress, or difficulty ○ *They put
us on the rack when we were 2–1 up but we
came back well and it was great to win with
such a late goal.*

> The rack was an instrument of torture
> which was used in the past. Prisoners
> were tied to the rack, and their arms
> and legs were stretched until they
> confessed or told secrets, or died.

rack and ruin something that is going to
rack and ruin is falling into a very bad
condition, because nobody is looking
after it or dealing properly with it ○ *The
country is going to rack and ruin under this
government.*

> The old-fashioned spelling of 'rack' –
> 'wrack' means the same as 'wreck',
> something that has been destroyed.

radar

drop off the radar to be forgotten or
ignored because people's attention has
moved to something more important
○ *Stories in the news drop off the radar with
people after a couple of weeks.*

> When a plane or other moving object
> drops off the radar, it can no longer be
> detected by the system of radio waves
> used to find its position and track its
> movement.

rag

lose your rag (*British*) to suddenly lose
your temper with someone and get very
angry ○ *Everyone said Wright did well
simply because he didn't lose his rag with
anyone.*

a red rag to a bull → see **bull**

ragged

run someone ragged to make
someone do so much that they get
extremely tired ○ *He tends to produce his
best football before half-time, though often
coming back to run defenders ragged in the
closing minutes.*

rags

★ **rags to riches** said to describe the life of someone who was very poor when they were young, and who later became very rich and successful ○ *His life sounds to me like the classic rags to riches story. He married some money, I gather, but he made a lot more himself.*

rails

★ **go off the rails** *(mainly British)*

1 to start behaving in an unacceptable or strange way ○ *Our family was so happy until our daughter went off the rails. She left school at 15, left home, and now lives rough.*

2 to start to go wrong ○ *By the spring, the project seemed to be going off the rails. No major sponsor had come forward with the extra £1 million or so needed.*

jump the rails *(British, journalism)* to suddenly go wrong ○ *There is a point in the movie where it seems to jump the rails.*

on the rails

1 *(mainly British)* in a situation where you are operating successfully, especially after a period of difficulty ○ *Co-ordinated action is needed more than ever to put the European economy back on the rails.*

2 living and behaving in a way that is acceptable and orderly, especially after a period when life was going badly ○ *I was released from prison last year. I have managed to get part of my life back on the rails by finding a flat and a part-time job.*

rain

come rain or shine done regularly, regardless of the weather or other problems ○ *He plays golf, come rain or shine, every Monday.*

it never rains but it pours said to mean that when one bad thing happens, other bad things often happen too and make the situation worse ○ *He had a legitimate goal disallowed for 'handball' and later had a shot handled by a defender, only to see no penalty given. It never rains but it pours.*

take a rain check to refuse an offer or invitation politely, or say that you would like to accept it, but at a different time ○ *She says she'd like to take a rain check on it and do it in May.*

This expression refers to baseball. If a baseball game was cancelled because of rain, people were entitled to see another game by showing their original ticket or receipt. This ticket was called a rain check.

rainbows

chase rainbows to waste your time trying to get something that you can never have ○ *Kemp could see why there had been that open verdict, and why the police were having difficulty finding proof; they might as well be chasing rainbows.*

ranch

bet the ranch *(American)* to spend all the money that you have in order to achieve something, and risk losing it if you fail ○ *We thought that if we could do it, it would give us an important lead over our competition in future years. We've taken risks before and so we bet the ranch.*

rank

pull rank to make unfair use of your power or position to make people do what you want ○ *The Federal Government threatened to pull rank and override the states with its own legislation.*

ranks

A rank of soldiers is a line of them standing side by side.

★ **break ranks** to disobey the instructions of a group or organization of which you are a member, and express your own opinion ○ *Would you break ranks with your party and vote against the president's tax bill?*

When soldiers break ranks, they stop standing in a line and move apart.

★ **close ranks** to support the other

members of a group totally and oppose any criticism or attacks from outside ○ *Malaysian Cabinet ministers have closed ranks behind Prime Minister Mahathir Mohamad, saying there was no question of his stepping down.*

≡ When soldiers close ranks, they stand closer together so that it is hard for anyone to break through the line.

ransom

★ **hold someone to ransom** (British) to use your power or influence to force someone to do something they do not want to do ○ *But who are the powerful men at the Bundesbank who have the power to hold Europe to ransom?*

a king's ransom → see **king**

rap

take the rap to accept the blame or responsibility for something that has been done badly or has gone wrong, even if it is not your fault ○ *He had tried, and failed, to get someone to take the rap for a corruption scandal.*

≡ 'Rap' is slang for a criminal charge.

rat

look like a drowned rat to be very wet, for example because you have been caught in the rain or because your hair is wet ○ *By the time I got there I looked like a drowned rat.*

★ **the rat race** a job or way of life in which people compete aggressively with each other in order to be successful ○ *I had to get out of the rat race for a while and take a look at the real world again.*

★ **smell a rat** to suspect that something is wrong in a particular situation, for example that someone is trying to deceive you or harm you ○ *If only I'd used my head, I'd have smelt a rat straight away and never touched the proposition.*

rate

at a rate of knots (British) very quickly

○ *By 1935, Blyton was publishing at a rate of knots – adventures, fairy tales, mysteries.*

≡ The speed of ships is measured in knots. A knot is one nautical mile per hour, equivalent to 1.15 land miles per hour.

ray

a ray of sunshine someone or something that makes you feel better because there is something positive and refreshing about them ○ *I am looking forward to the wedding, it's the one ray of sunshine for the future.*

reap

> To reap a crop such as corn means to cut and gather it.

reap the harvest to suffer or benefit as a result of past actions ○ *Tonight we reap the bitter harvest of a decade of national indulgence.*

reap the whirlwind (literary) to suffer now because of mistakes that were made in the past ○ *We are reaping the whirlwind from parents who grew up in the sixties, and who themselves were encouraged to question everything.*

≡ This is a quotation from the Bible (Hosea 8:7). It refers to the punishment of the Israelites for disobeying God. It says that they have planted the wind, and that they will now harvest a whirlwind (= a storm).

you reap what you sow said to mean that everything that happens is a result of things which you have done in the past ○ *It seems to me that if we create areas of such bleakness and social deprivation we should expect to reap what we sow.*

≡ This is based on a quotation from the Bible (Galatians 6:7). It says that whatever you plant, that is what you will harvest (or, in other words, if you behave well, good things will happen to you, and if you behave badly, bad things will happen to you).

rearguard

★ **fight a rearguard action** to try hard to stop something happening, without much hope of success ○ *National telephone companies are fighting a rearguard action against competition from beyond their frontiers.*

The rearguard of a retreating army is a unit which separates from the rest and acts as a defence while the rest of the army is getting away.

record

★ **off the record** used for saying that you do not want anyone to report what you have said ○ *That's off the record. Don't go repeating what I've said, you hear.*

★ **on the record** used for saying that you are willing for people to report and repeat what you are saying ○ *We are on the record as saying we will protect our friends in the war zone, and we mean that.*

★ **set the record straight** to correct a mistake or misunderstanding ○ *But a company seeing wrong information about itself on a report can have a frustrating time setting the record straight.*

red

★ **in the red** owing money to someone or to another organization ○ *The company was already in the red to the extent of more than three million pounds.*

This expression comes from the practice in the past of using red ink to fill in entries on the debit side of a book of accounts.

red as a beetroot (British) having a very red face, for example because you are very hot or very embarrassed ○ *He turned as red as beetroot when I told him.*

a red letter day a day when something very important or exciting happens ○ *Back in 1986 Jim had his first picture published in BBC Wildlife Magazine. 'That was a real red letter day for me!' he confesses.*

In the past, important feast days and saints' days were printed in red in some calendars.

★ **see red** to suddenly become very angry or annoyed because of something which has been said or done ○ *The programmes so far have simply reinforced negative stereotype images of young Black people. It makes me see red.*

This is a reference to the traditional belief that the colour red makes bulls angry. In bullfighting, the matador waves a red cape to make the bull charge.

red-handed

★ **catch someone red-handed** to catch someone while they are doing something illegal or wrong ○ *In fact, the burglar wasn't inside the flat, but on the roof, and was caught red-handed by the police.*

The reference here is to a guilty person whose hands are covered in blood.

reed

a broken reed (British, literary) one of the members of a group who is very weak and cannot be depended on in difficult situations ○ *They recognized that their allies were a broken reed.*

reign

★ **a reign of terror** a period during which there is a lot of violence and killing, especially by people who are in positions of power ○ *The president last night dismissed the government, accusing it of having unleashed a reign of terror against its political opponents.*

The original Reign of Terror was during the French Revolution between April 1793 and July 1794, when many thousands were put to death by the government.

rein

The reference in these expressions is to a rider using the reins to control a horse.

★ **give someone free rein** to give someone all the freedom they want or need to do something ○ *He was given free rein to manage the cavalry as he wished.*

★ **keep a tight rein on someone or something** to control someone or something firmly ○ *The recession has forced people to keep a very tight rein on their finances when on holiday.*

rest

the rest is history → see **history**

rhyme

without rhyme or reason happening without any logical or obvious reason ○ *Cuts are being made without rhyme or reason. The only motive is to save money to meet Treasury targets.*

rich

rich as Croesus (*British*) very rich ○ *He may be nearly as rich as Croesus, but that's still not rich enough for him.*

> Croesus was the ruler of Lydia, a kingdom in Asia Minor, in the 6th century BC. He was famous for being very rich.

strike it rich to suddenly earn or win a large amount of money ○ *I've been thinking, prospecting might be just what we've been looking for: a quick way to strike it rich.*

riddles

talk in riddles to not say clearly and directly what you mean ○ *For several days, he dropped enigmatic clues to Ann, and talked in riddles about his unpredictable absences of the past months.*

ride

★ **a free ride** a situation in which someone gets some benefit from a situation without putting any effort into achieving it themselves ○ *I never wanted anyone to think I was getting a free ride or special treatment from the boss.*

go along for the ride to decide to join in an activity without doing it seriously or getting deeply involved in it ○ *Your boyfriend is not likely to be serious about anything this week except having a good time. Go along for the ride.*

★ **a rough ride** a situation in which you have a lot of problems and it is very difficult for you to achieve something ○ *The government is likely to face a rough ride in parliament.*

★ **take someone for a ride** to deceive or cheat someone ○ *You've been taken for a ride. Why did you give him five thousand francs?*

> This expression comes from American gangsters' slang. When gangsters 'took someone for a ride', they took them away in a car in order to kidnap them or kill them.

right

right as rain feeling well or healthy again after an illness or injury ○ *We put a bandage on his knee, gave him a biscuit and a cup of tea and he was right as rain.*

rights

bang to rights

1 having enough evidence against someone to accuse them of a crime and to prove that they are guilty ○ *You've got your man – got him bang to rights – evidence, witnesses, the lot.*

2 showing a good understanding of someone and describing them accurately ○ *I read Matthew Sura's piece on you last month and I thought he got you bang to rights.*

> This is probably connected with the expression 'bang-on' or 'dead-on', meaning 'exactly'.

ringer

★ **a dead ringer for someone** someone who looks or sounds exactly like another person ○ *An ordinary guy from Baltimore, Dave Kovic is extraordinary in one respect: he's a dead ringer for the US President.*

The word 'ringer' may originally have come from a name for dishonest traders at fairs who sold brass rings, pretending they were gold. In American horse racing, a 'ringer' is a horse that has been dishonestly substituted for another in a race.

rings

run rings round someone to be much better at a particular activity than someone else, and be able to beat or outwit them ○ *Mentally, he can still run rings round men half his age.*

ringside

a ringside seat an excellent and clear view of what is happening somewhere ○ *The first US presidential election for which I had a ringside seat was that which brought John F. Kennedy to office over 30 years ago.*

In boxing, the ringside seats are the seats that are closest to the ring and have the best view.

riot

read the riot act to angrily tell someone off for having done something stupid or wrong ○ *The president read the riot act to his party, warning those who sought to preserve the old system that power was already slipping from their grasp.*

The Riot Act was a law passed in Britain in 1715. It made it an offence for a group of twelve or more people to refuse to break up and leave if someone in authority read them the relevant section of the Act.

★ **run riot**

1 to get out of control ○ *There can be no parts of Britain which are no-go areas, where gangs run riot terrorising the innocent while the police stay safely away.*
2 if something such as imagination or speculation runs riot, it expresses itself or spreads in an uncontrolled way ○ *We have no proof and when there is no proof, rumour runs riot.*

In hunting, if the hounds run riot, they follow the scents of other animals rather than the one they are supposed to be chasing.

rip

★ **let rip**

1 to do something without restraint ○ *I give a dinner party for ten people about every three weeks. It's a big number where I can really let rip and make things look beautiful.*
2 to suddenly start talking about something that you feel strongly about but had previously been quiet about ○ *He sometimes wondered if it wouldn't be better if she let rip as she used to do over his inadequacies in the past.*

rise

The reference in these expressions is to a fish rising to the surface of the water to take the bait.

get a rise out of someone to deliberately make someone angry by teasing them or making fun of them ○ *Johnson stopped bothering him once he saw he couldn't get a rise out of him.*

take the rise out of someone to make fun of someone ○ *They had the game won by half-time but they weren't satisfied with that. They were taking the rise out of us and we won't forget that in a hurry.*

river

sell someone down the river to betray someone or do something which harms them in order to gain an advantage for yourself ○ *He has been sold down the river by the people who were supposed to protect him. It had a devastating effect on his health.*

This is a reference to slave-owners on the Mississippi river selling unwanted slaves to other slave-owners further down the river, where the conditions were harsher.

road

★ **down the road** after a particular amount of time ○ *Twenty-five years down the road from independence, we have to start making some new priorities.*

★ **hit the road** to begin a journey ○ *Urban commuters are having to hit the road earlier to be sure of beating the jams and finding a parking space.*

take the high road (American) to follow the course of action which is the most moral or most correct and which is least likely to harm or upset other people ○ *US diplomats say the president is likely to take the high road in his statements about trade.*

robbery

daylight robbery (British) or **highway robbery** (American) a situation in which you are charged a lot of money for something that should cost a lot less or even nothing at all ○ *They are charging three bucks for the comics, which sounds like highway robbery to us.*

rock

between a rock and a hard place in a difficult situation where you have to choose between two equally unpleasant courses of action ○ *We're caught between a rock and a hard place. Either we spend two months planning the operation and end up being late, or we come in right now and risk making mistakes.*

★ **hit rock bottom**
1 to be at an extremely low level and be unable go any lower ○ *The UK motor industry slumped to one of its blackest days yesterday as new car sales hit rock bottom.*
2 to be in a hopeless or difficult situation which makes you feel very depressed ○ *When my girlfriend asked me to move out of our flat and end our relationship, I hit rock bottom.*

≣ This expression comes from mining, and refers to the layer of rock that is reached once the supply of minerals being taken from the mine has been used up.

rocker

off your rocker (informal) crazy ○ *Mrs. Stevens will think I'm off my rocker handing out my money like that before the bankruptcy business is even settled.*

rocket

not rocket science very easy to learn or understand ○ *In 1981, it didn't take long for our people at CBS to learn these techniques. As I'd told Sauter, this isn't rocket science.*

rocks

on the rocks experiencing difficulties and likely to end or fail ○ *Their marriage was on the rocks, but they had determined not to divorce until the children were grown up.*

≣ The image here is of a ship that is stuck on rocks.

rod

make a rod for your own back (British) to unintentionally do something which will cause you many problems ○ *If you give in to your children, you'll just be making a rod for your own back.*

≣ This expression refers to someone providing the stick with which they themselves will be beaten.

roll

★ **be on a roll** to be in a situation where things are going very well for you, and you are making a lot of progress ○ *We're on a roll and we're winning, which gives the players that extra belief in themselves.*

≣ This expression probably comes from surfing.

be rolling in it (informal) to be very rich ○ *She's only 25 and she's rolling in it.*

Rome

fiddle while Rome burns to do nothing or spend your time on unimportant things when you have very serious issues or problems to deal with ○ *Fighting with one another over small details is like fiddling while Rome burns: it is a distraction from the main issue.*

⫶ There is a story that the Emperor Nero set fire to Rome, and then played his lyre and sang as he watched the flames. Afterwards he denied this and blamed the Christians for the destruction.

Rome was not built in a day said to mean that it takes a long time to do a job or task properly, and you should not rush it or expect to do it quickly ○ *I know Rome wasn't built in a day but I don't want to wait 200 years.*

when in Rome said to mean that people should follow the customs of the people they are visiting or living with ○ *We had a leisurely lunch, followed by a little sleep - when in Rome!*

⫶ This was probably first used by St Ambrose (died 397 AD) in answer to a question about whether religious fasting should take place on the day set aside in Milan or the day used in Rome.

roof

★ **go through the roof**

1 if the level of something such as the price of a product goes through the roof, it suddenly increases very rapidly ○ *House prices were going through the roof.*

2 to suddenly become very angry, and usually show your anger by shouting at someone ○ *I admitted I had ordered a racing car, and found myself in terrible trouble. He went through the roof!*

raise the roof to make a very loud noise, for example by cheering, singing, or shouting ○ *Best audience I've ever had in my life – they practically raised the roof.*

rooftops

shout something from the rooftops to let a lot of people know about something that you are particularly angry or excited about ○ *I would love to be able to shout our results from the rooftops.*

room

★ **a smoke-filled room** if a political or business decision is made in a smoke-filled room, it is made by a small group of people in a private meeting, rather than in a more democratic or open way ○ *Richards doesn't think that a return to the smoke-filled room, in which a few bosses make the decision, would be possible.*

⫶ This was first used to refer to the suite in the Blackstone Hotel in Chicago where Warren Harding was chosen as the Republican presidential candidate in 1920.

roost

★ **come home to roost** if something bad or unacceptable that someone has done comes home to roost, they will now have to deal with the unpleasant results of their actions ○ *You ought to have known that your lies would come home to roost in the end.*

⫶ This expression is taken from the poem 'The Curse of Kehama' by the English poet Robert Southey: 'Curses are like young chickens, they always come home to roost.'

★ **rule the roost** to be the most powerful and important person in a group ○ *In Germany, scientists will be found at the top of many manufacturing companies; in Britain, accountants rule the roost.*

⫶ This expression seems to refer to the dominant cock in a chicken coop. However, 'rule the roost' may have developed from the earlier expression 'rule the roast', which refers to the head of the household who carves and serves the meat.

root

★ **root and branch** if something is changed root and branch, it is changed completely, so that none of the old or traditional parts remain ○ *These measures should change our economic system root and branch.*

> In 1641 the Root and Branch Bill abolishing the government of the church by bishops was presented to the English Parliament. Those who supported the bill were known as 'root-and-branch men', and the term has been used to refer to reform ever since.

★ **take root** to become established or begin to develop ○ *The idea of starting up his own picture library began to take root.*

roots

put down roots
1 to make a place your home, for example by taking part in activities or making a lot of friends there ○ *Servicemen and women are seldom in the same place long enough to put down roots and buy their own home.*
2 if something puts down roots somewhere, it becomes firmly established there, so that it is likely to last and to be successful in the future ○ *Not only did the party increase its share of the poll but it also put down roots in areas where it had previously been weak or even non-existent.*

rope

at the end of your rope (*American*) feeling desperate because you are in a difficult situation and do not know how to deal with it. The usual British expression is **at the end of your tether**. ○ *Everything is dreadful and I am at the end of my rope.*

> The image here is of an animal which cannot move very far because it is tied to something with a length of rope.

give someone enough rope to hang themselves to give someone the freedom to do something in the way they want to do it, usually in the hope that they will fail or become weak by doing it the wrong way ○ *The King has simply given the politicians enough rope to hang themselves: once the party system has been discredited by political in-fighting, he will present himself once again as an absolute ruler.*

ropes

★ **learn the ropes** to learn how to do a particular job or task ○ *By the time he was 34, he had learnt the ropes of the jewellery trade.*

> The origin of this expression is from sailing ships, where the sailors had to get to know the complicated system of ropes which made up the rigging.

★ **on the ropes** very close to failing or being defeated ○ *The Denver-based developer has been on the ropes because of depressed housing markets in Denver, Texas and Arizona.*

> The image here is of a boxer who has been pushed back against the ropes around the edge of the ring.

show someone the ropes to show someone how to do a particular job or task ○ *We had a patrol out on the border, breaking in some young soldiers, showing them the ropes.*

> The origin of this expression is from sailing ships, where the sailors had to get to know the complicated system of ropes which made up the rigging.

roses

come up smelling of roses to be in a better or stronger situation than before, after experiencing a difficult situation ○ *Ellis, who was sacked on Monday, has come up smelling of roses. He has been taken on by a rival company and his financial package is even healthier.*

everything is coming up roses
said to mean that someone is having a lot of success and everything is going well for them ○ *For Rachel Ashwell, everything's coming up roses both in her home and her working life.*

This was the title of a song from the musical 'Gypsy' (1959), with words by Stephen Sondheim.

rough

cut up rough (British) to suddenly become extremely angry or violent ○ *We took a police officer in case he cut up rough.*

★ **rough and ready**
1 done in a hurry, and so rather basic, or not very exact ○ *The rough and ready method used to limit total costs worked reasonably well.*
2 not polite or well educated ○ *At first the rough and ready sailors did not know what to make of the young cleric.*

★ **rough and tumble** a situation in which the people involved try hard to get what they want, and do not worry about upsetting or harming others ○ *Whoever expected leaders in the rough and tumble of electoral politics to be nice or fair?*

Originally, a rough and tumble was a boxing match in which there were no rules or restrictions.

take the rough with the smooth
(British) to be willing to accept both the unpleasant and the pleasant aspects of something ○ *You have to take the rough with the smooth. I never promised there would be no risk.*

roughshod

★ **ride roughshod over someone**
to pay no attention to what someone wants, or take decisions without considering their feelings or interests ○ *Bosses nowadays seem to think they can ride roughshod over unions and I like to see them fighting back.*

In the past, a roughshod horse had nail heads sticking out from its shoes, so it would not slip on icy roads. These shoes could cause terrible injuries if the horse was ridden over a person in a battle or by accident.

roulette

★ **play Russian roulette** to do something that is very dangerous because it involves big risks ○ *America's space agency has been accused of mismanagement and playing Russian roulette in launching some of its missions.*

If someone plays Russian roulette, they fire a revolver containing only one bullet at their head without knowing whether the bullet will be released or not.

row

a tough row to hoe a situation which is very difficult to deal with ○ *I think, however, that in a criminal prosecution against the police, the prosecutor has a very tough row to hoe.*

rub

don't rub it in (spoken) said to mean that someone should not draw attention to something that is unpleasant or embarrassing for you ○ *Of course too much good fortune could give rise to someone else's envy, so don't rub it in by boasting.*

the rub of the green (mainly British) good luck in an activity or sport ○ *Providing we have the rub of the green, there is no reason why we can't do really well in the summer.*

This expression probably comes from golf or bowls. The 'rub' is the direction in which the grass is bent when it is cut, which affects the movement of the ball.

★ **there's the rub** said to mean that there is a problem or contradiction which is difficult or impossible to deal with ○ *'I am* *definitely not part of the club. They think I am this ferocious feminist who doesn't approve of them.' And there's the rub. Women are much more likely to imagine they are being criticised even when they are not.*

≡ This is from the well-known speech
≡ that begins 'to be or not to be' in
≡ Shakespeare's play 'Hamlet', act 3
≡ scene 1, when Hamlet is wondering
≡ whether or not to commit suicide:
≡ 'To die, to sleep; To sleep, perchance to
≡ dream. Ay there's the rub; For in that
≡ sleep of death what dreams may
≡ come...'

Rubicon

cross the Rubicon to make an important decision which cannot be changed and which will have very important consequences ○ *Today the Government has crossed the Rubicon in favour of the Euro.*

≡ The Rubicon was a small river which
≡ separated Roman Italy from Gaul, the
≡ province ruled by Julius Caesar. Caesar
≡ crossed the Rubicon in 49 BC, invaded
≡ Roman Italy, and started a civil war.
≡ 'The die is cast' is based on the same
≡ incident.

rug

★ **pull the rug from under someone's feet** to suddenly stop helping and supporting someone ○ *Every time we have been close to saving the shipyard, the Government has pulled the rug from under our feet.*

sweep something under the rug (*American*) to try to forget about something and hide it because you find it embarrassing or shameful ○ *By sweeping the wrongdoing under the rug, executives seek to avoid being accused of mismanagement by directors and shareholders.*

rule

★ **a rule of thumb** a general rule about something which you can be confident will be right in most cases ○ *A good rule of thumb for any type of studio photography is to use no more light sources than are strictly necessary.*

≡ This expression probably dates back to
≡ the use of the first joint of the thumb
≡ as a unit of measurement.

rules

★ **bend the rules** to do something which is not normally allowed, either to help someone else or for your own advantage ○ *The river authorities said they were willing to bend the rules for us and allowed us to go through the first lock.*

run

a dummy run (*British*) a trial or test procedure which you carry out in order to see if a plan or process will work properly ○ *Before we started we did a dummy run, checking out all the streets and offices we would use, and planning our escape route.*

★ **give someone a run for their money** to put up a very strong challenge in a contest which someone else is expected to win fairly easily ○ *The British team gave the host side a run for its money to finish a close second in the team competition.*

have someone on the run to be in a stronger position than your opponent, so that you can control their actions and defeat them ○ *It is clear that the Opposition thinks it has him on the run.*

run before you can walk (*British*) to try to do something which is very difficult or advanced before you have made sure that you can successfully achieve something simpler ○ *They tried to run before they could walk. They made it too complicated.*

runaround

give someone the runaround to deliberately try to mislead or confuse someone and not tell them the truth about something which they need or want to know ○ *In early August, someone close could give you the runaround, especially where it concerns money or other joint matters.*

runes

read the runes (British, literary) to understand a situation in a particular way, and decide what is likely to happen ○ *The management has proved itself innovative and imaginative. They read the runes and knew what would happen.*

Runes were an alphabet used in northern Europe until medieval times. The letters were often thought to have magical properties.

running

★ **be in the running** to have a good chance of getting a job or winning a prize ○ *The US needs a win tonight to still be in the running for the gold.*

If a horse is 'in the running', it has a good chance of winning a race.

rush

a rush of blood a sudden foolish or daring action which someone would not normally do ○ *Hughes' rush of blood may have cost Manchester United a couple of million pounds.*

Ss

sabre

'Sabre' is spelled 'saber' in American English.

★ **sabre-rattling** a situation in which someone is behaving very aggressively and making threats, often of military action, although it is not certain how serious they are or whether they will actually carry out their threats ○ *After more than a week of sabre-rattling, the two countries have agreed to talk about their differences.*

≣ A sabre is a heavy sword with a curved blade that was used in the past by soldiers on horseback.

sack

hit the sack to go to bed ○ *It was raining and we were tired, so we only half-unpacked the car and then hit the sack.*

≣ In the past, people sometimes used sacks and hay as bedding.

saddle

in the saddle in charge of the affairs of a particular country, or making the important decisions in an organization ○ *It is his bad luck to be in the saddle when his country has to decide which road it is now going to follow.*

ride high in the saddle to currently be very successful, and to show this in your behaviour and attitudes ○ *The Australian cricket team are riding high in the saddle after their recent victory against England.*

safe

★ **play it safe** to not take any risks ○ *The pilot decided that Christchurch was too far away, and played it safe, landing at Wellington.*

safe as houses (British) very safe and reliable ○ *Both managers can count on one thing – their jobs are safe as houses.*

sailing

★ **plain sailing** (British) or
smooth sailing (American) easy to do or achieve ○ *Once I got used to the diet it was plain sailing. I lost 2 stones in weight over a four month period and the weight loss has been maintained.*

≣ 'Plain sailing' is sailing in favourable conditions, without any difficulties. However, the expression may have come from 'plane sailing', a method of working out the position of a ship and planning its route using calculations based on the earth being flat rather than round. This is a simple and easy method which is fairly accurate over short distances, especially near the equator.

sails

trim your sails to change your behaviour to deal with a difficult situation, for example by limiting your demands, needs, or expectations ○ *Mr Lee, for his part, has already begun trimming his sails in preparation for dealing with the new government.*

≣ To trim sails means to adjust them according to the strength and direction of the wind.

salad

someone's salad days (literary) the time when someone was young and inexperienced ○ *The Grand Hotel did not seem to have changed since her salad days.*

= This is a quotation from Shakespeare's

'Antony and Cleopatra' (Act 1, Scene 5), when Cleopatra is talking about her youth: 'My salad days, When I was green in judgment'.

saloon

the last chance saloon for someone (British) the final opportunity for someone to succeed in what they are doing ○ *The boxers understand one thing clearly. As far as the world title goes, Saturday is the last chance saloon for both of them.*

salt

★ **no-one worth their salt would do something** said to mean that no-one who was good at their job would consider doing a particular thing ○ *No player worth his salt wants to play in the lower divisions.*

> In the past, salt was expensive and rare. Roman soldiers were paid a 'salarium' or salt money, so they could buy salt and stay healthy.

★ **rub salt into the wound** to make something even worse for someone, for example by reminding them of their failures or faults or by increasing their difficulties ○ *Compensation paid to criminals is rubbing salt into the wounds of victims of serious crimes.*

the salt of the earth a person or people whom you admire for their honesty and reliability. This expression is used mainly by upper class people when they are talking about working people. ○ *These are good people, rather rough-and-ready, but the salt of the earth.*

> This expression comes from the Bible, when Jesus tells his followers that they are the salt that gives the earth its flavour. (Matthew 5:13)

★ **take something with a pinch of salt** (mainly British) or
take something with a grain of salt (American) to not rely on something, such as a piece of information, because it may

not be accurate or true ○ *You have to take these questionnaire results with a pinch of salt because respondents in such surveys tend to give the answers they feel they should.*

> A pinch of salt is a small amount of salt held between your thumb and your first finger. Some people believe that this expression refers to the King of Pontus, Mithridates VI, who lived in the first century BC. It is said that he made himself immune to poison by swallowing small amounts of it with a grain of salt. However, other people think that it is a medieval English expression, which suggests that you need to be suspicious of unlikely stories in the same way that you need salt with food.

sand

be built on sand to not have a strong or a proper basis, and therefore to be likely to fail or come to an end ○ *He moved into the newspaper business in the Seventies. It was an empire built on sand. The newspapers folded, and by 1981 he was bankrupt.*

> This expression relates to a story in the Bible (Matthew 7:24-27), where Jesus compares the people who follow his teachings to a wise man, who built his house on rock. When floods came, the house built on rock remained standing, while others collapsed.

sands

shifting sands a situation that keeps changing and is therefore difficult to deal with ○ *Even his critics in the West have acknowledged his shrewd tactical skills in the shifting sands of Arab politics.*

sandwich

someone is one sandwich short of a picnic said to indicate in a humorous way that you think someone is very stupid or is behaving very strangely ○ *His daughter confirmed that her father was definitely one sandwich short of a picnic.*

sardines

be packed like sardines to be fitted tightly into a small space and therefore to be unable to move about easily ○ *The people are in appalling conditions. They're packed like sardines on the ship. They can barely move so the sanitary conditions are very, very bad.*

≣ The image here is of tinned sardines ≣ which have been tightly packed.

sauce

what's sauce for the goose is sauce for the gander (*old-fashioned*) said to mean that what applies to one person should apply to others, because people should be treated fairly and equally ○ *Unless Washington acknowledges that what is sauce for the goose is sauce for the gander, these talks with Russia and China are unlikely to make progress.*

say

it goes without saying said to mean that something is so obvious that it does not need to be said or explained ○ *And of course it goes without saying that if there's anything you should need while you're out here, please don't hesitate to call me here at the embassy.*

scales

the scales have fallen from someone's eyes (*literary*) said to mean that someone suddenly realizes the truth about something after a long period of not understanding it or of being deceived about it ○ *The scales have finally fallen from his eyes and he realises that he's made a dreadful mistake.*

≣ This is a reference to the Bible story of ≣ Saul, who became blind after he had a ≣ vision of God on the road to Damascus ≣ (Acts 9:18). Saul became a Christian ≣ after a follower of Jesus restored his ≣ sight. The Bible says that at the ≣ moment when Saul's sight was

≣ restored, it was as if scales had ≣ suddenly fallen from his eyes.

scene

★ **set the scene for something**
1 (*journalism*) to briefly tell people what they need to know about a subject or topic, so that they can understand what is going to happen or be said next ○ *To set the scene for this latest programme exploring the improvement in East-West relations, here's Kevin Connolly from Moscow.*
2 to create the conditions in which a particular event is likely to happen ○ *The first hour's cricket set the scene for a superbly entertaining day as England and South Africa battled to win the match.*

scenes

★ **behind the scenes** in private or in secret, rather than publicly ○ *The Prime Minister's remarks put in the public arena a debate which has been going on behind the scenes for months.* ○ *The debate was postponed for a third time after another day of intensive behind-the-scenes negotiations.*

≣ This refers to the scenes or scenery ≣ used on the stage in the theatre, and ≣ was originally used to refer to those ≣ events in a play that took place off-≣ stage.

scent

throw someone off the scent to deliberately confuse or deceive someone who is trying to find out the truth about something, by making them believe something that is not true ○ *The murderer tried to throw the cops off the scent by claiming that he saw another man attacking the woman.*

≣ This is a reference to hounds that ≣ get distracted from the trail of an ≣ animal they are hunting, for ≣ example because of another ≣ smell.

school

★ **of the old school** having traditional ideas and values, and being fairly old-fashioned ○ *As a builder of the old school, he did not always see eye to eye with designers of new houses.* ○ *She is very much an old-school nurse and her outlook leads to clashes with other staff*

the old school tie (British) said to refer to the belief that men who have been to the most famous British private schools use their positions of influence to help other men who went to the same school as themselves ○ *Most of these men claim that school made little difference to the professional paths they followed and try to deny the notion of the old school tie.*

the school of hard knocks a very difficult or unpleasant life ○ *He graduated from the school of hard knocks as well – most of his family perished in the war.*

This is being contrasted with a formal academic education and the qualifications obtained by studying at a school or college. A similar phrase sometimes used is 'the University of Life'.

science

blind someone with science to tell someone about something in a complex or technical way so that they have great difficulty in understanding it ○ *As a teenage, amateur photographer, I learned all the technical jargon so I could impress people by blinding them with science.*

score

★ **know the score** to know what the real facts of a situation are and how they affect you, even though you may not like them ○ *Taylor knows the score now, and what will happen if he fails.*

★ **settle a score** or
settle an old score to take revenge for something that someone has done to you in the past ○ *The ethnic groups turned*

on each other to settle old scores, leaving millions dead.

scratch

★ **something or someone is not up to scratch** or
something or someone does not come up to scratch (British) said to mean that something or someone is not as good as they ought to be ○ *Athletes have no one to blame but themselves if their performances are not up to scratch.*

In the past, boxers started a fight with their left feet on a line drawn on the ground, known as the scratch. When a boxer was knocked down, they were allowed thirty seconds' rest before coming 'up to the scratch' once more. A boxer who was not at the line in time lost the fight.

★ **start from scratch** to create something completely new, rather than adding to something that already exists ○ *She moved to a strange place where she had to make new friends and start a new life from scratch.*

In the past, the starting line for races was often a line scratched in the earth.

screw

have a screw loose (informal) to be slightly crazy ○ *My sister looked at me as if I had a screw loose.*

The image is of a piece of machinery that needs to be adjusted or repaired.

★ **turn the screw on someone** or
tighten the screw on someone to increase the pressure on someone to make them do what you want ○ *NATO is turning the screw on the president and piling on the pressure.*

This is a reference to a method of torture called the thumbscrew. The prisoner's thumbs were pressed between two bars of iron which were then tightened by means of a screw.

screws

put the screws on someone to use pressure or threats to make someone do what you want ○ *They had to put the screws on Harper. So far, he was the only person who might know something.*

This is a reference to a method of torture called the thumbscrew; see the explanation at 'turn the screw on someone'.

sea

★ **all at sea** (British) or
at sea very confused by a situation; unable to understand a situation ○ *When he was in prison, he knew at least where he stood. Now that he's been released, he's all at sea.*

The reference here is to a ship or a boat that has got lost.

★ **a sea change** (literary) a complete change in someone's attitudes or behaviour ○ *Supermarkets have a huge influence on what we eat and will continue to do so until there is a sea change in political thinking on food.*

This phrase is taken from act 1 scene 2 of Shakespeare's play 'The Tempest' (1611), which begins with a storm at sea and is a tale of magic and transformation: 'Full fathom five thy father lies; Of his bones are coral made: Those are pearls that were his eyes: Nothing of him that doth fade, But doth suffer a sea-change Into something rich and strange.'

seams

The seams of a piece of clothing are the places where the separate pieces of cloth used to make it are stitched together.

★ **burst at the seams** to be completely full of people or things ○ *If your shed is bursting at the seams or you can't get your*

car into the garage because of the clutter, it's time to get organised.

come apart at the seams

1 to be in a very bad state and about to fail ○ *University lecturers have given a warning that Britain's university system is in danger of coming apart at the seams because of cuts in government funding.*

2 to behave in a strange or illogical way, because you are under severe mental strain ○ *He stood for a moment, breathing deeply; he was coming apart at the seams, something he had never thought would happen to him.*

season

★ **open season on someone or something** when a lot of people are criticizing or attacking someone or something ○ *It seems that, as far as the media are concerned, it's open season on the royal family.*

In hunting, the open season is the period of the year when it is legal to hunt particular types of animals or birds.

seat

fly by the seat of your pants to do something difficult or dangerous using only your instincts, because you lack the right kind of experience or information about it ○ *The truth is that neither experts nor mothers know as much as each might wish; to a great extent, all of us fly by the seat of our pants and try to learn quickly from experience.*

If you fly an aircraft by the seat of your pants, you do not use maps or instruments.

★ **in the driving seat** (British) or
in the driver's seat (American) in control of a situation ○ *Politically, the radicals were in the driving seat, much to the anxiety of the moderates.*

★ **in the hot seat** in a position where you have to make important or difficult decisions, or answer difficult questions ○ *The club was formed in 1900 and since 1902 they have had only seven managers. Syd King was the longest-serving with 30 years in the hot seat from 1902.*

★ **take a back seat**

1 to allow other people to have all the power, importance, or responsibility ○ *You will be aware that there are some situations when it is wise to take a back seat and some where it is appropriate to fight for your, and others', rights.*

2 if one thing takes a back seat to another, people give the first thing less attention because they think that it is less important or less interesting than the other thing ○ *Dr McLaren's own private life takes a back seat to the problems and difficulties of his patients.*

security

a security blanket something that provides someone with a feeling of safety and comfort when they are in a situation which worries them or makes them nervous ○ *To small children, teachers are security blankets – loved, respected, trusted.*

A young child's security blanket is a piece of cloth or clothing which the child holds and often chews in order to feel comforted.

seed

go to seed

1 to allow yourself to become unfit, untidy, or fat as you grow older ○ *Once he had carried a lot of muscle but now he was going to seed.*

2 to become dirty and neglected because of lack of care ○ *The report painted a grim picture of an America going to seed, its bridges and roads falling apart, its national parks neglected.*

When vegetables such as lettuce go to seed, they produce flowers and seeds, and are no longer fit to eat.

seed corn resources or people that will produce benefits in the future rather than immediately ○ *I regard the teachers as the people who are planting the seed corn for the future and therefore I regard their work as crucially important.*

A farmer's seed corn is the grain that is used for planting rather than being sold or eaten.

seeds

★ **sow the seeds of something** or **plant the seeds of something** to start the process which causes a particular problem or benefit to develop ○ *Shortly after that came foreign armies, foreign settlers and foreign apartheid, which planted the seeds of today's crises in Africa.*

send

★ **send someone packing** to tell someone very forcefully or in an unsympathetic way to leave a place, job or position ○ *We had an idyllic life in the country until I decided I wanted to live alone for the first time in my life and I sent my boyfriend packing.*

shade

put someone in the shade to be so impressive that you make another person or thing seem unimportant by comparison ○ *Although now in her seventies, Joan Collins always stuns the crowds with her chic outfits and still manages to put younger women in the shade.*

Shade here means the shadow or darkness produced by blocking the light.

shades

shades of someone or something said to mean that someone or something reminds you of another person or thing ○ *Andie MacDowell stars in the bizarre mystery thriller Ruby Cairo, as the wife of a crook who has faked his death (shades of The Third Man, perhaps?).*

'Shade' is an old word for 'ghost'.

shadow

afraid of your own shadow very timid or nervous ○ *They're all afraid of their own shadows. Can't say I blame them. After all, this is a police state.*

★ **cast a long shadow over something** to have a bad influence over something that lasts for a long time ○ *Cancer has cast its long shadow over almost every family in the country.*

★ **a shadow of someone's or something's former self** said to mean that someone or something is much less powerful or capable than they used to be ○ *Kevin dreaded going downhill as a football player. He hated the thought of ending up a shadow of his former self.*

shake

shake like a leaf to shake because you are cold, afraid, or nervous ○ *At three o'clock in the morning she sat up suddenly in bed, shaking like a leaf.*

shakes

in two shakes of a lamb's tail (old-fashioned, spoken) very soon or very quickly ○ *I'll be back in two shakes of a lamb's tail.*

no great shakes ineffective, useless, or of poor quality ○ *This restaurant is no great shakes gastronomically, but the portions are huge.*

≣ This expression probably refers to shaking dice and getting a poor result, although there are other possible explanations.

shape

★ **knock something into shape** or **whip something into shape** to use whatever methods are necessary to change or improve something, so that it is in the condition that you want it to be in ○ *After a successful career at the Italian central bank, few people doubt his ability to whip the economy into shape.*

shape up or ship out said to mean that someone should start behaving in a more reasonable or responsible way, or else they should leave the place where they are or give up what they are doing ○ *The message to every player in the team is clear – shape up or ship out.*

shave

have a close shave to very nearly have an accident or disaster or to very nearly suffer a defeat ○ *Gingrich had a close shave in the 1990 general election.*

sheep

★ **the black sheep** or **the black sheep of the family** someone who is very different from the other people in their family or group and who is considered bad or worthless by them ○ *My aunt was very famous in those days, but because she was the black sheep of the family I was never encouraged to talk about her.*

≣ Black sheep are less valuable than white sheep since their wool cannot be dyed. In addition, people used to associate the colour black with evil and wrongdoing.

separate the sheep from the goats to examine a group of things or people and decide which ones are good and which are bad ○ *It is getting harder and harder to separate the sheep from the goats among the 4,000 or so titles for children that are published every year.*

≣ The Bible says that on the Day of Judgment, Jesus will divide His sheep from the goats (Matthew 25:32). The sheep represent those who are going to heaven, and the goats represent those who are going to hell.

someone might as well be hanged for a sheep as a lamb said to mean that someone will suffer or be punished whatever they do, so they might as well do something really bad if they can get some enjoyment or profit from it ○ *This* seductive thought process – I might as well be hanged for a sheep as a lamb – is a trap which awaits all dieters. After succumbing to one biscuit you feel such a failure you consume the whole packet.

For a long time in the past in England, the penalty for sheep stealing was death.

sheet

keep a clean sheet (British, journalism) in a football match, if a team keeps a clean sheet, no goals are scored against them ○ *Tottenham's most successful season was 1944-45: on twelve occasions they kept a clean sheet.*

start with a clean sheet to be allowed to forget previous debts or mistakes, and so be given a new chance to succeed at something ○ *The Christmas break has erased unhappy memories and allowed the Government to start the new year with a clean sheet.*

shelf

on the shelf (British) used to describe a middle-aged woman who some people consider to be too old to be attractive to men, and who is therefore unlikely to ever marry. Many people dislike this expression because of the attitude which it represents. ○ *I certainly don't equate being single with being on the shelf!*

shelf life the length of time that something will last ○ *A large proportion of small businesses have a short shelf life.*

shell

★ **come out of your shell** to become less shy, and more talkative and friendly ○ *She used to be very timid and shy but I think she's come out of her shell.*

play a shell game (mainly American) to deliberately deceive people, for example by changing things or pretending to change things, in order to gain an advantage ○ *The union accused the mine-owners of playing a shell game, planning to*

open mines in the future with the intention of hiring non-union miners.

The shell game is an old confidence trick. An object is hidden under one of three cups, which are then moved out of their original order. The victim bets on where the object is, and typically gets it wrong. The trick may have become known as the shell game because it was originally done with walnut shells rather than cups.

shine

take the shine off something (mainly British) to make something less enjoyable than it should be ○ *There are two factors which may take the shine off the immediate euphoria following the end of the coup.*

take a shine to someone (British) to like someone a lot from the very first time that you meet them ○ *Laura took a shine to her at the interview and offered her the job on the spot.*

ship

abandon a sinking ship to leave an organization or cause which is about to fail completely ○ *When the party leader resigned, opposition MPs accused him of abandoning a sinking ship.*

★ **jump ship** to leave an organization or cause, either because you think it is about to fail or because you want to join a rival organization ○ *The Liberal Democrat government lost a vote of confidence last week. Some ruling party members immediately jumped ship and created new parties.*

If sailors jump ship, they leave their ship without permission and do not return.

run a tight ship to keep firm control of the way your business or organization is run, so that it is well organized and efficient ○ *Andy, our team coach, is very organized and confident. He runs a tight ship and he does a great job.*

when someone's ship comes in said to talk about what someone will do if they become rich and successful ○ *When my ship comes in, I'll buy a big house in the country.*

This is a reference to a merchant's ship returning home with a heavy load of goods.

shirt

keep your shirt on (mainly American) to calm down and not be angry or impatient. The usual British expression is **keep your hair on**. ○ *'For heaven's sake, hurry up, Pete!' – 'All right. Keep your shirt on! I'm just coming.'*

lose your shirt (mainly British) to lose all your money on a bad investment or bet ○ *If you play cards with these guys, you can lose your shirt.*

put your shirt on something (mainly British) to bet or risk a large amount of money on something because you are convinced that it will win or succeed ○ *I was just thinking you might put your shirt on Golden Boy in the next race. It's bound to be a winner, isn't it?*

a stuffed shirt someone in an important position who behaves in a very formal or pompous way ○ *His seminars work because he keeps things simple. He walks around talking like an ordinary person, rather than a stuffed shirt.*

This refers to a shirt being displayed on a dummy or mannequin in a clothing shop. The dummy is hollow and has no use apart from filling the space occupied by the shirt.

shoe

drop the other shoe (American) to complete a task by doing the second and final part of it ○ *Last week, Time Warner Inc. dropped the other shoe in its two-step $13.86 billion acquisition of Warner Communications Inc.*

if the shoe fits (American) used to tell someone that unpleasant or critical remarks which have been made about them are probably true or fair. The usual British expression is **if the cap fits**. ○ *Although I trained as an architect, I have always been interested in interior design too. So, when people saw my work and said 'You're an interior designer', I thought 'If the shoe fits.'*

the shoe is on the other foot → see **foot**

shoes

dead men's shoes (British) said to talk about a situation in which people cannot make progress in their careers until someone senior to them retires or dies ○ *At that particular time, jobs were very difficult to obtain. It was more or less dead men's shoes.*

fill someone's shoes to do someone's job or hold their position as well as they did ○ *It'll take a good man to fill our old boss's shoes.*

★ **put yourself in someone's shoes** to make an effort to imagine how you would feel or act if you were in the same situation as a particular person ○ *You should be kinder when considering others, and put yourself in their shoes once in a while.*

quake in your shoes to be very frightened or anxious about something that is about to happen ○ *The prospect of having to give evidence against him in court made the witnesses quake in their shoes.*

smudge your own shoes (British) to damage your own reputation while trying to harm someone else's reputation ○ *He dishes the dirt on his buddies and smudges his own shoes with admissions of gambling.*

someone wouldn't like to be in another person's shoes said to mean that someone would not like to be in the same situation as a particular person ○ *He hasn't made any friends and has upset a lot of powerful people. I wouldn't like to be in his shoes if he comes back to work.*

★ **step into someone's shoes** to take over someone's job or position ○ *In America, if a president resigns or dies in office, the vice-president steps into his shoes.*

shoestring

★ **on a shoestring** using very little money ○ *Newly divorced with two children to raise, she was living on a shoestring.* ○ *A British science fiction film made on a shoestring budget is taking America by storm.*

> In American English, shoelaces are called shoestrings. The reference here is to the very small amount of money that is needed to buy shoelaces.

shoo-in

> 'Shoo-in' is sometimes spelled 'shoe-in'.

be a shoo-in for something to be certain to win something, such as an election or a contest ○ *The president looks as though he's a shoo-in for another four years.*

shop

all over the shop (*British*) spread across a large area or over a wide range of things. The usual American expression is **all over the lot**. ○ *When the pipe in the kitchen burst this morning, it sprayed water all over the shop.*

shut up shop (*British*) or

close up shop (*mainly American*) to be forced to close your business, for example because of difficult economic conditions ○ *Unless business picks up soon, some of the 245 foreign-owned banks in Switzerland may have to shut up shop.*

★ **a talking shop** (*mainly British*) something such as a conference or an organization where discussions have no practical results ○ *Governments which used to dismiss the UN as a mere 'talking shop' now see possibilities for the international body to act more as a world policeman.*

talk shop to talk about work to other people who do the same type of work, in a way that is boring for other people to hear ○ *Although I get on well with my colleagues, if you hang around together all the time you just end up talking shop, which gets boring.*

shopping

a shopping list a list of demands or requirements that someone wants to get from a particular person or organization ○ *Mr Baker presented a shopping list of additional help the United States was requiring from its allies.*

short

have someone by the short and curlies (*British*) to have someone completely in your power ○ *The unions' chief negotiator last night said: 'We had the company by the short and curlies.'*

> In this expression, 'short and curlies' may refer to a person's pubic hair, to hair on the back of their neck, or to the hair in their beard.

sell someone short to fail to provide someone with all the things that they think you ought to provide ○ *The president accused his former aides of failing to support him, of selling him short.*

> The reference here is to someone being cheated by being given less of something than they have paid for.

sell yourself short to be modest about your achievements and good qualities, so that other people do not realize just how good you are ○ *Be confident in your ideas and ability, and don't sell yourself short.*

> The reference here is to someone being cheated by being given less of something than they have paid for.

shot

by a long shot used to add emphasis to a statement, especially a negative statement or one that contains a superlative ○ *We have to know what is going on, and we don't, not yet, not by a long shot.*

do something like a shot to do something immediately, because you are very eager to do it or because something forces you to do it ○ *If I won the lottery, I would give up my job like a shot.*

★ **fire a warning shot across someone's bows** or
fire a shot across someone's bows to do something which shows that you are prepared to oppose someone strongly if they do not stop or change what they are doing ○ *Britain's agriculture minister departed from his prepared speech to fire a shot across Norway's bows.*

≣ The bows are the front part of a ship.

get shot of something or someone (British) to get rid of something or someone as quickly as possible ○ *He didn't want to talk to me, and didn't invite me into the house. He couldn't wait to get shot of me.*

★ **give something your best shot** to try as hard as you can to achieve something, even though you know how difficult it is ○ *I gave it my best shot, but I wasn't quite good enough to win.*

have one shot in your locker to have only one thing left that you can do in order to achieve success so that, if this fails, you will have to give up ○ *They had one hope left – one shot in their locker – an appeal to the Supreme Court.*

≣ A locker is a small cupboard with a lock. In this case, it might be a cupboard containing ammunition.

a long shot
1 a way of solving a difficulty or problem that, although it has little chance of success, is still worth trying ○ *You could try to find her. It's a long shot but you could look in the phone book.*
2 something that is very unlikely to happen ○ *Observers say a deal between the White House and Congress is a long shot in an election year, when both political parties are trying to get the upper hand.*

≣ The reference here is to someone shooting at a target from a very long distance.

someone's best shot at something said to mean that something is the best chance that someone has of achieving something ○ *Mazankowski and other analysts say Canada's best shot at economic recovery is continued growth in the United States.*

★ **a shot in the arm** help and encouragement at a time when you badly need it ○ *The remaining problems can be dealt with in weeks, and to risk further delay would be to deny the world economy a desperately needed shot in the arm.*

≣ A 'shot' is an injection, in this case an injection of a drug that stimulates you.

shots

★ **call the shots** to make all the important decisions in an organization or situation ○ *Is the military really the power behind the President now? Who really calls the shots?*

≣ This may refer to someone shooting and saying which part of the target they intend to hit. Alternatively, it may refer to a snooker or pool player saying which ball they intend to hit or which pocket they intend to hit it into.

shoulder

come straight from the shoulder to be direct and completely honest ○ *His opinions about top politicians in Washington and New York come straight from the shoulder. 'The president,' he says, 'was out of touch with reality.'*

≣ In boxing, a blow that is straight from the shoulder is a direct and powerful blow, delivered with a straight arm.

★ **give someone the cold shoulder** to deliberately ignore someone ○ *He gave me the cold shoulder at the party; he didn't talk to me at all.*

A shoulder is a cut of meat which includes the upper part of the animal's front leg. This expression refers to a medieval practice where important guests were given roast meat. Less important people were only given cold meat left over from previous meals.

put your shoulder to the wheel to put a great deal of effort into a difficult task ○ *These hard-working and decent people are prepared to put their shoulders to the wheel, to build a better society.*

In the days when people travelled in carriages or carts on roads that often got very muddy, people would help free vehicles that were stuck by leaning against a wheel and pushing.

★ **a shoulder to cry on** someone you can rely on to give you emotional support when you are upset or anxious ○ *For a lot of new mums the health visitor becomes a real friend, full of sound advice and the perfect shoulder to cry on when it all gets too much.*

★ **stand shoulder to shoulder** to work co-operatively with and support someone else in order to achieve a common aim ○ *The prime minister said that Britain stood shoulder to shoulder with the US in response to the terrorist atrocities.*

shoulders

★ **rub shoulders with someone** (*mainly British*) to associate with someone important or famous for a while. The usual American expression is **rub elbows with someone**. ○ *Johnson had always loved rubbing shoulders with celebrities.*

show

The show referred to in the following expressions is a theatrical performance.

get the show on the road to put a plan or an idea into action ○ *He checked his watch. 'Shouldn't we get this show on the road, now that Rolfe's here?'*

keep the show on the road to ensure that a plan or an idea continues to operate successfully ○ *The government is going to have to find something to offer the unions during these talks if it is to keep the show on the road.*

★ **run the show** to be in control of an organization, event, or situation ○ *The fear is that you have on paper the restoration of democracy, but in reality the military still run the show.*

★ **steal the show** to get more attention or praise than the other people or things in a show or other event ○ *It was the Chinese swimmers who stole the show on the first day of competition. They set new Asian records in almost every race.*

★ **stop the show** to give an outstanding performance in a show or other event ○ *Twelve-year-old Reggie Jackson stopped the show last night, singing 'America the Beautiful'.* ○ *She got a standing ovation for her show-stopping number at the concert yesterday evening.*

showers

send someone to the showers (*American*) to disqualify someone from a game or exclude them from an activity, because of their bad behaviour or poor performance ○ *Within the first 15 minutes, four players had been sent to the showers for fighting.*

In baseball and other sports, players who are sent off cannot return to the field and so can take a shower before the game is finished.

shrift

★ **get short shrift** to be treated very rudely or to receive very little attention ○ *Employees' complaints are getting short shrift.*

'Shrift' is an old word meaning confession to a priest. In the past, condemned criminals were allowed only a few minutes to make their confession before they were executed.

shuffle

get lost in the shuffle (mainly American) to not be noticed and have no attention paid to you ○ He worries campaign finance reform will get lost in the shuffle of White House priorities.

> When packs of cards are properly shuffled, it is impossible to know where a particular card is.

sick

sick as a dog very ill or very upset ○ In the children's story The Chocolate Wedding, the main character, Lulu, eats 16 chocolate eggs and is as sick as a dog.

sick as a parrot (British) very annoyed or disappointed about something ○ I can't believe Ronaldo missed the goal with that shot. He must be sick as a parrot about it.

> The origin of this expression is uncertain. References to people being 'as melancholy as a sick parrot' have been found as early as the 17th century. In the 1970s in West Africa, there was an outbreak of the disease of psittacosis or parrot fever, which humans can catch from birds. At about this time, footballers and football managers started using this expression a lot to say how they felt when they had lost a match.

sick as a pig (British) very annoyed and upset about something ○ Les has just been sacked from his job. He's as sick as a pig.

side

★ **be on the safe side** to do something as a precaution, although it is unlikely to be necessary ○ You probably won't need to apply for planning permission to build a shed in your garden, but to be on the safe side, check with your local planning department.

be on your side to give you an advantage and help you to achieve something ○ Having time and money on your side always helps, of course.

give someone the rough side of your tongue → see **tongue**

laugh out of the other side of your mouth → see **mouth**

let the side down (British) to disappoint people by doing something badly or by doing something which people do not approve of ○ The workers are the best in the world – it is the managers who let the side down.

> A side is one of the teams in a game or competition.

★ **look on the bright side** to try to be cheerful about a bad situation by concentrating on the few good things in it or by thinking about how it could have been even worse ○ I tried to look on the bright side, to be grateful that I was healthy. I didn't talk to other people at all about my disastrous relationship with my boyfriend.

on the side of the angels → see **angels**

sunny side up
1 (mainly British, journalism) bright and cheerful ○ It's not always easy to be sunny side up.
2 (mainly American) used to describe a fried egg that has been cooked on one side only and not turned over in the pan ○ Nicole cooked his eggs the way he liked them – sunny side up with a drizzle of melted butter on top.

sides

talk out of both sides of your mouth → see **mouth**

two sides of the same coin or **opposite sides of the same coin** two opposite aspects of the same situation or idea ○ He says he draws no line between tragedy and comedy. 'I've always felt that they are inseparable, that they are two sides of the same coin.'

sight

★ **at first sight** used to describe your first impression of someone or something, usually to indicate that this first impression was wrong or incomplete ○ *Nothing is ever quite as good or quite as bad as it looks at first sight.*

look a sight (*mainly British, informal*) to look untidy, ridiculous, etc. ○ *By the time we got to the restaurant, I was soaking wet and I must have looked a sight.*

★ **lose sight of something** to forget or ignore an important aspect of something because you have other things to think about ○ *As so often happened, Peter, Tommy and Henry had totally lost sight of their real objective.*

out of sight, out of mind said to mean that it is easy to forget about someone or something, or to stop caring about them, when you have not seen them for a long time ○ *My boyfriend and I broke up when he went to work in China – it was a case of out of sight, out of mind.*

a sight for sore eyes said to mean that something gives you a lot of pleasure when you look at it ○ *The sunset over the Strait of Malacca is a sight for sore eyes.*

sights

The sights on a weapon such as a rifle are the part that helps you to aim it more accurately.

★ **have something in your sights** to be aiming or trying hard to achieve something, and to have a good chance of success ○ *I am studying at university, with good job prospects firmly in my sights.*

This expression is often used more literally to say that someone is looking at a target through the sights of a gun.

★ **set your sights on something** to decide that you want something and to try very hard to get it ○ *Although she came from a family of bankers, Fiona set her sights on a career in medicine.*

This expression are also used literally to say that someone is looking at a target through the sights of a gun.

signed

★ **signed and sealed** official and unable to be changed ○ *Well, the agreement is signed and sealed, and there's nothing you can do or say about it.*

In the past, documents were 'sealed' with wax into which a special mark or design was pressed using a device called a seal. The mark or design in the wax proved that the document was authentic and had not been opened.

silk

you can't make a silk purse out of a sow's ear said to mean that it is impossible to make something really successful or of high quality out of something which is unsuccessful or of poor quality ○ *Well, this just goes to show that you can't make a silk purse out of a sow's ear. It's a truly awful novel, and even when you throw famous stars at it, you can't make it into a great movie.*

silver

born with a silver spoon in your mouth born into a very rich family and having a privileged upbringing. This expression is usually used to show resentment or disapproval. ○ *Samantha was born with a silver spoon in her mouth; there's always someone to pay her bills if her inheritance isn't enough.*

This expression goes back to the 17th century. The reference is to babies from wealthy families being fed using silver spoons.

hand someone something on a silver platter → see **platter**

sing

sing the same tune or **sing the same song**

1 to continue to express the same ideas or opinions that you have expressed before ○ *The president keeps singing the same tune he's been singing for years, which* presumably he believes.

2 if a group of people are singing the same tune, they are all expressing the same opinions about something ○ *Everyone was singing the same tune – one politician after another stood up to declare that there was only one solution to the crisis.*

sink

leave someone to sink or swim
to leave someone to do something on their own, with their success or failure depending entirely on their own efforts or abilities ○ *The sad part is that many of these wounded soldiers have been left to sink or swim on their own after serving their country.*

sitting

★ **do something in one sitting** or **do something at one sitting** to not stop doing something until you have finished it ○ *She can easily go through a box of chocolates in one sitting.*

six

★ **knock someone for six** (British) to give someone a surprise or shock which they have difficulty recovering from ○ *Many people are very positive and see redundancy as a chance to start a new career, but the emotional impact of being made redundant can knock other people for six.*

> In cricket, six runs are scored when a batsman hits the ball so that it lands outside the playing area without bouncing. When this happens, you can say the bowler has been hit for six.

six of one and half a dozen of the other said to mean that both of two people, situations or possible courses of action are equally bad or equally good ○ *To me it was six of one and half a dozen of the other. They were both at fault.*

sixes

at sixes and sevens (mainly British) disorganized and confused ○ *Everything in the office is at sixes and sevens. None of us knows what we should be doing.*

> Two origins have been suggested for this phrase. The first is from a dice game, and the second is from a dispute that arose between two of the guilds or craft organizations in medieval London about who was to go sixth and who seventh in the annual procession through the city. The dispute was resolved by the guilds taking turns, and this still happens today.

size

★ **cut someone down to size** to do or say something to someone who is behaving arrogantly, to show them that they are less important or impressive than they think they are ○ *It may be that people are drawn to work in journalism because of the chance to cut everyone else down to size.*

try something on for size to consider something carefully in order to decide whether you believe it or to try using something in order to decide whether you think that it is good ○ *'Jarvis killed Mr Rownall?' he said slowly, trying on the idea for size and seeming to find it plausible.*

skates

get your skates on (mainly British) to hurry up ○ *Bargain hunters had better get their skates on – the best properties are selling fast.*

skeleton

★ **have a skeleton in the closet** or **have a skeleton in the cupboard** (British) to keep secret something which would be scandalous or embarrassing for you if other people knew about it ○ *But everybody's got secrets, haven't they? Everybody has a skeleton in the closet.*

skid

be on skid row to have lost everything in your life, for example because you have become alcoholic or gone bankrupt

○ *Gamblers can get through huge amounts of money. They spend their savings, then the mortgage payments stop. It's a downhill spiral and soon they're on Skid Row.*

Skid row is used, especially in American English, to refer a poor part of a city where many drunks and homeless people live.

skids

★ **on the skids** doing badly and very likely to fail ○ *My marriage was on the skids.*

put the skids under something or someone (British) to cause something or someone to do badly or fail ○ *Two new witnesses in the murder case have put the skids under the accused man's alibi.*

skin

★ **do something by the skin of your teeth** to just manage to do something, although you very nearly fail ○ *Chelsea won the title by the skin of their teeth.*

This expression seems to come from the book of Job in the Bible, although its meaning has completely changed. Job loses everything and then says 'I am escaped with the skin of my teeth' (Job 19:20), meaning that the skin of his teeth is all he has left.

get under someone's skin
1 to annoy or worry someone ○ *The continuing criticism of his behaviour is getting under his skin a little bit.*
2 to cause someone to feel interest or affection ○ *After a slow start, the film gets under your skin because of its affection for its characters and sympathy with the frustrations of small-town life.*
3 to try to find out how someone feels and thinks, so that you are able to understand them better ○ *It is only through getting right under the skin of your colleagues and loved ones that you will be able to relate to them as equals.*

it's no skin off my nose (British, informal) said to mean that you are not worried about something bad that has happened because it only affects or harms other people, or because it is not your responsibility ○ *When I heard she'd got the sack, I thought, it's no skin off my nose. She's not what you'd call a mate, and losing a lousy job like that's no big deal, is it?*

jump out of your skin to receive a sudden unpleasant shock or surprise ○ *When I heard gunshots, I jumped out of my skin.*

make your skin crawl to make you feel disgust ○ *He gave a laugh that made my skin crawl.*

★ **save your own skin** to try to save yourself from something dangerous or unpleasant, often without caring what happens to anyone else ○ *The government is trying to save its own skin rather than trying to help the victims of the disaster.*

★ **skin and bone(s)** very thin, because of lack of food or serious illness ○ *Many villages are deserted. In one we found nomads looking for water. They were skin and bones. They had no food.*

★ **a thick skin** an ability to not be upset by criticism ○ *A woman politician needs a thick skin.*

★ **a thin skin** a tendency to be easily upset by criticism ○ *He has a thin skin and lacks determination – he's certainly not cut out to be a journalist.*

sky

blow something sky-high to do or say something which completely destroys something, such as someone's hopes or beliefs ○ *All our hopes, plans and dreams have just been blown sky-high.*

out of a clear blue sky completely unexpectedly ○ *Out of a clear blue sky and after 34 months of successive increases, unemployment has dropped by 22,000.*

This expression compares an unexpected event to a bolt of lightning from a blue sky. The expressions 'out of the blue' and 'a bolt from the blue' are based on a similar idea.

★ **the sky's the limit** said to mean that it is possible that someone or something will be very successful ○ *'How much are you hoping to make for this charity of yours?' 'Well, loads hopefully. I mean the sky's the limit.'*

slack

cut someone some slack to make things slightly easier for someone than you normally would, because of their special circumstances or situation ○ *When you're new at a job, colleagues and bosses cut you a little slack. They forgive minor mistakes because you're new.*

★ **take up the slack** or
pick up the slack to start making full use of all of the resources or potential of, for example, an industry, economy, or organization ○ *Losing one of our best players was tough. However, the rest of the team came together and picked up the slack.*

▤ If you take up the slack in a rope, you tighten it.

slap

★ **a slap in the face** a situation in which someone upsets you by insulting you or appearing to reject you ○ *The daughter of a murdered terrorist victim said that it is a slap in the face when convicted terrorist killers are being treated like national heroes.*

a slap on the wrist a very light punishment or reprimand ○ *Other than a few slaps on the wrist, the General went unpunished.*

slate

In the past, people used pieces of slate for writing on, for example in schools, shops, and pubs. Shopkeepers and publicans would write customers' debts on their slates, and wipe them clean when the debts were paid.

put something on the slate (British) to buy something on credit and pay for it later ○ *'Give me another coffee and put it on the slate.'*

★ **wipe the slate clean**
1 to get rid of an existing system so that you can replace it with a new one ○ *There's a strong desire among the public to wipe the slate clean and to call for early presidential and legislative elections.*
2 to earn enough money to pay off your debts, so that you no longer owe money to anyone ○ *Over a decade he wiped the firm's slate clean of debt and brought it into healthy profit.*
3 to be punished for something wrong that you have done, or to make amends for it by your good behaviour, so that you can start your life again without feeling guilty about it ○ *Serving a prison sentence makes some people believe they have wiped the slate clean.*

sledgehammer

a sledgehammer to crack a nut (British) said to mean that the methods someone is using to solve a problem are far stronger than is necessary ○ *Bankers say that the proposed law is a sledgehammer to crack a nut.*

▤ A sledgehammer is a large heavy hammer which is used for smashing rocks and concrete.

sleep

★ **not lose any sleep over something** to not worry about something at all ○ *I'd like to have a little more money – who wouldn't – but I won't lose any sleep over it.*

sleep on it to wait until the next day to make a decision, so that you have some time to consider it carefully ○ *Don't make any promises today. We'll talk about it tomorrow when you've had a chance to sleep on it.*

sleeve

★ **have something up your sleeve** to have a secret idea or plan which you can use to gain an advantage over other people ○ *The company's strategy for improvement is simple, according to Mr Pearse: 'We've got nothing fancy up our sleeves. We just have to be better.'*

≣ If someone wanted to cheat at cards, they could hide a good card up their sleeve to use at an appropriate time.

laugh up your sleeve to be secretly amused by something, for example because someone has done something very badly, or because you know something that nobody else knows. This expression is usually used to show disapproval. ○ *He wondered just how smugly she was laughing up her sleeve at his ineptitude.*

≣ The image here is of someone trying to hide the fact that they are laughing by putting their hand or arm in front of their mouth.

sleeves

roll up your sleeves to get ready to work hard, often as part of a group of people ○ *He was very much a team player, rolling up his sleeves and getting down to work.*

slings

the slings and arrows of something (mainly British) the unpleasant things that happen to you which are not your fault ○ *She was very ill at that time, which reduced her ability to cope with the slings and arrows of life.*

≣ This is a quotation from a speech in Shakespeare's play 'Hamlet', where Hamlet is considering whether or not to kill himself: 'To be, or not to be - that is the question; Whether 'tis nobler in the mind to suffer The slings and arrows of outrageous fortune, Or to take arms against a sea of troubles, And by opposing end them?' (Act 3, Scene 1)

slice

a slice of the action → see **action**

slip

a slip of the tongue something that you said by mistake ○ *The interviewer asked Mr Clarke about the time he said that The Mirror was read by morons. Mr Clarke replied that the comment was a slip of the tongue. He added: 'I meant to say it was written by morons.'*

there is many a slip twixt cup and lip (literary) said to mean that a plan may easily go wrong before it is completed, and you can never be sure of what will happen ○ *Joe must be a hot favourite to win in Belfast, but there's many a slip twixt cup and lip.*

≣ 'Twixt' is an old-fashioned word meaning 'between'.

slippery

slippery as an eel used to describe someone whom it is very difficult to catch, or from whom it is very difficult to get the information that you want ○ *His opponent in the boxing ring was as slippery as an eel, as cunning as a fox and as quick as lightning.*

slope

★ **on a slippery slope** involved in a course of action that cannot be stopped and that will lead to failure or serious trouble ○ *These young people are already on the slippery slope to criminality.*

small

make someone feel small or **make someone look small** to deliberately say or do something which makes someone look or feel stupid, especially in front of other people. ○ *He made me feel small, like an idiot.* ○ *I could see he was going to do whatever he could to make me look small.*

smoke

blow smoke (mainly American) to deliberately confuse or mislead someone in order to deceive them ○ *It was time to see if Sam was just blowing smoke or if he* *actually had some useful information for us.*

★ **go up in smoke** to fail or end without anything being achieved ○ *But with just eight minutes to go, their dreams of glory went up in smoke. Liverpool scored twice within minutes and went three-two ahead.*

send out smoke signals to give an indication of your views or intentions, often in an unclear or vague form which then needs to be interpreted ○ *I'll tell you exactly what I think we ought to do, but what kind of smoke signals ought to be sent by the White House is up to them to figure out.*

≣ Smoke signals are columns of smoke which were used to send messages over long distances, for example by Native American tribes.

smoke and mirrors (*mainly American*) things which are intended to deceive or confuse people ○ *The president claims that his economic plan is free of the smoke and mirrors that have characterized earlier budget plans.*

≣ Magicians sometimes use smoke and mirrors when they are performing tricks, in order to confuse or deceive people.

there's no smoke without fire said to mean that an unpleasant rumour or unlikely story is likely to be at least partly true, as otherwise nobody would be talking about it ○ *I was incredibly upset by the story. It was the main item on the news and people were bound to think there was no smoke without fire.*

smooth

★ **smooth the way** to make it easier for something to happen or more likely for something to happen ○ *For several weeks now, the president has been trying to smooth the way for this package of spending cuts and tax increases.*

snail

★ **at a snail's pace** very slowly, often too slowly ○ *The economy grew at a snail's pace in the first three months of this year.*

snake

a snake in the grass someone that you strongly dislike and disapprove of because, although they pretend to be your friend, they are actually your enemy and betray you ○ *He's just a snake in the grass. You can't trust that guy.*

≣ This phrase was first used by the Roman poet Virgil in his work 'The Eclogues' to refer to a hidden danger.

snake oil (*mainly American*) something which someone is trying to sell you or make you believe in when you think it is false and is not to be trusted ○ *He said he was in the oil business. He just omitted to say it was the snake oil business.*

≣ In the United States, snake oil was a substance typically made from the plant snakeroot. Dishonest salesmen tried to persuade people to buy it, claiming that it was a medicine which would cure their illnesses.

snow

a snow job (*mainly American*) lies and exaggerations, intended to deceive or flatter someone. ○ *They have the experience to know the difference between getting information and getting a snow job.*

snowball

not a snowball's chance in hell → see **chance**

snug

be as snug as a bug in a rug (*British, old-fashioned*) to be in a very comfortable situation ○ *Jamieson sat down beside McKinnon. 'Ideal working conditions, you said. Snug as a bug in a rug, one might say.'*

soap

no soap (*American*) said to mean that you have tried to do something but that you have failed ○ *I looked everywhere for him, then finally I went home. I called him at home this morning. No soap.*

sober

sober as a judge (British, old-fashioned) used to emphasize that someone is not drunk ○ 'Have you been drinking?' the policeman asked. Les looked up at him and shook his head. 'No. Sober as a judge, officer.'

sock

put a sock in it (British, old-fashioned) used to tell someone, in a rude way, to stop talking ○ 'Put a sock in it, all of you. I need to tell you something.'

socks

pull your socks up (British) to try hard to improve your behaviour or work ○ Listen, it's about time you pulled your socks up and worked a bit harder because you're falling behind in your school work.

someone or something will knock your socks off said to mean that someone or something is very good and that you are very impressed by them ○ This band will knock your socks off!

work your socks off to work very hard ○ We've all worked our socks off to produce this show.

song

★ **be on song** (British, journalism) to be playing a sport very well ○ It only needs one or two players to play badly and we'll be in trouble. The whole team must be on song.

sing the same song → see **sing**

★ **go for a song** to be sold for an unexpectedly low price ○ I bought this rug from a second-hand shop. I couldn't resist it when I saw it – it was going for a song.

> This expression may be a reference to printed song sheets, which were very cheap. Alternatively, it may refer to small amounts of money that passers-by give to someone who is singing in the street.

make a song and dance about something (mainly British) to react in a very anxious, excited, or angry way to something that is not important ○ Jan made a great song and dance about the change of plan at first, but she calmed down soon enough.

sorrows

drown your sorrows to drink a lot of alcohol in order to forget something sad or upsetting that has happened to you ○ His girlfriend has just dumped him so he's gone off to the pub to drown his sorrows.

soul

bare your soul to someone to tell someone all the thoughts and feelings that are most important to you ○ We all need someone we can bare our souls to, someone we can confide in.

★ **sell your soul for something** to do whatever you need to in order to get what you want, even if it involves abandoning your principles or doing something you consider wrong ○ They have sold their soul to the devil; they do anything for money.

> There are many stories about people who sold their souls to the devil in return for wealth, success, or pleasure. The most famous is about Dr Faustus, whose story was first told in a book published in Germany in 1587, and later told by writers such as the English writer Marlowe and the German poet Goethe.

sound

sound as a bell in a very good condition and very reliable ○ The doctor says that granddad's heart's as sound as a bell.

> 'Sound' in this expression means whole and undamaged. A bell that has a crack in it will not ring clearly.

soup

in the soup in trouble ○ She has a knack of landing herself right in the soup.

spade

call a spade a spade to speak honestly and directly about something, especially if it is controversial or embarrassing, rather than being careful about what you say ○ *I'm not at all secretive, and I'm not afraid to call a spade a spade.*

> In a play by the Ancient Greek dramatist Menander, one of the characters says 'I call a fig a fig, and a spade a spade'.

spades

★ **have something in spades** to have a lot of something ○ *This Glaswegian band have got talent in spades.*

spanner

★ **throw a spanner in the works** (*British*) to cause problems which prevent something from happening in the way that it was planned. The usual American expression is **throw a wrench into the works**. ○ *If Britain objects, this would throw a spanner in the works and could damage the prospects of the treaty being successfully concluded.*

spare

spare no expense to spend as much money as is necessary to achieve or do something ○ *Their stadium is magnificent and the club is ambitious and they plan to spare no expense to catch up with Celtic once more.*

spark

a bright spark (*mainly British*) an intelligent and lively person ○ *Our poor exam results were totally demoralizing because in the third form we'd been real bright sparks.*

sparks

sparks fly

1 if sparks fly between two people, they discuss something in an angry or excited way ○ *From what I have seen of this TV discussion programme, the presenters are not afraid to tackle serious issues or let the sparks fly when necessary.*

2 used to describe a situation or relationship that is very exciting

○ *Whenever two such temperamental artists meet, you know sparks will fly.*

strike sparks off each other (*mainly British*) if people who are trying to achieve something together strike sparks off each other, they react to each other in a very exciting or creative way ○ *It was a productive partnership, the two designers striking creative sparks off each other, ensuring whatever they worked on was fresh and edgy.*

spectacles

★ **look at something through rose-tinted spectacles** to notice only the good things about a situation, so that your opinion is unrealistic ○ *He accused diplomats of looking at the world through rose-tinted spectacles.*

spectre

> 'Spectre' is a literary word for 'ghost'.

the spectre at the feast (*British*) someone who spoils other people's enjoyment, for example because they remind them of an unhappy event or situation ○ *The overwhelming good humour was only marred by some catcalls when the US delegation arrived, but no one directly criticised the spectre at the feast.*

> According to the Greek writer Plutarch, the Ancient Egyptians used to place a skeleton at the table during a feast, to remind them that they would die one day.

speed

bring someone up to speed to give someone all the latest information about something ○ *I guess I should bring you up to speed on what's happened since I came to see you yesterday.*

bring something up to speed to make something reach its highest level of efficiency ○ *The fear is that the system will not be cheap to bring up to speed.*

spick

> 'Spick' is sometimes spelled 'spic'.

spick and span very clean, neat, and tidy ○ *When she arrived, she found Ann dusting the furniture, making sure the house was spick and span.*

≣ This expression has developed from an old-fashioned expression 'spick and span-new', meaning 'very new'. 'Spick' probably came from a Dutch word meaning 'new', and 'span-new' meant 'completely new'.

spin

in a spin (mainly British) so angry, confused, or excited that you cannot act sensibly or concentrate on what you are doing ○ *This news came right out of the blue and it's left me in a spin.*

≣ If a plane goes into a spin, it goes out of control and falls very rapidly towards the ground in a spiralling movement. If it goes into a flat spin, it turns round and round as it falls, but remains horizontal.

spit

be the spitting image of someone if one person is the spitting image of another person, the first person looks exactly like the second ○ *Sam is the spitting image of his father. He's tall and dark, just like his dad.*

≣ The origin of this expression is uncertain, but it may have developed from 'spirit and image'. If one person was the spirit and image of another, they were alike both in character and physical appearance.

spit and polish used to talk about a place that is very clean or that is being made very clean ○ *The bar, which had been open for two months now, was all spit and polish.*

spit and sawdust (British) said to mean that somewhere, such as a pub or a bar, looks dirty, untidy, and not very respectable ○ *There's Hogan's Bar in the High Street if it's spit and sawdust you're after.*

≣ In the past, the public bars of many pubs had sawdust on the floor to soak up the mess caused by people spitting and spilling their drinks.

splash

★ **make a splash** to attract a lot of attention because of something successful that you do or by the way you behave on a particular occasion ○ *She made quite a splash at the party with her outspoken views and colourful and expensive clothes.*

spoke

put a spoke in someone's wheel (mainly British) to deliberately make it difficult for someone to do what they are planning to do ○ *If she had known he was seeing Tinsley, she undoubtedly would have tried to put a spoke in his wheel.*

≣ Cartwheels used to be made of solid wood, with holes in them through which a wooden bar or 'spoke' could be pushed in order to make the cart slow down or stop.

spoon

★ **get the wooden spoon** (British) to be last in a race or competition or to be the worst at a particular activity ○ *England must beat Scotland today to avoid getting the wooden spoon.*

≣ At one time, the student who got the lowest marks in their final mathematics exam at Cambridge University was given a wooden spoon.

spot

★ **be on the spot** to be in the place where something that you are talking about is actually happening ○ *Ironically, the first that reporters on the spot knew about the release of Mr Mann was when they heard a news flash on a local radio station.* ○ *The*

Austrian government has dispatched a group of experts to Thailand to begin an on-the-spot investigation.

★ **a blind spot** something that you do not understand or know anything about, although you feel that perhaps you should ○ Computers are a blind spot with me.

★ **do something on the spot** to do something immediately ○ Watch out for sales staff who say you'll get a special discount or prize if you sign on the spot.

★ **have a soft spot for someone** to like or care about someone à lot ○ It looked to me as if Tom had a soft spot for Emily.

hit the spot to be very good and to succeed in pleasing people ○ The company's new advert really hits the spot.

★ **put someone on the spot** to put someone in a difficult situation which they cannot avoid, for example by making them answer awkward questions ○ You shouldn't have asked Gary whether he's asked Linda to marry him. You put him on the spot and that's very unfair.

spots

knock spots off something or someone (British) if one thing or person knocks spots off another, the first is much better than the second ○ I'm looking forward to the return of their chat show. It knocks spots off all the others.

The reference here is probably to someone who is shooting so well that they are able to knock out the spots or marks on a playing card that they are aiming at.

spout

up the spout (British, informal)
1 completely ruined or hopeless
○ The economy's up the spout.
2 pregnant. This expression is usually used when the pregnancy is considered to be a problem rather than a good thing. ○ In the village where I grew up, there was always somebody up the spout.

Originally, this expression was used to refer to items which had been pawned. The 'spout' was the lift in which an item was taken from the pawnbroker's shop to the storeroom above.

spring

no spring chicken someone who is no longer young. This expression is often used when you think someone's appearance or behaviour is surprising for their age. ○ At 85, he is no spring chicken, but Enrico Cuccia is busier than ever.

A spring chicken was a young chicken that was ready to be eaten in the spring time, as opposed to an older bird.

spur

★ **do something on the spur of the moment** to do something suddenly and without planning it in advance ○ He had decided on the spur of the moment to make the journey south to Newcastle. ○ Judges currently cannot reflect in their sentencing the difference between a planned killing and a spur-of-the-moment emotional crime.

spurs

★ **earn your spurs** (mainly British) to have shown that you are capable of doing something well, and that you can be relied on to do it well in the future ○ How did he earn his spurs for the toughest police job in the country?

In medieval times, when a man was made a knight, he was sometimes given a pair of golden spurs.

square

★ **be back to square one** to have failed completely in what you were trying to do, so that now you have to start again ○ So we are back to square one. Their costly intervention has been for nothing, a carefully-constructed peace process lies in ruins.

This expression may refer to board games where the players move counters along a series of squares, and sometimes have to start again at the beginning.

on the square *(mainly American)* honest ○ *Are you sure this guy's on the square?*

This expression probably comes from the use of a square, a measuring device used to check that a right angle is completely accurate.

squib

★ **a damp squib** *(mainly British)* something that is much less impressive or exciting than you expected it to be ○ *As political scandals go it was a damp squib, and in Central Office it was greeted with hilarity and relief rather than indignation.*

A squib is a small firework. A damp squib would not go off properly, and so it would be a disappointment.

stable

closing the stable door after the horse has bolted → see **door**

stack

blow your stack *(mainly American)* to become very angry with someone and shout at them ○ *My father really blew his stack over this.*

stack the deck *(American)* to arrange a situation unfairly against someone, or in your own favour ○ *The President is doing everything in his power to stack the deck in his favour and guarantee his regime's return to power.*

The literal meaning of this expression is to cheat when shuffling cards by secretly putting them in an order which is to your advantage.

stage

★ **set the stage for something** to make preparations so that something can happen ○ *Jamaica's prime minister set the stage for a snap election this month by announcing candidates for his People's National Party.*

stake

go to the stake to defend something *(mainly British, old-fashioned)* to be absolutely certain that you are right about something, and to be prepared to suffer the consequences of defending it ○ *English biologist Thomas Henry Huxley was prepared to go to the stake to defend Darwin's theory of evolution.*

A stake is a wooden post. In the past, people were sometimes tied to a stake and burned alive for refusing to give up beliefs which the church considered heretical and wrong.

stall

set out your stall *(British)* to make all the necessary plans or arrangements that you need to achieve something, and show that you are determined to achieve it ○ *He has set out his stall to retain his place in Europe's Ryder Cup team.*

stand

★ **stand up and be counted** to state publicly your support for or rejection of something, especially when this is difficult or controversial ○ *We must have the courage to stand up and be counted on this issue.*

standard

★ **the standard bearer of something** someone who acts as the leader or representative of a particular organization or group of people ○ *Inevitably, the public perception of her is that of a standard bearer for women jockeys.*

A standard is a flag with badges or symbols on it, which represent a person or organization. In the past, a standard bearer was the person who led an army into battle carrying a standard.

stars

have stars in your eyes to be very hopeful and excited about things which you expect to happen to you in the future. This expression is often used to suggest that someone is naive and that their hopes are unlikely to come true. ○ *We had stars in our eyes last weekend. Now we understand the reality of the situation.*

★ **reach for the stars** to be very ambitious and try hard to achieve something, even though it may be very difficult ○ *If you're ready to move on in your career, keep your feet firmly on the ground while reaching for the stars!*

starter

under starter's orders (British) ready to do a task or job, and able to begin doing it immediately if necessary ○ *The Vice-President is under starter's orders – his job exists to provide a legitimate successor if a president dies.*

state

★ **the state of play** (British) the current situation ○ *Ben Willmott gives you the state of play on marijuana and the law.*

steam

The following expressions refer to the use of steam to provide power for a machine, especially a steam engine.

do something under your own steam to do something on your own, without help from anyone else ○ *He left the group convinced he could do better under his own steam.*

go full steam ahead to start to carry out a particular project in a thorough and determined way ○ *The prime minister declared it was full steam ahead for a fourth term of government.*

go somewhere under your own steam to make your own arrangements for a journey, rather than letting someone else organize it for you ○ *Most hotels organise tours to inland beauty spots, but car hire is cheap enough to consider taking off into the hills under your own steam.*

★ **let off steam** (mainly British) or **blow off steam** (mainly American) to do or say something which helps you to get rid of your strong feelings about something ○ *I was so upset that I pulled the car over to the side of the road, got out, and took a long walk. I just had to let off steam.*

≡ The reference here is to steam escaping noisily from the safety valve of a steam engine.

pick up steam to start to become stronger or more active ○ *Boskin said the economy should pick up steam next year.*

run out of steam to become weaker or less active, and often to stop completely ○ *The US is in a triple dip of recession. The promised recovery ran out of steam, the economy is slowing sharply and consumer spending is falling.*

stew

in a stew (old-fashioned) very worried about something ○ *He's been in a stew ever since he took that phone call early this morning.*

let someone stew or **let someone stew in their own juice** to deliberately leave someone to worry about something, for example the consequence of their actions, and to not do anything to comfort or help them ○ *He was very nasty to everyone and now no one will speak to him; let him stew in his own juice.*

stick

carry a big stick to have a lot of power, and therefore be able to get what you want ○ *The company carries a big stick. Over the past 107 years it has built itself up into the biggest brand in the world and now controls 44 per cent of the global market.*

≡ This expression comes from a saying which became widely known through a speech made by Theodore Roosevelt in 1903: 'There is a homely old adage which runs, "Speak softly and carry a big stick; you will go far."'

★ **get a lot of stick** (British) to be criticized, often in an unfair way, or for something that is not your fault ○ *The cricket team got a lot of stick when they returned from their tour of India, but they deserved it as they had played so badly.*

get the short end of the stick (mainly American) to end up in a worse position than other people in a particular situation, although this is not your fault ○ *As usual it's the consumer who gets the short end of the stick.*

get the wrong end of the stick to completely misunderstand something ○ *People are so easily confused, and so often get the wrong end of the stick.*

have more things than you can shake a stick at to have a very large number of a particular thing ○ *My daughter has more pairs of shoes than you can shake a stick at.*

in a cleft stick (British) in a difficult situation which you cannot get out of easily ○ *Debbie now finds herself in a cleft stick. If she pays her rent, she won't have any money to buy food.*

This expression may refer to the practice of trapping snakes by holding them down behind the head with a forked stick.

★ **a stick to beat someone with** (British) something that can be used to cause embarrassment or difficulty for someone ○ *Surprisingly, the opposition, usually eager to find any stick to beat the government with, is refusing to comment on the affair.*

stiff

be as stiff as a board to have a very stiff body ○ *When you start to do yoga, you can gain flexibility very quickly – even if you are as stiff as a board at your first session.*

sting

★ **something has a sting in the tail** (British) said to mean that although a remark or proposal seems, initially, welcome or pleasing, it contains an unpleasant part at the end ○ *The agreement had a sting in the tail. It said that the entire aid package would be suspended if the country did not make progress on the economic front.*

This is a reference to a scorpion, which is small and looks harmless, but has a poisonous sting in its tail.

take the sting out of something to make something less unpleasant or painful ○ *The most serious situation can be viewed with humour and that always helps to take the sting out of hard facts.*

stitch

a stitch in time or
a stitch in time saves nine said to mean that it is better to deal with a problem in its early stages, in order to prevent it getting worse ○ *The saying 'a stitch in time saves nine' is never more true than with a boat's paintwork: one must be immediately ready to touch up the chips that occur in order to prevent a bigger job later.*

stitches

someone or something has you in stitches said to mean that someone or something makes you laugh a lot ○ *The outrageous comedienne plans to have the north of England in stitches when she performs at the Liverpool Festival of Comedy.*

stone

★ **leave no stone unturned** to consider or try every possible way of doing something ○ *In the difficult weeks ahead, we'll leave no stone unturned in our search for a peaceful solution to the crisis.*

a rolling stone gathers no moss said to mean that, if a person keeps moving from one place to another, they will not get many friends or possessions ○ *He said that a rolling stone gathers no moss, that I'd never have a family if I spent my life touring with the band. I was determined to prove him wrong.*

something is not set in stone
said to mean that something such as
an agreement, policy or rule is not
permanent and that it can be changed
○ *Promises made two or three years before an
election are not set in stone and can be
changed.*

★ **a stone's throw from somewhere**
very close to a particular place ○ *Burke
found employment and rented a flat a stone's
throw from his new office.*

stools

fall between two stools (*mainly
British*) to be in an unsatisfactory
situation because you do not belong to
either of two groups or categories, or
because you are trying to do two
different things at once and are failing at
both ○ *Labour says that young people on
waiting lists for youth training fall between
two stools. They can't get unemployment
benefit, nor can they get the allowance for the
scheme they're waiting to get on.*

stops

★ **pull out all the stops** to do everything
you possibly can to make something
happen in the way that you want it to
○ *The government has pulled out all the stops
to try and ensure an election victory.*

On a church organ, the stops are the
knobs which you pull or push in order
to control the type of sound that
comes out of the pipes. The organ
plays loudest when all the stops are
out.

storage

put something into cold storage
to delay doing something or dealing with
something, for example because other
more important things need your
attention or because you are not ready
to do it ○ *The author's illness means that he
has put completion of his fourth novel into
cold storage.*

storm

a storm in a teacup (*British*) said
to mean that something is not very
important but people are making a lot of
unnecessary fuss about it. The usual
American expression is **a tempest in a
teapot**. ○ *I know how much Ella likes you.
I'm sure this disagreement is all a storm in a
teacup. It'll blow over in no time.*

★ **take somewhere by storm** to be very
successful or popular in a particular
place, and to make a good impression on
people there ○ *The film has taken America
by storm.*

This expression originally meant to
capture something such as a fort or a
military position by means of a
sudden, violent attack.

★ **weather the storm** to survive a
difficult situation or period without being
seriously harmed or very badly affected
by it ○ *The company has weathered the
storm of the current recession better than
most. As car sales have plummeted, it's seen
its share of the market actually increase.*

story

★ **to cut a long story short** (*British*) or
to make a long story short
(*American*) said to mean that you are only
going to mention the final result or point
of a complicated account of something,
without giving any further details ○ *I met
Paul at a party two years ago – he was the
most handsome man I'd ever seen – and, to
cut a long story short, we're getting married
next year.*

straight

★ **keep someone on the straight and
narrow** to help someone to live an
honest, decent life and prevent them
from doing immoral or illegal things
○ *Our goal is to keep these vulnerable young
people on the straight and narrow.*

'Straight' was originally 'strait', which
meant 'narrow'. The expression

probably refers to a passage in the Bible: 'Because strait is the gate, and narrow is the way which leads to life, and there are few that find it.' (Matthew 7:14)

straight as a die

1 (British) completely honest ○ *Tom's not the devious type – he's as straight as a die.*
2 very straight ○ *The streets are lined up, straight as a die, along the left bank of the Guadiana estuary.*

A die is a specially shaped block of metal which is used to cut or form other metal into a particular shape. This expression may refer to dies which were used to produce designs on coins. The metalworkers needed to strike the die with a hard straight blow from a hammer, in order to leave a clear impression on the coin.

straw

draw the short straw (mainly British) to be chosen from a number of people to perform a task or duty that nobody else wants to do ○ *Jim drew the short straw: he had to drive forty miles to the airport at midnight to pick up Elizabeth.*

This expression comes from the practice of using pieces of straw to draw lots. One person holds several pieces of straw in their hand with the ends poking out. Each person in the group takes a piece of straw and the person with the shortest piece loses.

★ **the final straw** the latest in a series of unpleasant or difficult events that makes you feel that you cannot tolerate a situation any longer ○ *Mr Elton was already distraught over his mother's death. When his wife asked him for a divorce, it was the final straw.*

a man of straw (British, formal) a man who does not have the ability or the courage necessary to carry out a particular task or to fulfil a particular role

○ *The problem of the Labour Party is that it is once again firmly in the grip of men of straw without guts and without principles.*

the straw that breaks the camel's back the latest in a series of unpleasant or difficult events that makes you feel that you cannot tolerate a situation any longer ○ *Last week, I broke my wrist skateboarding for the second time. That was the straw that broke the camel's back. My dad has told me to give up the sport.*

The reference here is to an animal which is already carrying a great deal on its back and which collapses when one more thing is added.

straws

clutch at straws to rely on ideas, hopes, or methods which are unlikely to be successful, because you are desperate and cannot think of anything else to try ○ *This extraordinary speech was made by a man clutching at straws to gain much-desired publicity.*

The image here is of a drowning person who is desperately trying to grab hold of anything to save himself or herself, even a straw.

straws in the wind (British, journalism) signs of the way in which a situation may develop ○ *There is new evidence that the economy is starting to climb out of recession. The latest straws in the wind are improved retail sales and an increase in property sales.*

People sometimes drop pieces of straw in order to see which way they move as they fall, so that they can tell which way the wind is blowing.

streak

talk a blue streak (American) to talk a lot and very fast ○ *Although I'm usually shy, that night I talked a blue streak from the moment I arrived at the party.*

This expression refers to a blue streak of lightning flashing quickly across the sky.

stream

★ **come on stream** (mainly British) to begin to operate fully. The usual American expression is **come on line**. ○ Faults at Romania's first nuclear power plant must be repaired before it comes on stream.

street

★ **the man in the street** an ordinary, average person ○ But how do these massive changes appear to the man in the street?

something is right up your street (mainly British) said to mean that something is exactly the kind of thing you like or know about ○ Actor Roy Barraclough has taken on a role that's right up his street, as Sherlock Holmes' bumbling sidekick Watson.

streets

★ **be streets ahead of something or someone** (British) to be much better than something or someone else ○ Bill had a great imagination and was always streets ahead of his fellow-teachers in seeing children's needs and in arranging ways to meet them.

stretch

★ **be at full stretch** (British) to be unable to work any harder or more efficiently, because you are already using all your resources ○ Police are warning that emergency services are at full stretch and they are advising motorists to travel only if their journey is absolutely necessary.

stride

★ **hit your stride** or
get into your stride to start to do something easily and confidently, after being slow and uncertain at the beginning ○ The Government is getting into its stride and seems, for the moment, to be fulfilling its promises.

put someone off their stride (British) to stop someone from concentrating on what they are doing, so that they do not do it as well as usual ○ The player's bad behaviour is a tactic designed to put his opponent off his stride.

★ **take something in your stride** (British) or
take something in stride (American) to deal with a difficult situation calmly and successfully ○ Ridley didn't start shouting, or anything like that. In fact, right until the end he seemed to be taking it all in his stride.

strikes

In baseball, a 'strike' is a legal pitch or ball which the batter fails to hit. The batter is out after three strikes.

three strikes against someone or something (mainly American) three factors which make it impossible for someone or something to be successful ○ He said to me, 'Listen, you've got three strikes against you. You're poor, you're uneducated and you're homeless.'

three strikes and you're out said to mean that a country or an organization has a policy or law, according to which people who commit three offences are punished very severely, even if the individual offences are not very serious ○ California has recently introduced a law known as three strikes and you're out, meaning that after a third conviction, you are put in prison.

string

have another string to your bow (British) to have more than one useful skill, ability, or thing that you can use in case you are unsuccessful with the first skill, ability, or thing. In this expression, 'bow' is pronounced with the same vowel sound as the word 'show'. ○ Stephanie has another string to her bow. Before her career in interior design, she was a photographer.

Archers used to carry a spare bowstring in case the first one broke.

have someone on a string to make someone do whatever you want, because you control them completely ○ *For the rest of his life he had her on a string, spending her money and controlling every aspect of her life.*

strings

★ **pull strings** to get something you want, not by your own merit but by using your friendships with powerful and influential people. This expression is usually used in a disapproving way. ○ *Many of Anna's colleagues felt that she was pulling strings to advance her career.*

★ **pull the strings** to control everything that another person or an organization does ○ *Having engineered many of these political changes and pulled the strings from behind the stage, he now feels it's his due, as it were, to become national leader.*

The image here is of a puppet which is controlled by means of strings.

★ **with no strings attached** said to mean that an offer of help has no unpleasant conditions which must be accepted as part of the offer, or that the person making it does not expect anything in return ○ *This is an extremely generous offer, which comes with no strings attached. I think that we should accept.*

with strings attached said to mean that an offer has unpleasant conditions which must be accepted as part of the offer, or that the person making it expects something in return ○ *The charity has a very strict rule that it refuses to accept any donations with strings attached.*

strip

tear a strip off someone or **tear someone off a strip** (British) to speak angrily or seriously to someone because they have done something wrong ○ *We were sent to the headmaster's office and he tore strips off both of us.*

stroke

different strokes for different folks said to mean that people are different, and that some individuals or groups have different needs and wants from others ○ *The federal government has always been respectful of local customs in local communities, and therefore you had different strokes for different folks.*

put someone off their stroke (British) to stop someone from concentrating on what they are doing, so that they do not do it as well as usual ○ *'You wanted to see me?' – 'What? Oh, yes. Sorry, everything that's been happening has quite put me off my stroke.'*

The reference here is to rowing, in which all the members of a team have to pull on their oars at exactly the same moment. Each pull of the oars is called a stroke.

strokes

in broad strokes in general terms rather than in detail ○ *The speech will lay out in broad strokes the two candidates' differing approaches towards how best to stimulate the economy.*

The image here is of an artist painting a picture roughly or quickly.

strong

strong as an ox extremely strong ○ *Big Beppe, as everybody calls him, is enormous and as strong as an ox.*

stubborn

stubborn as a mule determined to do what you want and unwilling to change your mind, often in a way that annoys other people ○ *He is, without question, a man of his word, but he can certainly be stubborn as a mule.*

stuff

★ **strut your stuff** to do something which you know you are good at in a proud and confident way in order to impress other people ○ *He was the type of guy who liked to show off and strut his stuff.*

stuffing

knock the stuffing out of someone to destroy someone's energy and self-confidence, and leave them feeling weak and nervous ○ *The opposition knocked the stuffing out of us early on and we never got into the game.*

stump

★ **be on the stump** (mainly American) if politicians are on the stump, they are travelling to different places and speaking to voters as part of their election campaign ○ *Despite his falling popularity, the president braved it on the stump today on behalf of his fellow Republicans.*

> This expression comes from politicians using tree stumps as platforms when giving a speech in the open air.

style

cramp someone's style to prevent someone from behaving freely in the way that they want ○ *Like many women with good jobs, independent spirits and high standards, she believes marriage would cramp her style.*

suck

suck it and see (British) said to mean that the only way to find out if something new is a good idea and is likely to be successful is to actually try it ○ *These results do not mean that the Japanese will like these Western products. The only sure way to prove that is to suck it and see.*

suit

> The following expressions refer to the four suits in a pack of cards: diamonds, hearts, clubs, and spades.

★ **follow suit** to do the same thing that someone else has just done ○ *If Tim decided to have pancakes for breakfast, Pam would follow suit.*

> If you follow suit in a card game, you play a card of the same suit as the previous player.

something is someone's long suit said to mean that someone is good at something, or knows a lot about it, which gives them an advantage ○ *Looking after children is not her long suit. She's definitely a career woman.*

> If a large number of a player's cards belong to a particular suit, you can call that suit their long suit.

summer

an Indian summer (mainly British) a period of great success late in your life or career, often after a period of not being successful ○ *The recent revival in international fashion is proving an Indian summer for Mr Rabanne, better known for his perfumes in the Seventies and Eighties.*

> An Indian summer is a period of unusually warm sunny weather during the autumn.

supper

sing for your supper (old-fashioned) to have to do a particular job before you are allowed to do or have something that you want ○ *'You're going to have to sing for your supper,' said the organizer. 'While the guests are eating, I want you to sit at the end of the table and perform for us.'*

sure

sure as eggs is eggs (British) said to mean that you are very certain something will happen ○ *He'll be back later on. Sure as eggs is eggs.*

> This expression may be a corruption or mishearing of 'as sure as x is x', referring to the use of x to represent a variable in algebra and logic.

surface

★ **scratch the surface of something** to deal with or experience only a small part of something ○ *Officials say they've*

only scratched the surface of the city's
political corruption.

swallow

**one swallow doesn't make a
summer** said to mean that, although
something good has happened, the
situation may not continue to be good,
and you cannot rely on it ○ *Sales are up by
1%, which is a vast improvement on the last
six months. One swallow, however, doesn't
make a summer and business could still be
better.*

Swallows are a type of bird. The
reference here is to the arrival of
swallows in Europe at the beginning of
summer, after spending the winter
further south.

swear

swear up and down → see **up**

sweat

**do something by the sweat of your
brow** (literary) to do something through
hard physical work, without any help
from anyone else ○ *Most people are no
longer earning their bread by the sweat of
their brow.*

in a cold sweat very frightened, anxious,
or embarrassed ○ *It was a terrifying
experience, a nightmare. I still come out in a
cold sweat thinking about it.*

sweep

make a clean sweep if someone who
has just taken up a position of authority
in an organization makes a clean sweep,
they make a lot of changes, for example
getting rid of a large number of
employees, in order to make the
organization more efficient or profitable
○ *The new CEO made a clean sweep of
longtime employees, firing the managers, one
by one.*

★ **make a clean sweep of something**
to win something or a series of things
very easily ○ *The USA has made a clean

sweep of all 5 titles in the Women's
Gymnastics event.*

sweet

cop it sweet (mainly Australian)
to accept harsh treatment or a
punishment without reacting violently
or complaining ○ *Bullies tend to lose
interest in a victim very quickly if that victim
refuses to 'cop it sweet'.*

★ **keep someone sweet** (British) to do
something to please someone so that
they will treat you well in return ○ *Some
firms reserve boxes at football grounds and at
theatres that can be used by high-flying staff
they want to keep sweet.*

sweet as pie (mainly British) very kind,
friendly, and charming ○ *She really is
sweet as pie, as well as being original, honest
and very funny.*

swing

★ **be in full swing** to be operating fully or
to have already been happening for some
time, rather than just having started
○ *Twelve days after Hurricane Andrew left its
trail of destruction and misery across South
Florida, officials say recovery efforts are at
last in full swing.*

get into the swing of something to
get used to something and to start doing
it well or start enjoying it ○ *I assumed
everything would be okay once I got into the
swing of college but I had no idea how lonely
I would be.*

go with a swing (British) to happen in a
lively and exciting way ○ *These impressive
recipes are guaranteed to make the party go
with a swing.*

swings

swings and roundabouts (British)
said to mean that there are as many
advantages as there are disadvantages in
a particular situation ○ *When it rains,
high-street pubs will do better than country
pubs because people may not want to leave
town. When the sun shines, pubs with

gardens benefit. It's very much swings and roundabouts.

sword

★ **a double-edged sword** something that has both a good and a bad side ○ *The strong currency is a double-edged sword. It helps the nation's banks, but it also raises the costs of exports for car and electronics manufacturers.*

have the Sword of Damocles hanging over your head to be in a situation in which something very bad could happen to you at any time ○ *As a Grand Prix driver you have the Sword of Damocles hanging over your head at every moment.*

This expression comes from a Greek legend. Dionysius, the ruler of Syracuse, was annoyed by Damocles, who kept flattering him and saying how much he admired him. Dionysius invited Damocles to a feast, and asked him to sit in his own seat. When Damocles looked up during the feast, he noticed a sword hanging by a single thread above his head, and so he could no longer enjoy the feast. The sword symbolized the dangers and fears that rulers have, in addition to all the privileges.

swords

'Ploughshares' is spelled 'plowshares' in American English.

beat swords into ploughshares to try to stop war or conflict, and to use the resources and technology of warfare to do other things to improve people's lives ○ *For Ukrainians, beating swords into*

ploughshares and turning rocket plants into car factories is an economic necessity.

A ploughshare is one of the blades on a plough. This expression may come from the Bible (Isaiah 2:4), which says that people should make their swords into ploughshares; they should stop fighting wars, and start working together productively.

cross swords with someone to disagree and argue with someone, or oppose them ○ *These two politicians have crossed swords on many occasions.*

system

★ **get something out of your system** to say or do something that you have been wanting to say or do for a long time, and therefore begin to feel less worried or angry about it ○ *If something awful happens to you at least you can write about it. I'm sure you feel better if you get it out of your system.*

systems

it's all systems go said to mean that people are very busy with a particular project, or that you expect there will be a lot of activity in a particular field ○ *Work started on the indoor sports arena at the beginning of the year and it's now all systems go, with a huge team of builders working on the project.*

This expression became popular as a result of its use during the launch of spacecraft in the United Sates in the 1960s and 1970s. It indicated that the spacecraft was functioning correctly and was ready for takeoff.

Tt

tab

★ **pick up the tab** to pay a bill or pay the costs of something, especially something that you are not responsible for ○ *Pollard picked up the tab for dinner.*

table

can drink someone under the table to be able to drink much more alcohol than someone else can without getting drunk ○ *Donna is the only person I know who can drink me under the table.*

do something under the table *(mainly American)* to do something secretly because it is dishonest or illegal. The usual British expression is **do something under the counter**.
○ *Some staff made deals under the table with freight companies by charging extra money for express delivery when sometimes the express service did not exist.*

★ **put something on the table** to present something, such as a proposal, plan or offer, formally to other people, so that it can be discussed and agreed on ○ *The United States said Europe must put a new offer on the table to save the talks.*

tables

★ **turn the tables on someone** to do something to change a situation so that you gain an advantage over someone or cause them problems, following a time when they had the advantages or caused problems for you ○ *The Prime Minister has turned the tables on his many enemies and has given them something to worry about for a change.*

> The image here is of a player in a game such as chess turning the board through 180 degrees, so that the situations of the two players are reversed.

tabs

★ **keep tabs on someone** to make sure that you always know where someone is and what they are doing, often in order to control them ○ *The FBI kept close tabs on the novelist, at times opening his mail and recording his conversations.*

> Originally, this was an American expression which uses an American sense of 'tab', meaning an account or bill, which can be used to keep a record of what someone spends.

tail

chase your own tail or
chase your tail to spend a lot of time and energy doing something, but achieving nothing ○ *It feels great to be making some progress on this project at last, and not just chasing my own tail.*

go off with your tail between your legs to go away feeling very ashamed and embarrassed because of a defeat or a foolish mistake that you have made ○ *I ran out of money, lost my job, my house, my girlfriend. I came home to Sydney with my tail between my legs, absolutely broke and shattered.*

★ **on someone's tail** following someone closely, often chasing them ○ *Juarez entered the finishing lap with Zadrobilek right on his tail. Only three kilometres remained.*

the tail wags the dog said to mean that a small or unimportant part of something is becoming too important and is controlling the whole thing ○ *To avoid the impression of the tail wagging the* dog, the prime minister cannot be seen to be giving in to the wishes of a minority party.

turn tail to turn and run away from someone or something because you are frightened of them ○ *Rebels were forced back from position after position until they turned tail and fled.*

with your tail up feeling very happy or confident about your chances of success ○ *We'll go to court with our tails up.*

tale

live to tell the tale to survive a dangerous or frightening experience ○ *Michael Sproule was attacked by a shark. He lived to tell the tale but underwent emergency surgery for multiple injuries.*

something tells its own tale said to mean that something reveals the truth about a particular situation ○ *The fact that we originally booked for only one night but ended up staying eight tells its own tale. We can't recommend the hotel highly enough.*

tales

tell tales to tell lies or reveal secrets about someone, so that they get into trouble ○ *She had no right to tell tales to his mother!*

talk

someone is all talk or **someone is all talk and no action** said to mean that someone talks about doing something without ever doing it ○ *No wonder people no longer believe a word he says. He's all talk and no action. No matter what he promises, nobody will be able to trust him.*

tall

★ **tall tales** stories or statements which are difficult to believe because they are so exaggerated or unlikely ○ *Pollard was described as someone whose rich imagination and keen intellect were convincing; some of his college chums believed his tall tales.*

'Tall' used to be used to describe language that was considered extremely formal or exaggerated.

tangent

go off on a tangent to start saying or thinking something that is not directly connected with what you were saying or thinking before ○ *Our teacher occasionally goes off on a tangent, talking about things totally unrelated to our textbooks or the curriculum.*

In geometry, a tangent is a straight line which touches a curve at one point but does not cross it.

tango

it takes two to tango said to mean that a situation or argument involves two people and they are both therefore responsible for it ○ *I've tried everything to stop our marriage falling apart. But it takes two to tango and, so far, my husband has made no effort to save our relationship.*

This is the title of a song by Hoffman and Manning, written in 1952.

tank

someone or something is built like a tank said to mean that someone is very big and strong, or that something has been made very well and very solidly, and will last for a long time ○ *Nick's built like a tank and lots of people are afraid of him when they first meet him, but he's actually a really friendly, gentle guy.*

tap

★ **on tap**
1 available and ready for immediate use ○ *The enterprise agency's close links with both the university and several business institutions provides local businesses with a wealth of knowledge on tap.*
2 (American) scheduled to happen very soon ○ *More military and medical experiments are on tap for Atlantis astronauts today.*

If drink such as beer is available on tap, it is kept in a barrel fitted with a tap, so it can be drawn off as required.

tape

★ **red tape** official rules and procedures that seem complicated and unnecessary and that cause delay ○ *Two lawyers have written a book in a bid to help people cut through the red tape when dealing with British immigration and nationality laws.*

Lawyers and government officials used to tie documents together with red or pink tape.

taped

have got something taped (British) to think that you fully understand something and are in control of it ○ *The one certainty of parenthood is that whenever you feel you've got it taped, something will happen and prove you wrong!*

target

be shooting for the same target if two people are shooting for the same target, they are in agreement about what they are trying to achieve together ○ *We'll only succeed if we're both shooting for the same target.*

task

take someone to task to criticize someone strongly for something they have done ○ *One day she took me to task for never using her name when I was talking to her.*

taste

something leaves a bad taste in your mouth or
something leaves a nasty taste in your mouth said to mean that something that someone does makes you feel angry or disgusted with them because it was a very unpleasant thing to do ○ *Some people are abusive in shops, in buses and on trains. They seem to think it is smart. For the victim it leaves a nasty taste in the mouth.*

tea

someone would not do something for all the tea in China said to emphasize that someone definitely does not want to do something ○ *He would not change his job for all the tea in China.*

In the past, all tea came from China.

tee

★ **to a tee** or
to a T perfectly, or in exactly the right way ○ *His job suits him to a tee.*

T stands for 'tittle', a small mark in printing such as the dot over an i. The expression refers to writing being very clear and exactly right.

teeth

armed to the teeth having or carrying a lot of weapons or very effective weapons ○ *The police are grossly underpaid and underequipped while the criminals are armed to the teeth with the latest weapons.*

★ **cut your teeth doing something** to do something new which gives you experience and helps you learn how to do more advanced or complicated things ○ *Dennis cut his teeth with theatre roles before taking on parts in TV series and films.*

When a child cuts a tooth, the tooth begins to appear through the gum.

fed up to the back teeth with something or
sick to the back teeth of something (British) annoyed or tired because something has been happening for a long time and you think it should be stopped or changed ○ *I've always supported the Conservative Party but I'm fed up to the back teeth with them at the moment.*

★ **get your teeth into something** to become deeply involved with something and do it with a lot of energy and enthusiasm ○ *Half the trouble is having nothing interesting to do. We've not had a project to get our teeth into for weeks.*

gnashing of teeth when people become very worried or upset by something that has happened, especially when they are overreacting or showing their concern in an excessive way ○ *In times of widespread strife and much gnashing of teeth, a sense of community is needed to stop everyone plummeting into the dark depths of despair.*

> The phrases 'weeping and gnashing of teeth' and 'wailing and gnashing of teeth' both appear several times in the Bible in descriptions of the people who are sent to hell.

★ **gnash your teeth** to show your anger about something in a very obvious way ○ *He stood glaring at me, gnashing his teeth.*

grind your teeth to be very angry or frustrated about something, but feel that you cannot say or do anything about it ○ *Lucy appeared to think this over for a moment and then walked away, grinding her teeth in frustration.*

★ **grit your teeth** to decide to continue even though the situation you are in is very difficult ○ *He says that there are no simple solutions and that it will be hard work, but we just have to grit our teeth and get on with it.*

kick someone in the teeth to unexpectedly treat someone very badly and unfairly ○ *The union expected that the coalfield would be given favourable treatment: 'Instead we have been kicked in the teeth.'*

lie through your teeth to tell very obvious lies while appearing not to be embarrassed about this ○ *It's clear that the government are lying through their teeth.*

like pulling teeth very difficult to do ○ *Getting this information out of him was like pulling teeth.*

> When a dentist pulls someone's tooth, they pull it out of their gum. In the past, this was done without anaesthetic and so it was difficult and painful.

set your teeth on edge if something sets your teeth on edge, you find it extremely irritating or unpleasant ○ *His casual arrogance never failed to set my teeth on edge.*

show your teeth to show that you are capable of fighting or defending yourself ○ *We need to show our teeth if we are going to overturn the council's plan to build new houses in our village.*

something has teeth said to mean that something, such as an organization or a law, has the necessary authority or power to make people obey it ○ *The prison operates under a contract service level agreement which has teeth – financial penalties can be imposed and it's independently monitored.*

teething

★ **teething problems** (British) small problems in the early stages of a new project, or when a new product first becomes available ○ *The company conceded there have been teething problems with the new system but said that these were now being corrected.*

tell

tell someone where to get off to tell someone in a rude and forceful way that you cannot accept what they are saying or doing ○ *If somebody said that to me, I'd tell them where to get off.*

tempest

a tempest in a teapot (American) something that is not important but that people are making a lot of unnecessary fuss about. The usual British expression is **a storm in a teacup**. ○ *'It's a tempest in a teapot,' he said of the controversy over the painting.*

tenterhooks

on tenterhooks very nervous or excited, because you are keen to know what is going to happen ○ *'It was a good match wasn't it? Very exciting.' 'Yes, we were on tenterhooks.'*

In the past, when cloth had been woven, it was stretched on a frame called a tenter and held in place by hooks. The person's emotional state is being compared to the tension in the cloth.

territory

something goes with the territory said to mean that something often occurs in a particular kind of situation or activity, and so you have to be prepared for it ○ *People often point me out and ask me for photos and autographs, but that goes with the territory. I chose to become an actor and I'm not going to complain about that.*

test

★ **something has stood the test of time** said to mean that something has proved its value and has not failed or has not gone out of fashion since it first appeared ○ *Since it began manufacturing in 1933, Gossen has built easy-to-use, reliable equipment that has stood the test of time.*

tether

★ **at the end of your tether** (mainly British) feeling desperate because you are in a difficult situation and you do not know how to deal with it. The usual American expression is **at the end of your rope**. ○ *She was at the end of her tether. She needed someone she could talk to, someone she could trust.*

A tether is a length of rope, used for tying animals up. The image is of an animal which cannot move very far because it is tied to something with a tether.

Thames

not set the Thames on fire to not be very exciting or successful ○ *They both had reasonably successful careers in London, without exactly setting the Thames on fire.*

there

★ **be there for someone** (spoken) to always be ready to listen to someone's

problems and to help and support them ○ *Jimmy's a good friend to me – he's always been there for me with support and advice.*

someone is not all there said to mean that someone is not very intelligent, or that they are slightly mentally ill ○ *You could tell that she wasn't all there. You could see it in her eyes.*

thick

★ **do something through thick and thin** to continue doing something even when the situation makes it very difficult for you ○ *I'll love you through thick and thin, no matter what happens.*

This comes from a hunting expression 'through thicket and thin wood'. A thicket is a small group of trees or bushes which are growing closely together.

★ **in the thick of it** deeply involved in a particular activity or situation ○ *A fight broke out in the bar and he suddenly found himself in the thick of it.*

lay it on thick to exaggerate something such as a statement, an experience, or an emotion, in order to impress people ○ *Sue was laying it on a bit thick when she said that Tom was the best dancer she'd ever seen.*

thick as mince (mainly Scottish) very stupid ○ *He's bound to fail the exam – he's thick as mince.*

thick as thieves if two or more people are as thick as thieves, they are very friendly with each other ○ *Jones and Cook have known each other since the age of ten – they're thick as thieves.*

thick as two short planks (British) very stupid ○ *His people regarded him as a great and wise monarch. In fact he was as thick as two short planks.*

thin

spread yourself too thin to try to do a lot of different things at the same time, with the result that you cannot do any of them properly ○ *The company grew too fast and spread itself too thin across too many diverse areas.*

thin as a rake extremely thin ○ *I'd always been as thin as a rake but in London my weight went up to more than 12 stone.*

thing

★ **do your own thing** to live or behave in the way you want to, without paying attention to convention and without depending on other people ○ *Her parents let her do her own thing as long as she keeps in touch by phone to say she is okay.*

★ **one thing led to another** said, when you are giving an account of something, to mean that you do not think you need to give any details of events, because they happened in an obvious way ○ *Elsa got in with the wrong crowd of people. They were bad news. One thing led to another and she started shoplifting.*

thorn

★ **a thorn in someone's side** someone or something that continually annoys or causes trouble for someone else ○ *She has become a thorn in the side of the government since publishing a number of reports pointing out that public cash was being mishandled.*

This refers to a passage in the Bible (2 Corinthians 12:7), in which St Paul says that the Devil gave him an illness (or a 'thorn in his flesh') to make him suffer, and to stop him from becoming too proud.

thread

hang by a thread to be very likely to fail soon ○ *It's clear that the ceasefire is hanging by a thread and may be broken at any time.*

someone's life hangs by a thread said to mean that someone is seriously ill and that they are very likely to die soon ○ *The*

baby was delivered by emergency Caesarean and the life of her mother hung by a thread.

This expression may relate to the story of the Sword of Damocles: see the explanation at 'sword'.

throat

cut your own throat to make a mistake by doing something which is going to result in disaster for you ○ *I think the union is cutting its own throat because, if the company can't reduce its costs, then even more jobs will be lost.*

grab something by the throat to make a determined attempt to control, defeat, or deal with something ○ *Instead of being passive and waiting for things to happen, you must get out there and grab life by the throat.*

jump down someone's throat to react to something someone has said in a very impatient, angry, and unpleasant way ○ *Even if I just asked her how she was, she'd jump down my throat, as if I were interrogating her.*

★ **ram something down someone's throat** to try to force someone to accept, believe, or learn something against their will ○ *When I was a kid, my parents rammed religion down my throat.*

something grabs you by the throat said to mean that something is so powerful, interesting, or exciting that you are forced to pay attention to it ○ *Fifty years after it was made, the film still grabs you by the throat.*

something sticks in your throat
1 said to mean that something makes you annoyed or impatient ○ *It sticks in my throat that politicians think that they still have something to tell the rest of us about morality.*
2 said to mean that you cannot say a particular word, or you dislike saying it, because it does not express your real feelings or because it makes you feel uncomfortable ○ *She found it impossible*

to utter the usual terms of maternal endearment: words such as 'darling' or 'pet' stuck in her throat.

throats

★ **be at each other's throats** if two people or groups are at each other's throats, they are continually arguing or fighting ○ He and Stevens didn't get on; they'd been at each other's throats for years.

throes

★ **in the throes of something** busy doing or deeply involved in something, especially something difficult or unpleasant ○ The newspaper's future looks bleak. It's in the throes of a four-month-old strike and is losing nearly a million dollars a day.

throttle

do something at full throttle to do something with all your energy and effort ○ She's a high-powered businesswoman who always goes at things at full throttle.

⦀ If an engine is operating at full throttle, it is operating at its maximum speed.

throw

throw a wobbly or
throw a wobbler (British) to lose your temper in a noisy, uncontrolled, and childish way, often about something unimportant ○ I can't even lie in the bath without him throwing a wobbly because there are a few shampoo bottles with the lids off.

thumb

★ **be under someone's thumb** be under the control or influence of another person ○ Ian was completely under his wife's thumb. She controlled the money, told him what to do and wouldn't allow him to have any friends of his own.

have a green thumb (American) to be very good at gardening. The usual British expression is **have green fingers**. ○ She had a green thumb and, using only instinct

and loads of manure, casually grew huge crops of fruit.

someone or something sticks out like a sore thumb said to mean that someone or something is very noticeable because they are very different from the other people or things around them ○ 'First impressions are very important,' says Baines. 'You don't want a new house to stick out like a sore thumb; it should blend into its surroundings.'

thumbs

be all fingers and thumbs or
be all thumbs to do something with your hands in a clumsy way and keep making mistakes while you are doing it ○ Can you open this packet for me? I'm all fingers and thumbs.

★ **give something the thumbs down** or
give the thumbs down to something to show that you do not approve of something, such as a plan, a suggestion, or an activity, and are not willing to accept it ○ Out of 58,000 replies to the questionnaire, 79 per cent gave the thumbs down to the proposal.

⦀ A thumbs down or a thumbs-down sign is a sign that you make by pointing your thumb downwards in order to show dissatisfaction or disagreement, or to show that things are going badly. In ancient Rome, a signal in which the thumb was bent down was used at the games to tell a victorious gladiator not to kill his opponent.

★ **give something the thumbs up** or
give the thumbs up to something to show that you approve of something, such as a plan, a suggestion, or an activity, and are willing to accept it ○ A big US oil company has given the thumbs up to the president's energy plan.

⦀ A thumbs up or a thumbs-up sign is a sign that you make by pointing your thumb upwards in order to show satisfaction or agreement, or to show that everything is all right. In ancient Rome, a signal in which the thumb was straight was used at the games to tell a victorious gladiator to kill his opponent.

twiddle your thumbs to waste your time and achieve nothing because you have nothing to do ○ *Graduates who have invested time and their parents' money to go to university do not want to sit twiddling their thumbs on the dole.*

thunder

steal someone's thunder to stop someone from getting attention or praise by doing something better than them or doing something before them ○ *He's a very insecure boss – he's always afraid that his staff might steal his thunder.*

This expression may come from an incident in the early 18th century. A British playwright, John Dennis, invented a new way of making the sound of thunder for his play 'Appius and Virginia'. However, the play was unsuccessful and soon closed. Soon afterwards, Dennis went to see a production of 'Macbeth' by another company and found that they had stolen his idea for making thunder sounds. He is said to have jumped up and accused them of stealing his thunder.

ticket

a one-way ticket to something something that is certain to lead to a particular situation or state, usually an undesirable or unpleasant one ○ *Having strong feelings for someone when those feelings aren't returned is a one-way ticket to unhappiness.*

tide

★ **stem the tide of something** to get control of something bad that is happening on a large scale, and stop it ○ *The authorities seem powerless to stem the tide of violence.*

swim against the tide to do or say something which is the opposite of what most other people are doing or saying ○ *Adenauer generally appeared to be swimming against the tide in international politics.*

tight

★ **sit tight** to wait and see how a difficult situation develops before taking any action ○ *In a recession, the message is that those who want to sell their houses should sit tight for a couple of years if they can.*

tightrope

★ **walk a tightrope** to be in a difficult situation where you must be very careful about what you do or say, because you are trying to satisfy opposing groups ○ *He is walking a tightrope between the young activists and the more traditional elements within the democracy movement.*

tiles

be out on the tiles (British) to go out in the evening, for example to a bar or club, and not return home until very late or until the following morning ○ *You look as though you've been out on the tiles, Ken.*

This may be a reference to cats spending the night out on the rooftops.

time

★ **be living on borrowed time** to not be expected to survive for much longer ○ *From this moment onwards, this government is living on borrowed time.*

big time used to emphasize the importance or extent of something that is happening ○ *With a little luck we could make this plan work, and work big time.*

★ **call time on something** (mainly British, journalism) to put an end to something ○ *Scott Hastings has called time* on his international rugby career by cutting short his contract.

> This expression originates in British pubs where the landlord calls time to tell drinkers that the pub is about to close.

★ **have time on your hands** to have a lot of free time and not know what to do with it ○ *Children need discipline and planned activities. If they have too much time on their hands, they can get into trouble.*

★ **hit the big time** to become very famous and successful ○ *The fashion designer hit the big time in 1935, when he was chosen to design the Duchess of Gloucester's wedding dress.*

in no time very quickly or very soon ○ *You're going to be OK, buddy. We'll get some back-up out here and you'll be on your way to hospital in no time at all.*

★ **mark time** to not do anything new or decisive, because you are waiting to see how a situation will develop ○ *We feel we're just marking time until our new boss arrives.*

> When soldiers mark time, they march on the spot without moving forward.

★ **play for time** to try to delay doing or saying something definite until you have decided what is the best course of action to take ○ *He poured himself a drink, playing for time, giving himself a moment to think before he answered her question.*

tin

behave like a little tin god or
behave like a tin god (mainly British) to behave as if you are much more important and powerful than you really are ○ *He accused the officials of behaving like tin gods.*

have a tin ear for something to be unable to appreciate or understand music or something else that you can hear ○ *For a playwright specializing in characters who use the vernacular, he has a tin ear for dialogue.*

tip

★ **just the tip of the iceberg** something that is part of a very large problem or a very serious situation, although other aspects of the problem or situation may not yet be obvious ○ *We get about 2,000 complaints every year but this is just the tip of the iceberg. Many more people just suffer in silence.*

> Only a very small part of an iceberg can be seen above the water. About nine-tenths of it is below the surface.

something is on the tip of your tongue said to mean that you are sure you know something, such as a word, an answer, or a name, but that you cannot remember it at the moment ○ *I know the answer to this question. No, no, don't tell me. Oh, it's on the tip of my tongue.*

something was on the tip of your tongue said to mean that you really wanted to make a remark or ask a question about something, but that you decided not to ○ *'Do you know anything about this?' he asked after a while. It was on the tip of my tongue to tell him what I'd seen but, in the end, I said nothing.*

★ **tip the balance** or
tip the scales to produce one result in a particular situation where, before, two possible results seemed equally likely ○ *As the election looms, the two main parties appear so evenly matched that just one issue could tip the balance.*

toast

someone is toast (informal) said to mean that someone is no longer important or powerful, or that their position is under threat ○ *'Hit your sales targets next year or you're toast,' my manager told me.*

tod

on your tod (British, informal, old-fashioned) by yourself, without help from anyone else ○ *I can't believe that you managed to work this out on your tod.*

This expression comes from Cockney rhyming slang 'on your Tod Sloan' meaning 'on your own'. Tod Sloan was a famous American jockey at the beginning of the 20th century.

today

here today, gone tomorrow said to mean that someone or something is only present for a short time. You often use this expression to suggest that this is a bad thing. ○ *Most gang members live day to day and their philosophy is 'Here today, gone tomorrow.'*

toe

dip your toe in the water or
dip a toe in the water (mainly British) to start doing something that you have not done before in a slow and careful way because you are not sure if you will like it or if it will be successful ○ *After years of selling her jewellery through fashion stores, she finally dipped a toe in the water and opened her own jewellery shop in London.*

go toe to toe with someone (mainly American) to start to fight, argue, or compete with someone fiercely and directly ○ *They're confident that the company is now strong enough to go toe to toe with its rivals.*

toes

★ **keep someone on their toes** to cause or force someone to be alert and ready for anything that might happen ○ *Our new boss has kept us on our toes right from the moment she took over the job.*

make your toes curl to make you feel very embarrassed for someone else ○ *There are moments of tenderness and some very funny scenes in Nigel Charnock's direction. And there are scenes, too, that make your toes curl.* ○ *Movies about famous explorers rarely work, as some recent toe-curling efforts show.*

★ **step on someone's toes** or
tread on someone's toes to offend

someone by criticizing the way they do something or by interfering in something that is their responsibility ○ *Women often feel ridiculously inhibited and duty-bound not to antagonize the men they work with or tread on too many toes.*

turn up your toes (British) to die. This expression is used to refer to death in a light-hearted or humorous way. ○ *I've discovered that all my old admirers have turned up their toes to the daises. Now I feel old!*

toffee

someone can't do something for toffee (British) said to mean that someone is extremely bad at doing something ○ *She can't sing for toffee.*

Tom

every Tom, Dick, and Harry any person, even an ordinary person with no special skills or qualities ○ *This hotel used to be exclusive. Nowadays they let in every Tom, Dick and Harry.*

All of these names used to be very common, and so they began to be used to refer to ordinary people in general.

tomorrow

like there's no tomorrow without thinking about the results of your behaviour ○ *In the property boom of the 1980s, the banks lent to property companies in Britain like there was no tomorrow.*

tomorrow is another day said to mean that, although you have just had a bad experience, you are confident or hopeful that your life will be much better in the future ○ *Everything went wrong. I didn't play well. However, tomorrow is another day.*

ton

come down on someone like a ton of bricks to speak very angrily to someone because they have done something wrong or to punish them severely ○ *If you make even the tiniest mistake, they all come down on you like a ton of bricks.*

like a ton of bricks very suddenly and dramatically ○ *The reality of the situation hit her like a ton of bricks.*

tongue

be unable to get your tongue round something (British) to have difficulty pronouncing a word or phrase ○ *When my brother was little, he couldn't get his tongue round the word 'bicycle'; it always came out as 'bi-ci-click'.*

★ **bite your tongue** to not say a particular thing, even though you want to, because it would be the wrong thing to say at the time, or because you are waiting for a better time to speak ○ *I wanted to tell him how much I would miss him, but I bit my tongue.*

find your tongue to begin to talk, when you have previously been too shy or frightened to say anything ○ *After a lon silence, Tom eventually found his tongue.*

give someone the rough side of your tongue or

give someone the rough edge of your tongue (British, old-fashioned) to speak angrily or harshly to someone about something that they have done wrong ○ *He's really going to give the boy the rough side of his tongue.*

give someone a tongue-lashing to speak harshly or angrily to someone about something that they have done ○ *The President of the EU Commission was given a tongue-lashing from Mr Major and told to drop his objections to a world trade deal.*

speak with forked tongue to lie or deliberately mislead people ○ *He speaks with forked tongue. I don't trust him and I don't like him.*

★ **tongue in cheek** used to describe a remark or a piece of writing that is meant to be funny and ironic, and is not meant to be taken seriously ○ *I think people are taking all this more seriously than we intended. It was supposed to be tongue in cheek.*

tongues

tongues are wagging said to mean that people are gossiping as a result of someone's behaviour ○ *They spent an evening together at his Knightsbridge flat. He said they talked and played cards but added: 'No doubt tongues will be wagging.'*

tools

down tools (British) if a group of people down tools, they stop working, for example in order to protest about something ○ *In August 1980, the workers at this shipyard downed tools and went on strike for pay increases.*

the tools of the trade the skills and equipment that you need to do your job properly ○ *As a pianist, Grace's fingers were the tools of her trade.*

tooth

be long in the tooth to be getting old ○ *'Why don't you enrol in the University and take a course?' 'Aren't I a bit long in the tooth to start being an undergraduate?'*

This expression refers to the fact that you can judge the age of a horse by looking at its teeth. As horses get older, their teeth look longer because their gums are receding.

fight tooth and nail to make a determined effort to keep or get something, when other people are trying to take it away from you or prevent you from having it ○ *The prime minister let it be known that she would fight tooth and nail to stay in office.*

★ **have a sweet tooth** to like eating things that are sugary or taste sweet ○ *She has a sweet tooth; she can't resist chocolate cake and peppermint creams.*

red in tooth and claw (literary)
behaving competitively and ruthlessly
○ *His intention was to demonstrate that Labour is no longer red in tooth and claw, but a serious and sober political party.*

> This is a quotation from the poem 'In Memoriam' (1850) by the English poet Alfred, Lord Tennyson. (Part 56, stanza 4)

top

at the top of the heap → see **heap**
at the top of the pile → see **pile**
blow your top to become very angry with someone and shout at them ○ *I never asked her personal questions because, for some reason, she'd always blow her top and tell me I was being nosy.*

★ **from top to bottom** very thoroughly ○ *She cleaned the house from top to bottom.*

★ **from top to toe** (mainly British) used to talk about the whole of someone's body ○ *She was trembling from top to toe.*

get on top of you to make you feel anxious and that you are not managing a situation well because there is too much work or too many problems ○ *Most of us are irritable or bad-tempered when things get on top of us.*

off the top of your head → see **head**

★ **on top of something** dealing with a difficult task or a situation successfully ○ *With two young children and a full-time job, I'm so busy that I'm not keeping on top of the housework.*

on top of the world → see **world**

★ **over the top** or

  OTT extreme and exaggerated. This expression is usually used disapprovingly. ○ *I'm sorry. I realize now that I was a bit over the top, accusing you of being a traitor.* ○ *Each design is very different in style. Some are subtle, some gloriously OTT.*

> During the First World War, 'to go over the top' meant to climb out of the trenches and run into no-man's land in order to attack the enemy.

push someone over the top (American) in a competition or contest, if something pushes someone over the top, it results in them winning ○ *The advertising campaign pushed the company over the top, allowing them to replace their rivals as the number-one soft drink in supermarkets.*

torch

> The torch referred to in these expressions is a long stick with burning material at one end which provides a light. This kind of torch is sometimes used in processions or parades.

carry a torch for someone to be in love with someone who does not love you, or who is already involved with another person ○ *What makes a woman so special that a man will carry a torch for her all his life?*

carry the torch for something to support something, such as a political party or a particular belief, very strongly and try to persuade other people to support it too ○ *This group carries the torch for the millions of people who demonstrated against the regime, and the thousands who died.*

toss

argue the toss (British) to waste your time by arguing about something which is not important or which cannot be changed ○ *Arguing the toss over whether Sydney or Melbourne is a better place to live is an Australian pastime.*

> This may refer to someone tossing a coin in the air in order to reach a decision.

★ **not give a toss about something** (British, informal) to not care at all about something ○ *'We don't give a toss what journalists think about us,' says Dave Chambers, the band's drummer.*

toss-up

★ **it's a toss-up** said to mean that two or more courses of action seem equally likely to succeed or fail, or that two or more things are equally likely to happen ○ *It's a toss-up whether oil prices will go up or down over the days ahead.*

≣ When you toss a coin, there is an equal chance that the coin will land heads or tails.

touch

be kicked into touch (mainly British) to be rejected or postponed ○ *Trish Johnson's challenge for the US Women's Open Championship was kicked into touch by a foot injury yesterday.*

≣ In rugby football, when the ball is kicked into touch it is kicked over one of the boundary lines along each side of the pitch.

★ **the common touch** the quality that some people in a position of power have of being able to understand how ordinary people think and feel and of being able to communicate with them ○ *Yudhoyono is seen as a politician with the common touch, who sings, writes poetry and plays guitar in a band.*

★ **it's touch and go** said to mean that you cannot be certain whether something will happen or not ○ *I thought I was going to win the race, but it was still touch and go.*

★ **someone is a soft touch** said to mean that it is easy to make someone do what you want, or to make them agree with you ○ *Pamela was always a soft touch when Michael needed some cash.*

≣ To touch a person for money means to approach them and persuade them to let you have some money as a loan or a gift.

touch paper

light the blue touch paper or **light the touch paper** (British) to do something which causes other people to react in an angry or aggressive way ○ *This kind of remark is guaranteed to light the blue touch paper with some Labour politicians.*

≣ The touch paper on a firework is a small piece of dark blue paper attached to one end. When it is lit, it burns slowly until it sets off the firework.

tough

tough as old boots (British) or **tough as nails** having a strong and independent character ○ *He was a very easy-going type of person in a large group, but across a negotiating table, he was tough as nails.*

towel

★ **throw in the towel** to stop trying to do something, because you know that you cannot succeed ○ *It seemed, initially, as if the police had thrown in the towel and were planning to abandon the investigation, but the following day the interviews resumed.*

≣ In boxing, a fighter's trainer sometimes throws a towel or sponge into the ring as a signal of defeat in order to stop the fight before there are any more injuries.

tower

★ **a tower of strength** someone who gives you a lot of help or support during a difficult period of your life ○ *In her terrible sadness she has found Charles to be a tower of strength.*

town

go to town on something to deal with something with a lot of enthusiasm or energy ○ *They really went to town on the decorations for the party.*

paint the town red to go out and enjoy yourself ○ *Let's go out and paint the town red!*

≣ This expression is said to have originated in the Wild West. It may have been used to describe groups of Native Americans setting fire to towns. Another possibility is that it referred to cowboys threatening to 'paint the town red' with the blood of anyone who tried to stop their drunken behaviour.

traces

kick over the traces to pay no attention to rules and conventions, and behave exactly as you want to ○ *Young people always want to kick over the traces, refusing to accept old values without question.*

When a horse pulling a cart or carriage kicks over the traces, it steps over the side straps attached to its harness, so it can no longer be controlled effectively by the driver.

track

★ **the fast track to something** the quickest way of achieving something ○ *Like many of his classmates, Chris Urwin believes a university degree will be the fast track to corporate success.* ○ *The company offers fast-track promotion schemes for promising young executives.*

A track here is a running track or racing track.

★ **have the inside track** (*mainly American, journalism*) to have an advantage, for example special knowledge about something ○ *Denver has the inside track among 10 sites being considered for the airline's new $1 billion maintenance facility.*

On a racing track, the inside track is the shortest, and so the competitors want to use it in order to take advantage of this fact.

★ **keep track of something or someone** to make sure that you have accurate and up-to-date information about something or someone all the time

○ *I could never keep track of all the visitors to the mansion.*

★ **lose track of someone or something** to no longer know where someone or something is or what is happening to them ○ *You may wonder how the administrators of this fund can lose track of £20 million meant to help the poorest citizens.*

★ **off the beaten track** if a place is off the beaten track, it is isolated and quiet, because it is far from large cities or their centres, and so few people go there or live there ○ *The village is sufficiently off the beaten track to deter all but a few tourists.*

A track here is a footpath or narrow road.

★ **on the right track** acting or progressing in a way that is likely to result in success ○ *Guests are returning to our hotel in increasing numbers – a sure sign that we are on the right track.*

★ **on the wrong track** acting or progressing in a way that is likely to result in failure ○ *Polls show that around 55 per cent of voters believe the country is headed on the wrong track.*

★ **a track record** the reputation that a person, a company, or a product has, which is based on all their successes and failures in the past ○ *This corporation has a high-quality management team with a good track record.*

An athlete's track record is a record of the performances he or she has achieved.

tracks

come from the wrong side of the tracks to come from a poor, unfashionable, and lower-class area of town ○ *Here are two sisters who come from the wrong side of the tracks in Los Angeles and have come to dominate the world of women's tennis.*

Railway tracks sometimes mark boundaries between different parts of a town, for example between richer and poorer areas.

★ **cover your tracks** to hide or destroy evidence of your identity or actions, because you want to keep them secret ○ *The killer may have returned to the scene of the crime to cover his tracks.*

Tracks here are footprints.

make tracks to leave the place where you are, usually in a hurry ○ *Webb looked at the bar clock. 'Ten past nine. We must make tracks or we'll be late for the meeting.'*

In this expression, 'tracks' are footprints.

★ **stop someone in their tracks** or **stop someone dead in their tracks** to make someone suddenly stop moving or doing something because they are very surprised, impressed, or frightened ○ *The sound of gunfire stopped them dead in their tracks.*

★ **stop something in its tracks** or **stop something dead in its tracks** to make something, such as a process or an activity, immediately stop continuing or developing ○ *If the Chancellor pulls the plug on the £22 billion programme, the resulting job losses could stop Britain's economic revival dead in its tracks.*

trail

★ **blaze a trail** to be the first person to do or discover something new and important, which will make it easier for other people to do something similar in the future ○ *The party is blazing a trail for the advancement of women in politics.* ○ *A trailblazer in the treatment of mental illness, Bateman has served as a psychiatrist, administrator and teacher.*

New trails or routes through forests were often marked by 'blazing', which involved making white marks called 'blazes' on tree trunks, usually by chipping off a piece of bark.

trap

★ **fall into the trap of doing something** to make a very common mistake, or one that is very easy to make ○ *School administrators often fall into the trap of thinking that discipline problems, not unsatisfying education, are the cause of low levels of achievement among pupils.*

tree

bark up the wrong tree to follow the wrong course of action because your beliefs or ideas about something are incorrect ○ *If you plan to become a writer because it will make you lots of money, you're barking up the wrong tree.*

This expression comes from raccoon hunting, which takes place at night. Dogs that are trained to show where raccoons are hiding by barking sometimes indicate the wrong tree.

★ **be at the top of the tree** (British) to have reached the highest level in a career or profession ○ *She has been at the top of the acting tree for 35 years.*

out of your tree (informal) crazy or behaving very strangely, sometimes as a result of drinking alcohol ○ *It was obvious they had been drinking. They were both out of their tree.*

trees

someone cannot see the wood for the trees (British) or

someone cannot see the forest for the trees (American) said to mean that someone is so involved in the details of something that they forget or do not realize the real purpose or importance of the thing as a whole ○ *The staff here are working so hard and are so tired that they can't see the wood for the trees.*

something or someone does not grow on trees (mainly British) said to mean that something or someone is very rare and difficult to obtain ○ *Mitchell will* *not be replaced in a hurry: managers with his expertise do not grow on trees.*

trial

★ **a trial balloon** (*mainly American*) an idea or plan which is suggested in order to find out about public opinion on a subject that causes many arguments ○ *The administration has not officially released details of the economic plan, although numerous trial balloons have been floated and hints have been dropped.*

Balloons were formerly used to find out about weather conditions.

trick

★ **do the trick** to achieve the result that you want ○ *If these self-help remedies don't do the trick, consult a qualified homoeopath.*

it's the oldest trick in the book said to mean that people should have expected something dishonest or unfair that someone has done because it is a very common or obvious thing to do ○ *Well, that's the oldest trick in the book – to blame someone else for your problems.*

★ **not miss a trick** to always know what is happening and take advantage of every situation ○ *My assistant, Eileen, has a good eye for detail and never misses a trick.*

The reference here is to a player winning every trick in a card game such as whist or bridge.

use every trick in the book to do everything you can think of in order to succeed in something ○ *Companies are using every trick in the book to stay one step ahead of their competitors.*

tricks

★ **be up to your old tricks** to be behaving in a dishonest or foolish way which is typical of you ○ *They're up to their old tricks of promising one thing and doing the opposite.*

trim

in fighting trim (*mainly American*) in very good condition ○ *The company needs to be in fighting trim for the next decade, when domestic competition may increase.*

A boxer who is in fighting trim is fit and ready to fight.

trolley

off your trolley (*British, informal*) crazy or very foolish ○ *She has decided to leave London to go and live on a remote island. Most people think she's off her trolley, but she's never been so sure of anything in her life.*

trooper

swear like a trooper to use a lot of swearwords ○ *Mo was rude and abusive and swore like a trooper.*

A trooper is a soldier.

trot

★ **on the trot** (*British, informal*) if something happens several times on the trot, it happens that number of times without a break ○ *It was the team's fifth win on the trot, a club record.*

trousers

wear the trousers → see **wear**

trowel

lay it on with a trowel (*British*) to exaggerate a statement, experience, or emotion, in order to impress people ○ *To make sure the significance of his remarks was not missed, the Prime Minister laid it on with a trowel.*

truck

★ **have no truck with something** to strongly disapprove of something and refuse to become involved with it ○ *Smith stated clearly that his party will have no truck with any extremist attitudes or views.*

'Truck' is an old term which referred to trading goods by bartering. 'To have no truck with someone' literally means to have no dealings with them.

true

ring true if a statement or a promise rings true, it seems to be true or sincere ○ *He said he was sorry for upsetting me but his apology just didn't ring true.*

trump

play your trump card to do something unexpected which gives you a definite advantage over other people ○ *If she wished, she could threaten to play her trump card, publishing an autobiography of embarrassing disclosures.*

In card games such as whist and bridge, one of the four suits is chosen as trumps for each hand. Cards of that suit then rank higher than cards of the other three suits.

★ **a trump card** something which gives you a definite advantage over other people ○ *Only two days into the strike, the distribution of goods was suffering: and that, ultimately is the railwaymen's trump card.*

trumpet

★ **blow your own trumpet** (British) to tell other people that you have done very good things and have very good qualities in order to make them admire you. The usual American expression is **blow** your **own horn**. ○ *The three candidates traded insults and blew their own trumpets yesterday as each one claimed to be heading for victory.*

In the past, the arrival of important people in a place was announced by the playing of trumpets.

trumps

★ **come up trumps** (British)
1 to achieve an unexpectedly good result ○ *Sylvester Stallone came up trumps at the US box office with his movie Cliffhanger.*
2 to unexpectedly help someone with a problems ○ *In moments of crisis for me, you always come up trumps!*

In card games such as whist and bridge, one of the four suits is chosen as trumps for each hand. Cards of that suit then rank higher than cards of the other three suits. The reference here is to a player drawing a trump from the pack.

truth

★ **be economical with the truth** to deceive people by deliberately not telling them the whole truth about something. People use this expression when they want to suggest that someone is being dishonest, but do not actually want to accuse them of lying. ○ *She asked repeated questions but only received answers which were at best economical with the truth, at worst deliberately designed to deceive.*

tub

tub-thumping (British, journalism) describes people's attitudes or behaviour when they are supporting an idea or course of action in a very vigorous and sometimes aggressive way. This expression is usually used to show disapproval of this kind of behaviour. ○ *Recovery does not depend on tub-thumping speeches from politicians, but on the Government creating jobs.*

People sometimes used to refer to pulpits as 'tubs', especially when talking humorously about nonconformist preachers. The image is of a preacher banging the pulpit with his fist to emphasize his message.

tubes

be going down the tubes or **go down the tubes** → see **down**

tune

★ **call the tune** to be in control of a situation and make all the important decisions ○ *My husband spends lots of money on his hobbies but moans when I want to buy anything. He thinks he has the right to call the tune as he earns more money than I do.*

This expression comes from the proverb 'he who pays the piper calls the tune'.

★ **change your tune** to express a different opinion about something or someone from the one you had expressed before ○ *He had maintained for many years that the Earl was dead. But these days he has changed his tune.*

dance to someone's tune to do whatever someone wants or tells you to do, usually without questioning them or hesitating. This expression is often used to criticize someone for allowing themselves to be controlled in this way. ○ *Supermarkets buy huge quantities of meat from farmers, but at the lowest possible price. So farmers have, unfortunately, been forced to dance to their tune.*

sing a different tune

1 to express ideas or opinions which are in complete contrast to the ones which you were expressing a short time ago ○ *She declared herself at peak fitness. Just 24 hours later, she was singing a different tune after losing badly in her match against Williams. 'I wasn't prepared,' she said. 'And I was suffering from jet lag.'*

2 if a group of people are singing a different tune, they are all expressing different opinions about something ○ *The problem of homelessness is great enough without two Government departments singing different tunes.*

sing the same tune → see **sing**

tunnel

★ **have tunnel vision** to focus all your energy and skill on the task which is most important to you and ignore things that other people might consider important ○ *They always say that you have to have tunnel vision to be a champion. You can't have any outside distractions at all.*

Tunnel vision is a medical condition in which someone can only see things that are immediately in front of them,

and cannot see things that are to the side.

turkey

talk turkey (*mainly American*) to discuss something in an honest, direct and serious way ○ *Suddenly government and industry are talking turkey. Last month the Prime Minister promised a partnership to improve the climate for business.*

This expression is said to have its origin in an American story about a white man who went hunting with a Native American. They caught several wild turkeys and some other birds. After the trip the white man divided the birds unfairly, keeping the turkeys for himself and giving the Native American the less tasty birds. The Native American protested, saying he wanted to 'talk turkey'.

a turkey shoot a battle or other conflict in which one side is so much stronger or better armed than the other that the weaker side has no chance at all. This expression is usually used to suggest that the situation is unfair. ○ *After weeks of bombing, it was a one-sided battle. The fighting stopped earlier than expected partly because of public disquiet at the 'turkey-shoot'.*

A turkey shoot is an occasion when people hunt turkeys, which are very easy to shoot.

turkeys

like turkeys voting for Christmas (*British*) said to mean that it is very unlikely that someone will choose to do a particular thing because it would very obviously be bad for them ○ *If we accept this proposal, it would be like turkeys voting for Christmas. It's just not going to happen.*

In Britain and some other countries, people traditionally eat turkey at Christmas.

turn

★ **at every turn** if something happens at every turn, it happens very frequently or continuously, and usually prevents you from doing what you want to do ○ *Although the government has had a coherent economic plan, parliament has set out to block it at every turn.*

turn-up

a turn-up for the books (British) something that is very surprising and unexpected, and usually very pleasing ○ *'This is a real turn-up for the books for me,' he chuckled, leaning on his bike at the finish. 'I've never won a race before.'*

> The reference here is to a horse that unexpectedly wins a race. The 'books' are the bookmakers' records of the bets taken on the race.

turtle

turn turtle if a boat turns turtle, it turns upside down when it is in the water ○ *The dinghy nearly turned turtle twice, but I managed to keep her upright.*

> Turtles are helpless when they are turned onto their backs.

twain

never the twain shall meet or **ne'er the twain shall meet** (literary) said to mean that there are so many differences between two groups of people or two groups of things that people believe that they can never exist together in the same place or situation ○ *The education system is notorious for separating the sciences and the humanities. This academic 'ne'er the twain shall meet' policy unfortunately does not always reflect the needs of the real world.*

> 'Twain' is an old-fashioned word meaning two. This is a quotation from 'The Ballad of East and West' (1889) by the English poet Rudyard Kipling: 'Oh, East is East, and West is West, and never the twain shall meet.'

twist

round the twist (British) crazy ○ *This man's clearly round the twist.*

two

be two of a kind to be two very similar people ○ *We're two of a kind, Ed. That's probably why our friendship's lasted this long.*

★ **put two and two together** to correctly guess the truth about something from the information that you have ○ *It's not going to be long before the police put two and two together and come looking for you.*

it takes two to tango → see **tango**

unbowed

bloodied but unbowed (literary)
not defeated or destroyed after a bad
experience ○ *He went out there and worked
for every single vote. It was a narrow victory
but an important one. He is bloodied but
unbowed.*

> Unbowed means standing upright
> without showing fear or pain.

unglued

come unglued (American)
1 to lose control of your emotions and to
behave in a strange or crazy way ○ *She had
apparently come unglued since losing her job.*
2 to fail. The British expression is **come
unstuck**. ○ *Their marriage finally came
unglued.*

unstuck

★ **come unstuck** (British) to fail. The
American expression is **come unglued**.
○ *Australia's Greg Norman came badly
unstuck in the third round of the Memorial
golf tournament yesterday.*

up

★ **on the up and up**
1 (British) becoming very successful and
doing well ○ *Their career path has flattened
out slightly rather than still being on the up
and up.*
2 (American) honest or legal ○ *If you're
honest and on the up and up, I'll be able to tell
it, feel it. If you're hiding something, I can tell
that too.*

swear up and down (American) to insist

that you are telling the truth. The usual
British expression is **swear blind**. ○ *He'd
sworn up and down he was going to get the
cash and bring it right back.*

★ **up and coming** likely to be successful
in the future ○ *He was one of our very up
and coming young ministers and I feel he had
a great future in front of him.*

★ **up and running** working or
functioning successfully after a good
start ○ *We've invested in the people, tools,
and technology to get your system up and
running quickly and keep it that way.*

uppers

on your uppers (British) having very
little money ○ *The company is on its uppers
and shareholders can forget about receiving
dividends for a couple of years.*

> The upper of a shoe is the top part of it,
> which is attached to the sole and heel.
> If you are on your uppers, you have
> worn through the sole and heel.

upstairs

kick someone upstairs (British)
to give someone a job or position which
appears to have a higher status but
actually has less power or influence
○ *The radicals kicked him upstairs to the
ceremonial job of president.*

use

it's no use crying over spilled milk
→ see **milk**
no use to man or beast → see **man**

vacuum

★ **in a vacuum** separately from the things that you would expect something to be connected with ○ *Such decisions do not occur in a political vacuum, but have serious political implications both at home and abroad.*

variety

variety is the spice of life said to mean that doing and seeing a lot of different things makes life more enjoyable and interesting ○ *It is important to vary the training program so that boredom is avoided. Exercise should be fun and variety is the spice of life.*

veil

draw a veil over something to deliberately not talk about something or give any details, because you want to keep it private or because it is embarrassing ○ *Most of us have something in our past career over which we choose to draw a veil.*

≡ A veil is a piece of cloth used by
≡ a woman to cover her face.

vessels

empty vessels make the most sound (old-fashioned) said to mean that people who talk a lot about their knowledge, talent or experience are often not as knowledgeable, talented or experienced as they claim to be ○ *The trouble is that empty vessels seem to be making the most sound and getting the most words in print.*

≡ A vessel is a container such as a jug,
≡ pot or jar.

view

a bird's-eye view a clear impression of what is happening ○ *Before I left England, I was a parliamentary lobby correspondent, getting a bird's eye view of the way politicians encourage people to believe in dreams.*

★ **take a dim view of something** to disapprove of something ○ *Back in 1989 he took a dim view of lotteries, and wrote to a proposer: 'I do not support your proposal for a lottery and would wish not to be involved at this stage.'*

a worm's eye view an impression of what is happening in a situation from the point of view of someone who has a low status, or is considered inferior in some way ○ *They were considered to be leaders who, for the most part, 'were complete fools, with a worm's eye view of the world and a poor understanding of their jobs'.*

villain

★ **the villain of the piece** (British) the person who is responsible for all the trouble or all the problems in a situation ○ *If he is indeed the villain of the piece, as the police claim he is, he should have been more carefully watched.*

≡ In this expression, the 'piece' is
≡ a play.

vine

wither on the vine or **die on the vine** (literary) to die or gradually come to an end ○ *I talked to senior citizens and ordinary people all over this state who are worried that the American dream is dying on the vine.*

violet

a shrinking violet a person who is very shy and timid ○ *None of the women he paints could be described as shrinking violets.*

In the past, violets were considered to be a symbol of modesty, because of their small size and the fact that the flowers remain hidden among the leaves until they open.

volumes

★ **speak volumes** to reveal or imply a lot about a situation ○ *What you wear speaks volumes, and it can lie, too.*

In this expression, a 'volume' is a book.

Ww

wagon

be on the wagon to have stopped drinking alcohol ○ *He was an alcoholic, but he's been on the wagon for more than 10 years.*

Originally the expression was 'on the water wagon' or 'water cart'. Water carts were horse-drawn carts used for transporting water or for sprinkling the streets. If someone was 'on the wagon', they were drinking water and not alcohol.

hitch your wagon to someone to try to become more successful by forming a relationship with someone who is already successful ○ *The increasing power of the Pacific rim provides a reason why Russia should not hitch its wagon too closely to America.*

This is a quotation from the essay 'Civilization' (1870) by the American writer Ralph Waldo Emerson: 'Now that is the wisdom of a man, in every instance of his labor, to hitch his wagon to a star, and see his chore done by the gods themselves.'

wagons

circle the wagons to unite with the other people in a group in order to protect yourselves and fight whoever is attacking you ○ *Some African-Americans who initially opposed Thomas because of his politics are circling the wagons to support him because of his race.*

According to some Wild West stories, when wagon trains were attacked by Native Americans, the settlers drove the wagons into a circle in order to defend themselves better.

wake

The wake of a ship is the trail of white foaming water behind it.

★ **in something's wake** if an event leaves an unpleasant situation in its wake, that situation happens after that event or is caused by it ○ *A deadly cloud of gas swept along the valleys north of Lake Nyos in western Cameroon, leaving a trail of death and devastation in its wake.*

★ **in the wake of something** happening after an earlier event, especially an unpleasant one, often as a result of it ○ *The trouble at Shotts prison follows in the wake of unrest at several prisons in England.*

wake-up

★ **a wake-up call** an event that shocks people into taking action about a difficult or dangerous situation ○ *The jury said the damages were intended to send a wake-up call to the firm and other big companies that sexual harassment would not be tolerated.*

If you have a wake-up call, you arrange for someone to telephone you at a certain time in the morning so that you are sure to wake up at that time.

walk

take a walk to go away or to stop interfering ○ *The Coastguard broke in almost immediately, asking if we required any assistance. 'Tell him to take a walk,' said Steve.*

a walk in the park something that is very easy ○ *I thought marriage was tough, but that's a walk in the park compared to golf.*

walk the walk (*informal*) to act in a way that matches the things that you say ○ *But the time has come for Mr Coleman to* prove that he can walk the walk to the same level as he can talk the talk.

wall

drive someone up the wall to annoy someone a lot ○ *He's so uncooperative - he's beginning to drive me up the wall.*

★ **go to the wall** *(British)* if a person or company goes to the wall, they lose all their money and their business fails ○ *A total of 1,776 companies went to the wall in the three months to March – a drop of 14 per cent on the first three months of 1992.*

hit the wall to reach a point where you cannot go any further or achieve any more ○ *To ensure their businesses do not hit the wall, operators must ensure their financial management is strong and streamlined.*

nail someone to the wall to make someone suffer, because you are very angry with them ○ *If he could not pay off his debt, they would nail him to the wall.*

★ **off the wall** unusual, unconventional, or eccentric ○ *The new channel is so off the wall and unlike anything we see at the moment that you really have to watch it to appreciate how it will be.* ○ *At other times the band plays a kind of off-the-wall lounge music, a kind of soundtrack to a hip science fiction movie.*

This may be a reference to a shot in a game such as squash or handball, where the ball bounces off the wall at an unexpected angle.

someone will go to the wall for someone or something *(British)* said to mean that someone is prepared to suffer on behalf of a person or a principle that they support strongly ○ *Above all, he prizes loyalty. He'll go to the wall for someone or something he believes in.*

One explanation for this expression is that it refers to someone who is trapped with their back to a wall and no way of escape. Another explanation is that it refers to medieval chapels in

which healthy people used to stand, but which had seats around the walls for sick people. A third explanation is that it refers to someone standing in front of a wall before being executed by a firing squad.

★ **the writing is on the wall** *(mainly British)* or

the handwriting is on the wall *(mainly American)* said to mean that you have noticed things which strongly suggest that a situation is going to become difficult or unpleasant ○ *The writing is clearly on the wall. If we do nothing about it, we shall only have ourselves to blame.*

This expression comes from a Bible story (Daniel 5) in which a mysterious hand appears and writes a message on the wall, announcing that Belshazzar's kingdom will soon come to an end.

walls

climb the walls to feel very frustrated, nervous, or anxious ○ *I'm climbing the walls now because I have not got a job. I have been searching hard for six months without success.*

walls have ears said to warn someone that they should be careful about what they are saying because people might be listening ○ *Take care. This place is like a village. Assume all walls have ears.*

war

a war of nerves → see **nerves**

★ **a war of words** *(journalism)* a situation in which two people or groups of people argue or criticize each other because they strongly disagree about a particular issue ○ *A war of words has blown up over who is to blame for a confrontation between police and fans outside the venue.*

warpath

on the warpath very angry and getting ready for a fight or quarrel ○ *St Vincent and Grenadines' biggest* *businessmen are on the warpath after claims that foreign nationals are trying to con them out of thousands of dollars.*

> Native Americans were said to be 'on the warpath' when they were on an expedition to attack their enemies. The warpath was the path or route that they took.

wars

in the wars having been hurt or injured ○ *Charlotte's four-year-old brother, Ben, has also been in the wars. He is still in plaster after breaking a leg.*

warts

★ **warts and all** used for describing someone or something as they are, including all their faults ○ *Judith would not be the first wife to have got the measure of her husband and decided that he is still the man for her, warts and all.*

> The 17th century English leader Oliver Cromwell is said to have told an artist who was painting his portrait that he did not wish to be flattered: 'Remark all these roughnesses, pimples, warts, and everything as you see me, otherwise I will never pay a farthing for it.'

wash

everything will come out in the wash said to reassure someone that everything will be all right ○ *That will be the end of that. Everything will come out in the wash – I promise you.*

something will come out in the wash said to mean that people will eventually find out the truth about something ○ *It will make great listening at an industrial tribunal. Everything will come out in the wash, and Flashman will deserve it all.*

waste

a waste of space (British) someone who is completely useless. ○ *Even Sarah, a tall 13-year-old with a white face and black-*

ringed eyes, treated him as if he were a waste of space.

watch

★ **on someone's watch** during a period when someone is in a position of power, and is therefore considered to be responsible for what happens ○ *Mistakes were made on my watch, and accordingly I believe my decision to retire, while painful, is appropriate.*

> When someone such as a soldier is on watch, they have been ordered to remain alert, usually while others sleep, so that they can warn of danger or an attack.

water

★ **be dead in the water** (*journalism*) to have failed and to have little hope of success in the future ○ *People are not spending money: they're not buying houses; they're not going into stores. This economy is dead in the water.*

> The image here is of a sailing boat which cannot move because there is no wind.

blow something out of the water to destroy something completely, suddenly, and violently. ○ *The government is in a state of paralysis. Its main economic and foreign policies have been blown out of the water.*

> The image here is of a ship which is completely destroyed by a missile or torpedo.

in deep water in a difficult or awkward situation ○ *You certainly seem to be in deep water and doing your utmost to reverse the negative trends of the past couple of months or so.*

★ **in hot water** in a situation in which you have done something wrong and people are angry with you ○ *Debbie is in hot water when Rick discovers her attempt to sabotage his relationship with Sarah.*

like water off a duck's back if criticism is like water off a duck's back, it is not having any effect at all on the person being criticized ○ *Every time you discipline him he will smile sweetly so that you may think your rebukes are streaming away like water off a duck's back.*

The feathers on a duck's back are covered with an oily substance which stops them absorbing water so that it flows straight off them.

★ **pour cold water on something** or **throw cold water on something** to point out all the problems of an idea or plan, rather than sharing other people's enthusiasm for it ○ *They poured cold water on the French proposal for a peace conference involving both the EU and the UN.*

someone can talk under water *(mainly Australian)* said to mean that someone always talk a lot in any situation, and it is sometimes difficult to stop them talking ○ *My friends tell me that I can talk under water.*

★ **something does not hold water** said to mean that you do not believe that a theory or an argument can possibly be true or right ○ *They make it clear that the British Government's argument does not hold water.*

★ **test the water** or **test the waters** to try to find out what the reaction to an idea or plan might be before taking action to put it into effect ○ *I was a bit sceptical. I decided to test the water before committing the complete management team.*

★ **tread water** to be in an unsatisfactory situation where you are not progressing, but are just continuing doing the same things ○ *I could either tread water until I was promoted, which looked to be a few years away, or I could change what I was doing.*

When swimmers tread water, they move their arms and legs in order to keep their head above the water without actually making progress in any direction.

water over the dam *(American)* or **water under the bridge** used for describing an event or situation that happened in the past and so is no longer worth thinking about or worrying about ○ *Mr Bruce said that he was relieved it was over and that he regarded his time in jail as water under the bridge.*

waterfront

cover the waterfront *(mainly American)* to cover a very wide range of things, or cover every aspect of something ○ *We have five employees looking after this whole project. They cover the entire waterfront: oil, real estate, high-tech, and everything else.*

Waterloo

meet your Waterloo to suffer a very severe defeat or failure, especially one which causes you to finally give up what you are trying to do ○ *At the foot of cliff I met my Waterloo. The face of the cliff rose sheer above us, and it was clear even to me that we would not be able to climb it.*

In 1815, the French leader Napoleon suffered his final defeat at the Battle of Waterloo in Belgium.

waters

fish in troubled waters to be involved in a very difficult or delicate situation, which could cause you problems ○ *They had had boundary disputes with their previous neighbours, and did not want to appear to be fishing in troubled waters.*

muddy the waters to deliberately try to make a situation or an issue more confusing and complicated than it really is ○ *This ruling seems only to have muddied the waters. It seems a bit confusing and we are seeking clarification.*

still waters run deep said to mean that someone who seems to be unemotional or who is hard to get to know is in fact interesting and complex ○ *He's extremely shy and withdrawn, though it may be that still waters run very deep.*

test the waters → see **water**

wave

catch the wave to seize an opportunity that is presented to you, especially an opportunity to do something new ○ *With parliamentary elections still officially scheduled for October, politicians are hoping to catch the wave of rising discontent.*

 Surfers need to catch a wave just as it breaks in order to ride it successfully.

wavelength

★ **on the same wavelength** if two people are on the same wavelength, they understand each other well because they share the same attitudes, interests, and opinions ○ *We could complete each other's sentences because we were on the same wavelength.*

 A radio programme cannot be heard unless the radio is tuned to the correct wavelength.

waves

★ **make waves** to disturb a situation by changing things or by challenging the way things are done, often in a way that improves the situation ○ *Maathai has a history of making waves. In 1971 she became the first woman in East and Central Africa to earn a PhD.*

way

★ **the easy way out** doing what is easiest for yourself in a difficult situation, rather than dealing with the problem properly ○ *It is the easy way out to blame others for our failure, and this is bad practice.*

go back a long way (mainly British) or
go way back (mainly American) to have been friends or associates for a very long time ○ *We go back a long way, and she's always kept in touch, always been there for me.*

★ **look the other way** to deliberately ignore something unpleasant, immoral, or illegal that is happening when you should be trying to deal with it or stop it from happening ○ *Stolen goods are sold unashamedly in broad daylight but you tend to look the other way and mind your own business.*

★ **pave the way for something** to make it easier for another thing to happen ○ *A peace agreement last year paved the way for this week's elections.*

rub someone up the wrong way (British) or
rub someone the wrong way (American) to annoy someone a great deal ○ *Ella had an uncommon knack of rubbing everyone up the wrong way.*

 Cats do not like having their fur rubbed 'the wrong way', that is in the opposite direction to the way it naturally grows.

someone can't fight their way out of a paper bag → see **paper**

ways

cut both ways to have two different effects, usually one good and one bad ○ *For Britain, the impact cuts both ways. The immediate effect of cheaper oil is to reduce North Sea oil revenue. But it also produces lower domestic inflation and stronger export markets.*

★ **mend your ways** to stop behaving badly or illegally and improve your behaviour ○ *He seemed to accept his sentence meekly, promising to work hard in prison and to mend his ways.*

set in your ways having very fixed habits and ideas which you are unlikely or unwilling to change ○ *Try not to become set in your ways. It's very easy to develop personal routines and not to accept that other people have other ways of doing things.*

wayside

★ **fall by the wayside**
 1 to fail in something you were doing and

give up trying to achieve success in it ○ *The average player's lifespan at the top is five years. You either play well, deal with the pressure, or you fall by the wayside.*

2 if an activity has fallen by the wayside, people have stopped doing it and forgotten about it ○ *Each year our birthday parties grow more and more polite. We still have a birthday cake and give presents, but dancing seems to have fallen by the wayside.*

⸽ This expression comes from the story of the sower (= a person who plants seeds) told by Jesus in the Bible (Mark 4:4). The seed that falls by the wayside represents the people who do not pay attention to Jesus's teachings.

wear

wear the trousers *(British)* or **wear the pants** to be the person in a couple who makes all the important decisions ○ *She may give the impression that she wears the trousers but it's Tim who makes the final decisions.*

weather

keep a weather eye on something or someone *(British)* to watch something or someone carefully so that you are ready to take action when difficulties arise or anything goes wrong ○ *It is necessary always to keep a weather eye on your symptoms and stay alert to the changes which occur.*

⸽ This expression was originally used by sailors, who had to keep a constant watch on the weather and wind direction.

make heavy weather of something *(British)* to make an activity or task much more difficult or take more time than it needs to ○ *To an outsider, though, the surprising thing is not that Spain's conservatives are inching ahead but that they are making such heavy weather of it.*

⸽ Ships were said to make heavy weather when they handled badly and were difficult to control in rough seas.

★ **under the weather** not feeling very well ○ *If you're feeling a bit under the weather but can't work out what's wrong, try our DIY guide to self-diagnosis.*

web

a tangled web something that is very confused and difficult to understand ○ *It is sometimes difficult to cut through the tangled web of government information in order to know the benefits you can claim.*

wedge

★ **drive a wedge between people** to cause bad feelings between two people who are close in order to weaken their relationship ○ *I did try to reassure her, but that only seemed to irritate her more. That made me upset, and I started to feel Toby was driving a wedge between us.*

the thin end of the wedge *(British)* the beginning of something which seems harmless or unimportant at present but is likely to become important, serious, or harmful in the future ○ *I think it's the thin end of the wedge when you have armed police permanently on patrol round a city.*

weight

★ **carry weight** to be respected and able to influence people ○ *El Tiempo is Colombia's leading newspaper. Its opinions carry considerable weight in the country.*

carry the weight of the world on your shoulders to have very many troubles or responsibilities ○ *You look as if you're carrying the weight of the world on those lovely shoulders.*

⸽ This expression may be a reference to Atlas, a giant in Greek mythology, who was punished by Zeus by being made to carry the heavens on his shoulders, and who is often portrayed with the world on his back.

a dead weight something that makes change or progress extremely difficult ○ *It's time for him to see that Labour must be* *free of the dead weight of union power.*

★ **pull your weight** to work as hard as everyone else who is involved in the same task or activity ○ *Your performance will be judged by the performance of your team, and you cannot afford to carry members who are not pulling their weight.*

punch above your weight *(British, journalism)* to have more influence or power than you would be expected to have ○ *The small Florida city of Tallahassee has always considered itself to punch above its weight when it comes to sport.*

punch your weight *(British, journalism)* to have as much influence or power as you would be expected to have ○ *There are some North-Easterners who feel that the North will never be able to punch its weight against the affluent South-East.*

★ **throw your weight about** *(British)* or **throw your weight around** to behave aggressively and use your authority over other people more forcefully than you need to ○ *Jonathon Rose, defending, told the jury: 'My client is the sort of person who likes to throw his weight around after he's been watching rugby with the lads.'*

★ **throw your weight behind someone or something** to do everything you can to support a person, plan, or campaign ○ *The U.S. government is promising now to throw its weight behind the peace negotiations.*

worth your weight in gold very useful, helpful, or valuable ○ *Successful television is about having ideas. People with ideas are worth their weight in gold.*

west

go west *(old-fashioned)*
1 to die ○ *When he went west, he wanted to be remembered.*
2 to stop existing or working ○ *His hopes of a professional singing career went west long ago.*

> The sun 'goes west' when it sinks below the horizon in the west at the end of the day. The comparison between going west and dying has been used in many different languages and cultures for many centuries. For example, people sometimes associate this expression with Native Americans, who used to say that a dying person went west to meet the sinking sun.

whale

have a whale of a time to enjoy yourself a lot ○ *I had a whale of a time in Birmingham.*

wheat

separate the wheat from the chaff to decide which things or people in a group are good or necessary, and which are not ○ *The reality is often blurred by the propaganda. It is becoming more and more difficult to separate the wheat from the chaff.*

> The 'chaff' is the outer part of wheat that has been separated from the grain. In the Bible (Matthew 3:12; Luke 3:17), John the Baptist uses the image of someone separating the wheat from the chaff to describe how Jesus will separate those who go to heaven from those who go to hell.

wheel

a big wheel someone who has an important and powerful position in an organization or society ○ *They flew Robin to New York, where George's uncle was a big wheel at Memorial Hospital.*

a fifth wheel or
a third wheel *(American)* someone who is unwanted and unimportant in a situation ○ *Women really do suffer more as widows. The fifth woman at a couples dinner party is a fifth wheel; the fifth man is a social coup.*

> A fifth wheel on a car or a third wheel on a bicycle would be unnecessary.

reinvent the wheel to work on an idea or project that you consider new or different, when it is really no better than something that already exists ○ *Learn from Scandinavia. We have created foundations for other countries to follow. Each country's organization does not need to reinvent the wheel.*

the wheel has come full circle → see **circle**

wheels

oil the wheels (British) or

grease the wheels to help things to run smoothly and successfully ○ *Credit cards greased the wheels of the consumer boom by allowing us to buy what we want, when we want.*

set the wheels in motion to do what is necessary to start carrying out an important plan or project ○ *I have set the wheels in motion to sell Endsleigh Court: the sooner I get out of this block, the better.*

spin your wheels (mainly American) to fail to do or achieve anything satisfactory ○ *He is not getting anywhere. He's just spinning his wheels.*

the wheels are turning said to mean that a process or situation is continuing to develop and progress ○ *The wheels are turning on plans to convert the building into a bookstore.*

wheels within wheels used for describing a situation that is very complicated because many different things, which influence one another, are involved in it ○ *Our culture is more complex than he knows. Wheels within wheels. Hierarchies.*

> This expression comes from the Bible: 'The wheels looked the same. They looked like a wheel within a wheel.' (Ezekiel 1:16)

whip

crack the whip to make people work very hard and treat them strictly and perhaps harshly ○ *They run the chapel, I don't. They crack the whip and I have to jump to it.*

a fair crack of the whip (British) a chance to prove how good you are at something ○ *None of them is expecting any favours, just a fair crack of the whip.*

have the whip hand or

hold the whip hand to have more power than the other people involved in a situation, and so have an advantage or control over them ○ *The biggest party in that government should have the whip hand in decision-making.*

whirl

give something a whirl to try something in order to see whether you like it or think you can be successful doing it ○ *Why not give acupuncture a whirl?*

whirlwind

reap the whirlwind → see **reap**

whisker

be within a whisker of something to be almost a particular amount ○ *Unemployment, at 6.4 per cent of the labour force, is now within a whisker of the rate at which inflation has often started to climb.*

by a whisker if you succeed in doing something by a whisker, you almost fail. If you fail to do something by a whisker, you almost succeed. ○ *At the end we lost by a whisker and I feel terribly disappointed.*

★ **come within a whisker of doing something** to nearly succeed in doing something. ○ *He came within a whisker of scoring a spectacular goal.*

whisper

whisper sweet nothings to speak to someone in a romantic or affectionate way ○ *Some women are turned on by romantic men who'll hold their hand in the street and whisper sweet nothings in their ears.*

whistle

★ **blow the whistle on someone or something** to tell the authorities about something secret or illegal, or someone who is doing something illegal, dishonest, or immoral because you feel strongly that what they are doing is wrong and they should be stopped ○ *Members of Queensland coastal communities are being asked to blow the whistle on activities that damage the marine environment.* ○ *The department needs to protect whistle-blowers, health professionals who want and care to make a change in the system.*

> In games such as football, the referee blows a whistle to stop play when a player has committed a foul.

someone can whistle for something said rudely to mean that you will not give something to someone ○ *She refused to open her books to the auditors, closed the show and told the city it could whistle for its money.*

> There was an old superstition among sailors that they could make the wind blow by whistling.

white

white as a sheet or
white as a ghost very pale and frightened ○ *There was another lady lorry driver who pulled in in front of me, who it affected badly. She was as white as a sheet.*

white as snow very white in colour ○ *When it's warm enough to go bare-legged but your skin's as white as snow, a fake tan's the answer.*

whiter than white used for describing someone whose actions are always honest and moral. You usually use this expression when you are referring to doubts about the person's character or behaviour, or when you are being ironic and trying to suggest that the person is less honest or moral than they appear to be. ○ *He is prepared to forgive Atherton's deceit this time, but it has left him in no doubt that his behaviour must be whiter than white in future.*

whys

the whys and wherefores the reasons for something ○ *Even successful bosses need to be queried about the whys and wherefores of their actions.*

> 'Wherefore' is an old-fashioned word meaning 'for what' or 'why'.

wick

get on someone's wick (British, informal) to irritate someone a great deal ○ *Let's face it, after three or four songs that voice really does get on your wick.*

wicket

be on a sticky wicket or
bat on a sticky wicket (British) to be in a difficult situation in which you find it hard to deal with your problems ○ *Mr Hughes is batting on a very sticky wicket indeed. Should he succeed in proving his outrageous claims, he would lay himself open to a charge of treason.*

> On a cricket pitch, the wicket is the area of grass between the two sets of stumps. When a lot of rain has fallen on the wicket it becomes soft or 'sticky', and in these conditions, it is difficult for the batsmen to predict which way the ball will bounce.

wilderness

★ **in the wilderness** (British, journalism) used for describing a part of someone's career when they are inactive and ignored, and do not have an influential role ○ *He is delighted to get another chance to represent his country after a period in the wilderness.*

a voice crying in the wilderness or
a lone voice in the wilderness someone who is pointing out the dangers in a situation or the truth about it, but nobody is paying any attention ○ *For years, he was a lone voice in the wilderness, and a lot of it came across as self-serving. But I'll tell you, the man was right.*

This is from the Bible (Matthew 3:3), and refers to John the Baptist who preached the coming of the Messiah but was often ignored.

wildfire

★ **spread like wildfire** to very quickly reach or affect a lot of people ○ *When final confirmation of his release came, the news spread like wildfire.*

This expression may refer to the way that fires which start in the countryside spread very quickly and are difficult to control.

willies

give you the willies to make you feel very nervous or frightened ○ *Living on the mountainside is enough to give anyone the willies – especially when the wolves howl like the wind at night.*

wind

blow in the wind to be thought about and discussed, but not decided upon or resolved ○ *The agreement blowing in the wind at Montreal signalled a change in business conditions, and du Pont decided to jump in.*

★ **get wind of something** to get to know about a plan or information, often when other people did not want you to ○ *I want nothing said about this until I give the word. I don't want the public, and especially not the press, to get wind of it at this stage.*

This expression refers to animals being able to smell hunters or other animals when they are some way off, because the smell is carried to them on the wind.

in the wind likely to happen ○ *Change is in the wind and this England team will alter as the year unfolds.*

it's an ill wind or

it's an ill wind that blows nobody any good said to point out that unpleasant events and difficult situations often have unexpected good effects ○ *It's an ill wind, of course, and what is bad for the oil companies is good for the consumer and inflation.*

like the wind very quickly ○ *Out on the water, the boat goes like the wind.*

put the wind up someone (mainly British) to make someone scared or worried ○ *The front door was jammed and they couldn't open it. The delay put the wind up me because, by then, I knew something was very wrong.*

sail close to the wind (mainly British) to take a risk by doing or saying something which may get you into trouble ○ *Max warned her she was sailing dangerously close to the wind and risked prosecution.*

If someone sails a boat too close to the wind, they try to sail in the direction from which the wind is blowing, and stop or capsize as a result.

a second wind the strength or motivation to go on and succeed in what you are doing when you are tired or unsuccessful ○ *It was great tennis and it was fun. I got a second wind midway through the fourth set.*

If runners who are out of breath get their 'second wind', their breathing becomes easier and they are able to continue.

see which way the wind is blowing or
see how the wind is blowing to understand or realize how a situation is developing and use this in deciding what to do ○ *He wasn't one to make pronouncements before he had seen which way the wind was blowing.*

spit in the wind to waste your time by trying to do something which has little or no chance of success ○ *But the idea that you can talk about a single currency today is to spit in the wind of economic reality.*

take the wind out of someone's sail (American) or

take the wind out of someone's sails
to make someone feel much less confident in what they are doing or saying ○ *We hit a bad patch after losing in the semi-final. The effort and disappointment took the wind out of our sails for a while.*

twisting in the wind or
swinging in the wind *(mainly American)*
left in a very difficult and weak position, often by people who hope to gain advantage from this for themselves ○ *The Prime Minister left the minister swinging in the wind, neither giving him his support, nor being prepared to end the agony by sacking him.*

whistle in the wind to say something empty or pointless. ○ *Prior to going out, he had confided to some Spanish journalists that he was going to win the tournament, but that turned out to be whistling in the wind.*

windmills

tilt at windmills to waste your time on problems or issues which in other people's opinion are not really problems at all ○ *I have spent my life tilting at windmills. Will I never learn?*

≡ This expression refers to the novel 'Don Quixote' (1605) by the Spanish writer Cervantes, in which Don Quixote sees some windmills, thinks that they are giants, and tries to attack them.

window

★ **go out the window** or
fly out the window if a plan or a particular way of thinking or behaving goes out the window, it disappears completely ○ *Three years later she met Mick, and her good intentions flew out the window.*

wing

do something on a wing and a prayer
to do something in the hope that you will succeed, even though you do not have the proper resources for it, or are not properly equipped or prepared ○ *Whatever the cause, large parts of the government seem to be running on a wing and a prayer.*

≡ This is the title of a song by H. Adamson, written in 1943, which referred to the emergency landing of an aircraft: 'Tho' there's one motor gone, we can still carry on, Comin' In On A Wing And A Pray'r.'

★ **take someone under your wing**
to protect someone and make sure that they are all right ○ *I let him tag along because he had not been too well recently. I took him under my wing and looked after him.*

≡ The image here is of a hen gathering her chicks under her wing.

under the wing of someone in a situation in which someone controls you or takes responsibility for you ○ *If their problems are picked up at school and they come under the wing of an educational psychologist, they may be found a place in a special school.*

≡ The image here is of a hen gathering her chicks under her wing.

wings

★ **clip someone's wings** to limit someone's freedom to do what they want ○ *The opposition has been trying to clip his wings by making his actions and his appointments subject to parliamentary approval.*

≡ People sometimes clip the wings of captive birds to prevent them from flying away.

★ **spread your wings** to do something new that is more ambitious than anything you have done before ○ *I've always had a very strong musical direction and I was able to really flourish and spread my wings.*

try your wings to try to do something new to see if you can succeed ○ *He was very keen to try his wings and be a deputy on his own.*

★ **wait in the wings** to wait for an

opportunity to take action, especially to take over another person's job or position ○ *He was one of a number of young, up and coming American players who were waiting in the wings for the next Major Championship.*

In a theatre, the wings are the hidden areas to the left and right of a stage, where the actors wait before going on to the stage.

wink

not sleep a wink or

not get a wink of sleep to not be able to go to sleep ○ *This was my first Grand Prix win of the season and I was so excited I couldn't sleep a wink that night.*

tip someone the wink (British, old-fashioned) to quietly or secretly give someone information that could be important or helpful to them ○ *The commission may tip him the wink that certain compromises might prove acceptable to EU governments.*

winks

forty winks (old-fashioned) a short sleep or rest ○ *There's nothing like forty winks to ease away the tension and stresses of a hard day.*

wire

★ **down to the wire** (mainly American) until the last possible moment ○ *As Congress worked down to the wire to reach a compromise, the president lectured a group of White House interns on the budget crisis.*

get in under the wire (mainly American) to get in somewhere or do something at the last possible moment ○ *On first reading it looks like they'll get in under the wire because they have a US partner on the team.*

The 'wire' here is an imaginary one which the horses pass under at the end of a race. A horse that gets in 'under the wire' just manages to beat another horse and finish in one of the winning places.

a live wire someone who is very lively and energetic ○ *She is a wonderful girl, a real live wire and full of fun.*

A live wire is an electric wire or cable that has an electric current running through it.

wires

get your wires crossed to be mistaken about what someone else means or thinks ○ *Despite her tone of voice, she still looked vaguely confused. He began to wonder if they'd got their wires crossed.*

witless

scare someone witless to make someone very frightened or worried ○ *The door used to blow open and scare me witless.*

wits

★ **at your wits' end** very worried and desperate about something and not knowing what to do about it ○ *People are at their wits' end about crime and they want to do something. They want action.*

collect your wits or

gather your wits (literary) to make an effort to control yourself and become calm again, after you have had a frightening or shocking experience ○ *For a bone-jarred moment all he knew was the shocked terror of being left in a hail of gunfire; then he collected his wits, scrambled up and fled.*

have to have your wits about you or

have to keep your wits about you or

need your wits about you to need to be alert and ready to take action in a difficult or new situation ○ *You've got to have your wits about you when you're driving a car.*

pit your wits against someone (British) to use your intelligence to try to defeat someone ○ *He has to pit his wits against an adversary who is cool, clever, cunning and desperate not to be caught.*

scare someone out of their wits or **scare the wits out of someone** to make someone very frightened or worried ○ *The tree crashed through the conservatory and set off all the alarms, which joined with the sound of the gale to scare me out of my wits.*

wives

★ **an old wives' tale** a commonly held belief that is based on traditional ideas, often ones which have been proved to be incorrect or inaccurate ○ *My mother used to tell me to feed a cold and starve a fever. Is it just an old wives' tale?*

wobbler

throw a wobbler → see **throw**

wobbly

throw a wobbly → see **throw**

wolf

★ **cry wolf** to continually ask for help when it is not needed, or warn about danger when it does not really exist, so that people stop believing you and will not help you when it is really necessary ○ *Knowing when to order an evacuation is crucial. If it is issued too early, the storm could veer off in another direction, then officials could be accused of crying wolf and future orders might not be taken seriously.*

In one of Aesop's fables, a little boy who looks after sheep amuses himself by calling for help and making the villagers rush to rescue him when in fact there is no danger. One day a wolf comes and attacks the sheep, but the villagers do not believe him when he calls for help, and the sheep are all killed.

keep the wolf from the door to provide you with enough money to live on ○ *Your pension will keep the wolf from the door, but for a comfortable old age you need to make maximum use of the financial choices now open to you.*

For many centuries in the past, wolves were symbols of hunger.

a lone wolf someone who is independent and likes doing things on their own, rather than doing them with other people ○ *Among his peers, he is something of a lone wolf.*

a wolf in sheep's clothing someone who appears harmless or ordinary, but is really very dangerous or powerful ○ *Major's grey image may disguise a wolf in sheep's clothing.*

In one of Aesop's fables, a wolf wraps itself in a fleece and manages to get into a sheepfold without being noticed. It then attacks the sheep and eats them. This image is also used in the Bible (Matthew 7:15), where people are advised to beware of false teachers of God's word; they may appear harmless, but in fact they are dangerous and destructive.

wolves

throw someone to the wolves to allow someone to be criticized severely or treated roughly, and not try to protect them ○ *What I fear most is the thought of being released into the general prison population. I don't know what will happen if they throw me to the wolves.*

wonder

a one-day wonder or **a nine-day wonder** something or someone that is interesting, exciting, or successful for only a very short time, and does not have any lasting value ○ *If the goal was simply to make people aware of environmental problems it was a great success. The fear of environmentalists, though, is that this may prove to be a one-day wonder.*

'A nine-day wonder' may be related to the Catholic 'Novena' festivals, which last for nine days.

wood

dead wood someone or something that is no longer useful or effective in a

particular organization or situation
○ *Now is the time for the dead wood at the top of the party to be cut away. Since the elections, the leadership has received a great deal of criticism.*

★ **touch wood** (*mainly British*) or **knock on wood** (*mainly American*) or **knock wood** (*mainly American*)
said to mean that you hope a situation will continue to be good and that you will not have any bad luck ○ *She's never even been to the doctor's, touch wood. She's a healthy happy child and anyone can see that.*

This expression may come from the ancient belief that good spirits lived in trees and people used to tap on them to ask the spirits for help or protection. Alternatively, it may be related to the Christian practice of touching a rosary or crucifix. People sometimes actually touch or knock on a wooden surface as they say this.

someone cannot see the wood for the trees → see **trees**

woods

★ **not out of the woods** still having difficulties with something or still in a bad condition ○ *One economist warns the nation's economy is not out of the woods yet, that there has to be concern about financial shocks coming from abroad.*

This may come from the proverb 'Don't halloo till you are out of the wood', which is a warning not to celebrate something before you have actually achieved your aim.

woodwork

come out of the woodwork to suddenly start publicly doing something or saying something, when previously you did nothing or kept quiet ○ *People are starting to come out of the woodwork to talk about fraudulent practices in the industry.*

wool

★ **dyed-in-the-wool** used to describe a supporter of a particular philosophy or a member of a particular group to suggest that they have very strong beliefs or feelings about that philosophy or group, and are unlikely ever to change ○ *Mr Purves has made Hong Kong his home for the past 38 years but he remains a dyed-in-the-wool Scotsman.*

In medieval times, wool was often dyed before it was spun and woven. This meant that colour was more evenly distributed in the wool, and lasted longer.

pull the wool over someone's eyes to try to deceive someone in order to get an advantage over them ○ *'I just told them I was ten years younger than I really was,' says Liliana, speaking yesterday about how she pulled the wool over the medical profession's eyes.*

In the past, wigs for men were sometimes called 'wool' because they looked like a sheep's fleece. It was easy to pull wigs over people's eyes, either as a joke or in order to rob them.

word

★ **a dirty word** something that someone disapproves of and does not want to have anything to do with ○ *At the root of their problems was the misplaced belief that good products sell themselves. Marketing became a dirty word at the company.*

★ **from the word go** from the very beginning of an activity ○ *Right from the word go, many of the players looked out of breath and out of their depth.*

get a word in edgeways (*British*) or **get a word in edgewise** (*mainly American*) to manage to say something even though someone else is talking so much ○ *For heaven's sake, Sue, will you let me get a word in edgeways!*

not breathe a word to not tell anyone

about something ○ *Don't breathe a word of this to anyone.*

someone's word is law said to mean that everyone in an organization or group has to obey someone, even if this is unreasonable. ○ *His father was the kind of parent who saw no reason to discuss anything with his son; his word was law.*

a word in someone's ear (British) a situation in which you speak to someone quietly and privately about a delicate or difficult matter ○ *I'll go and see him. It won't be official, mind. Just a word in his ear over lunch.*

words

★ **eat your words** to be proved to be wrong when you have given an opinion about something ○ *England made Denmark eat their words with a brilliant victory in the European championship. The Danish coach had criticised England prior to their semi-final clash.*

famous last words said to mean that it is quite possible that your claim that something will definitely happen in a certain way will be proved wrong ○ *'All under control,' said Bertie. 'Famous last words,' added Idris with a wide grin.*

in words of one syllable as simply and clearly as possible. You often use this expression to suggest that the person you are talking to is stupid or slow to understand something. ○ *I'm sure I don't have to spell things out in words of one syllable to you.*

★ **lost for words** or
at a loss for words so amazed, shocked, or moved by something that you do not know what to say or how to express your feelings in words ○ *I had the feeling they were all waiting for me to say something. But for the first time in my life I felt at a loss for words.*

★ **not mince your words** to state an opinion clearly and directly, even though you know that some people will not like

what you are saying ○ *She did not mince her words when she came to the platform to demand a vote of no confidence in the president.*

put words into someone's mouth to try to make someone give opinions or make statements which they have never actually given or made ○ *You're trying to get me to say things! You're putting words into my mouth which have got nothing to do with me or my book!*

take the words out of someone's mouth to say the thing that someone was just about to say ○ *'Well, it's been amazing,' she said in closing. 'You took the words right out of my mouth, Lisa.'*

work

★ **do someone's dirty work** to do something unpleasant or difficult on someone's behalf because they do not want to do it themselves ○ *He's always got other people to do his dirty work for him.*

★ **have your work cut out** to have a very big problem to deal with that you will not find easy to do. ○ *The Prime Minister has his work cut out for him as most analysts see little chance of resolving the constitutional crisis.*

a nasty piece of work a very unpleasant person ○ *What about the husband, then. He's a real nasty piece of work.*

a piece of work (American) a very surprising, unusual, or impressive person ○ *Her next role is to play the most highly decorated policewoman in New York City. She's a real piece of work – very controversial.*

works

★ **in the works** (mainly American) being planned or in progress. ○ *The Office of Development for the city says that a shopping center is in the works.*

the works or
the whole works said after mentioning a number of things, to mean many other things of the same kind ○ *Amazing place*

he's got there – squash courts, swimming pool, jacuzzi, the works.

world

come down in the world or

go down in the world (old-fashioned) to have less money than you had before and now have a lower social status ○ Young women of middle class families which had come down in the world also found work in the upper ranges of domestic service.

come up in the world or

go up in the world (old-fashioned) to have more money than you had before and now have a higher social status ○ A well brought-up young man: he was said to have been an ordinary worker who had come up in the world.

dead to the world sleeping very deeply ○ Sarah was dead to the world and would probably sleep for twelve hours.

it's a small world or .

small world said to express your surprise when you unexpectedly meet someone you know in an unusual place ○ I'm only just recovering from the surprise of running into you like this. Small world.

not long for this world likely to die soon ○ Peter asked Ian to become his assistant earlier that year, perhaps knowing that he was not long for this world. When he died in June, Ian became chairman.

not set the world on fire to not be exciting and to be unlikely to be very successful ○ Munton is a good bowler, but hardly likely to set the world of cricket on fire.

★ **on top of the world** extremely happy ○ When she came back from that holiday she was so happy, on top of the world.

★ **out of this world** very good or impressive ○ The show was really good. The music was great and the costumes were out of this world.

think the world of someone to like and admire someone very much or be very fond of them ○ He is an involved and caring father, and Sam thinks the world of him.

the world is your oyster said to mean that someone has the opportunity to achieve great success in their life ○ You've got a wonderful watershed in your life, Johnny. You're young, you've got a lot of opportunity. The world is your oyster.

This expression suggests that success can be taken from the world in the same way that pearls can be taken from oysters. This idea was used by Shakespeare in 'The Merry Wives Of Windsor': 'Why, then the world's mine oyster, Which I with sword will open.' (Act 2, Scene 2)

worlds

★ **the best of both worlds** all the benefits and advantages of two different things, without any of the problems or disadvantages ○ These locations combine the best of both worlds. They're in the town yet close to the beautiful countryside of Worcestershire and Warwickshire.

★ **the worst of both worlds** all the problems and disadvantages of two different things without any of the benefits and advantages ○ Fans got the worst of both worlds: higher prices and more low-quality football.

worm

the worm has turned said to mean that someone who has tolerated a lot of bad treatment from other people without complaining unexpectedly changes their behaviour and starts to behave in a more forceful way ○ Then my mother came home and started bossing us around. She said, 'The worm has turned. Things are going to be different around here.'

worms

★ **a can of worms** or

a bag of worms a situation that is much more complicated, unpleasant, or difficult than it seems at first ○ Now we have uncovered a can of worms in which there has not only been shameful abuse of power, but *a failure of moral authority of the worst kind.*

worried

worried sick extremely worried ○ *Where have you been? I've been worried sick about you.*

worse

★ **the worse for wear** looking tired or in a bad state, especially because you have been working hard or drinking a lot of alcohol ○ *He turned up at important functions two hours late and noticeably the worse for wear.*

worst

the worst of both worlds → see **worlds**

wounds

★ **lick your wounds** to feel sorry for yourself after being thoroughly defeated or humiliated ○ *England's cricketers are licking their wounds after being soundly defeated in the second Test against Australia at Melbourne.*

≡ Some animals, such as cats, lick their ≡ wounds when they are injured.

open old wounds to remind people of an unpleasant or embarrassing experience in the past that they would rather forget about ○ *But that afternoon my world was overturned. Ted's diagnosis had opened old wounds and I no longer felt secure.*

wraps

★ **keep something under wraps** to keep something secret and not reveal it to anyone ○ *The official report has been kept under wraps for months by legal objections from BA.*

take the wraps off something to tell people about something such as a proposal or a new product for the first time ○ *Later this year, Porsche will take the wraps off their Ferrari-bashing 911 Turbo.*

wrench

throw a wrench into the works or **throw a monkey wrench into the works** (American) to cause problems which prevent something from happening in the way that it was planned. The British expression is **throw a spanner in the works**. ○ *When Elton was robbed it threw a monkey wrench into the works.*

wringer

go through the wringer or **be put through the wringer** to go through a very difficult period or situation which upsets you greatly and makes you ill or unhappy ○ *I felt as though I'd been through the wringer. My life seemed a wreck.*

XYZ

yards

go the whole nine yards (American) to do something to the fullest extent possible ○ *She's been the whole nine yards with the disease, has come through it, and has now taken up sailing.*

This expression refers to the amount of cement, nine cubic yards, which is contained in a cement-mixer truck.

yesterday

not born yesterday not as naive or as easily deceived as people seem to think ○ *He was rewarded with a disbelieving smirk. 'Now you really do sound like my father. I wasn't born yesterday, you know.'*

yonder

into the wide blue yonder or **into the wild blue yonder** (literary) on a journey to a faraway place which is unfamiliar or mysterious ○ *Sailing into the wide blue yonder, Colin discovers his very own Treasure Island.*

zero-sum

a zero-sum game (journalism) a situation in which if one person gains an advantage, someone else involved must suffer an equivalent disadvantage ○ *In New York people pursue money, which is not a zero-sum game. No one has to lose money for you to make money.*

A zero-sum game is one in which the winnings and losses of all the players add up to zero.

zone

be in the zone to be performing particularly well ○ *I remember riding back to the stables on a rising tide of emotion and hugging my dad. By now I was in the zone and brimming with confidence.*